TAHOE

ANN MARIE BROWN

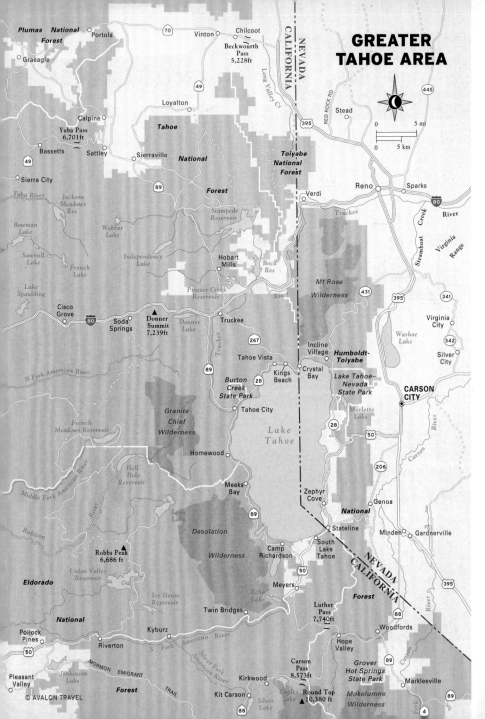

GREATER TAHOE AREA

Plumas National Forest

Portola
Graeagle
Vinton
Chilcoot
Beckwourth Pass 5,228ft

CALIFORNIA
NEVADA

Long Valley Cr.

445
395
Red Rock Rd
Stead

Calpine
Loyalton

Tahoe

49
70

Yuba Pass 6,701ft
Bassetts
Sattley
Sierraville

National

49
Sierra City

89

Toiyabe National Forest

Verdi
Reno
Sparks
80
Truckee River
Steamboat Creek
Virginia Range

Yuba River
Jackson Meadows Res
Webber Lake
Stampede Reservoir
Boca Res
Hobart Mills

Forest

Bowman Lake
Sawmill Lake
French Lake
Independence Lake
Prosser Creek Reservoir

Mt Rose Wilderness

431
395
341

Lake Spaulding

Cisco Grove
Soda Springs
80
Donner Summit 7,239ft
Donner Lake
Truckee
267
Tahoe Vista
Incline Village
Crystal Bay
Humboldt-Toiyabe
Virginia City
342
Silver City
Washoe Lake

N Fork American River

CARSON CITY

89
28
Kings Beach
Burton Creek State Park
Tahoe City

Lake Tahoe–Nevada State Park

Marlette Lake
28
50

French Meadows Reservoir

Granite Chief Wilderness

Lake Tahoe

206

Homewood

Middle Fork American River

Hell Hole Reservoir
Meeks Bay

Carson River

Loon Lake

89

Zephyr Cove
Genoa

Rubicon

Desolation Wilderness

Camp Richardson
Stateline
Minden
Gardnerville

National

Robbs Peak 6,686 ft

Eldorado

Union Valley Reservoir
Ice House Reservoir

Echo Lake

Meyers
50

South Lake Tahoe

395

NEVADA CALIFORNIA

National

Twin Bridges
Luther Pass 7,740ft
Woodfords
88

Forest

Pollock Pines
50
Kyburz
Riverton
S Fork American River

Hope Valley

Silver Fork American River

Grover Hot Springs State Park

89
Carson River

Pleasant Valley
Jenkinson Lake
MORMON EMIGRANT TRAIL

Carson Pass 8,573ft

Forest

Kit Carson
Kirkwood
88
Silver Lake
Ceples Lake
Round Top 10,380ft

Mokelumne Wilderness

Markleeville
89

4

© AVALON TRAVEL

0   5 mi
0   5 km

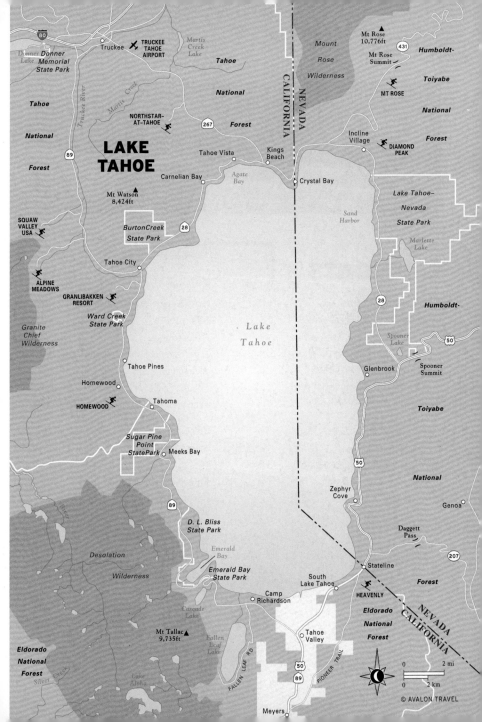

Contents

Discover Tahoe

To most visitors, the Tahoe region is clearly defined by its 22-mile-long, azure blue lake, "a noble sheet of blue water lifted six thousand three hundred feet above the level of the sea, and walled in by a rim of snow-clad mountain peaks," in the oft-quoted words of Mark Twain. The 10th-deepest lake in the world—1,645 feet at its deepest point—and 3rd deepest in North America, Lake Tahoe is blessed with remarkable water clarity and a boulder-lined, sandy shoreline that makes it one of the most photogenic lakes in the West. By any measure, Lake Tahoe can be counted among the notable treasures of North America's landscape.

Bordered by three federally designated wilderness areas, plus a huge swath of national forest and multiple California and Nevada state parks, the Tahoe basin is a veritable playground for outdoor enthusiasts. It's also a major tourist destination, with more than 250,000 visitors per day pouring in on summer holidays. Besides ogling the world-famous lake, most summer visitors come to hike, bike ride, or enjoy a wide variety of other outdoor sports. If you ever wanted to try rock climbing, fishing, horseback riding, sailing, ballooning, or boating, Tahoe is the place to do it. If you want more "civilized" outdoor fun, 14 golf courses around the lake provide it.

Although a greater number of people visit Tahoe in summer than in winter, it is Tahoe's wealth of ski resorts that has made the lake

an internationally recognized destination. More than a dozen alpine resorts are located near the lake, the largest concentration anywhere in the United States. A wide range of "nonvertical" activities are also available in Tahoe's snowy wonderland—from ice-skating to snowshoeing to dogsled rides to snowmobile tours to sipping hot chocolate beside a roaring fire.

Year-round, travelers arrive in droves to play the odds at high-rise casinos on the Nevada side of the lake, where gambling is legal. A half-dozen Stateline casinos, plus a few more on the northeast shore, attract thousands of visitors who flock to Tahoe purely for its indoor recreation opportunities, including big-name entertainment, first-class restaurants, and ample nightlife.

Add up this bounty of opportunity and there lies the crux of the region's popularity: Lake Tahoe is one of few places on earth where, if you choose to, you can hike or ski to a pristine wilderness area, shop for a dinner dress, dine at a trendy bistro, and gamble the night away, all in a single day at the lake.

Planning Your Trip

▶ WHEN TO GO

Which season is best at Lake Tahoe? The region enjoys about 275 days of sunshine per year on average, so visitors can enjoy pleasant days around the lake year-round. Each season has its charms, so plan your visit according to which recreational activities you enjoy the most.

While snow can fall as early as mid-October, and spring snowmelt may not happen until June, the most dependable months for skiing and winter sports are usually December-mid-April. If you are going to Tahoe during these months, be sure your tires and brakes are in good condition and that you carry chains for your vehicle, even if it has four-wheel drive or all-wheel drive.

Summer is a too-brief season that lasts only about three months (mid-June-mid-September), and in that time thousands of hikers, mountain bikers, boaters, and swimmers visit the lake. This is the most popular time of year for travel to Lake Tahoe, so make advance reservations for lodging and camping.

As a general rule of thumb, it is wise to avoid a trip to Tahoe on summer and winter holiday weekends. To completely avoid the crowds, consider a trip in the autumn off-season (September and October). This is one of the most pleasant periods at the lake, when Tahoe's abundant aspen groves put on their annual golden-colored show and the

The colors of autumn inspire local Tahoe artists.

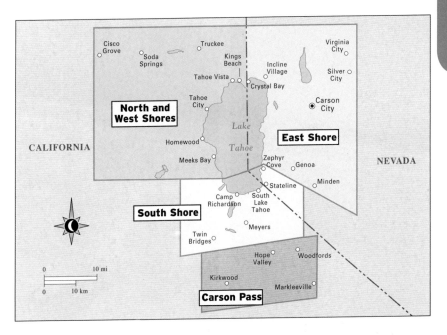

weather is still warm and mild. The peaks, trails, and passes of the high country usually remain open and accessible until sometime in October when the first snowfall arrives. After Labor Day, rates at most Tahoe lodgings drop considerably, and they remain low until the Thanksgiving holiday.

Tahoe's lowest visitation months are April and May, even in years when the ski resorts stay open until the end of April. Just like in autumn, this spring "shoulder season" is a great time for Tahoe travel bargains, although outdoor activities are limited because the ski season is waning but there is still too much snow for hiking, mountain biking, and other summertime sports.

▶ WHERE TO GO

South Shore

Perched on either side of the California-Nevada border, the twin cities of South Lake Tahoe and Stateline are comprised of a mix of high-rise casino resorts, upscale restaurants, fast-food joints, low-budget motels, luxury condos, and quaint cabins. A big attraction is Heavenly Ski Resort and its year-round gondola. The South Shore atmosphere is decidedly urban, with myriad activities located within blocks of downtown, including skiing, golfing, swimming, boating, and sightseeing cruises on the lake.

North and West Shores

Tahoe City, the North Shore's biggest town, offers plenty of lodgings, restaurants, and recreation activities, but is somewhat more

dawn at Tahoe

snowmobiles on Spooner Summit

laid-back than the South Shore's cities. The West Shore is even more sedate, with small hamlets offering a few visitor services in the midst of two state parks and miles of national forest land. To the north of Tahoe City lies Truckee, Donner Lake, and Donner Summit, home to major ski resorts, including famous Squaw Valley, Alpine Meadows, and Northstar-at-Tahoe.

East Shore

On the Nevada side of the lake, the East Shore boasts an abundance of shoreline protected as public parkland. A 20-mile stretch from Incline Village south to Zephyr Cove is almost entirely undeveloped. Here beach lovers have the best chance at claiming a private cove, and hikers and mountain bikers enjoy panoramic lake views. Most visitor services are located north at the twin towns of Crystal Bay and Incline Village. Two ski resorts are found here: Diamond Peak and Mount Rose.

Carson Pass

Carson Pass is less than an hour from the bustling South Shore, but psychologically it's a world away. With only a few scattered cabin resorts providing visitor services, the region attracts those who seek high peaks, alpine lakes, fields of wildflowers, and dramatic Sierra scenery. The biggest town, Markleeville, has a population of only 1,000 people. Its numbers are boosted substantially by the visitors who flock to the area in summer for hiking, mountain biking, and fishing, and in winter head up the hill to Kirkwood Ski Resort for downhill and cross-country skiing.

Explore Tahoe

► SOUTH SHORE SUMMER GETAWAY

It's a travesty to have only a short time to spend at Lake Tahoe's South Shore, but if a three-day stay is all your travel plans allow, you'll have to cram in as much as you can. Here's how to make the most of a brief but action-packed summer trip.

Day 1

Get up before sunrise and begin your trip to Lake Tahoe in dramatic style, by taking a scenic hot-air balloon flight over the lake. The views from 2,500 feet above the lake's surface are unforgettable, and the flight ends with a champagne toast to that glorious body of water. Or, if you can't stand to get up early on your first day of vacation, start your day mid-morning with a ride on the Heavenly gondola. This man-made marvel whisks sightseers up an incline of almost 2,800 feet in a mere 12 minutes, providing panoramic lake views. Be sure to disembark at the observation platform and take a look around. Picnic tables abound, so pack along some sandwiches and have lunch at 9,123 feet.

Once the hot-air balloon or gondola has delivered you back down to earth, spend the rest of the day in a more sedate fashion. There's no better place to kick back than on a strip of Tahoe sand. To enjoy a beach-party atmosphere, complete with colorful cocktails, head to Zephyr Cove. If you want tranquility, head to Nevada Beach. When it's time to start thinking about dinner, make a reservation for sunset at Bistro on the Pier or Camp Richardson's The Beacon, so you can watch that bright golden orb disappear behind Mount Tallac.

Go up, up, and away in a hot-air balloon over Lake Tahoe.

DINNER WITH A LAKE VIEW

Chambers Landing

SOUTH SHORE

- **Edgewood Restaurant,** Stateline: With a high, vaulted ceiling and big windows overlooking the lake, it's hard to focus your eyes on the upscale continental-style menu.

- **The Beacon,** South Lake Tahoe: Order a Rum Runner and grab a spot under the umbrellas on the huge outdoor deck, which opens onto a sandy beach.

NORTH SHORE

- **Wild Goose,** Tahoe Vista: It's tough to beat the up-close water views and outstanding California cuisine served here.

- **Gar Woods Grill and Pier,** Carnelian Bay: The lake view from the outdoor deck is divine, which makes Sunday brunch wildly popular in the summer months.

- **Jake's on the Lake,** Tahoe City: Peaceful marina and lake views and outdoor deck dining make this a great spot for happy hour. Order an Alpine Sunset and watch the sun go down.

- **Christy Hill,** Tahoe City: The food has been lauded by *Zagat* and *Bon Appétit,* but the panoramic blue-water vista is what keeps diners coming back.

WEST SHORE

- **Sunnyside,** Tahoe City: Boasting the largest lakeside deck anywhere at Tahoe, Sunnyside's casual atmosphere and grill menu keep diners of all ages happy.

- **Chambers Landing,** Homewood: This charming river-rock and wood-beamed pavilion enjoys a park-like setting right on the beach. It's like dining at your own private lakeside club.

- **West Shore Café,** Tahoe City: A perfect spot for a wintertime après-ski snack or a summer meal on the deck, the waterfront West Shore Café is a lakeview-lover's dream.

EAST SHORE

- **Lone Eagle Grille,** Incline Village: This restaurant at Hyatt Regency Lake Tahoe Resort is best patronized at lunch or brunch, when diners can get the most out of its stellar waterfront location.

Fannette Island is an intriguing sight in Emerald Bay.

Day 2

The best way to gain a sense of Tahoe's mind-boggling size is to get out on a boat in the middle of it, so a boat excursion on the lake is a must. Your choices for mode of travel are wide ranging: Passenger service is available on huge stern-wheeler paddleboats, sailboats, yachts, and speedboats. For a more intimate cruising experience, your best bet is to choose one of the smaller-capacity vessels, like the 50-passenger sailboat *Woodwind II* or the 76-foot classic yacht *Safari Rose* on the South Shore. Do-it-yourselfers should opt for a self-propelled kayaking or paddleboarding trip instead. Morning is the best time to paddle or cruise, before the midday wind comes up on the lake.

Come afternoon, it's time to take a tour around all or part of the lakeshore. If you choose to drive your own car, circumnavigating the entire lake requires about three hours to cover the full 72 miles. Be sure to drive in a clockwise direction so you are always on the lake side of the highway. Or leave your car parked and choose from a few ecofriendly transportation options: Take advantage of the Nifty Fifty Trolley, which offers narrated tours on open-sided buses that travel from Stateline to Emerald Bay and beyond, where you can get on and off as you please. Or go for a bike ride on the South Shore's paved Pope-Baldwin Bike Path. Bike rentals are easy to come by, and the trail passes by several interesting sites, including the Tallac Historic Site and the Stream Profile Chamber, plus a few of the South Shore's loveliest beaches.

You'll need a big dinner after this day of exploring, so make a reservation at Scusa or Café Fiore and do a little carbo-loading on freshly made pasta. Afterward, cap off your day by soaking in the hot tubs at Nepheles.

Day 3

When in Tahoe, it's almost a prerequisite that you go for a hike. If you're not into high

setting up camp

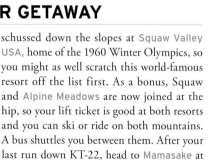

Horses graze at Kirkwood.

mileage and thigh-burning ascents, consider some of the easier trails around Lake Tahoe's South Shore, such as the one-mile trail to Vikingsholm at Emerald Bay, or the similar-length path to Eagle Lake. Get an early start on either trail in order to beat the crowds to these deservedly popular destinations. Those inclined to more serious hiking have dozens of longer trails to choose from. Two excellent close-by options would be Mount Tallac or Dicks Lake. At the end of the day, you'll probably want to wash the trail dust off and cool yourself down, so head over to Baldwin Beach and go for a swim in Lake Tahoe. Sure, it's cold, but that's what the locals call "refreshing." To celebrate your last night on the South Shore, tonight's dinner should be something spectacular, so score a reservation for Edgewood Tahoe or Evan's and make a toast to another fine Tahoe day.

► NORTH SHORE WINTER GETAWAY

Fake a note from your doctor, email it to your boss, and turn your two-day ski or snowboard weekend into three days. Deep powder stashes are just waiting to be discovered on the North Shore, and you're going to need adequate time to experience them all.

Day 1

You can't say you've skied at Tahoe until you've schussed down the slopes at Squaw Valley USA, home of the 1960 Winter Olympics, so you might as well scratch this world-famous resort off the list first. As a bonus, Squaw and Alpine Meadows are now joined at the hip, so your lift ticket is good at both resorts and you can ski or ride on both mountains. A bus shuttles you between them. After your last run down KT-22, head to Mamasake at

TOP PICKS FOR FAMILIES

Snow tubing is fun for all ages.

- **Best boat cruise:** Let your kids feel the wind in their hair on a *Woodwind II* sailing cruise. Or take a ride on the blazing fast *Tahoe Thunder.*

- **Best food:** Head for the kid-friendly **Burger Lounge** or **Hard Rock Café** on the South Shore, or **Rosie's Café** in Tahoe City.

- **Best water fun:** Just northwest of the Tahoe City Y, you can rent a raft and float lazily down the **Truckee River** to River Ranch Lodge.

- **Best snow-play fun: Soda Springs** at Donner Summit places just as much emphasis on tubing as it does on skiing. Kids can also hop on their very own pint-size snowmobiles and race around a circular track.

- **Best place to ride bikes:** On the North Shore, pedal the five-mile **Truckee River Recreation Trail** that parallels the rolling river. On the South Shore, ride the **Pope-Baldwin Bike Path.**

- **Best kid-friendly hike:** On the South Shore, hike one easy mile to Angora Lakes. Buy a pitcher of lemonade at the 1920s-era cabin resort, then go for a swim in the lake, or rent a kayak or paddleboard.

- **Best playground:** Take the kids to Tahoe City's **Commons Beach,** where the playground includes a mini-boulder for junior "rock climbers" ages six and older.

- **Best place to tire out the kids: Squaw Valley USA** offers ice-skating and swimming at High Camp Bath and Tennis Club, horseback riding, a ropes course, two rock climbing walls, and the Skyjump Bungee Trampoline.

- **Best field trip:** Take a drive to Nevada's **Virginia City,** site of the 1860s Comstock gold- and silver-mining boom. The under-12 set will want to take a ride on the Virginia and Truckee Railroad and tour the underground mine in the Ponderosa Saloon.

- **Best ice cream:** Summer isn't summer until you've taken the kids to Camp Richardson for an ice-cream cone.

A ride on the chairlift at Heavenly offers visual rewards.

The Village at Squaw for bountiful servings of sushi and sake to take your mind off your burning thighs.

Day 2

Time for another big day on the slopes, and that means heading for another of the North Shore's "steep and deep" resorts. Sugar Bowl is the grande dame of Tahoe resorts, having first opened in 1936. Try carving a few turns on its longest run, Crowley's off Mount Lincoln, which is a whopping three miles long with a 1,500-foot vertical drop. Alternatively, if your legs need a rest from all the shredding you did yesterday, consider buying a lift ticket at Northstar-at-Tahoe instead and spending the day on its mellower blue runs.

No matter where you ski or ride, finish off your day with drinks and dinner in nearby Truckee. Try Cottonwood for a sophisticated meal or Tacos Jalisco if you just want to fill your empty belly with great, cheap Mexican food. After dinner, head over to Moody's Bistro to listen to some jazz and swap stories with the bartender about your awesome day on the slopes.

Day 3

Now that you've skied or snowboarded at some of the North Shore's megaresorts, it's time to head for the locals' favorite, Homewood. Sure, it doesn't look like much from the road, but wait until you get up high and see the stupendous lake views from the top of the chairlift. Perhaps best of all, a day on Homewood's slopes won't break the bank; the resort has some of the most reasonable lift ticket rates anywhere around the lake. To celebrate your good financial sense, après-ski get a table for dinner at West Shore Café, just across the road, or head into Tahoe City to Christy Hill or Wolfdale's.

► THE NONSKIER'S WINTER WONDERLAND

Your partner is addicted to skiing and snowboarding, and will spend his/her vacation pushing the envelope on double-black-diamond runs, terrain parks, and half-pipes. You, on the other hand, can never quite figure out how to gracefully dismount the chairlift and often end your day at the first-aid station. Three words of advice: Give it up. There is plenty of other fun stuff to do in the snow at Lake Tahoe, and none of it will leave you strapped to a sled pulled by the ski patrol.

Day 1

Go snowshoeing. No experience is required; snowshoeing is as easy as walking, and rentals are a real bargain compared to skiing equipment. Beginners can snowshoe along the lakeshore at Camp Richardson and the Tallac Historic Site, around the meadow at Squaw Creek, or on easy trails at Spooner Lake. More experienced snowshoers can set off into the backcountry on a multitude of trails.

Day 2

Now that you're feeling more confident in the snow, try cross-country skiing. Even those who shun the downhill slopes can have a great time cross-country skiing on beginner-level, flat trails. It's a fun way for nonskiers to play in the snow without risking a broken leg. Most people can quickly learn the basics of cross-country skiing. (Skate skiing is much harder; start with basic gliding, or classic skiing.) Great places for beginners to get a lesson and rental package are Spooner Lake on the East Shore, Royal Gorge near Truckee, Tahoe Cross-Country near Tahoe City, or Kirkwood Cross-Country at Carson Pass. You'll be kicking and gliding like a pro in only a couple of hours.

Costumed skaters re-live the 1970s at Heavenly Village ice rink.

BEST CAMPGROUNDS

The Tahoe region provides many great spots to pitch your tent.

- **Best for boaters:** With a kayak or boat (your own or a rented vessel), you can stay at one of two dozen sites at Emerald Bay Boat-in Camp. Park your boat at a mooring buoy and savor Emerald Bay from lake level. Moonlit nights are magical here.

- **Best for hot-springs lovers:** The camp at Grover Hot Springs State Park works for people who prefer warm mineral waters to the ice-bath water of the lake. The camp and the park's two pools—one hot and one cooler—are open year-round.

- **Best for swimmers and sunbathers:** Nevada Beach Campground is bare-bones, but it's just 100 yards from the water on Tahoe's southeast shore. The beach is a long and wide stretch of sand, with a picturesque view of the West Shore.

- **Best for winter camping:** Snow camping doesn't appeal to everybody, but for serious cross-country skiers and snowshoers, General Creek Campground at Ed Z'berg Sugar Pine Point State Park is a perfect base of operations. Follow ski trails right from your tent door.

- **Best for luxury lovers:** Fallen Leaf Lake Campground is huge and popular. But for those who are reluctant about the whole tent-and-sleeping bag idea, the camp offers hot showers, flush toilets, and yurts with sleeping platforms, space heaters, and electric lights.

- **Best for lake-view sites:** Eagle Point Campground at Emerald Bay State Park is perched on a high point above Emerald Bay, and a few of the sites have to-die-for lake views. The best sites are 66-70 on the Emerald Bay side of the loop. Equally divine are the views from sites 148-153 at neighboring D. L. Bliss State Park.

- **Best for wildflower fans:** In Carson Pass, Woods Lake Campground has a compelling view of Round Top Peak from many of its sites, and easy access to the Winnemucca and Round Top Lakes Loop, one of California's premier wildflower walks.

- **Best for peak-baggers:** Mount Rose Campground is perched at 9,300 feet near the slopes of Mount Rose, a few miles from Incline Village.

Dogs and their people admire the wildflowers in Carson Pass.

Day 3

If you are feeling a bit tired from the last two days of snow play, let Trigger or Rover and their friends do the work of pulling you through the snow. Horse-drawn sleigh rides are available in Squaw Valley on the North Shore, and Camp Richardson and Stateline on the South Shore. Dogsled tours led by eager, panting huskies are available at the Resort at Squaw Creek on the North Shore and Kirkwood in Carson Pass.

Day 4

Go ice-skating in the morning and tubing in the afternoon. Outdoor rinks are found at Squaw Valley's High Camp, Northstar-at-Tahoe, and at the base of Heavenly, but if you'd rather skate where the climate is controlled, South Lake Tahoe has a regulation-size indoor rink. For an afternoon of tubing or sledding, head to Hansen's Resort in South Lake Tahoe or North Tahoe Regional Park in Tahoe Vista. All of Lake Tahoe's alpine ski resorts offer tubing or sledding, too.

Day 5

Do a little winter sightseeing. In the morning, ride the scenic cable car at Squaw Valley or the gondola at Heavenly. In the afternoon, take a sightseeing cruise aboard the *Tahoe Queen* or *MS Dixie II* stern-wheeler paddleboats. If it's too cold on the upper deck, you can always enjoy the view from down below in one of the heated, enclosed cabins.

Day 6

Go snowmobiling. Since there is horse-power involved, your adrenaline-addicted snowboarding spouse might even join you. No experience is required, and proper clothing (snowsuits, snow boots, and helmet) is usually included in the tour fee. Snowmobiling tours are offered on the North Shore along the high ridges of Tahoe National Forest, on the South Shore above Zephyr Cove, and in the Blue Lakes area of Carson Pass.

BEST PLACES TO TAKE A DIP

The East Shore's Chimney Beach is scenic and secluded.

Sure, the water is icy cold, but one look at the azure blue waters of Lake Tahoe, and you'll want to dive in anyway. Best bets:

- **North Shore:** Speedboat Beach, near Cal-Neva Casino at Stateline. Large boulders and white sand, plus a great view of the far-off South Shore. A few miles to the west, any strip of sand in Kings Beach is great for swimming, with its south-facing beachfronts getting lots of sun.

- **West Shore:** D. L. Bliss State Park, 17 miles south of Tahoe City. Calawee Cove is hands-down the loveliest beach at Lake Tahoe, but for more privacy, hike the Rubicon Trail to find your own cove.

- **South Shore:** Baldwin Beach, four miles north of the South Lake "Y." Very shallow water along the shore makes the temperature reasonable for swimming. If your dog likes to swim with you, head to neighboring Kiva Beach, where canines are permitted.

- **East Shore:** Sand Harbor, 2.5 miles south of Incline Village. Of course it's crowded, but it's worth it. Sand Harbor's gentle turquoise coves, backed by granite boulders, have a fine-grained, soft white sand, unlike the coarse gravel and rocks so common around the lake. For a more private patch of sand, drive 2.5 miles farther south on Highway 28 and hike 0.5 mile to Secret Cove and Chimney Beach. You might get an anatomy lesson here; some Secret Cove beachgoers don't get tan lines.

▶ THE PEAK-BAGGER

You've come to Lake Tahoe with a purpose. You have one week of vacation time, and you want to hike all of the Tahoe basin's highest summits—a worthwhile mission, to be sure. Okay, lace up your boots, fill your pack with plenty of snacks and water, and let's get climbing.

Day 1

Start with a warm-up peak, so you can get used to the high-elevation air around the lake. The lofty 9,235-foot summit of Ralston Peak is no slacker in the view department. Start at the Ralston Peak Trailhead off U.S. 50 for a heart-pumping climb, or for an easier ascent, take the boat taxi across Echo Lakes and follow the Pacific Crest Trail to the Ralston Trail. This 8.6-mile round-trip has a mere 1,800-foot elevation gain, and Ralston's summit view is a stunner: Nearly a dozen lakes of the Desolation Wilderness are in sight, as well as mighty Pyramid Peak and Mount Tallac.

Day 2

So much for your easy day. Today, while you are still fresh, it's time to tackle Mount Tallac. This mighty 9,735-foot summit may not be the tallest mountain around the lake, but it scores high marks for its summit view. Getting there is a bit of a butt-kicker, especially since the first 2 miles of the hike are deceptively easy. From the 2.1-mile mark at Cathedral Lake, the trail gains 2,100 feet in only 2.6 miles—a grade that gives pause to even the fittest of hikers. The entire hike is 9.4 miles round-trip with a 3,400-foot elevation gain. The summit view takes in Lake Tahoe, Emerald Bay, Fallen Leaf Lake, the lake-filled basins of the Desolation Wilderness, and distinctive Ralston and Pyramid Peaks.

Day 3

Since you are still on the south side of the lake, and to rest up a bit from your day at

Dicks Lake in Desolation Wilderness is a great day-hiking destination.

Tahoe wildflowers

Tallac, head for the summit of Echo Peak above Upper Angora Lake. It's an easy stroll to the lake, but make sure you enjoy a glass of lemonade at the Angora Lakes Resort before beginning the attack on Echo Peak, elevation 8,588 feet, which is more than 1,200 feet higher, but accessible in about a mile. You'll long remember the merciless grade on this short stretch, but you'll also remember the view—a 360-degree panorama that includes the Echo Lakes, Fallen Leaf Lake, Lake Tahoe, and numerous other lakes and peaks in the Desolation Wilderness.

Day 4

Take a drive down to Carson Pass to summit mighty Round Top Peak. The trek starts easily enough from either Carson Pass Summit or Woods Lake Campground, but once you reach Round Top Lake the work commences. The summit towers imposingly 1,000 feet above you, and a rough path struggles up, up, and up over the peak's volcanic slopes. You may need to use your hands as well as your feet. From Round Top's summit ridge, you take in

a vista of the Dardanelles, Lake Tahoe, Caples Lake, Woods Lake, and Round Top Lake. Even more dramatic is the southward view of Summit City Canyon, 3,000 feet below.

Day 5

With luck, your peak-bagging vacation just happens to coincide with the summer wildflower bloom, because your next trail passes through acres of flower fields. Start at the West Shore's Twin Peaks Trailhead for the Tahoe Rim Trail and follow an initially mellow course along Ward Creek, which becomes increasingly steep as you go. After six miles one-way and a 2,400-foot elevation gain, you'll be standing on the eastern summit of Twin Peaks, elevation 8,878 feet. Easily identifiable landmarks include Granite Chief, Tinker Knob, Mount Rose, Freel Peak, and Mount Tallac. Heck, while you're up here, you might as well bag the western summit of Twin Peaks, too.

Day 6

Castle Peak beckons, and you must answer. You can hike to this summit via a shorter path (5.4 miles round-trip) on a dirt road from the north side of I-80 near Boreal Ridge, or a longer route (9.4 miles round-trip) from the south side of I-80. The elevation gain is about 2,100 feet. The throat of an ancient volcano, the multi-turreted summit of 9,103-foot Castle Peak provides a horizon-expanding view, reaching as far as the Diablo Range 100 miles to the west and equally as far to the north. No matter which way you go, the trail is relatively easy until you reach Castle Pass; from there the last 1.2 miles to the top are steep. The eastern turret of the "castle" is the highest summit.

Day 7

Hope for cool temperatures today, because you are heading for the volcanic summit of 10,778-foot Mount Rose. Much of the route is treeless, waterless, and exposed. The 10-mile round-trip has a meager 2,300-foot elevation gain, which sounds quite manageable until you realize that the vast majority of that gain occurs in the final 2.6 miles to the summit. The final 0.5 mile is the most challenging, because of the high-elevation air and the exposed volcanic terrain. On clear days, the summit view spreads so far and wide that it is easy to pick out Mount Lassen, nearly 100 miles to the north.

When you have finished your hike, drive back down the Mount Rose Highway to the Big Water Grille above Incline Village. Enjoy a few drinks at the bar and pat yourself on the back for being such a fine mountaineer.

▶ THE ADRENALINE JUNKIE

In an average day, your biggest risk-taking is driving in rush-hour traffic while simultaneously talking on your cell phone. If you want to experience some genuine thrills, you came to the right place. Fuel up with a few shots of espresso, and let's go!

bloodcurdling 24-mile loop, so instead arrange a shuttle pickup with the Spooner Lake Outdoor Company and ride the trail point to point, an adrenaline-inducing 13 miles. Along the way, watch out for the 1,600-foot near-vertical drop-offs.

Day 1

Get on your mountain bike (or rent one, if yours is at home) and pedal the world-famous Flume Trail on Tahoe's East Shore. Since it's your first day of vacation, you probably don't want to go crazy and ride the entire

Day 2

Get a bird's-eye view of the lake courtesy of HeliTahoe Helicopters, based at South Lake Tahoe Airport. Sign up for the hour-long tour, in which your pilot will buzz over Emerald Bay, Sand Harbor, and the South

A mountain bike ride on the Flume Trail is a must for fit cyclists.

Shore. Want more adrenaline? Ask the pilot to take the doors off so you can take better pictures. When the flight is over, drive down to Kirkwood and let gravity be your thrill ride on Zip Tahoe's zipline course. You'll fly through the tree canopy at about 30 miles per hour and 80 feet above the ground.

Day 3

Today is the day to feel nothing but air under your feet and experience the absolute thrill of hanging onto a rock wall with only your fingers and toes (okay, you'll be roped in, but the psychological effect is similar). Sign up with the Tahoe Adventure Company or Alpine Skills International for one of the rock climbing classes on Lover's Leap, a chunk of granite that rises 600 feet straight up from the American River. You'll be performing vertical acrobatics in the time it takes to say "on belay."

Day 4

Start by getting up at the crack of dawn to go for a 5 A.M. hot-air balloon flight. Your one-hour ride will take you as high as 2,500 feet above the lake's surface, providing dizzying views of the Tahoe basin. After the postflight champagne toast, head over to Timber Cove Marina to feel some g-forces aboard the *Tahoe Thunder*. This is the fastest tour speedboat on the lake, boasting over 800 horsepower. You'll come away with a new understanding of the word *fast*.

Day 5

Time to get back on the mountain bike. If you love the feel of gravity-induced speed, you'll love Mr. Toad's Wild Ride, aka the Saxon Creek Trail. This is the South Shore's most famous (or infamous) ride, with an extremely technical, obstacle-ridden downhill stretch suitable for advanced riders only. Bring your first-aid kit.

Day 6

Head over to the Truckee River for a day of rafting, and not the leisurely, floating kind that everyone does on the stretch from Tahoe City to River Ranch. Instead, sign up for a guided trip on the Lower Truckee River, which offers Class II and III rapids almost all summer long. Compared to what you've been doing all week, this white water may seem mild, but maybe that will ease the transition back to your no-thrills office job. Vacation's over, but here's the good news: It's time to start planning for next year.

Tahoe Thunder

SOUTH SHORE

Far and away the most populated stretch of Lake Tahoe shoreline is the South Shore, with most of the development centered around the twin cities of South Lake Tahoe (in California) and Stateline (in Nevada). However, at first glance neither of these cities delivers much in the way of alpine charm. Consisting mainly of a haphazard, unplanned strip of commercial enterprises lined up along U.S. 50 (which is euphemistically called "Lake Tahoe Boulevard" in this in-town stretch), the cities of the South Shore have long suffered from a mild case of urban blight. If you are expecting to see a quaint mountain village perched along the shores of the lake, you won't find it here, at least not along the main thoroughfare.

Fortunately, an effort at self-improvement is being made. Since the late 1990s, the construction of two new "village" complexes, comprised of lodgings, restaurants, and shops—one at Ski Run Boulevard and the other clustered around the Heavenly gondola between Heavenly Village Way and Stateline Avenue—has forced the removal of many old and unsightly motels, fast-food restaurants, and gas stations. Since these new village centers encourage walking, not driving, they are much more in tune with Lake Tahoe's natural environment, and they have added a certain mountain-style metropolitan flair to the downtown area of the South Shore.

Despite the preponderance of strip malls and a near-constant parade of automobile traffic,

© ANN MARIE BROWN

HIGHLIGHTS

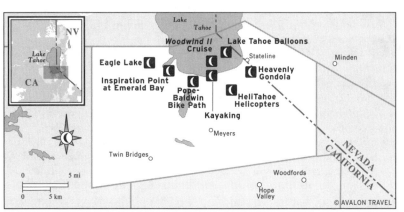

LOOK FOR 【 TO FIND RECOMMENDED SIGHTS, ACTIVITIES, DINING, AND LODGING.

【 *Woodwind II* **Cruise:** Among many possible choices, one of the best Tahoe cruising excursions is on board the 50-passenger *Woodwind II* sailboat, which has glass-bottom viewing windows that allow guests to peer beneath the surface of the lake (page 30).

【 **HeliTahoe Helicopters:** For a little shot of adrenaline, sign up for a helicopter tour out of South Lake Tahoe Airport. Tours of various lengths are available, offering bird's-eye views of Emerald Bay, Sand Harbor, and the South Shore (page 32).

【 **Lake Tahoe Balloons:** This memorable excursion with Lake Tahoe Balloons includes an early-morning boat cruise on the lake, launch of the hot-air balloon from the boat deck, a view-filled flight through the skies above Lake Tahoe, and a champagne toast after landing (page 33).

【 **Heavenly Gondola:** No matter what time of year, don't miss taking a scenic gondola ride at Heavenly Ski Resort. On the uphill leg, be sure to disembark at the overlook platform and check out the view from 9,123 feet in elevation (page 35).

【 **Inspiration Point at Emerald Bay:** The blue-green expanse of Emerald Bay, with mag-ical Fannette Island poking up from the lake's surface, is one of the most photographed sights in the United States. The drive-up overlook at Inspiration Point is one of the best spots to get a good look and a few snapshots (page 38).

【 **Eagle Lake:** You'll need to get a very early start to beat the crowds on the trail to Eagle Lake, but this short although somewhat steep walk is worth the effort. The hike takes in the sight and sound of cascading Eagle Creek, the granite shores of a picturesque glacial cirque lake in the Desolation Wilderness, and fine views of distant Emerald Bay (page 48).

【 **Pope-Baldwin Bike Path:** You don't have to be Lance Armstrong, or even especially athletic, to ride this level, paved bike trail, which travels past some of the South Shore's greatest sights, including Baldwin Beach, the Tallac Historic Site, and the Stream Profile Chamber (page 58).

【 **Kayaking:** Sign up for a tour with Kayak Tahoe, and you'll paddle your own boat through the sparkling waters of Emerald Bay or along the boulder-strewn beaches of the East Shore in the company of a knowledgeable guide. Confident beginners can forego the tour, simply rent a kayak, and set out on their own (page 60).

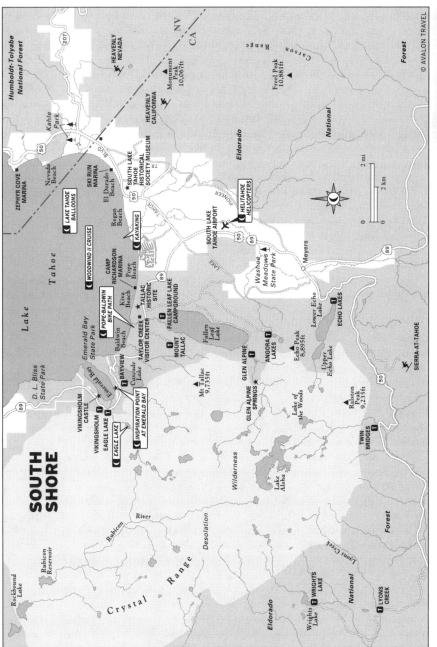

SOUTH SHORE

SOUTH SHORE

© AVALON TRAVEL

there is still a wealth of scenic beauty to be found on the South Shore. Even busy U.S. 50 has occasional spots where drivers are treated to views of Lake Tahoe's mesmerizing blue waters. And just a short drive from the "Y"—the busiest intersection in South Lake Tahoe, where U.S. 50 and Highway 89 divide—lies the eastern stretch of the Desolation Wilderness, one of the most stunning glacier-sculpted landscapes in the Sierra Nevada. Hikers and backpackers can spend weeks exploring its miles of trails, visiting dozens of alpine lakes, and climbing a banquet of peaks and precipices. Outside the wilderness area, a host of other outdoor activities are possible in the grand Tahoe scenery—mountain biking, boating, golfing, fishing, horseback riding, and rock climbing, to name a few—as well as the obvious multitude of winter sports—alpine skiing, cross-country skiing, snowshoeing, snowmobiling, and sledding, among others.

For the less ambitious, much can be seen right from your car windows. Heading west and north from the cities of the South Shore, travelers enjoy a scenic ride up Highway 89/Emerald Bay Road to Emerald Bay itself, one of the most photographed places in the United States. Along the way, pristine stretches of Tahoe shoreline await your blanket and picnic basket. There are historic sites to be toured, boat cruises to take, open-air trolleys to ride, and outdoor festivals to enjoy. For those more inclined toward indoor recreation, there are shops and art galleries to browse in, and the 24-hour lure of the casinos. Quite simply, there is such an abundance of fun things to do in the South Shore region that it's impossible not to enjoy a vacation here.

PLANNING YOUR TIME

Many visitors spend a week or more in and around the South Shore, both in the winter and summer seasons. Even if you aren't a casino-and-nightlife kind of person, the South Shore

offers enough activities to keep anyone busy for several days, no matter what their interests, and no matter what the season. Just visiting a few of the South Shore's sightseeing highlights will require a minimum of two days. Be sure to plan enough time to ride the **Heavenly gondola,** take a boat cruise on the *Tahoe Queen* or the *Woodwind II,* and drive or ride public transportation to scenic **Inspiration Point at Emerald Bay.** History buffs will want to allow a few days just to visit the numerous museums and historic sites in the area, including **Vikingsholm Castle** and **Tallac Historic Site.** Outdoor recreationists will be hard-pressed to squeeze in enough hiking, biking, boating, fishing, or snow-related sports before their vacation ends, no matter how much time they have allotted. At a minimum, even the most casual adventurer should take the short hike to **Eagle Lake,** go for a spin on the paved **Pope-Baldwin Bike Path,** and spend a few hours paddling around the lake in a rental kayak.

TOUR BOATS AND CRUISES
Tahoe Queen and MS Dixie II

One of the most popular activities at Lake Tahoe is cruising around the lake in a Mark Twain–style stern-wheeler paddleboat. On the South Shore, the *Tahoe Queen* operates out of Ski Run Marina and the MS *Dixie II* departs from Zephyr Cove Marina. Both boats are operated year-round by Lake Tahoe Cruises (775/589-4906 or 800/238-2463, www.zephyrcove.com). The vessels are large enough to hold a few hundred people, but even so, the tours are so popular that they sometimes sell out.

The 400-passenger MS *Dixie II* offers daily cruises year-round, including a Sunday brunch cruise along Tahoe's East Shore, a sunset dinner/dance cruise, and an Emerald Bay sightseeing cruise. The video *Sunken Treasures of Lake Tahoe* plays below deck during the daytime cruises, but few passengers bother to watch it. Instead, most head above deck to

the *Tahoe Queen* paddlewheeler

enjoy the fresh air, sunshine, and lake views. In winter, guests can choose to relax on the enclosed, lower decks, or head out onto the open third deck for snapping pictures and soaking up the winter sun. Daytime cruises last about 2 hours; the sunset dinner/dance cruise lasts 3.5 hours and includes a four-course meal and a live band. Cocktails and wine are available for purchase. Rates are $39 for adults and $15 for children under 12, except for dinner cruises, which are $69 adults and $35 children. There is an additional $8 fee to park your car at Zephyr Cove Marina.

The *Tahoe Queen,* a smaller paddleboat based out of Ski Run Marina, offers a similar array of cruises and also features a glass bottom that permits riders to peer into the clear Tahoe depths. The *Tahoe Queen* holds a few cruises that are more interesting than the standard tours, including Santa's Christmas cruise on a few December dates, and in the summer months, Mark Twain's Tales of Tahoe Cruise,

with actor McAvoy Layne portraying the ghost of Mark Twain. Layne, playing Twain, regales guests with tales of his adventures at Lake Tahoe in 1861. Most cruises last 2.5 hours ($39 adults, $15 children 11 and under). The *Tahoe Queen*'s sunset dinner cruise with appetizers, dinner, and dessert, plus a live band, costs $69 adults and $41 children.

If authenticity is important to you, you'll choose the *Tahoe Queen* over the MS *Dixie II.* The *Tahoe Queen* is an honest-to-goodness Mississippi paddle wheeler, with its paddles actually propelling the boat. It's also the smaller of the two cruising vessels, so you get a more intimate experience.

In winter, the *Tahoe Queen* also runs a skier/boarder shuttle from the South Shore to Incline Village, where passengers disembark and board a bus to Northstar Ski Resort. Breakfast is served on the morning ride to Incline Village; the boat trip back to the South Shore is a big, fun, après-ski party with live

© ANN MARIE BROWN

The captain sails the *Woodwind II* out of its harbor.

entertainment. The ski shuttle cruise operates only on Tuesdays and Thursdays, mid-January–early April ($59 adults, $30 children 11 and under).

◖ Woodwind II Cruise

If you'd rather not set sail with a couple hundred strangers, more intimate cruises are available. The sailboat *Woodwind II* (888/867-6394 or 775/588-3000, www.sailwoodwind.com, $34–49 adults, $15 children) offers lake excursions for 50 passengers maximum, complete with billowing white sails, sturdy masts, tinkling halyards, full bar service, and glass-bottom viewing windows that allow passengers to look beneath Tahoe's surface. The on-board crew does all the work of sailing; guests relax on the deck or down below in enclosed cabins and enjoy the ride. The *Woodwind II* is a 55-foot catamaran that sails from Zephyr Cove along the lake's East Shore, passing Cave Rock and then heading out into the center of the

1,600-foot-deep lake for a 360-degree Tahoe panorama. Cruises are offered multiple times per day in summer, but the best choice is the sunset champagne cruise, complete with beer, wine, and champagne.

Safari Rose

An elegant addition to the *Woodwind* fleet is the 80-foot classic yacht *Safari Rose* (888/867-6394 or 775/588-1881, www.tahoeboatcruises.com, $105 adults, $65 children 12 and under, although bringing children on this cruise is discouraged). This teak-paneled, plushly upholstered vessel offers a half-day sightseeing cruise to Lake Tahoe's West Shore, including a walking tour of the historic Ehrman Mansion at Sugar Pine Point State Park, and special summer evening tours such as the Wednesday Wine Tasting Cruise. Lunch is included on the daytime cruises; cocktails and appetizers are served in the evening. The *Safari Rose* departs from Tahoe Keys Marina.

Tahoe

For more than half a decade, the wooden cruiser *Tahoe* (888/867-6394 or 775/588-1881, www.tahoeboatcruises.com, $135 adults, $65 children 12 and under, although bringing children on this cruise is discouraged) has been carrying visitors across the waters of Lake Tahoe. This meticulously restored 40-foot yacht sails up to 18 passengers from Tahoe Keys Marina to the East Shore's Thunderbird Lodge, where they take a guided walking tour of this architectural oddity, which was recently added to the National Register of Historic Places. The walking tour covers the estate's grounds, lighthouse room, old lodge, maid's quarters, original kitchen, and the 600-foot-long underground tunnel leading to the boathouse. A buffet lunch is served on the boat.

Tahoe Star

Harrah's and Harveys casinos offer a cruise on Bill Harrah's formerly private 54-foot yacht, the *Tahoe Star* (775/586-6534, www.harveystahoe.com, $40 adults, $28 children). This same yacht has played host to the likes of Sammy Davis Jr., Frank Sinatra, Natalie Cole, Bill Cosby, and David Letterman. A shuttle leaves from the casinos and takes passengers to Round Hill Pines Marina, about five miles away, where the cruise departs. The yacht holds 36 passengers. A 90-minute cruise to Emerald Bay and back departs daily in summer (times vary). Passengers must be 21 or older for the evening cruises.

Bleu Wave

Not to be outdone by the other casinos, MontBleu has its own tour boat (775/588-9283 or 866/413-0985, www.tahoebleuwave.com) plying the blue waters of Lake Tahoe. The 1966 classic yacht *Bleu Wave* is 72 feet long and can accommodate up to 49 passengers. The boat departs from Round Hill Pines Marina and cruises to Emerald Bay almost daily year-round,

with lunch and drinks provided along the way ($59 adults, free for children under 12). But the summer evening "sushi cruise" is their specialty, a 1.5-hour tour that includes a sushi dinner ($45 per adult, offered 5–6:30 P.M. Wed. and Sat.). In winter, the *Bleu Wave* offers a ski cruise to Homewood Ski Resort. Skiers and riders leave Round Hill Pines Marina at 8 A.M. and arrive in about an hour at West Shore Café and Inn, which is right across the road from Homewood. The $99 price includes an all-day lift ticket and discounted lunch from Homewood's West Shore Café.

Tahoe Thunder

For some people, the only speed that holds their interest is "fast." The *Tahoe Thunder* (530/544-5387 or 530/544-2942, www.action-watersports.com, $59 adults, $30 children 12 and under) boasts the fastest Coast Guard–inspected public speedboat ride on the lake. Operating out of Timber Cove Marina, across the highway from the Safeway store, the *Tahoe Thunder* is a 33-foot bullet boat with horsepower that tops 800. Don't forget your jacket for the chilling breeze brought on by the high g-forces, and maybe your earplugs for the roar of the engine. Only 12 passengers fit on board this little speedster, so the ride to Emerald Bay is intimate as well as fast.

Windsong

At the other end of the spectrum from the loud speedboat *Tahoe Thunder* is the 65-foot sailing yacht *Windsong*, which operates out of Timber Cove Marina, across the highway from the Safeway store (530/544-5387 or 530/544-2942, www.action-watersports.com, $49 adults, $25 children 12 and under). The sailing yacht holds only 24 passengers, guaranteeing that you'll hear only the sound of the wind rippling through the sails. The summer-only two-hour cruise plies the waters along the South Shore.

The *Tahoe Thunder* was built to go one speed: fast.

Rum Runner

On the north side of the "Y," historic Camp Richardson has its own cruising yacht, the 55-foot *Rum Runner* (530/542-6570, www.camprichardson.com, $39 adults, $19 children 12 and under), named for one of the South Shore's most popular cocktails. Heading to Emerald Bay and back, the 1.5-hour tours leave twice a day in summer (1 and 3:30 P.M.) with only 30 passengers on board. Beer, wine, and cocktails are available for purchase.

Tahoe Duck

Perhaps the strangest of all the possible ways to cruise Lake Tahoe is aboard the *Tahoe Duck* (530/525-7825, www.tahoeducktours.com, $30 adults, $19 children 3–17, free for children under 3), a World War II amphibious truck that can travel by land and by sea. A total of 21,000 of these vehicles were built between 1942 and 1945 for use in the war, and remained in service as late as 1974. The *Tahoe Duck* drives down

U.S. 50 from Heavenly Village to the Tahoe Keys Marina, then splashes into the water for a 30-minute cruise (the entire tour lasts about 75 minutes). The *Duck* usually operates only May–September.

TOURS BY AIR
◖ HeliTahoe Helicopters

Lake Tahoe looks huge from the ground, so just imagine what it looks like from an aerial perspective. To see if you've imagined correctly, take a tour with HeliTahoe Helicopters (1901 Airport Rd., South Lake Tahoe, 530/544-2211, www.helitahoe.com, $70–325 per person). The only helicopter tour operator on the lake, owner Claudio Bellotto has two flying machines based at South Lake Tahoe Airport. Both are surprisingly quiet for both passengers and passersby (unlike the helicopters that buzz the Hawaiian Islands, these can't be heard from the ground). Choose from tours that last from 10 minutes ($70 per person) to an hour ($325 per person), offering bird'-eye views of Emerald Bay, Sand Harbor, and the South Shore. In 2010, Bellotto began offering "flying weddings" in addition to his regular tours. His Bell 206 helicopter has adequate room for a minister, best man, and maid of honor in addition to the bride and groom.

◖ Lake Tahoe Balloons

South Shore visitors longing to go up, up, and away can do just that with Lake Tahoe Balloons (530/544-1221 or 800/872-9294, www.laketahoeballoons.com, $250 per person). The company launches their hot air balloon not from land but from the surface of the lake, via the *Tahoe Flyer,* the world's only certified balloon launch and recovery boat. Balloon rides are offered in the early-morning hours only (5–7 A.M. launch time, May–Oct.), when the wind is relatively calm.

See Lake Tahoe from the basket of a hot-air balloon.

© ANN MARIE BROWN

A continental breakfast is served on board the boat as it cruises to the designated launch site on the lake. Passengers watch as the balloon is inflated mid-lake, then they climb aboard its wicker basket, or gondola, for a one-hour flight. During the flight, passengers will fly as high as 3,000 feet above the water's surface, enjoying a bird's-eye view of the entire Tahoe basin, and on the clearest days, a southward view all the way to the peaks of Yosemite National Park. It's an amazing and somewhat daunting sensation to be propelled only by blasts of hot air, the skill of the balloon pilot, and the whim of the wind. After the flight, passengers are treated to a traditional post-flight champagne toast. The entire adventure takes about four hours.

Lake Tahoe Paragliding

If helicopters and hot-air balloons are too tame for you, consider a tour in a para-glider with a professional USHPA Certified Tandem Instructor at Lake Tahoe Paragliding (530/318-1859, www.laketahoeparagliding.com, $200 per person). Yes, it's just you and your tandem instructor, tethered to what amounts to little more than a parachute, soaring above Lake Tahoe. No motor, no fuselage, just the two of you at the mercy of the Tahoe breeze. Anyone who weighs more than 60 and less than 215 pounds can take part in this adventure, regardless of fitness level. Both pilot and passenger are hooked into the glider, with the passenger positioned in front for the best view. As passenger, your only job is to lean left or right when your pilot tells you to do so. After an hour's flight, you'll land on the Tahoe sand and help to pack up the gear. Still not enough of an adrenaline rush? Then learn how to fly solo at Lake Tahoe Paragliding's school; an array of courses provide all the instruction you need to get your beginner, intermediate, or advanced rating.

Sights

KAHLE PARK

Just a few blocks east of the Stateline casinos at Kahle Drive and U.S. 50 lies a beautiful preserved area that is popular with joggers, dog walkers, and nature lovers. Kahle Park (775/586-7271), which lies on the Nevada side of the state line, features a one-mile interpretive trail that focuses on Tahoe's human and natural history. Named for the Washoe Indian word for the rock-grinding tools used by the tribe to prepare food, Lam Watah Trail visits a meadow that was the traditional site of a Washoe spring encampment. Signs explain the importance of Tahoe's meadows and wetlands as a filtering system for the lake. The trail winds its way to the lakeshore at Nevada Beach, one of the largest and widest stretches of coarse white sand in all of Tahoe. A bonus here is that this trail is often snow-free (or well packed by boot prints), even in winter. Bring snowshoes just in case, however.

VAN SICKLE BI-STATE PARK

As winter skiers and summer sightseers ride the Heavenly gondola from Lake Tahoe's South Shore to the slopes above, they soar above the 725 woodsy acres of Van Sickle Bi-State Park (530/542-5580 or 530/543-6038), which opened to the public in July 2011. Although the trail system is still under development, Van Sickle is already popular with hikers, dog walkers, and mountain bikers. The park contains a few historic buildings, including an old 1860s barn that belonged to Henry Van Sickle. The Van Sickle family operated the Stateline Stables on this site until 1993, and over the years, thousands of vacationing families enjoyed trail rides on this property. Today the

© ANN MARIE BROWN

Historic barns and buildings can be seen at Van Sickle Bi-State Park.

SOUTH SHORE

park's main attraction is the Daggett Summit Connector Trail, which runs uphill from the large paved parking lot. A 1.5-mile walk up this trail leads to a fire-scarred area with spectacular views over South Lake Tahoe and the casino area. A short distance farther, the trail crosses a small waterfall, then heads east and in another 1.8 miles connects to the Tahoe Rim Trail at Daggett Summit. The park entrance is closed to cars Nov.–May, but visitors can still walk in or snowshoe past the gates. Enter the park behind the Raley's supermarket at Heavenly Village Way and Lake Parkway, or off the Loop Road behind Harrah's.

◖ HEAVENLY GONDOLA

Spring, summer, fall, or winter, take a ride on the Heavenly Ski Resort gondola (1001 Heavenly Village Way, 775/586-7000, www. skiheavenly.com, 9 A.M.–4 P.M. weekdays and 8:30 A.M.–4 P.M. weekends and holidays in winter, 10 A.M.–5 P.M. daily in summer). The lower terminal for the eight-passenger tram cars is in downtown Stateline at Heavenly Village; the upper end is 2.4 miles up the mountain. The gondola whisks sightseers up an incline of almost 2,800 feet in a mere 12 minutes, providing nonstop panoramic views. On the uphill trip, be sure to disembark at the 14,000-square-foot observation platform perched amid the granite at 9,123 feet in elevation (the gondola doesn't stop there on the way back down). The 360-degree views include the Carson Valley and surrounding desert to the east, the Desolation Wilderness to the west, and the entire expanse of Lake Tahoe laid out from south to north. A short paved trail circles the overlook, and the views change with every step. A small café serves appetizers, sandwiches, wine, and espresso, and you can sit at the outdoor tables and marvel at the view while you nosh. Then hop back on the gondola for the final stint to the top, where you can ski, snowboard, or go tubing in winter,

the view from the observation platform near the top of the Heavenly Gondola

© ANN MARIE BROWN

or in summer, try your hand at a 26-foot rock climbing wall or go for a hike (choose from three different trails of varying difficulty). The Tamarack Lodge, built in 2010, is located at the top of the gondola and serves surprisingly gourmet food.

Gondola tickets vary in price by season; plan on paying about $32 for adults, $28 for seniors over 65 and teens 13–18, and $21 for children 5–12. Children 4 and under ride free. The easiest parking for the gondola is at the city-owned garage on Bellamy Court, off Heavenly Village Way ($3.75 per hour or $25 per day). Don't try to park for free in the neighboring Raley's parking lot; you may get towed.

A summer attraction accessible only with a gondola ride is the **Heavenly Flyer ZipRider,** an 80-second-long thrill ride that travels a distance of 3,100 feet. From the top of the gondola, riders hop onto the Tamarack Express chair to get to the ZipRider take-off deck. Riders are clipped into a seat between two elevated cables, and then gravity zips them down the mountain at speeds approaching 50 miles per hour (there is a 525-foot drop in elevation from the top of Tamarack Express to the top of the gondola). As riders zoom through the treetops, the views are spectacular. Check before you go, though: As of winter 2012, the Heavenly Flyer ZipRider is not in operation as a result of an accident in August 2009 that led to one man's death and a subsequent lawsuit. Officials at Heavenly state that they plan to reopen the zipline, but it's anybody's guess when that will happen. If it is still closed when you visit, you can always ride the zipline at Kirkwood Ski Resort (see the Carson Pass chapter).

SOUTH LAKE TAHOE HISTORICAL SOCIETY MUSEUM

At this small but surprising museum (3058 Hwy. 50, South Lake Tahoe, 530/541-5458, www.laketahoemuseum.org, 11 A.M.–3 P.M. Wed.–Mon. in summer, Sat. only in winter, free admission) located next to the Lake Tahoe Visitors Authority, visitors can see the lake through the eyes of its early explorers and residents. Housing the region's most comprehensive collection of early photographs, pioneer tools, farm implements, and Washoe Indian baskets, the museum showcases an entirely different way of life at the lake than what we know today. Exhibits document eclectic bits and pieces of Tahoe history, from the Pony Express to the gold- and silver-mining era, from the invention of snow sports to the beginning of the casino industry. Several displays of photographs and memorabilia highlight Tahoe's early tourist resorts (the Tahoe Tavern, the Tallac Hotel, and Fallen Leaf Lake Lodge). An entire section is devoted to the Lake Valley Railroad and the massive steamships that transported passengers around the lake in the late 19th century, before the development of highways and widespread use of the automobile. A highlight is the model of the historic vessel SS *Tahoe,* which was the largest of the steamers that plied Lake Tahoe's waters, measuring nearly 170 feet in length and with a carrying capacity of 200 passengers. Eventually the ship was scuttled near Glenbrook Bay because maintaining her was no longer economical.

On the grounds behind the museum is the Tahoe basin's oldest still-standing building, Osgood's Toll House, circa 1859, and a 1930s-era log cabin.

TALLAC HISTORIC SITE

Located near the U.S. Forest Service's visitors center is the Tallac Historic Site (2.7 miles north of the Y on Hwy. 89/Emerald Bay Rd., 530/541-5227, www.tahoeheritage.org, dawn–dusk June–Sept., free admission, guided tours $7 mid-June–mid-Sept.), a 150-acre chunk of lakeshore property that is home to a cluster of late-1800s and early-1900s summer homes and mansions—a total of 28 buildings in all.

The impressive structures were built by prominent San Francisco families with money acquired in banking, railroad building, and land speculation.

Three grand homes from Tahoe's "Era of Opulence," still housing some of their original furnishings, can be seen at Tallac—the Baldwin, Pope, and Heller Estates. All three estates are on the National Register of Historic Places. The **Baldwin Estate**, built in 1921, is now home to the **Tallac Museum**, which features an impressive display of Washoe Indian exhibits. The neighboring **Pope Estate**, built in 1894 by George Tallant and later owned by the Lloyd Tevis and George Pope families, is the interpretive center for the Tallac site. The building can be visited on docent-led tours in the summer months. On summer weekends, living-history programs often take place, featuring costumed docents playing the roles of real people from Tallac's history.

Those interested in gardening shouldn't miss the Pope Estate's arboretum, a tranquil spot with a pond, small waterfall, and a collection of plants and trees from around the world put together by Mrs. William Tevis, the daughter of a California governor, in the early 20th century. (The Tevis family purchased the Pope Estate from its original owners.)

The **Heller Estate**, constructed in 1923, is also known as **Valhalla** and is the home of the annual Valhalla Arts and Music Festival, a series of concerts and dramatic performances held throughout the summer. (For program information and tickets, phone 530/541-4975 or go to www.valhallatahoe.com.) Arts and crafts are sold at two small twin cabins on the estate. Valhalla includes a grand hall with a 40-foot-high fireplace, and can be rented for weddings and events.

A few archaeological remains of the **Tallac Resort** can also be seen at the Tallac Historic Site. The opulent resort, which owner/entrepreneur Elias "Lucky" Baldwin called the "Greatest Casino in America," had its heyday in the 1890s, when the wealthy would come from all over California and Nevada to dine, dance, and gamble in elegance on the shores of Lake Tahoe. In addition to the casino, the Tallac Resort included two large and lavish hotels with a ballroom and tennis courts. Guests at the resort would enjoy orchestra concerts, steamer rides across the lake, croquet, and other organized activities. Visitors today can see the remains of the casino foundation and walk the resort's rock-lined promenade.

Present-day Tallac visitors can also stop in at the boathouse on the grounds of the Pope Estate, where an organization called Tahoe Classic Yacht (530/544-2307, www.tahoeclassicyacht.org) runs a small maritime museum highlighting the history of watercraft on Lake Tahoe. Under restoration at the boathouse is the *Quic Chakidn,* a 38-foot cruiser built in 1921, which once operated as a tour boat on Emerald Bay and was used to tow the famous steamer *Tahoe* when she reached the end of her useful life. A few other antique boats are also on display, plus a collection of outboard motors.

The Tallac site enjoys an incredibly scenic location on Lake Tahoe's shore, so don't miss the chance to stroll along the beach or walk out on the pier behind the boathouse. And take note of the trees on the Tallac grounds. Because they were protected by the wealthy Tallac landowners during the great logging era of the late 1800s, they are some of the finest examples of old-growth conifers remaining in the Tahoe basin.

TAYLOR CREEK VISITOR CENTER

Managed by the U.S. Forest Service, the Taylor Creek Visitor Center (three miles north of the South Lake Tahoe Y on Hwy. 89/Emerald Bay Rd., 530/543-2674, 8 A.M.–5:30 P.M. daily mid-June–Sept., 8 A.M.–4:30 P.M. Oct.) provides in-depth information on the natural ecology of the

Lake Tahoe basin. Maps and guides are for sale, and interpretive programs are held regularly in summer. Visitors could easily spend most of a day here attending free lectures and nature walks. The Taylor Creek Visitor Center is the starting point for four short interpretive trails: Rainbow Trail, Smokey's Trail, Lake of the Sky Trail, and Forest Tree Trail, as well as a trail that leads to the neighboring Tallac Historic Site. The wheelchair-accessible Rainbow Trail travels to the center's main attraction: the **Stream Profile Chamber,** an underground structure that allows visitors to walk alongside the depths of Taylor Creek. Through large glass windows, you can peer into the water to watch rainbow trout, kokanee salmon, and other fishy creatures going about their business. Autumn is the most interesting season here, when the colorful kokanee swim up Taylor Creek to spawn and die. The visitors center holds a Kokanee Salmon Festival each year during the first weekend in October.

GLEN ALPINE SPRINGS

A pleasant one-mile walk along a cascading stream from near the western edge of Fallen Leaf Lake will bring you to the Glen Alpine Springs Historic Site, where one of the first resorts in the Lake Tahoe basin was located. Glen Alpine became popular in the 1860s when naturally carbonated spring water was discovered on the land. A resort with tent cabins and a dining hall was constructed around the spring. Resort guests would take part in a host of outdoor activities, like fishing and hiking, while enjoying the supposed health benefits of the spring water. Through the years, the resort changed hands several times and became progressively more developed and less rustic. A handful of buildings still stand from the resort's zenith in the 1890s, including a few designed by the famous architect Bernard Maybeck, the genius behind the San Francisco Palace of Fine Art. On-site docents staff an interpretive

center (530/541-4308, 10:30 A.M.–3:30 P.M. daily mid-June–mid-Sept.). Guided tours of the grounds and buildings are offered on weekends at 1 P.M. Be sure to wear sturdy walking shoes for the rocky dirt and gravel road/trail; the entire hike is two miles round-trip but mostly level. The Glen Alpine Trailhead is located at the end of Fallen Leaf Lake Road, 5.4 miles west of Highway 89.

POPE, KIVA, AND BALDWIN BEACHES

Summer visitors can enjoy the U.S. Forest Service's Baldwin Beach (dawn–dusk June–Sept.), a stunning stretch of coarse white sand on the shores of South Tahoe. Bring your kayaks, rubber rafts, or inner tubes; launching is easy here. A natural lagoon where Tallac Creek empties into Lake Tahoe on the northwest end of the beach is a popular swimming area for families with young children, because the water is shallow and surprisingly warm. Nearby, two other beaches—Pope and Kiva—are also managed by the Forest Service. Parking fee is $7 per car, except at Kiva Beach, where parking is free (enter at the Tallac Historic Site sign). Kiva Beach is the only one of the three where dogs are permitted. Pope, Kiva, and Baldwin Beaches are 2, 2.5, and 4 miles north of the South Lake Tahoe Y, respectively, on Highway 89/Emerald Bay Road.

◖ INSPIRATION POINT AT EMERALD BAY

Lake Tahoe's Emerald Bay, with its blue-green water and single, dramatic island, is one of the most photographed spots in the United States. Get your own snapshot at well-named Inspiration Point, perched hundreds of feet above Emerald Bay's three-mile-long cove. From this drive-up overlook, it is easy to imagine the glacial forces that carved out this remarkable scene. As the glaciers moved through, Emerald Bay very nearly became a separate lake, like nearby Fallen Leaf and Cascade Lakes, except that the terminal moraine at its mouth was never completed. So the beautiful bay remains an "add-on" to Lake Tahoe, connected to the main body of the lake on only one edge. Interpretive signs at the overlook relay some impressive figures about the lake, including the fact that if Lake Tahoe was drained, its massive volume of water would cover the entire state of California to a depth of more than a foot. The Inspiration Point parking lot is 7.5 miles north of the South Lake Tahoe Y on Highway 89/Emerald Bay Road, directly across from the entrance to Bayview Campground.

VIKINGSHOLM CASTLE

The curious can take a one-mile walk downhill (and uphill on the way back!) to see Vikingsholm Castle at Emerald Bay State Park (530/525-7232 or 530/541-6498, www.vikingsholm.org or www.sierrastateparks.org, 10:30 A.M.–4:30 P.M. daily Memorial Day–Sept. 30, parking fee $8; tours $8 adults, $5 children 6–12, free for children 5 and under), a Scandinavian-style mansion built in 1929 on some of Tahoe's most beautiful shoreline. Lora Josephine Knight, a wealthy Chicago widow, purchased this land at the edge of Emerald Bay and had her dream home constructed out of native stone and timber, without disturbing any of the property's existing trees. A short distance offshore, Ms. Knight had a stone teahouse built on the highest point on Fannette Island, the only island in Lake Tahoe. Guests would be shuttled by boat to the island, and servants would help them up the steep pathway to the teahouse, where they would sip Earl Grey and make polite conversation.

Considered to be one of the finest examples of Scandinavian architecture in North America, the 38-room Vikingsholm Castle is both beautiful and strange. Modeled in the style of a Norse fortress of about A.D. 800, the structure is capped with turrets and towers. Design

© ANN MARIE BROWN

The easy walk to Vikingsholm Castle offers great views of Emerald Bay.

motifs include hand-hewn beams carved with dragon heads and decorated with hand-painted flowers. Inside, the castle is furnished with authentic Scandinavian antiques as well as precisely crafted museum replicas. Part of the roof is sod, which is kept thoroughly watered so that it stays green all summer and can support wildflowers. A short distance behind the castle is the lower cascade of Eagle Falls.

Whatever you think about the building itself, its setting is spectacular. It's well worth the down-and-then-up walk just to enjoy the beautiful stretch of Emerald Bay shoreline that Lora Knight so dearly loved. (She spent 16 summers here until her death in 1945.) The hike does have a 500-foot elevation gain on the return uphill, so wear sturdy shoes and try to avoid the heat of midday. Regardless of whether or not you take a tour of the castle, the $8 parking fee is charged at the Vikingsholm parking lot, which is located 8.5 miles north of the South Lake Tahoe Y on Highway 89/ Emerald Bay Road.

Recreation

HIKING

One of the most popular activities on the South Shore is going for a hike, as the spectacular Sierra scenery quite naturally inspires the urge to explore. Before you set out on the trail, make sure you are prepared with a few essentials, such as bottled water (or some sort of water-filtering device), food, and a trail map. Because many of Tahoe's trails have rocky, uneven surfaces, hiking boots are highly recommended. Sunscreen and/or a sun hat are musts at this high elevation, and you don't want to be without mosquito repellent if the bugs are biting. And keep in mind that weather in the Sierra can change dramatically in a short period of time, so it's always wise to carry a lightweight rain poncho or jacket and additional clothing for layering.

For more information on the trails described in this section, contact the Lake Tahoe Basin Management Unit (35 College Dr., South Lake Tahoe, 530/543-2600, www.r5.fs.fed.us/ltbmu) or the Pacific Ranger District of Eldorado National Forest (7887 Hwy. 50, Pollock Pines, 530/647-5415, www.r5.fs.fed.us/eldorado).

The following hikes are listed from south to north along the Highway 89/Emerald Bay Road corridor, and from east to west along the U.S. 50/Lake Tahoe Boulevard corridor.

✷Angora Lakes

- Distance: 1.2 miles round-trip
- Duration: 1 hour
- Effort: Easy
- Elevation change: 250 feet
- Trailhead: Angora Lakes
- Directions: From the Y-junction of U.S. 50 and Hwy. 89 in South Lake Tahoe, drive 3 miles northwest on Hwy. 89 to Fallen Leaf Lake Rd. on the left (1 mile past Camp Richardson). Turn left and drive 2 miles to Tahoe Mountain Rd. Turn left and drive 0.4 mile, then turn right on Forest Service Rd. 12N14, which alternates as paved and unpaved. Drive 2.8 miles, passing the Angora Fire Lookout, to the parking lot at the road's end ($5 parking fee). The trailhead is on the left side of the upper parking lot.

Angora Lakes is especially popular with children's day camps and groups, so you may feel like an outsider on this trail if you aren't accompanied by someone under the age of 10. But this easy walk is a winner and requires so little effort that it can be done by almost anyone. The drive to the trailhead on a partially paved, partially dirt road offers scenic beauty of its own, especially as it climbs the ridge by the Angora Fire Lookout. At the upper parking lot at the road's end, you'll find the trail (a dirt road) on the left side.

In a mere 0.3 mile of walking through a pine-and-fir forest dotted with many rounded granite boulders, the road/trail reaches the first lake, Lower Angora, named after the angora goats that were grazed in this area in the 1870s. A few private houses are perched on the lake's far side. In another few minutes of walking, you arrive at Upper Angora Lake and Angora Lakes Resort, which was constructed in 1920 by the Hildinger family and has eight picturesque little cabins for rent. Members of the same family still run the resort today, but the cabins are so popular that getting a reservation is almost impossible. At 7,280 feet in elevation, Upper Angora Lake is set in a perfect bowl-shaped glacial cirque. Some people paddle around the lake in rubber rafts, and by midsummer, swimmers usually find the water warm enough to take a dip. Hikers can take advantage of the lake's small beach, fish from shore for trout, or rent rowboats for a few bucks an hour. No matter what else you choose to do at Upper Angora Lake, most everybody who visits here makes a stop at the refreshment stand to buy a big glass of lemonade. Given the sun-exposed hike, that lemonade stand is a gold mine.

Option: Energetic types who want to turn this easy walk into more of an adventure can ascend to the summit of Echo Peak, elevation 8,588 feet, from Upper Angora Lake. From the resort, head to the left around the lake and you'll see a use trail that ascends the ridge leading up to the peak. In fact, you'll probably see several use trails, all marked with rock cairns. Choose one and begin a grunt of a climb, gaining more than 1,200 feet in a little over a mile. Most people make it from the upper lake to the summit in under an hour, with some serious huffing and puffing. Echo Peak's view makes it all worthwhile. It's a 360-degree panorama that includes the Echo Lakes, Fallen Leaf Lake, Lake Tahoe, and numerous other lakes and peaks in the Desolation Wilderness to the west.

Fallen Leaf Lake's Moraine Trail

- Distance: 2.5 miles round-trip
- Duration: 1.5 hours
- Effort: Easy
- Elevation change: 50 feet
- Trailhead: Fallen Leaf Lake Campground
- Directions: From the Y-junction of U.S. 50 and Hwy. 89 in South Lake Tahoe, drive 3 miles northwest on Hwy. 89 to Fallen Leaf Lake Rd. on the left (1 mile past Camp Richardson). Turn left and drive 0.6 mile to the campground entrance on the right. The trail begins by campsite #75.

Picturesque Fallen Leaf Lake, measuring three miles long, is the second-largest alpine lake in the Tahoe basin. Much of the lakeshore is bounded by private property, so access to the lake is fairly limited. However, the short and easy Moraine Trail leads from near the entrance to Fallen Leaf Lake Campground to the lake's northwest edge. The narrow, sandy path meanders for 0.25 mile through groves of quaking aspen, then heads to the right when it reaches the lakeshore and crosses Fallen Leaf Lake's dam. On the far side, it skirts the edge of the west shore to Sawmill Cove, an ideal spot for swimming or picnicking. This is a remarkably easy walk, and a great place for a casual stroll with your dog. If possible, try to visit here in October, when you can see the aspens put on their fall color show. In winter, this trail is a popular beginner-level cross-country skiing route.

Grass, Susie, Heather, and Aloha Lakes

- Distance: 5.4–12.4 miles round-trip
- Duration: 3–7 hours
- Effort: Moderate
- Elevation change: 500–1,400 feet
- Trailhead: Glen Alpine
- Directions: From the Y-junction of U.S. 50 and Hwy. 89 in South Lake Tahoe, drive 3

HIKING ESSENTIALS

1. Food and water. Water is even more important than food, although it's unwise to get caught without some edible supplies for emergencies. Carry a couple of full water bottles as well as a purifier or filtering device so you can obtain water from streams, rivers, or lakes. Never drink water from a natural source without purifying it. What you carry for food is up to you. If you don't want to carry a lot of weight, stick with snacks like nutrition bars, nuts, dried fruit, turkey or beef jerky, and crackers.

2. Trail map. Never rely on trail signs or a GPS device alone; carry a map at all times. Maps are on sale at visitors centers and outdoor stores, or you can purchase them online. Try the Lake Tahoe Recreation Map or Desolation Wilderness Trail Map by Tom Harrison Maps (www.tomharrisonmaps.com) or the Lake Tahoe Basin Hiking and Biking Trail Map by Adventure Maps (www.adventuremaps.net).

3. Extra clothing. Not only can the weather suddenly turn windy, cloudy, or rainy, but your body's condition also changes: You'll perspire as you hike up a sunny hill, then get chilled at the top of a windy ridge or when you head into shade. Always carry a lightweight, waterproof, wind-resistant jacket, no matter how nice the weather is. Stay away from clothing made from cotton; once cotton gets wet, it stays wet. Polyester-blend fabrics dry faster. Some high-tech fabrics actually wick moisture away from your skin. In cool temperatures, or when heading to a mountain summit even on a hot day, carry gloves and a hat as well.

4. Flashlight. Mini-flashlights are available everywhere, weigh almost nothing, and can save the day. Tiny "squeeze" LED flashlights, the size and shape of a quarter, can clip onto any key ring. Make sure the batteries work. They are small, so take along a few extras.

5. Sunglasses and sunscreen. The higher the elevation, the more dangerous the sun is. Put on high-SPF sunscreen 30 minutes before you go out, and then reapply every couple hours. Also protect your face with a wide-brimmed hat and your lips with high-SPF lip balm.

6. Insect repellent. Find one that works for you and always have it in your pack. Many types of insect repellent use the active ingredient DEET, which is effective but also may be toxic, especially for children. Other types of repellent are made from natural substances such as lemon or eucalyptus oil.

7. First-aid kit. Supplies for blister repairs, an elastic bandage, an antibiotic ointment, and an anti-inflammatory medicine such as ibuprofen can be valuable tools in emergencies. If you're allergic to bee stings or anything else in the outdoors, carry medication.

8. Swiss Army-style pocketknife. Carry one with several blades, a can opener, scissors, and tweezers.

9. Compass. Know how to use one. If you prefer to use a GPS device, that's fine, but know that GPS may not work everywhere you go.

10. Emergency supplies. Ask, "What would I need if I had to spend the night outside?" Aside from food and water, these are supplies that will get you through an unplanned night in the wilderness:

· *Lightweight blanket.* Get a blanket or sleeping bag made of foil-like Mylar film designed to reflect radiating body heat. These make a great emergency shelter, and weigh and cost almost nothing.

· *Matches and a candle.* Keep matches in a waterproof container (or zippered bag), just in case you ever need to build a fire in an emergency.

· *Whistle.* If you need help, you can blow a whistle for a lot longer than you can shout.

· *Small signal mirror.* A flash from a mirror can be seen from far away.

11. Fun stuff. These aren't necessary, but can make your trip more fun: a wildflower or birding book, a pair of binoculars, a fishing license and lightweight fishing equipment, and extra socks (they feel like heaven halfway through a long hike).

large, island-dotted Susie Lake

here and walk 1 mile to the edge of Grass Lake, 2.7 miles from the trailhead. Swimming is the primary activity at this pretty, popular lake.

Those seeking more scenery and a longer day on the trail should skip the Grass Lake turnoff and instead continue another 1.6 miles to the next junction. There, bear left for Susie Lake, then left again 0.5 mile later. At 4.2 miles from your start you'll reach Susie Lake's scenic shoreline, which has an abundance of established backpacking sites tucked amid groves of whitebark pines and hemlocks. Many people make large, island-dotted Susie Lake their turnaround point for an 8.4-mile day, but it's a pity not to continue for another mile to even more dramatic Heather Lake, a treeless, granite-bound beauty. The additional ascent is minimal, and much of the walk is a lovely stroll around Susie's southwestern shore. Where the trail reaches Heather Lake, it skirts along its northern edge on a steep, rocky slope. Just beyond the lake's northwest shore, where a scarce few trees create shade and shelter for camping or picnicking, is the pass leading to Lake Aloha. If you still have the energy, walk onward for one more mile to the northern shore of Aloha, 6.2 miles from your start at Glen Alpine. Lake Aloha is a huge, shallow lake peppered with hundreds of tiny islands—a surreal but beautiful sight to behold. It was created when several small lakes were dammed to form one massive basin.

Gilmore and Half Moon Lakes

- Distance: 12.4 miles round-trip
- Duration: 6–7 hours
- Effort: Moderate
- Elevation change: 1,750 feet
- Trailhead: Glen Alpine
- Directions: From the Y-junction of U.S. 50 and Hwy. 89 in South Lake Tahoe, drive 3 miles northwest on Hwy. 89 to Fallen Leaf Lake Rd. on the left (1 mile past Camp Richardson). Turn left and drive 5.4 miles

miles northwest on Hwy. 89 to Fallen Leaf Lake Rd. on the left (1 mile past Camp Richardson). Turn left and drive 5.4 miles to the end of the road and the Glen Alpine Trailhead. Day hikers are required to fill out a self-serve wilderness permit at the trailhead.

To complete this entire lake-filled trip, the mileage may be long, but the trail's grade is so gentle that the hike is much easier than you'd expect. This trail visits three lakes directly and travels near a fourth, so you can tailor your hiking distance to whatever your mood, abilities, and schedule allow. The trailhead is at Glen Alpine at the end of Fallen Leaf Lake Road. After an easy walk up the gravel and dirt road, which travels 1 mile to the site of the historic Glen Alpine Springs Resort (an interpretive center and various displays are found here), the path narrows to a single-track trail and continues for another 0.7 mile to the Desolation Wilderness boundary and a left turnoff for Grass Lake. Hikers wanting a short, easy hike can turn left

© ANN MARIE BROWN

© ANN MARIE BROWN

Even as late as June, Gilmore Lake can be covered in snow.

to the end of the road and the Glen Alpine Trailhead. Day hikers are required to fill out a self-serve wilderness permit at the trailhead.

This hike follows the path less traveled to three scenic lakes in the Desolation Wilderness. The route is the same as the trail to Susie, Heather, and Aloha Lakes for the first 3.3 miles, but then heads right to join the Pacific Crest Trail heading north to Gilmore Lake, 1 mile farther. It's a pleasant hike all the way, gaining only 1,750 feet over 4.3 miles. Snuggled at the base of Mount Tallac's southwest slope, Gilmore Lake is a nearly circular body of water that is forested on its southern shore and backed by a steep talus slope to the north. It is visited mostly by hikers heading from Fallen Leaf Lake to Mount Tallac, and backpackers making their way on the Pacific Crest Trail over Dicks Pass. After enjoying a rest and perhaps a swim at Gilmore, simply retrace your steps 0.7 mile on the Pacific Crest Trail, then turn right on the trail to Half Moon Lake. A brief, easy climb followed by a mostly level

walk brings you around the north shore of the lake. Crescent-shaped Half Moon Lake and its tiny neighbor, Alta Morris Lake, are contained in a huge glacial cirque that rates among the most beautiful spots in all of the Desolation Wilderness, yet the lakes are not heavily visited. They are just far enough off the main trail (1.9 miles) that many hikers heading for other destinations won't bother to make the detour. That leaves you with a chance of solitude at the gorgeous lakes, which are set at the base of Dicks Peak (9,974 feet) and Jack's Peak (9,856 feet).

Mount Tallac

- Distance: 9.4 miles round-trip
- Duration: 5–6 hours
- Effort: Strenuous
- Elevation change: 3,400 feet
- Trailhead: Mount Tallac
- Directions: From the Y-junction of U.S. 50 and Hwy. 89 in South Lake Tahoe, drive

© ANN MARIE BROWN

The summit of Mount Tallac is a must-do hike for many Tahoe visitors.

3.5 miles northwest on Hwy. 89 to the left turnoff for the Mount Tallac Trailhead and Camp Shelly (across Hwy. 89 from the Baldwin Beach entrance). Turn left and drive 0.4 mile, then turn left and drive 0.6 mile to the signed trailhead. Day hikers are required to fill out a self-serve wilderness permit at the trailhead.

There are two popular trails that lead to Mount Tallac (pronounced "tull-ACK"), but the route that offers the most views almost all the way to the top is the one from the Mount Tallac Trailhead. This is a butt-kicker of a hike, with 3,400 feet of elevation gain from the bottom to the top, and two-thirds of it crammed into the last 2.6 miles. (The other route begins at the Glen Alpine Trailhead at Fallen Leaf Lake, is about 1 mile longer, and has slightly less elevation gain.) Regardless of its difficulty, this is one of the most popular hikes near South Lake Tahoe and also one of the most rewarding. The best way to avoid the heaviest crowds is to hike the trail on a weekday, preferably after Labor Day but before late October, when the 9,735-foot summit often sees its first snow.

The trail starts out deceptively easy, following an almost level course along a lateral moraine for 1.5 miles to tiny Floating Island Lake. The grass-edged lake once had a 20-foot-wide mat of soil and grass floating around its surface, earning its name, but the "floating island" has been absent for some years. A half mile farther is rocky but small Cathedral Lake, a relatively nondescript body of water, but a good place to rest up before the ensuing climb. And climb you will from here on out. At Cathedral Lake, you've completed 2.1 miles of the hike (almost halfway), but you've gained only 1,200 feet. You've got more than 2,100 feet left to gain over the next 2.6 miles—a punishing climb with almost no shade along the way. Fortunately, a nearly constant banquet of views awaits, with all of South Lake Tahoe spread out before you. The trail winds around to the less-steep southwest side of Mount Tallac, and

0.25 mile below the summit, it joins the other trail coming up from Gilmore Lake. The last few hundred feet seem to take forever, but finally you ascend the pile of jumbled rocks that mark the top. It's hard to decide which direction to face. To the east, of course, is Lake Tahoe, Emerald Bay, and Fallen Leaf Lake. To the west and south are the lake-laden basins of the Desolation Wilderness and distinctive Ralston and Pyramid Peaks. Unless the wind is fierce on top, you won't want to give up this summit vista anytime soon.

If you can arrange a car shuttle, a great way to hike Tallac is to go uphill from the Tallac Trailhead as described here, then come back down the west side of the mountain, passing by Gilmore Lake on the way to the Glen Alpine Trailhead at Fallen Leaf Lake. This provides the maximum amount of scenery in a hike of about 11 miles. Some people start at the Glen Alpine Trailhead and make a semi-loop by heading up Tallac's west side to the summit, then descending on the east side and taking a cutoff trail from Cathedral Lake to the Stanford High Sierra Camp at Fallen Leaf Lake. But since there is no parking at the Stanford camp unless you are a paying guest, hikers then have to walk back for a couple of miles along the road to the Glen Alpine Trailhead. A car shuttle from the Tallac Trailhead to the Glen Alpine Trailhead is a much better way to go.

Cascade Falls

- Distance: 1.5 miles round-trip
- Duration: 1 hour
- Effort: Easy
- Elevation change: 200 feet
- Trailhead: Bayview
- Directions: From the Y-junction of U.S. 50 and Hwy. 89 in South Lake Tahoe, drive 7.5 miles northwest on Hwy. 89 to Bayview Campground on the left. Turn left and drive to the trailhead parking area at the camp's far

end. If the lot is full, park in the dirt parking area along Hwy. 89, outside the camp entrance. Take the trail to the left from the trailhead signboard. (No wilderness permit is required for Cascade Falls hikers.)

The hike to Cascade Falls is one of the best easy hikes near South Lake Tahoe, but good timing is imperative. The waterfall is at its best only in the early summer months and dwindles to a meager dribble by August. In its peak season (May, June, and July), Cascade Falls is a wide stream of white water that plummets 200 feet over fractured granite into Cascade Lake's southwest end. At full flow, as it billows and scatters in the wind, creating a misty cloud of spray, it is easy to see why the waterfall was once known as White Cloud Falls.

The hike to Cascade Falls is remarkably level, following a hillside ridge high above azure blue Cascade Lake, elevation 6,464 feet. The route meanders in and out of Jeffrey-pine forest, alternately providing shade and open views. After a mere five minutes of walking, you're rewarded with a tremendous vista of the lake, which is separated from Lake Tahoe by a thin strip of land—the handiwork of glaciers. Soon the path follows an exposed granite ledge that drops off steeply to more dramatic views. The trail peters out near the edge of Cascade Creek, so how far you go is up to you. The best views of the waterfall are not right at the water's edge but about a quarter mile back on the trail. Upstream of the falls are some lovely aquamarine pools, surrounded by large shelves of granite that might inspire a picnic. In July, bright pink penstemon blooms in profusion among the rocky crevices of this trail.

Velma, Fontanillis, and Dicks Lakes Loop

- Distance: 10.5 miles round-trip
- Duration: 5–6 hours
- Effort: Strenuous
- Elevation change: 2,700 feet

© ANN MARIE BROWN

Dicks Lake is one of many pretty lakes in Desolation Wilderness.

- Trailhead: Bayview
- Directions: From the Y-junction of U.S. 50 and Hwy. 89 in South Lake Tahoe, drive 7.5 miles northwest on Hwy. 89 to Bayview Campground on the left. Turn left and drive to the trailhead parking area at the camp's far end. If the lot is full, park in the dirt parking area along Hwy. 89, outside the camp entrance. Day hikers are required to fill out a self-serve wilderness permit at the trailhead.

The Bayview Trailhead offers easy access from Highway 89 at Emerald Bay to the spectacular Desolation Wilderness, but it comes with the price of a steep climb. From the trailhead at Bayview Campground, hikers begin with an 850-foot ascent over a slope blanketed with white firs to Granite Lake at 1.2 miles out. Along the way, there are occasional overlook points where the trail breaks out of the trees to provide expansive views of Emerald Bay, Cascade Lake, and Lake Tahoe. Given the heart-pumping climb, it's not surprising

that many dog walkers and exercise seekers just make small but scenic Granite Lake their destination and turnaround point. Those who seek more adventure and are willing to pay for it can continue the even steeper ascent for another 0.9 mile and 800 feet of gain to the base of Maggie's Peaks, and scramble to the summit if they so desire. From Maggie's, the grade mellows out for a while before the trail descends to a junction with a path on the right coming in from Eagle Lake. Continue straight (left), and you'll reach the start of this lake-filled loop, now 3.7 miles from the trailhead. Most people go right first, heading for Upper and Middle Velma Lakes, which are located a short distance off the main trail. Shallow and marshy Upper Velma may not be worth the extra walk, but granite-backed Middle Velma certainly is. Continuing on the loop, you'll skirt along the shoreline of Fontanillis Lake, a remarkably long and narrow body of water named for its plentiful brook trout, and then reach Dicks Lake, the most scenic of the lot. Oval-shaped Dicks Lake is set in a dramatic glacial cirque, with Dicks Peak rising behind it. The final leg of the loop beyond Dicks Lake is a fascinating stroll over a series of low, glacially carved ridges and basins dotted with small ponds. For a genuine taste of the Desolation Wilderness landscape, you can't do much better than this hike.

【 Eagle Lake ⚡

- Distance: 2 miles round-trip
- Duration: 1.5 hours
- Effort: Easy/moderate
- Elevation change: 500 feet
- Trailhead: Eagle Lake
- Directions: From the Y-junction of U.S. 50 and Hwy. 89 in South Lake Tahoe, drive 8.5 miles northwest on Hwy. 89 to the Eagle Falls/Eagle Lake parking lot on the left. A $5 parking fee is charged unless you park outside the lot alongside the highway. Day hikers are required to fill out a self-serve wilderness permit at the trailhead.

On summer days, it can be difficult to find a parking spot at the trailhead for Eagle Lake. The reason, simply, is because you get so much bang for your buck on the relatively easy, 1-mile hike to the lake. Yes, the trail has a climb of 500 feet, and yes, it is rocky in places, but given enough time, even a three-year-old could make it to Eagle Lake. The lake is tucked into a beautiful glacial cirque in the Desolation Wilderness, and to get there, the trail crosses the cascading waters of Eagle Creek on a sturdy footbridge above Upper Eagle Falls. Many people just hike in the first 0.25 mile to the waterfall and then call it a day. If you do so, be sure to walk the short and informative interpretive loop that takes off from the footbridge; it provides lovely high views of Emerald Bay with little additional effort. The main trail parallels Eagle Creek much of the rest of the way to the lake. In addition to the up-close beauty

of this white-fir and Jeffrey-pine forest, the path offers splendid views of Emerald Bay; just turn around and take a look. Eagle Lake is a beauty, with a granite backdrop and a mix of rocky and forested shoreline that invites long picnics and leisurely swims. For many visitors, Eagle Lake is their first taste of the Desolation Wilderness, and it's compelling enough to get anyone hooked for life.

The only way to have a hope for solitude on this trail is to hike it very early in the morning—say 7 A.M.—or wait until an autumn weekday when most of the vacation crowds have dispersed.

Middle Velma Lake

- Distance: 10 miles round-trip
- Duration: 5–6 hours
- Effort: Strenuous
- Elevation change: 2,100 feet
- Trailhead: Eagle Lake
- Directions: From the Y-junction of U.S. 50 and Hwy. 89 in South Lake Tahoe, drive 8.5 miles northwest on Hwy. 89 to the Eagle Falls/Eagle Lake parking lot on the left. A $5 parking fee is charged unless you park outside the lot alongside the highway. Day hikers are required to fill out a self-serve wilderness permit at the trailhead.

The hike to Middle Velma Lake follows the same path as the trail to Eagle Lake, and the same rules apply: Parking can be difficult on summer days, and the crowds can be quite dense along the trail, even though Middle Velma Lake requires a much longer and more strenuous trek. Nonetheless, so many people get inspired by the scenery at Eagle Lake that they decide to continue along the trail to see more, and Middle Velma is the next destination. The junction for Velma Lakes is just 100 yards before the shore of Eagle Lake. At this junction, you gratefully leave a percentage of the crowds behind and ascend the hillside to a spectacular view of Eagle Lake and Lake Tahoe from up high. The ascent continues for the next 1.7 miles, with only occasional breaks for level walking. At 2.7 miles from the trailhead, a trail comes in on the left from the Bayview Trailhead; you continue straight for Middle Velma Lake. The grade becomes much easier, and in less than a mile you reach a major fork—left for Dicks Lake and Dicks Pass, and right for Middle Velma Lake. Head right and enjoy a long downhill stretch, followed by a few right turns in quick succession, all signed for Middle Velma. Five miles from your start you are on the shores of this lovely lake, which is dotted with rocky islands and popular with backpackers because of its hemlock-shaded shoreline. Anglers generally do well here. So do swimmers and picnickers.

Vikingsholm and Lower Eagle Falls

- Distance: 2.5 miles round-trip
- Duration: 1.5 hours
- Effort: Easy/moderate
- Elevation change: 500 feet
- Trailhead: Vikingsholm
- Directions: From the Y-junction of U.S. 50 and Hwy. 89 in South Lake Tahoe, drive 8.7 miles northwest on Hwy. 89 to the Vikingsholm parking lot on the right, just past the Eagle Falls/Eagle Lake parking lot on the left. An $8 parking fee is charged.

The busiest trail near the South Shore is the short hike to Vikingsholm, a Scandinavian-style mansion built in the 1920s on some of Lake Tahoe's most beautiful shoreline. The mansion belonged to Lora J. Knight, a wealthy Chicago widow who dreamed of building a home on glacier-carved Emerald Bay in the style of an ancient Viking castle. A short distance offshore, Knight also built a teahouse on Fannette Island, the only island in Lake Tahoe. The uniqueness of this property and its location attract a huge number of curiosity seekers

on every summer day, so solitude lovers should take this walk as early in the morning as possible, and preferably on a weekday. The path is a dirt road, not a trail, and leads downhill from Highway 89 to the lakeshore. Even from the parking area the views of Emerald Bay are spectacular; many people go no farther than the stone overlook constructed on granite slabs a few yards from the parking lot. But if you follow the dirt road, you'll enjoy an easy downhill stroll past sprays of summer wildflowers to the Vikingsholm grounds. For eight bucks, guided tours of the castle are available. Many hikers are content just to wander along the picnic-table-dotted shoreline or follow the trail behind Vikingsholm for another 0.25 mile to the base of Lower Eagle Falls, a refreshing cascade of white water in early summer. Near the castle the Vikingsholm Trail joins the Rubicon Trail, so those seeking a longer walk can follow Rubicon Trail south and then east for 1.6 miles to Emerald Bay State Park's Eagle Point Campground, or north for 4.5 miles to D. L. Bliss State Park. The vast majority of people just turn around at Vikingsholm and head back uphill, and many are unpleasantly surprised by the 500-foot elevation gain that awaits—especially since the trail is hot and shadeless at midday.

Rubicon Trail

- Distance: 5.5 miles one-way
- Duration: 2.5 hours
- Effort: Moderate
- Elevation change: 500 feet
- Trailhead: Vikingsholm
- Directions: From the Y-junction of U.S. 50 and Hwy. 89 in South Lake Tahoe, drive 8.7 miles northwest on Hwy. 89 to the Vikingsholm parking lot on the right, just past the Eagle Falls/Eagle Lake parking lot on the left. An $8 parking fee is charged.

The Rubicon Trail is Tahoe's premier lakeshore hike. If you want to get the maximum dose of

Lake Tahoe eye candy, with postcard-perfect views of rocky inlets, sandy coves, and boats bobbing in the water, this is your trail. Since the hike is 5.5 miles one-way and begins and ends at large trailheads at two state parks—Emerald Bay and D. L. Bliss—many hikers do this walk as a one-way trip by leaving one car at either trailhead, or coordinating with the Tahoe Trolley's schedule (800/736-6365 or 530/546-2912 www.laketahoetransit.com) for bus shuttle service. Most prefer to start at the Vikingsholm Trailhead by Emerald Bay and hike northward to the trail's end at D. L. Bliss, as there is less elevation gain traveling in this direction. Campers at Emerald Bay State Park's Eagle Point Campground are fortunate to have the option of hiking the Rubicon Trail right from camp. They get to explore an extra 1.6 miles of the Rubicon Trail, curving around the edge of Emerald Bay from the campground to Vikingsholm Castle—a stretch that is not seen by most Rubicon hikers because of the lack of day-use parking at the campground. And, of course, the ambitious can hike the trail in both directions instead of just one-way.

No matter how you do it, the path stays close to the lakeshore, although often high above it, and has a very relaxed grade. Highlights along the trail include Rubicon Point, Emerald Point, and Vikingsholm Castle, but really, the entire path is a highlight. Don't miss taking the short side trail that curves around the shoreline at Emerald Point, where the 1920s-era Emerald Bay Resort once stood, and allow some extra time so you can take the short tour of Vikingsholm Castle ($8 fee). Those who hike the 1.6-mile trail segment from Eagle Point Campground to Vikingsholm have an excellent chance of spotting bald eagles. For many years a pair has built a nest in a snag right next to the trail; lucky hikers can stand below and watch the mother eagle feeding her babies (don't forget binoculars).

Not surprisingly, the trail is extremely crowded, especially in the peak season, so you might want to plan this trip for after Labor Day. The most jammed-up section occurs as you near the end of the trail by Rubicon Point, where the drop-offs into the lake are so steep that the trail is lined with chain-link fencing, and the path is so narrow that only one person can pass through at a time. Still, even on the busiest days, everybody is in high spirits as they enjoy this eye-popping, film-burning lakeside scenery.

Lower and Upper Echo Lakes

- Distance: 2.7–5.4 miles round-trip
- Duration: 2–3 hours
- Effort: Easy
- Elevation change: 200 feet
- Trailhead: Echo Lakes
- Directions: From the Y-junction of U.S. 50 and Hwy. 89 in South Lake Tahoe, drive 9.8 miles southwest on U.S. 50 to the Echo Lakes/Berkeley Camp turnoff on the right, at Johnson Pass Rd. Turn right and drive 0.6 mile to Echo Lakes Rd. Turn left and drive 1 mile to the Echo Lakes parking lot, above the resort.

Many hikers use the twin Echo Lakes as their entry point to the Desolation Wilderness, with dozens of lakes accessible via short day hikes or longer backpacking trips. But those who just want a shorter, simpler trip will also enjoy a visit to Echo Lakes, where a small resort provides boat taxi service across the two beautiful alpine lakes. The boat service (530/659-7207, www.echochalet.com, one-way fare $10 per person, $5 dogs; round-trip fares are double) allows casual hikers to choose from a 5.4-mile round-trip hike out and back along the north shore of the lakes, or a shorter one-way walk of 2.7 miles combined with a scenic boat ride. The trail, which travels through stands of Jeffrey pines and white firs and offers nearly nonstop lake views, is nearly level and manageable even for nonhikers. Both the upper and lower lakes' shorelines are dotted with quaint private cabins, inspiring envy in all who visit here.

Tamarack, Ralston, and Cagwin Lakes

- Distance: 3.5–9 miles round-trip
- Duration: 2–5 hours
- Effort: Moderate
- Elevation change: 400 feet
- Trailhead: Echo Lakes
- Directions: From the Y-junction of U.S. 50 and Hwy. 89 in South Lake Tahoe, drive 9.8 miles southwest on U.S. 50 to the Echo Lakes/Berkeley Camp turnoff on the right, at Johnson Pass Rd. Turn right and drive 0.6 mile to Echo Lakes Rd. Turn left and drive 1 mile to the Echo Lakes parking lot, above the resort. Day hikers are required to fill out a self-serve wilderness permit.

Whether or not you utilize the Echo Lakes **boat taxi** (530/659-7207, www.echochalet. com, one-way $10 per person, $5 dogs; round-trip fares are double) will determine the exact distance and difficulty of this lovely hike. Taking the boat in both directions makes this an easy, 3.5-mile trip, but done entirely on foot, the hike is 9 miles. A one-way boat ride puts the mileage at 6.2. However you do it, this hike leads to three distinctly different lakes in the Desolation Wilderness. Deep, dark Tamarack Lake is marked by a tree-covered island and forested shoreline with an abundance of backpacking campsites. Ralston Lake sits in a glacially carved bowl with the steep walls of 9,235-foot Ralston Peak rising straight up from its shore. Tiny, peaceful Cagwin Lake is surrounded by forest and is the least dramatic of the three. The lakes are accessible via a nearly level walk on the Pacific Crest Trail, gaining less than 400 feet over 1.1 miles from the boat dock at Upper Echo Lake's west end. Turn left at the trail marker for Tamarack Lake, and you'll be

on its shoreline in a few minutes; the other two lakes lie less than a half mile beyond. The ease of this trail combined with the spectacular scenery means you are sure to have company at the lakes, but there's enough shoreline so that everybody can find their own private picnic or fishing spot.

Lake of the Woods and Ropi Lake

- Distance: 9.6 miles round-trip
- Duration: 5–6 hours
- Effort: Moderate/strenuous
- Elevation change: 1,800 feet
- Trailhead: Echo Lakes
- Directions: From the Y-junction of U.S. 50 and Hwy. 89 in South Lake Tahoe, drive 9.8 miles southwest on U.S. 50 to the Echo Lakes/Berkeley Camp turnoff on the right, at Johnson Pass Rd. Turn right and drive 0.6 mile to Echo Lakes Rd. Turn left and drive 1 mile to the Echo Lakes parking lot, above the resort. Take the **boat taxi** (530/659-7207, www.echochalet.com, one-way $10 per person, $5 dogs; round-trip fares are double) across Echo Lakes and begin your hike at the west end of Upper Echo Lake. Day hikers are required to fill out a self-serve wilderness permit at the boat drop-off point.

As with the hikes to Tamarack, Ralston, and Cagwin Lakes, the length of this trip is made much easier by utilizing the boat taxi service at Echo Lakes, which is both a time and energy saver, and quite enjoyable besides. From the boat dock at the western end of Echo Lakes, follow the gently graded Pacific Crest Trail (PCT) for 2.3 miles, gaining only 800 feet, but on a granite-lined trail that is exposed to the sun most of the day and can be hot. A left turn off the PCT near Haypress Meadows leads you to a junction with the Ralston Peak Trail. Take the trail signed for Lake of the Woods that leads west and downhill. It makes a steep descent over 0.5 mile, losing 350 feet and depositing you on the northeast shore of Lake of

© ANN MARIE BROWN

Hikers reach the rocky summit of Ralston Peak.

the Woods, one of the larger natural lakes in this basin and a popular backpacking, swimming, and picnicking spot. Many hikers make this their destination, or follow the popular trail that leads right (west) to Lake Aloha in less than a mile, another worthwhile destination. (Giant Lake Aloha was formed when dozens of smaller lakes were dammed, forming one huge, shallow body of water dotted with hundreds of small islands.) For this trip, head left (south) instead, following the path along the eastern edge of Lake of the Woods for 0.6 mile, then heading downhill, across Lake of the Woods' outlet stream and west to Ropi Lake. You'll lose another 500 feet in elevation along the way. Peppered with multiple dead snags, Ropi Lake is desolate but beautiful and has many good campsites on its shores. For the ambitious, it is an easy cross-country stroll from Ropi Lake to neighboring Osma and Toem Lakes (west) or Pitt and Avalanche Lakes (south). Avalanche Lake is perched above the upper cascades of

spectacular Horsetail Falls, the big waterfall that is easily seen from U.S. 50 near Strawberry.

Ralston Peak

- Distance: 8.2 or 8.6 miles round-trip
- Duration: 4–6 hours
- Effort: Moderate/strenuous
- Elevation change: 2,800 or 1,800 feet
- Trailhead: Echo Lakes or Ralston Peak
- Directions: From the Y-junction of U.S. 50 and Hwy. 89 in South Lake Tahoe, drive 9.8 miles southwest on U.S. 50 to the Echo Lakes/Berkeley Camp turnoff on the right, at Johnson Pass Rd. Turn right and drive 0.6 mile to Echo Lakes Rd. Turn left and drive 1 mile to the Echo Lakes parking lot, above the resort. Take the boat taxi (530/659-7207, www.echochalet.com, one-way $10 per person, $5 dogs; round-trip fares are double) across Echo Lakes and begin your hike at the west end of Upper Echo Lake. Day hikers

are required to fill out a self-serve wilderness permit at the boat drop-off point.

For the Ralston Peak Trailhead off U.S. 50, from the Y-junction of U.S. 50 and Hwy. 89 in South Lake Tahoe, drive 14 miles southwest on U.S. 50 to the turnoff for Camp Sacramento. Turn right (north) and park in the parking lot signed for Ralston Trail. Day hikers are required to fill out a self-serve wilderness permit at the trailhead.

There are two common routes to Ralston Peak: the easier route, which utilizes the boat taxi at Echo Lakes for an 8.6-mile round-trip with an 1,800-foot elevation gain; or the harder route, which begins at the Ralston Peak Trailhead off U.S. 50 for an 8.2-mile round-trip with a 2,800-foot elevation gain. Solitude seekers will enjoy the harder route since it gets less foot traffic. Pure pleasure seekers will enjoy the easier route, which passes near lovely Tamarack Lake on a remarkably mellow grade to Ralston's lofty 9,235-foot summit. Either path offers the same reward at the end: one of the best views possible in the Desolation Wilderness, with nearly a dozen lakes in sight, Pyramid Peak holding court to the west, and Mount Tallac towering directly north. The Ralston Trail from U.S. 50 begins with multiple switchbacks up a densely forested slope, and even after it breaks free of the trees it continues on a relentlessly steep ascent to the summit. The route from Echo Lakes follows the easy grade of the Pacific Crest Trail for the first 2.3 miles (be sure to take the 100-yard spur off the main trail to see Tamarack Lake), gaining only 800 feet in elevation. It's a walk in the park, except that there is little shade and the exposed granite can be hot. Then, after two left turns near Haypress Meadows, the grade steepens. The final 0.5 mile of trail to the summit can be a bit hard to discern (watch for trail cairns to aid you), but just keep heading uphill and you'll get there. When you do, you'll have a big smile on your face. Ralston's summit view is one you will long remember.

Horsetail Falls/Pyramid Creek Loop

- Distance: 1.5 miles round-trip
- Duration: 1 hour
- Effort: Easy/moderate
- Elevation change: 100 feet
- Trailhead: Twin Bridges
- Directions: From the Y-junction of U.S. 50 and Hwy. 89 in South Lake Tahoe, drive 15 miles southwest on U.S. 50 to Twin Bridges. Turn right into the parking lot signed for Pyramid Creek ($5 parking fee).

You'll know why they call it Horsetail Falls the minute you first see it while cruising along U.S. 50. Straight and narrow at the top and fanning out to a wide inverted V at the bottom, Horsetail Falls swishes hundreds of feet down Pyramid Creek's glacier-carved canyon. Its powerful stream is reinforced by four lakes: Toem, Ropi, Pitt, and Avalanche. The sight of this dramatic waterfall inspires thousands of highway drivers every day to stop and take a closer look, especially in the heavy snowmelt period from May to July. Few of them hike very far on the trail, as it soon becomes apparent that the waterfall is a long way from the parking lot. Most just pick a spot along the rushing cascades of Pyramid Creek and enjoy the wet and wonderful scenery, especially near a lacy cataract known as The Cascades. Technically the main trail doesn't go to Horsetail Falls at all. Instead, it follows a course known as the Pyramid Creek Loop, which is marked by small brown hiker signs nailed to trees. Much of the path traverses exposed slabs of granite, the handiwork of glaciers, and the open landscape provides good long-distance views of the falls.

Experienced hikers have the option of heading off the 1.5-mile Pyramid Creek Loop to the Desolation Wilderness boundary, where they must fill out a self-serve wilderness permit. From there, it is possible to make your way to the lower cascade of Horsetail Falls, although it is a trail-less route all the way and not advisable for the unprepared. If you choose to attempt the trip, use extra caution. Accidents happen in this area every year because of the slick rock and fast-moving water.

Twin and Island Lakes

- Distance: 6.6 miles round-trip
- Duration: 3–4 hours
- Effort: Moderate
- Elevation change: 1,200 feet
- Trailhead: Wrights Lake/Twin Lakes
- Directions: From the Y-junction of U.S. 50 and Hwy. 89 in South Lake Tahoe, drive 17 miles southwest on U.S. 50 to the signed Wrights Lake turnoff on the right (4.5 miles east of Kyburz). Drive 8 miles north on Wrights Lake Road to Wrights Lake Campground. Bear right at the information center and continue 1.2 miles to the road's end at the Twin Lakes Trailhead. Day hikers are required to fill out a self-serve wilderness permit at the trailhead.

Sculpted by glacial ice more than 1,000 feet deep during the last ice age, the granitic Crystal Range is one of the gems of Tahoe's Desolation Wilderness. The Crystal Basin Recreation Area provides convenient access to this rugged landscape of glaciated basins and saw-toothed peaks. Of a host of trail choices, the 3.3-mile day hike to Twin and Island Lakes offers the best payoffs in the least mileage: spectacular wildflower displays, excellent swimming opportunities in four rock-bound lakes, and miles of solid granite beneath your feet as you walk. Not surprisingly, this is the most popular day-hiking trail in the Crystal Basin.

The path's first stretch meanders past a lush, flower-filled meadow, overflowing with lupine and tiger lilies. A gentle climb through a red-fir and lodgepole-pine forest leads to a major junction just beyond the wilderness boundary, 1.3 miles out. Bear left and ascend more vigorously for 0.75 mile on exposed granite slabs.

At the top of the ridge, another wildflower garden awaits, this one bursting with fireweed, paintbrush, and ranger buttons. Vistas of stark, jagged peaks to the northeast produce an inspiring backdrop. At 2.4 miles you enter Twin Lakes's dramatic granite basin, where the receding glaciers polished each rock to a glowing sheen. The outlet stream from Upper Twin Lake cascades into the shimmering depths of Lower Twin Lake, forming a boisterous waterfall. If you can tear yourself away from the lake's inviting picnic spots, cross its old stone dam and continue along the northwest shore to well-named Boomerang Lake, shaped like an L, at 3 miles. Its tantalizing waters suggest a swim. Near the lakeshore you'll find the tiny, white, bell-shaped flowers of cassiope. Another 0.25 mile of climbing leads you to the shallow glacial valley that contains enchanting Island Lake, dotted with a multitude of rocky islands. From this high point, views of the Crystal Basin's granite-ringed cirque are the best of the trip.

Grouse, Hemlock, and Smith Lakes

- Distance: 6.8 miles round-trip
- Duration: 3–5 hours
- Effort: Strenuous
- Elevation change: 1,750 feet
- Trailhead: Wrights Lake/Twin Lake
- Directions: From the Y-junction of U.S. 50 and Hwy. 89 in South Lake Tahoe, drive 17 miles southwest on U.S. 50 to the signed Wrights Lake turnoff on the right (4.5 miles east of Kyburz). Drive 8 miles north on Wrights Lake Road to Wrights Lake Campground. Bear right at the information center and continue 1.2 miles to the road's end at the Twin Lakes Trailhead. Day hikers are required to fill out a self-serve wilderness permit at the trailhead.

The trail to Grouse, Hemlock, and Smith Lakes consists of an almost relentless climb,

granite-lined Hemlock Lake in the Crystal Basin

but the reward is a series of alpine lakes that get more scenic the higher you go. The trail follows the same wildflower-filled course as the path to Twin and Island Lakes for the first 1.3 miles to just past the wilderness boundary. Here, at a major junction, bear right. Small and pretty Grouse Lake is a heart-pumping, 1-mile climb away. Be sure to check out the views looking back toward Wrights Lake and Icehouse Reservoir as you ascend. Grouse Lake is a popular backpacking spot, with designated sites marked by wooden posts. Continue onward and upward for another 0.5 mile to small and stark Hemlock Lake, which is bounded by a forbidding granite slope on one side and a grove of scrawny hemlock trees on the other. This is a classic Desolation Wilderness lake, a perfect circle of sparkling blue surrounded by light-colored granite. You might be tempted to stop here, but Smith Lake lies another 0.5 mile beyond, way up high near tree line at 8,700 feet, and it's a stunner. Don't forget your bathing suit for this trip; at least one of these lakes is sure to lure you in.

Gertrude and Tyler Lakes

- Distance: 8.4 miles round-trip
- Duration: 4–6 hours
- Effort: Moderate/strenuous
- Elevation change: 1,350 feet
- Trailhead: Wrights Lake/Twin Lake
- Directions: From the Y-junction of U.S. 50 and Hwy. 89 in South Lake Tahoe, drive 17 miles southwest on U.S. 50 to the signed Wrights Lake turnoff on the right (4.5 miles east of Kyburz). Drive 8 miles north on Wrights Lake Rd. to Wrights Lake Campground. Bear right at the information center and continue 1.2 miles to the road's end at the Twin Lakes Trailhead. Day hikers are required to fill out a self-serve wilderness permit at the trailhead.

There's a whole lot of hiking to be done in

the Wrights Lake region of the Crystal Basin Recreation Area—so much that it can seem like too many trails to choose from. The trip to Gertrude and Tyler Lakes stands out because it offers great scenery, smaller crowds, and a chance to practice your cross-country skills on the way to Tyler Lake. A clearly defined trail leads to pretty Gertrude Lake, but Tyler Lake, slightly higher and lovelier, awaits only those who forge their own way. Start at the Twin Lakes Trailhead by taking the trail heading toward Rockbound Pass (not the main Twin Lakes Trail). You'll enjoy a remarkably easy grade until you reach a sign for Tyler Lake at 1.6 miles. Here, bear right and prepare to work a lot harder for the rest of this trip. One memorable 0.5-mile stretch goes almost straight uphill. The worst doesn't last long, thankfully, and the views of the spectacular peaks of the Crystal Range will spur you onward. Keep watch at 3.2 miles for an easy-to-miss spur trail on the left, 100 yards long, which leads to the grave of William Tyler, a rancher who died here in a blizzard in the 1920s. A half mile beyond this spur is Gertrude Lake, at 8,000 feet in elevation. But hold on: Before you head to Gertrude Lake, watch for the nearly invisible right fork just beyond the grave spur trail; this is an informal use trail to Tyler Lake. Occasional rock cairns signal the way. Even if you miss the use trail, you should be able to find Tyler Lake simply by heading cross-country 0.5 mile to the southeast of Gertrude Lake. Of the two lakes, Tyler is more beautiful, set in a granite basin with a few sparse whitebark pines on its shore. Since many hikers don't even bother trying to find it, you have a better chance at solitude here than at almost any of the lakes in the Crystal Basin.

Sylvia and Lyons Lakes

- Distance: 9.8 miles round-trip
- Duration: 5–6 hours
- Effort: Moderate/strenuous
- Elevation change: 1,700 feet
- Trailhead: Lyons Creek
- Directions: From the Y-junction of U.S. 50 and Hwy. 89 in South Lake Tahoe, drive 17 miles southwest on U.S. 50 to the signed Wrights Lake turnoff on the right (4.5 miles east of Kyburz). Drive 4 miles north on Wrights Lake Rd. to the signed turnoff for Lyons Creek Trail. Turn right and drive 0.5 mile to the trailhead. Day hikers are required to fill out a self-serve wilderness permit at the trailhead.

The entire Crystal Basin Recreation Area is well known for summer wildflowers, but the trail with the most rewards in the flower department is the Lyons Creek Trail to Sylvia and Lyons Lakes. Although the trail is no secret, it has the advantage of being a few miles away from busy Wrights Lake Campground and its multiple trailheads into the Desolation Wilderness, so this trail sees somewhat less traffic than others in the area. Even after the peak of the wildflower season ends, the path's final destination at Lyons Lake is always rewarding. The trail's grade is gentle almost all the way except for the final 0.5 mile to Lyons Lake. The path keeps to the south side of Lyons Creek for 4 miles, passing through a succession of woods and meadows, and offering occasional views of Pyramid Peak. After finally crossing the creek at 4.2 miles, the trail reaches a junction. Lyons Lake is to the left and steeply uphill; Sylvia Lake is 0.4 mile to the right on a mostly level course. If you are tiring out, you might skip the side trip to Sylvia Lake, which doesn't compare in size or beauty to Lyons Lake. Sylvia Lake is small and forested around its edges, and is often a breeding ground for mosquitoes. Lyons Lake is the prize on this trail, and a demanding 0.5-mile climb, gaining 400 feet, will get you there. After some huffing and puffing, you arrive at Lyons Lake's rock dam and gape in surprise at the visual impact of its commanding granite

© ANN MARIE BROWN

A steep final ascent brings hikers to Lyons Lake in the Desolation Wilderness, a great spot for a swim on a warm summer day.

amphitheater. Make sure you come well prepared with a picnic, a book, and a towel. You won't want to leave this spot anytime soon.

BIKING

Many consider Lake Tahoe to be a mecca for mountain biking in the Sierra Nevada. Bikes are allowed, even welcomed, on an abundance of trails, including large sections of the Tahoe Rim Trail.

Among the mountain biking community, the South Lake Tahoe region is well known for its abundance of rocks and hills, plus an abundance of well-constructed single-track, much of which was built in the last decade by the U.S. Forest Service. The trails here are well suited to riders seeking a challenge. But that's not to say there aren't opportunities for the more casual rider, both on dirt and on pavement. South Lake Tahoe is laced with paved bike paths, as well as places to rent bikes of all shapes and sizes, including beach cruisers and bikes towing

kid trailers. For people who want to ride around downtown South Lake Tahoe, the **South Lake Tahoe Bike Path** starts at El Dorado Beach on U.S. 50 and runs five miles west through town, connecting to other bike trails and bike lanes. Most of the ride has an urban feel to it, but a few scenic bridges cross over Trout Creek and the Upper Truckee River.

Last but not least, for those who want a leg up on the mountain, **Heavenly Ski Resort** (775/586-7000, www.skiheavenly.com) allows mountain bikers to bring their machines on the gondola so they can start their ride at the top of the hill, not the bottom. Check with Heavenly to see which trails are currently open to bikes.

Rentals

Anderson's Bike Rental (645 Hwy. 89, South Lake Tahoe, 530/541-0500) is located less than a half mile from the start of the Pope-Baldwin Bike Path. Rentals are also available just up the road at **Camp Richardson Outdoor Sports** (1900 Jameson Beach Rd., South Lake Tahoe, 530/542-6584).

If you need to rent a mountain bike, contact **Shore Line Bike Rentals and Sales** (775/588-8777 or 530/544-1105). With two locations in the Heavenly and Kingsbury Grade area, they will gladly set you up with a bike and a free map of the Powerline Trail. Two other places to rent bikes and get information are **Sierra Cycle Works** (3430 Hwy. 50, South Lake Tahoe, 530/541-7505) or **South Shore Bikes** (955 Emerald Bay Rd., South Lake Tahoe, 530/544-7433).

ⓒ Pope-Baldwin Bike Path

The bike path travels only 3.4 miles one-way, but it passes by some of South Lake Tahoe's greatest attractions. This is a trail for meandering and sightseeing; be sure to bring a bike lock so you can take advantage of all the things to do along the way.

© ANN MARIE BROWN

bicyclists along the Pope-Baldwin Bike Path

Don't miss getting off your bike to take a look at the underwater world at the Forest Service's Stream Profile Chamber at Taylor Creek. Autumn is the most fascinating time of year, when the kokanee salmon turn bright red and swim up the creek to spawn. You'll also want to step inside a few of the historic buildings at Tallac Historic Site, and if you pack along a picnic and a towel in a small knapsack, you can spend a few hours along the lakeshore at Pope or Baldwin Beaches. In between these highlights are pleasant stretches of trail for casual pedaling through the pines. The bike path begins just south of Camp Richardson along Highway 89. Rent bikes at Anderson's Bike Rental or at Camp Richardson Outdoor Sports just up the road.

Fallen Leaf Lake Road

This is another easy paved ride, although it isn't technically a bike path. This narrow, paved road winds 5.5 miles from Highway 89 along the edge of Fallen Leaf Lake and past dozens of charming cottages. It then continues beyond the lake to the Glen Alpine Trailhead for the Desolation Wilderness. Although cars travel on this road, they rarely drive as fast as you can ride, due to the narrowness of the road. Start the trip by parking near the entrance to Fallen Leaf Lake Campground; you also can access Fallen Leaf Lake Road from the Pope-Baldwin Bike Path.

Angora Ridge Lookout and Angora Lakes

More challenging, but still manageable for reasonably fit cyclists, is the 12-mile ride to Angora Ridge Lookout and Angora Lakes. Best suited for mountain bikes, the ride starts near Fallen Leaf Lake Campground, then follows Fallen Leaf Lake Road for 2 miles to Tahoe Mountain Road. A left here is followed by a right turn 0.4 mile later onto dirt Forest Service Road 1214, Angora Ridge Road. The road climbs to the top of Angora Ridge, elevation 7,290 feet. Views are good from the road, but walk a few feet to the fire lookout to get the best perspective on Fallen Leaf Lake, 1,000 feet below. From the lookout, the road descends slightly to the parking lot for Angora Lakes. The last mile to the lakes is on a car-free dirt trail, but the route is shared with a lot of hikers and dog walkers. You'll ride uphill to Lower Angora Lake, which has a few private homes on its edges, then proceed on level ground to more beautiful Upper Angora Lake, home to Angora Lakes Resort and its handful of picturesque cabins. (You must lock up your bike at the bike rack before entering the resort area.)

Powerline Trail

Mountain bikers of all abilities can handle the first few miles of Powerline Trail, a dirt road/trail that begins off Oneidas Street in South Lake Tahoe. Drive south of the Y on Highway 89, turn east on Pioneer Trail, and follow it to Oneidas Street. Turn right and drive to the Powerline Trailhead on the left (north) side of the road. The road/trail, which is also an off-highway vehicle route and runs more or less parallel to Pioneer Trail, starts with a gentle series of ups and downs as it follows underneath its namesake power lines. Where the trail crosses a creek and leaves the power lines behind, the more serious climbing begins. After a few switchbacks, the road reaches a T-junction. Bear right on High Meadow Trail, then 0.5 mile later, go left to get back on Powerline Trail. The path crosses Cold Creek on a well-constructed bridge and ascends gently behind the homes of Montgomery Estates to deliver you to Ski Run Boulevard by Heavenly Ski Resort. You can ride back on Ski Run to Pioneer Trail to your starting point on Oneidas Street for a 14-mile loop.

Corral Trail Loop

Another short, fun ride from Oneidas Street is the five-mile Corral Trail Loop, which starts just past the Trout Creek bridge on Oneidas (about two miles from Pioneer Trail). Follow the single-track Corral Trail up a short climb, then downhill through a rocky, technical stretch. Eventually the trail smooths out and offers some twisting, fast turns and small jumps. After about two miles, the trail junctions with Powerline Trail. Go left to head back to Oneidas, then left on the road for a paved climb back uphill to your car. If you'd rather get the climbing out of the way at the start of your ride, park near the Powerline Trailhead and begin the loop from there.

Mr. Toad's Wild Ride

Experienced mountain bikers favor Mr. Toad's Wild Ride, otherwise known as the Saxon Creek Trail. The East Shore has its famous Flume Trail; the South Shore has this much more treacherous point-to-point ride, which features an extremely technical, obstacle-ridden downhill stretch suitable for advanced riders only. The north end of the trail is at Forest Service Road 12N01A, on the south side of Oneidas Street. The south end of the trail is at the Big Meadow Trailhead for the Tahoe Rim Trail, 5.3 miles south of Meyers on Highway 89. In between is a drop of 2,200 feet in about 3 miles. Most riders start at the Big Meadow Trailhead and follow the Tahoe Rim Trail east and then north for 4.5 miles to Tucker Flat, elevation 8,830 feet. The route is single-track almost all the way and climbs through forest to a ridge, then makes a short descent to Tucker Flat and a junction of trails. If this first part proved to be too technical for you, turn around now; soon it will get much scarier. Turn left on Saxon Creek Trail and begin a highly technical downhill stretch, with lots of large rocks and big drop-offs. The trail follows the drainage of Saxon Creek, and the descent is fast and furious. Finally, the obstacles peter out, and the ride gets smoother with lots of fast, banked turns. Saxon Creek Trail eventually meets up with Forest Service Road 12N01A, and bearing right here delivers you to Oneidas Street, where your car shuttle should be waiting for you. Hope they brought some extra bandages.

BOATING AND WATER SPORTS

In winter at Lake Tahoe, it's all about the slopes. In summer, it's all about the lake—finding ways to get in it, on it, and around it. Whether you just want to look at the lake while enjoying an easygoing cruise, swim in the lake and then relax on its golden beaches, or race around the lake on a speedboat or personal watercraft, there are literally hundreds of ways to enjoy Lake Tahoe's mighty blue expanse.

◖ Kayaking

Whether you are a brand-new beginner or long-time expert, the waters of Lake Tahoe can provide hours of pleasure as you tool around its shimmering surface in a colorful, lightweight kayak. Much of the beauty of the experience lies in the fact that you are self-propelled, gliding along the lake without the noise and distraction of an engine. Traveling in this quiet fashion, and at a relatively slow pace, you are almost guaranteed to see wildlife. A family of ducks or a gaggle of geese may swim by your boat; an eagle or an osprey may soar overhead. Since most kayakers paddle close to the shoreline, deer and other land animals are also commonly seen.

A company called **Kayak Tahoe** (in Timber Cove Marina across from the Safeway, South Lake Tahoe, 530/544-2011, www.kayaktahoe.com) leads kayak tours, rents kayaks to do-it-yourselfers, and operates a kayaking school. No experience is necessary for rentals or tours; beginners are outfitted with a sit-on-top kayak, and with only a few minutes of instruction can set out on their own. Rental rates are $15 per hour for single kayaks and $28 per hour for doubles; kayaks can also be rented for a

Almost every type of watercraft is available for rent on the South Shore.

© ANN MARIE BROWN

two-hour window ($25–45) or all day ($65–85). Kayak Tahoe operates out of four locations: Timber Cove Marina, Nevada Beach, Pope Beach, and Baldwin Beach. If you have your heart set on paddling into Emerald Bay, rent your kayak at Baldwin Beach, the closest public launch spot. Strong, fit beginners and intermediates can handle the paddle to Emerald Bay, but a 9 A.M. start is recommended as there is usually less wind and fewer powerboats in the morning. Plan on a five-hour round-trip, including time to hang out at Fannette Island and Vikingsholm.

If you don't want to kayak on your own, guided tours along Tahoe's East Shore or into Emerald Bay are extremely popular ($65–85 per person), as are evening sunset and full moon tours ($30–35 for a two-hour tour). Be sure to make advance reservations for these tours.

Sit-on-top kayaks can also be rented at most of the South Shore's marinas, including Camp Richardson, Zephyr Cove, Ski Run, Lakeside, Round Hill, Timber Cove, and Tahoe Keys. Those who have brought their own kayaks to Lake Tahoe can put in at almost any public beach or marina they can drive to. The most popular area for kayaking on the South Shore is the sparkling waters of **Emerald Bay.** Most boaters launch from Baldwin Beach and paddle about 2 miles to Emerald Point, then steer around the point and into Emerald Bay. It's another 1.5 miles from Emerald Point to the back of the bay, where Vikingsholm Castle is located. Kayakers can stop for a rest on the beach, take a guided tour of the castle ($8), or pay a visit to Fannette Island, where the owner of Vikingsholm held tea parties. A **boat-in campground** (530/541-3030 or 530/525-7277, www.parks.ca.gov, $35) is located on the shores of Emerald Bay State Park for those who want to turn this into a two-day adventure.

Kayakers with bigger ambitions should check out the **Lake Tahoe Water Trail** map (800/849-6589, www.adventuremaps.net), which shows available boat launches, campsites, lodging, dining, and more for all 72 miles of lake shoreline. And visit the website of the **Lake Tahoe Water Trail Committee** (www.laketahoewatertrail.org) for information on trip planning, Tahoe paddling events, and the local kayaking community.

Stand-Up Paddleboarding

If you want to try the latest craze in nonmotorized water sports, rent a stand-up paddleboard, or SUP, from **South Tahoe Standup Paddle** (3115 Harrison Ave., South Lake Tahoe, 530/416-4829, www.tahoestanduppaddle.com, $35 per hour, $120 per day) or **Kayak Tahoe** (in Timber Cove Marina across from the Safeway, South Lake Tahoe, 530/544-2011, www.kayaktahoe.com, $20 per hour, $30 for two hours, $60 all day). Then fire your personal trainer; you'll work your core and abs as you paddle around the lake while standing up and maintaining your balance on these surfboard-like devices. The sport is easy to learn, at least on flat water, since the boards are very stable. For your first time, go early in the morning, when the lake is usually calm.

South Tahoe Standup Paddle also offers guided paddleboard tours (half day $150, full day $300), group and private lessons, and combination paddle-and-yoga classes. The shop also sponsors paddleboard races every Wednesday night in summer.

In 2011, Lake Tahoe hosted the fourth annual Tahoe Fall Classic paddleboard race, following a 22-mile course from Camp Richardson Marina to Kings Beach. The best paddlers completed the course in less than four hours, although many reported sore muscles and blisters on their hands.

Sailing

If the idea of plying Tahoe's waters by using only a combination of the wind and your own skill appeals to you, check out **Sailing**

Ventures in Tahoe Keys Marina (775/287-4356, www.sailingventures.com), which offers the South Shore's only professional sail training. Rates are $140 per person or $195 per couple for a two-hour demonstration class, or $325 per person for a more extensive two-day class. If you already know how to sail, sailboats can be rented in Tahoe Keys Marina or Ski Run Marina at **Tahoe Sports** (530/544-8888 or 530/544-0200, www.tahoesports.com). Rates are $95 per hour, $285 for a half day, or $570 for a full day.

Water-Sports Outfitters and Marinas

Literally dozens of water-sports companies are located around the South Shore, ready and willing to rent you a Jet Ski, Sea Doo, Waverunner, hydro bike, or powerboat for racing around the lake. Rates are typically about $100 per hour for most smaller vessels like Jet Skis and Waverunners. **Action Watersports** (3411 Hwy. 50, South Lake Tahoe, 530/544-5387, www.action-watersports.com), located at Timber Cove Marina behind the Best Western Timber Cove Lodge, rents all the aforementioned and also offers parasailing rides. For the uninitiated, this is an activity in which one, two, or three participants soar hundreds of feet above the lake, attached to a parachute being pulled by a boat. Potential parasailing passengers, be forewarned: Everyone on shore will stare at you while you "fly," so this is a poor activity for those inclined to shyness. Action Watersports has two other locations: one at Camp Richardson Marina (530/542-6570) and another at Lakeside Marina (530/541-9800).

Ski Run Boat Company (www.tahoesports.com) in Ski Run Marina (900 Ski Run Blvd., 530/544-0200) and Tahoe Keys Marina (2435 Venice Dr., 530/544-8888) rents powerboats, Jet Skis, hydro bikes, water tricycles, and other water toys by the hour or the day. In addition to a full array of rentals, they lead guided Jet Ski

tours to Emerald Bay. Their parasailing operation out of Ski Run Marina soars the highest of any company on the lake—more than 1,200 feet above the water.

Closer to the casinos, **Lakeside Marina** (Park Ave. and Lakeshore Dr., Stateline, 530/541-9800) has Waverunner, Sea Doo, and speedboat rentals. And on the Nevada side of the South Shore, **H2O Sports** (775/588-4155, www.rhpbeach.com) operates out of Round Hill Pines Beach, two miles northeast of Stateline. They rent Sea Doos, kayaks, paddleboats, and sea cycles, and offer parasailing rides. At nearby **Zephyr Cove Resort** (775/589-4901, www.zephyrcove.com), you can rent just about anything with horsepower—powerboats, Waverunners, ski boats—and yes, they have parasailing, too, with discounted rates if you "fly" before 10:30 A.M.

If you don't know how to water-ski or wakeboard, or would like to improve your skills, Lake Tahoe is a great place to learn. Try **Don Borges Water Ski School** at Round Hill Pines Beach, two miles northeast of Stateline (530/391-1215, www.rhpbeach.com).

If you brought your own boat or personal watercraft to Lake Tahoe and just need to find a boat ramp on the South Shore where you can put it in the water, you can do so at South Lake Tahoe Recreation Area (530/542-6056), Tahoe Keys Marina (530/541-2155), Timber Cove Marina (530/544-2942), Lakeside Marina (530/541-6626), or Camp Richardson Marina (530/542-6570).

SWIMMING

If it's a pristine Tahoe beach you desire, you have a handful of good choices on the South Shore. Three of the most scenic are **Baldwin, Kiva,** and **Pope Beaches,** all managed by the U.S. Forest Service, with restrooms and picnic facilities on-site. The beaches are located between two and four miles north of the South Lake Tahoe Y on Highway 89. A parking fee

© SABRINA YOUNG

Swimmers enjoy the pristine beaches of Tahoe.

of $7 is charged at Baldwin and Pope Beaches, but you can avoid the fee by riding your bike or walking instead of driving. The paved Pope-Baldwin Bike Path runs right through all three beach parking lots. There is no fee at Kiva Beach, but swimmers beware: There are lots of rocks in the water near the shoreline. On the positive side, views of Mount Tallac are divine, and dogs are allowed at Kiva Beach (but not at Pope and Baldwin). The neighboring **Camp Richardson Resort** also has a pay beach, but it is so crowded on summer days that it can be difficult to find a spot to lay down your towel.

Closer to downtown South Lake are two no-fee beaches. **El Dorado Beach** is located between Rufus Allen Boulevard and Lakeview Avenue and is visible from U.S. 50. Restrooms, a boat launch, and picnic facilities are provided. A grassy strip overlooking the lake makes a nice spot for a picnic. A couple of blocks away is **Regan Beach** (Lakeview Ave. and Sacramento Ave.), which has a food concession, restrooms,

picnic facilities, and a playground, but little sand, unless the lake level has dropped substantially over the course of a dry summer. It's more like a neighborhood park than a beach, but you can swim here. For parents with little ones, the grass might be easier to manage than sand anyway.

Also in the downtown area, just behind the Best Western Timber Cove Lodge, is **Timber Cove Beach,** a great choice for families because of its shallow water and the presence of a snack bar, kayak rentals, and a pier and restaurant.

Two miles northeast of Stateline, spectacular **Nevada Beach** is located at Elk Point Road, off U.S. 50. The beach is nearly a mile long and much wider than most Tahoe beaches. It's a wonderful place to spend a day, but note that it is often windy here by mid-afternoon, when the windsurfers and kiteboarders take over from the sunbathers and casual swimmers. Restrooms and picnic facilities are available. There is a $7 parking fee, but if you don't mind a short hike, you can forgo the fee by parking at Kahle Park (Kahle Dr. and U.S. 50) and walking the one-mile trail to Nevada Beach, or by parking at the end of Elk Point Road, near the Nevada Beach entrance, and walking in.

Also on the Nevada side of the South Shore, the private **Zephyr Cove Resort** (800/238-2463, www.zephyrcove.com) has a lovely strip of sand, as well as a restaurant, restrooms, beach volleyball, and the marina for the MS *Dixie II* and *Woodwind II* cruises. This is a serious "party beach," with plenty of action for all ages every day in summer. The parking fee is $8, but it's probably worth it just for the convenience of spending a few hours in the sun, then walking over and getting an ice cream or milk shake from the resort's famous soda fountain.

The same $8 rate is charged at nearby **Round Hill Pines Beach** (775/588-3055, www.rhp-beach.com), which provides a similar array of beach and boating activities on its half-mile-long strand of Tahoe sand. Food and drinks are available at the Round Hill deli and bar.

If you are willing to hike, **Emerald Bay Beach** by Vikingsholm Castle is a wonderful white-sand beach with picnic tables. Accessing the beach requires a two-mile round-trip hike with a 500-foot elevation gain on the return trip, and you still have to pay an $8 parking fee at the Vikingsholm Trailhead.

Finally, when you think about swimming or beachgoing, don't forget there's another lake around here besides Tahoe. **Fallen Leaf Lake,** south of Camp Richardson, has a lovely stretch of shoreline and a swimming beach on its northwest end, accessible by a short walk from Fallen Leaf Campground. Your dog is allowed to join you, too.

FISHING

Lake Tahoe is famous for its huge mackinaw trout, but the trophy fish don't just jump onto your line. Because of the lake's massive size and depth, the best fishing is always done by boat

and in the company of an experienced guide who knows the lake. Although mackinaw can be fished year-round, the bite is best in spring and early summer, when the fish move from the deepest parts of the lake into shallower water. The average size of a mackinaw is 3–5 pounds, but fish as large as 10 pounds are fairly common. Occasionally a 20–30 pounder will be caught; the lake record is more than 37 pounds.

The lake also offers an excellent kokanee salmon fishery, with most action occurring around midsummer. Kokanee, or landlocked salmon, are considerably smaller than mackinaw, but they are strong fighters and provide exciting fishing. The lake record kokanee was four pounds, 15 ounces. Brown and rainbow trout are also commonly caught in Lake Tahoe. The lake is open for fishing year-round, except for within 300 feet of its tributaries October 1–June 30.

Dozens of South Lake Tahoe guide services can take you out on the lake and greatly increase your chances of catching fish. Most services have a 90 percent or better catch rate. Bait, tackle, and beverages are usually provided, and your fish will be cleaned and bagged for you. One of the biggest and best guide services is **Tahoe Sport Fishing Company** (900 Ski Run Blvd., South Lake Tahoe, 530/541-5448 or 800/696-7797, www.tahoesportfishing.com), with a fleet of six boats available for private charter. They operate year-round out of Ski Run Marina and Zephyr Cove and offer four- or five-hour trips in the morning or afternoon ($85–95 per person), or all-day trips ($135). Fishing gear, bait, and tackle are provided, as well as snacks and drinks, and foul-weather gear if needed. If you catch fish, your guides will not only clean and bag it for you, they will even arrange to have it delivered to your favorite South Shore restaurant so it can be served to you at dinner.

There are too many other excellent **guide services** to list, but a few that come well recommended are Tahoe Topliners at Camp

© ANN MARIE BROWN

Every Tahoe angler hopes for a trophy-sized mackinaw, but the more common catch is in the three- to five-pound range.

Richardson Resort (530/721-0593, www.tahoetopliners.com), Four Reel Sport Fishing at the Tahoe Keys Marina (530/573-0141, www.southlaketahoesportfishing.com), Mile High Fishing Charters at the Tahoe Keys Marina (530/541-5312 or www.fish-tahoe.com), O'Malley's Fishing Charters at Zephyr Cove Marina (775/588-4102), Eagle Point Fishing Charters at Tahoe Keys Marina (530/577-6834), and Lake Tahoe Fishing Guides (530/541-5566 or 877/270-0742, www.tahoefishingguides.com).

Nearby, **Fallen Leaf Lake** also offers good boat fishing for mackinaw and rainbow trout. Shoreline anglers generally have better luck at this lake, too (try using worms, spinners, or lures). Access the lake by walking 0.25 mile from Fallen Leaf Lake Campground. Fishing within 250 feet of the dam is illegal. Captain Aaron Fox with Backwater Charters (530/544-1977 or 530/307-8906, call for rates) will take you out on Fallen Leaf Lake in his boat for guided fishing.

If you are a fly fisher hoping for some inside knowledge about the streams and rivers in the Tahoe area, pay a visit to **Tahoe Fly Fishing Outfitters** (2705 Hwy. 50, South Lake Tahoe, 530/541-8208 or 877/541-8208, www.tahoefly-fishing.com). In addition to their full-service fly shop, they offer guided trips and fly-fishing instruction, and complete equipment rentals (everything from waders to fly rods). The store sells a huge selection of hand-tied flies, many made by local experts. Guide rates are $175 for two hours, $250 for four hours, or $375 for eight hours. Beginners might want to sign up for the popular Introduction to Fly Fishing class, taught at a local stream ($50 per person).

If you just want your four-year-old to catch his or her first fish, head over to the **Tahoe Trout Farm** (1023 Blue Lake Ave., South Lake Tahoe, 530/541-1491, www.tahoetroutfarm.

com), a stocked pond for children 15 and under. No license is required and no limits apply; they charge by the size of the fish caught. Bait and tackle are provided. This family-owned business has been putting smiles on kids' faces since 1946. Another great spot for kid-oriented fishing is **Sawmill Pond** (2.5 miles west of the South Lake Tahoe Y, at Sawmill Rd. and Lake Tahoe Blvd.), where only kids 14 and under are allowed to fish (adults can watch, but they can't cast a line in the water). There is no charge, and kids can keep as many as five fish.

HORSEBACK RIDING

Feeling aerobically challenged? Let Trigger do the walking for you. A variety of guided one- to four-hour trail rides are offered by the trusty steeds at **Camp Richardson Corral** (Emerald Bay Rd. at Fallen Leaf Lake Rd., South Lake Tahoe, 530/541-3113 or 877/541-3113, www.camprichardsoncorral.com). If you don't want to commit much time, try the 55-minute, $40-per-person ride through the meadow and forest. There is also a two-hour ride ($78). The early-evening Steak Ride (4:30–6:30 P.M., $90 per person) is also popular. Riders follow trails through the forest and across Taylor Creek and back, returning to a hearty Western steak barbecue. The horses eat hay, of course. Children must be six years or older to ride; no experience is necessary. Camp Richardson also offers overnight horseback trips to several high mountain lakes; reservations are required.

A few miles to the east of South Lake Tahoe, **Zephyr Cove Stables** (775/588-5664, www.zephyrcovestables.com) provides equestrian services on the Nevada side of the South Shore. Breakfast, lunch, and dinner rides are available, or one- to two-hour rides without meals.

At all locations, riders should expect to pay about $40 per hour for a regular ride, or $50–75 for a ride that includes a meal.

ROCK CLIMBING

One look at the South Lake Tahoe shoreline, and the verdict is clear: This place rocks. Experts and beginners alike will find plenty of bouldering and climbing opportunities around the South Shore. A popular beginner area is located in **Eagle Creek Canyon** near Emerald Bay, 0.25 mile up the Eagle Lake Trail near the bridge over the creek. A 75-foot-tall cliff erroneously named **90-Foot Wall** can be climbed year-round. Various climbs and routes are possible, giving beginners and intermediates ample practice opportunities. Bolt anchors are positioned on top of the cliff, making toproping easy. Another popular toproping site is **Pie Shop,** named after a bakery that used to be near the rock's base. Pie Shop is located off Sawmill Road (one mile south of the South Lake Tahoe Airport).

A famous climbing area to the west of the South Shore is **Lover's Leap,** located off U.S. 50 by Strawberry. This distinctive chunk of granite that rises 600 feet from the American River Canyon floor was made famous by climbing legend Royal Robbins in the 1960s. Single- and multiple-pitch routes are available, offering variety for climbers of all levels. About 30 separate boulder problems also present good challenges. Farther west on U.S. 50, the Echo Lake and Kyburz areas offer more climbing opportunities, including the steep knobs of Phantom Spires near the Wrights Lake Road turnoff, and the smooth, solid cracks of Sugarloaf near Kyburz, where the hardest climb in the world was established by Tony Yaniro in 1978.

Generally the best months for climbing around the South Shore are May, June, September, and October. July and August are often too hot, except for shaded climbing areas like Eagle Lake Cliff. Winter is obviously too cold. For **climbing instruction** and/or **guide service,** contact the Tahoe Adventure Company (530/913-9212 or 866/830-6125, www.tahoeadventurecompany.com). Although the company is based on the North Shore, they offer classes at several South Shore locations, including Lover's Leap, Phantom Spires, and Sugarloaf. Beginner and intermediate lessons cost about $130 for a half-day session. Several other reputable companies offer guiding service and classes on the South Shore: Lover's Leap Guides (530/318-2939, www.loversleap. net) and Alpine Skills International (530/582-9170, www.alpineskills.com).

To purchase rock-climbing equipment on the South Shore, go to Tahoe Sports Ltd. (4008 Hwy. 50 in the Heavenly Village Shopping Center, South Lake Tahoe, 530/542-4000, www.tahoesportsltd.com).

GOLF

Golfers looking for a bargain should head to **Bijou Municipal Golf Course** (3464 Fairway Ave., South Lake Tahoe, 530/542-6097, www. cityofslt.us), run by the City of South Lake Tahoe Parks and Recreation Department. This nine-hole, par 32 course offers fine views of Freel Peak and Heavenly Ski Resort and is the perfect place to hit a few balls without breaking the bank. Green fees are only $15–22, and tee times are on a first-come, first-served basis, so you can golf at the spur of the moment.

Or, for a longer day on the greens, make a reservation at the 18-hole **Lake Tahoe Golf Course** (2500 Emerald Bay Rd., South Lake Tahoe, 530/577-0788, www.laketahoegc.com). This par 72 course, designed by Billy Bell Jr., boasts spacious fairways backed by snowcapped mountains. The Upper Truckee River comes into play on 13 holes. Breakfast and lunch are served, plus cocktails on the mountain-view sundeck. Private and group lessons are offered at the full-service pro shop. Green fees are $41–74 (spring and fall are best for bargain rates).

Another of South Lake Tahoe's scenic courses is **Tahoe Paradise** (3021 Hwy. 50, South Lake Tahoe, 530/577-2121, www.tahoe-paradisegc.com), an 18-hole beauty nestled among the sugar pines just four miles south of

the South Lake Tahoe Y. This par 66 executive course costs only $30–55 to play, but be prepared for narrow, tree-lined fairways. If you aren't a straight shooter, play somewhere else.

Just across the Nevada state line in the casino area is **Edgewood Tahoe Golf Course** (100 Lake Pkwy., Stateline, 775/588-3566 or 888/881-8659, www.edgewoodtahoe.com). This 18-hole, par 72 course, built by architect George Fazio and his nephew Tom Fazio in 1969, is a favorite of well-to-do golfers and celebrities. Green fees range from $110–240. Bordering Lake Tahoe, the course is remarkably scenic and has been lauded by *Golf Digest Magazine* as one of America's top 100 courses. You may have seen photographs of its 18th hole, which is surrounded by so much water, it's practically an island. Every July, Edgewood hosts the **American Century Celebrity Golf Championship** (www.tahoecelebritygolf.com), in which a host of famous actors and athletes pair up to raise money for charity. Charles Barkley, Michael Jordan, and John Elway are frequent contestants. But Edgewood is not just for golfers. Even if you don't play, tag along with someone who does and go hang out and enjoy the lake views at Edgewood's Brooks Bar and Deck, or have dinner in the fabulous Edgewood Restaurant (180 Lake Pkwy., South Lake Tahoe, 775/588-2787, www.edgewoodtahoe.com, 5:30–9 P.M. daily, $26–35).

And expect big changes at Edgewood in the coming years. The company that owns the course is in the process of getting permits to build a hotel property next to the current clubhouse. As proposed, the LEED-designed lodge will include 194 hotel rooms, a health spa, and a bistro-style restaurant.

WINTER SPORTS
Downhill Skiing and Snowboarding

Boasting the largest concentration of ski areas in North America, Lake Tahoe offers skiers and snowboarders plenty of terrain, plenty of variety, and most years, plenty of snow. Thanksgiving is the traditional opening day for downhill (alpine) skiing and snowboarding around Lake Tahoe, but this varies according to the whims of Mother Nature. The ski season usually lasts into early April. At Tahoe's lake level (6,200 feet), about 125 inches of snow fall each year, but the higher elevations receive as much as 500 inches. At most Tahoe ski resorts, snow bases are usually between 100 and 200 inches December–March.

Bargain hunters should understand that you hardly ever need to pay full price for lift tickets. You will have to do a little strategizing, though, which includes regularly scanning the resorts' websites for special deals, including discounted weekday skiing, stay-and-ski-free packages, or packages with lessons and/or rentals included. A great website to keep your eye on is **Snowbomb** (www.snowbomb.com), which offers vouchers for discounted tickets for most of the major resorts, plus discounts at local lodgings, ski shops, and restaurants. If you have a Costco store near your hometown, you can often buy discounted lift tickets there, or visit www.costco.com. SaveMart and Lucky stores in California also sometimes carry discounted lift tickets.

If you need to rent ski or snowboarding equipment and you don't want to do so at the resorts, where it is usually way overpriced, dozens of rental shops on the South Shore can set you up before you reach the slopes. **Heavenly Sports** has a whopping seven locations, including one at 988 Stateline Avenue in South Lake Tahoe (530/544-1921). **Powder House Lake Tahoe** (www.tahoepowderhouse.com) has six locations on the South Shore, including one that is across the street from Heavenly Village (4045 Hwy. 50, 530/542-6222), another at Lakeland Village condos (530/541-2886), and another at the Forest Suites condos (530/543-6550). And **House of Ski** (209 Kingsbury Grade, Stateline, 775/588-5935 or 800/475-4432, www.houseofski.com) has been renting ski equipment on the South Shore since 1979. They also typically have the best prices on equipment for sale. Typical rental rates at shops in town are about $25 per day for a basic alpine ski package (skis, boots, poles) and $32 per day for a snowboarding package (board and boots). If you want high-performance demo equipment, you'll pay as much as double that for the latest, greatest gear.

Skiers who need rental equipment but don't want to schlep around town can take advantage of ski rental delivery services. You simply book your rentals online, wait for the delivery truck to show up at your hotel or condo, try on your equipment to make sure everything fits, and off you go. Sure, it costs about double for this service over typical rental shop rates, but for many, the convenience is worth it. The best part is that if, while you're on the slopes, you find that your bindings don't work right or your boots pinch your toes, you call the delivery company and they come and replace them. The best of the South Shore ski delivery services is **Ski Butlers** (877/754-7754, www.skibutlers.com). In addition to their seven rental shops, **Powder House** also offers a ski delivery service (800/555-2065, www.powderhouseskidelivery.com).

For skiing on the South Shore, you have two close-by choices: Heavenly Ski Resort and Sierra-at-Tahoe. **Heavenly Ski Resort** (3860 Saddle Rd., South Lake Tahoe, 775/586-7000, www.skiheavenly.com, 9 A.M.–4 P.M. Mon.–Thurs., 8:30 A.M.–4 P.M. Fri.–Sun. and holidays) holds numerous Tahoe records, including the fact that it has the highest summit elevation of any resort around the lake (10,067 feet). With 4,800 skiable acres on and around the slopes of mighty Monument Peak, this is California's largest resort. Heavenly has 30 lifts, plus its famous gondola, serving 94 runs, the longest of which is a prodigious

© ANN MARIE BROWN

Lake Tahoe looks huge from the slopes of Heavenly Ski Resort.

5.5 miles. The resort's greatest vertical drop is 3,500 feet, considered to be the longest on the West Coast. Plus, Heavenly's acreage runs across the state line, so it is possible to ski from California to Nevada and back again. All in all, megaresort Heavenly can brag of a lot of "bests" and "mosts," and one of those "mosts" is most expensive lift tickets of any resort around the basin, and the fewest discounts and deals.

Heavenly isn't the best place for beginners to try out their first pair of skis, but it's tons of fun for intermediate and advanced skiers and riders. One-third of the mountain is for expert skiers (try the famous Gunbarrel or World Cup runs), nearly half is intermediate terrain, and beginners are left with a mere 20 percent. From a ridge near the top of Heavenly's Olympic chair, three gates access the backcountry for skiers and riders who want fresh lines, providing a route to two infamous runs: Palisades and Fire Break. These two backcountry canyons are now as popular, or more so, than Mott Canyon,

Heavenly's equally famous in-bounds expert area. Beginners do best staying close to the calm corduroy near the Boulder Lodge learning center.

The resort typically sees 360 inches of snow per season, and they have plenty of snowmaking equipment, so there's usually plenty of white stuff—but never as much as there is at some of Tahoe's other resorts, where the annual snowfall can be 100 inches greater. If Heavenly has one shortcoming, it's that the season often ends a bit early.

Heavenly was purchased by Vail Resorts Inc. in 2002, and a blizzard of success has fallen upon it ever since. The resort has been posting record seasons and is consistently rated one of the Top 20 Ski Resorts in North America by *Ski Magazine,* both for "overall best resort" and for "off-hill activities." Part of the reason for Heavenly's good fortune is the location of its $23 million **gondola,** which was completed in 2001 and sits smack in the middle of downtown at U.S. 50 and Heavenly Village Way. Skiers and riders can walk to the gondola from hundreds of lodgings on both sides of the California and Nevada state line. Traveling 2.4 miles in about 12 minutes, Heavenly's gondola is California's longest, and its 138 cabins carrying eight passengers apiece give it the most uphill carrying capacity of any gondola in the state. Even nonskiers enjoy riding the gondola; the lake views are sublime. On the uphill ride, skiers and nonskiers alike can disembark about two-thirds of the way up and take in the vista from a 14,000-square-foot observation deck. At the top of the gondola is a lodge and restaurant, as well as Heavenly's Adventure Peak snow park, where nonskiers can go tubing or snowshoeing.

Heavenly is notorious for having some of the priciest lift ticket rates of any of the big resorts around the lake. In fact, whether you are buying an adult ticket, a child's ticket, or a half-day ticket, expect to pay about 20 bucks more to ski here than you would at Kirkwood, Squaw, Northstar, Sugar Bowl, or Alpine Meadows. Like all the other resorts, Heavenly alters its ticket prices based on the peak periods of the ski season, with the highest prices usually occurring during the last two weeks of December and on other winter holidays, like Presidents Day weekend and Martin Luther King Day weekend. Pre-Thanksgiving and April tickets are usually the cheapest. For all-day tickets, adults can expect to pay anywhere between $70–92, seniors 65 and older and teenagers $70–80, and children 12 and under $35–55. To save a few bucks, purchase multiple-day tickets at least seven days in advance at Heavenly's website.

If you are staying on the South Shore, there's no need to drive and hassle with parking near Heavenly's gondola. Instead, take the free Heavenly Shuttle, which is operated by BlueGO (530/541-7149, www.bluego.org) and stops at all major casinos and hotels in town.

To the west on U.S. 50, 12 miles from South Lake Tahoe, lies **Sierra-at-Tahoe** (1111 Sierra-at-Tahoe Rd., Twin Bridges, 530/659-7453, www.sierraattahoe.com, 9 A.M.–4 P.M. weekdays, 8:30 A.M.–4 P.M. weekends and holidays). With a highest elevation of 8,852 feet, the Sierra-at-Tahoe ski area has several things going for it. For skiers and riders traveling from Sacramento or the San Francisco Bay Area, Sierra-at-Tahoe is within easy reach, shaving nearly 30 minutes off the trip to South Lake Tahoe. The resort has 2,000 mostly wind-protected acres and 46 runs, so there's no shortage of terrain. There's no snowmaking equipment, either, which can be a bummer in dry winters. Most years, though, the snowfall averages a prodigious 480 inches. Lastly, the mountain's summit hosts **360 Smokehouse Barbecue** inside the Grandview Lodge, where the pulled pork sandwiches are graced by big vistas from the outdoor deck. Maybe it's due to the dizzying view of distant Lake Tahoe, but here, barbecue sauce rises to new culinary heights.

Snowboarders are fond of Sierra-at-Tahoe because of its six terrain parks and two radical half-pipes, including a 17-foot-tall gem that has been ranked as one of the top 10 half-pipes in North America by *Transworld Snowboarding* magazine. Most years, Sierra also puts the time, money, and energy into building a superpipe. Expert skiers who like to have a few obstacles in their path enjoy the amount of tree skiing possible on the slopes. Five backcountry gates, when they are open, can get you onto the slopes less traveled in Huckleberry Canyon (the resort is hoping to incorporate this area into its in-bounds, but for now, it's open to advanced backcountry skiers only). And parents of wee ones will appreciate the fact that the resort has licensed day care for children ages 18 months to five years.

Ski and snowboard lessons and learning programs are a priority at Sierra-at-Tahoe. With their "Learn to Ski Guarantee," beginners are

© ANN MARIE BROWN

spring skiing and riding at Sierra-at-Tahoe

promised they will be able to ski or snowboard from the top of the mountain after three lessons, or the fourth lesson is free. A long and gentle, 2.5-mile, green-circle run travels all the way from the top of the mountain to the base, so many novices get to ride the lift to the summit on their first day. With all this, it is no surprise that Sierra-at-Tahoe has a well-earned reputation as a family-friendly resort. And even if you aren't a family-style skier or rider, this is still a great place to ski on a windy, stormy day, especially if you enjoy tree skiing.

Adult all-day tickets are $74–77, youths 13–22 are $64–67, children 5–12 are $19–24, and children 4 and under ski free. Seniors 65–69 pay $47–53; seniors 70-plus pay $22–28. Half-day tickets are $10 less across the board. But lots of people take advantage of Sierra's terrific three-day deal, which costs $160 for adults, meaning each of three days of skiing or riding costs a little more than 50 bucks.

If you are staying in South Lake Tahoe and don't want to drive through the snow over Echo Summit to get to Sierra-at-Tahoe, relax and take the free shuttle, which leaves from Stateline Transit Center, South Y Transit Center, and Meyers Chevron several times each morning starting at 6:30 A.M. (only resort employees ride those first early buses; the resort doesn't open until 8:30 or 9, depending on the day of the week). Buses make the return trip to the South Shore starting at 12:50 P.M. from Sierra-at-Tahoe. Check the resort's website for details: www.sierraattahoe.com.

Tahoe Queen Ski Shuttle to Northstar-at-Tahoe

Skiers and boarders who would like to head to Northstar's slopes but don't want to drive in the snow can take advantage of the *Tahoe Queen*'s **North Shore Ski Shuttle** (reservations: 775/589-4906 or 800/238-2463, www.zephyrcove.com), which departs at 7:30 A.M. on Tuesdays and Thursdays, mid-January–early

April, from Ski Run Marina. The *Tahoe Queen* cruises from the South Shore to the pier at the Hyatt Hotel in Incline Village, where passengers disembark and board a bus for a 30-minute ride to Northstar Ski Resort. Breakfast is served on the morning ride to Incline Village; the boat trip back to the South Shore is a big, fun, après-ski party with live entertainment ($59 adults, $30 children 11 and under).

Bleu Wave Ski Shuttle to Homewood

On Fridays, Saturdays, and Mondays in winter, usually beginning in mid-January and running until mid-April, the 72-foot yacht *Bleu Wave* (775/588-9283 or 866/413-0985, www.tahoebleuwave.com) offers a ski cruise from the Zephyr Cove area to Homewood Ski Resort. Skiers and riders leave Round Hill Pines Marina at 8 A.M. and nosh on a continental breakfast as the boat skims across Lake Tahoe to West Shore Café and Inn, which is right across the road from Homewood. The $99 price includes an all-day lift ticket and discounted lunch from the Homewood's West Shore Café.

Cross-Country Skiing

The South Shore alpine ski resorts don't particularly cater to cross-country (Nordic) skiers. The closest resort with a substantial number of groomed cross-country trails is **Kirkwood.** Instead, the South Shore's cross-country skiing hot spots are better suited to do-it-yourselfers who have their own equipment and know where to go. If you don't know the area, contact the U.S. Forest Service at 530/543-2600 for maps and trail guides.

One of the most popular areas is **Echo Lake Sno-Park,** on the north side of U.S. 50, one mile west of Echo Summit (0.5 mile in along the road to Echo Lakes). There is parking for about 60 cars, but you must purchase a Sno-Park permit November 1–May 30 ($5 per day

or $25 per year, 530/543-2600, www.ohv.parks.ca.gov). In South Lake Tahoe, you can buy a Sno-Park permit at any Longs Drugs location or U.S. Forest Service office; check www.ohv.parks.ca.gov for other locations. From Echo Lake Sno-Park, you can ski up to the twin Echo Lakes, then follow the trail along their north shores and beyond as far as you please. It's 3.5 miles to the far end of Upper Echo Lake, 6 miles to Lake Margery, and 7 miles to Lake Aloha.

A much smaller Sno-Park at **Taylor Creek,** on the west side of Highway 89 just north of Camp Richardson, offers beginner-level cross-country skiing trails to Fallen Leaf Lake (530/543-2600, www.ohv.parks.ca.gov). There is parking for about 15 cars, but again, you must have a Sno-Park permit. Those seeking more of a challenge can ski the hill leading up to the **Angora Fire Lookout** on Angora Ridge, or continue to the Angora Lakes. Another popular winter trailhead for accessing Angora Ridge, its fire lookout, and/or the lakes, is located off Tahoe Mountain Road. There is no fee for parking here, and a Sno-Park permit is not required, but parking is fairly limited. From the South Lake Tahoe Y, head west on Lake Tahoe Boulevard for 2.4 miles to Tahoe Mountain Road, then turn right. Drive 1 mile, then turn right on Glenmore Way, followed by an immediate left on Dundee Circle (follow the signs for Fallen Leaf Lake and Angora Ridge). Park at the end of the plowed road by the gated road/trail. You'll ski for about 2 miles, almost all of it uphill, to reach the fire lookout; it's a fast and furious descent on the way back. If you want to continue past the lookout to the lakes, they are 1.4 miles farther along the obvious road/trail.

Another no-fee area popular with South Lake Tahoe locals is located at the end of **Oneidas Street** (off Pioneer Trail near its junction with U.S. 50/Hwy. 89). From this trailhead you can ski the road/trail to Fountain Place, or a stretch of the Powerline Trail (both about four miles round-trip). **High Meadows Road,** also off Pioneer Trail but a few miles farther to the east near Sierra House Elementary School, has more Nordic skiing opportunities. Simply park at the gate (0.75 mile up High Meadows Rd.) and follow the road/trail as far as you wish; it leads to High Meadows in 3.5 miles and Star Lake a few miles beyond. Both the Oneidas and High Meadows trailheads see a fair amount of snowmobile use, but most everybody minds their manners, and the snowmobiles tend to pack down the snow nicely for skiing.

If you need a place to rent equipment or take a few hours of lessons, your best bet is **Camp Richardson Resort** (1900 Jameson Beach Rd., South Lake Tahoe, 530/541-1801 or 530/542-6584, www.camprichardson.com). The resort has 35 kilometers of groomed trails bordering Highway 89, including a few trails along the shore of Lake Tahoe and on the grounds of the Tallac Historic Site. Equipment rentals cost $9–19 per day; a full-day trail pass is $10. Stay-and-ski packages that include cross-country ski equipment rentals, trail passes, lodging, and a continental breakfast start at $55 per person (double occupancy).

Snowshoeing

The great thing about snowshoeing is that you don't need any experience to do it, and you don't need to go anywhere special to do it. If there is snow on the ground and you have two feet, you can snowshoe. Sure, you can ride the gondola to Heavenly's Adventure Peak and snowshoe there on a couple kilometers of trails, but you could just as easily (and much more cheaply) do so on any of South Lake Tahoe's bike paths, along the Baldwin Beach shoreline, at Fallen Leaf Lake, or almost anywhere else.

Still, if it's your first time and you prefer to be led by the hand, try the groomed trails by the **Mountain Sports Center** at Camp Richardson Resort (530/542-6584, www.camprichardson.

com) or **Sierra-at-Tahoe Ski Resort** (530/659-7453, www.sierrattahoe.com).

The Mountain Sports Center at Camp Richardson has the largest selection of snowshoe rentals at Lake Tahoe, including children's sizes; they also hold fun events like snowshoe cocktail races and full-moon snowshoe parties. Snowshoe rentals cost $15–20 for a half day, $18–30 for a full day. Kids under 12 get a free trail pass when accompanied by an adult.

Sierra-at-Tahoe maintains three miles of groomed snowshoe trails. Interpretive signs along the route describe the fauna and flora of the Sierra Nevada. Guides from the resort's Telemark and Backcountry Center occasionally lead guided nature walks on snowshoes, but for the most part, you'll be on your own to rent snowshoes and take a self-guided walk in the snow. Rent equipment for $25 per day at the resort.

Sledding and Tubing

If you want to feel like you are eight years old again, go sledding. It's the perfect activity to take decades off your personal clock. Sledding is fun, low-tech, and a guaranteed giggle-inducer. What you choose as your sledding device is up to you. Many swear by round saucers, others insist on traditional rectangular models in plastic or wood, and still others buck tradition by sledding in large, inflatable inner tubes. In fact, the latter has become so popular it has spawned its own winter sport, known simply as **tubing.** Many snow-play resorts now allow only tubes on their sledding hills because their insurance agencies believe this is a kinder, gentler, less accident-prone form of sledding.

An old-fashioned South Shore resort that offers tubing and sledding is **Hansen's Resort** (1360 Ski Run Blvd., South Lake Tahoe, 530/544-3361, www.hansensresort.com) where the tubing hill is a whopping 400 feet long, with banked turns and smooth downhill runs. Equipment is furnished with the

SNOWSHOEING 101

Snowshoeing is one of the fastest-growing winter sports in the United States. It is low impact, low cost, and can be enjoyed by people of all ages. The sport is gentle on the environment and requires a bare minimum of equipment. Compared to skiing or snowboarding, the learning curve for snowshoeing is mercifully brief. Basically, if you can walk, you can snowshoe.

Today's snowshoes are nothing like the huge wood-and-wicker "tennis racquets" used to travel across the snow a generation ago. Built with heat-treated aluminum frames, modern snowshoes are remarkably light and durable, and allow you to "float" over deep snow. The attached toe and heel crampons give you traction to climb steep hills and travel across icy surfaces. Snowshoe bindings strap on to almost any kind of boots; just make sure that yours are waterproof and warm. If you find that snow gets into the tops of your boots, a pair of gaiters can solve the problem.

The few techniques you need to master are fairly intuitive. You will figure them out on your own in short order. For example, your stance needs to be wider than it normally is for walking, so you don't step on the inside of your snowshoe frames. To go up a short, steep hill, you may need to "herringbone," or place your feet in a V shape—heels close together and toes spread out to the side. On very steep slopes, you may need to sidestep, or climb with your snowshoes parallel to the slope.

Many snowshoers like to use handheld poles to help their balance, especially on hills. Most poles are adjustable, and you'll quickly learn that you want to shorten them to go uphill and lengthen them to go downhill. If you are traversing a slope, or "side-hilling," you can lengthen one pole (on the downslope side) and shorten the other (on the upslope side) to aid your balance.

There's only one important rule of snowshoeing etiquette: If you are snowshoeing in an area where people cross-country ski, stay off the ski tracks so you don't ruin their smooth surface. Usually running parallel to the ski tracks are a separate set of snowshoe tracks, which you should follow. If not, make your own tracks.

If you decide to buy a pair of snowshoes instead of renting them, you'll find that there are many different styles. Casual snowshoers require the least expensive models, which are called "recreational" snowshoes. Often these can be purchased for less than $100, and they are suitable for snowshoeing on relatively level terrain. If you plan to head into the backcountry on snowshoes, you'll want one of the sturdier models that have stronger bindings and more aggressive crampons. These can run as high as $300. Typical rental rates for snowshoes at various shops around Lake Tahoe are about $15-20 per day.

$10-per-person, per-hour fee (no charge for kids ages 4 and under). No "outside" equipment is allowed. Hot chocolate and snacks are for sale. If you stay in one of their cabins, you can tube and sled for free.

If you are traveling with skiing friends, you can tube while they ski at **Sierra-at-Tahoe,** which brags of having 425 feet of smooth sailing and banked turns on its tubing run (noon–4 P.M. weekdays, 10 A.M.–4 P.M. weekends, $25 for two hours, including equipment).

Another sledding and tubing area is operated by **Lake Tahoe Adventures** (3071 Hwy. 50, South Lake Tahoe, 530/577-2940, www.laketahoeadventures.com) in the Meyers area, next to Lira's Supermarket.

Do-it-yourselfers should head to one of the state-run **Sno-Parks** in the South Lake vicinity. Sno-Parks, which are basically plowed parking lots alongside or near the highway, are marked by distinctive brown signs. Here, for the price of a $5 daily permit or $25 annual permit, you can slide down the hills on any piece of equipment you like. Heck, bring along your garbage-can lid if that's all you have. Sno-Park permits are sold at Longs Drugs stores, sporting-goods stores, businesses located near Sno-Parks, and many other locations. The Sno-Park program hotline (916/324-1222, www. ohv.parks.ca.gov) has information on where to buy permits and where Sno-Parks are located.

Three Sno-Parks are found in the South Shore region, but only one has good sledding and tubing opportunities. **Taylor Creek Sno-Park** (530/543-2600, www.ohv.parks.ca.gov), on the west side of Highway 89 near Camp Richardson, has a small sledding hill and parking for about 15 cars. This is the perfect spot to take very young children sledding.

The south side of Echo Summit on U.S. 50 used to have a Sno-Park named Echo Summit, but the area is now privately run and called **Adventure Mountain** (on U.S. 50, 2.8 miles east of Sierra-at-Tahoe, 530/577-4352, www. adventuremountaintahoe.com, 10 A.M.– 4:30 P.M. weekdays, 9 A.M.–5 P.M. weekends late November–April, conditions permitting). It still has the same great sledding hill, relatively clean restrooms, and ample parking. The parking fee is $18 per vehicle, and Sno-Park permits are not accepted. Bring your own sled, saucer, or inner tube, or rent one at the concession stand located adjacent to the hill, which also sells snacks, beverages, gloves, and hats. Three separate slopes of varying inclines allow you to choose your risk level. Thrill seekers will head for the longest, steepest slope, which used to be a ski run back in the days when a ski resort was located here. Only the most aerobically fit daredevils tackle this run—it's a long uphill hike to get to the top, especially when you are dragging a sled behind you.

Snowmobiling

If you are craving a winter sport with some horsepower behind it, snowmobiling might fit the bill. Two companies at South Lake offer guided snowmobile tours on groomed trails that lead to impressive high vistas of the lake. The largest snowmobile tour center on the West Coast, **Zephyr Cove Snowmobile Center** (760 Hwy. 50 at Zephyr Cove Resort, Zephyr Cove, 775/589-4906 or 800/238-2463, www. zephyrcove.com) has more than 100 Yamaha and Ski-Doo touring snowmobiles (including double-rider machines, so even children as young as five can go along for the trip, with Mom or Dad driving). The company caters to first-time riders with free shuttle service from the casino area of South Lake Tahoe to Zephyr Cove, and bus service from there to the snowmobiling trailhead. If you forgot to bring along your warmest gloves and boots, clothing rentals are available ($18 for a complete package consisting of jacket, bibs, boots, and gloves). Helmets are provided free with all rides. The standard two-hour Lakeview Tour leaves two to four times a day in winter, depending on demand; all drivers must be at least 16 years old. Cost is $119 for a single rider or $159 for two double riders, except for the weekend ride-and-dine tours, which are $122 per single rider, including dinner. Those seeking more adventure can sign up for the Sierra Summit Tour, a three-hour ride for $189 for single riders and $249 for double riders. If possible, try to make the trip on a weekday, as weekends are quite busy and tons of snowmobiles share the trails. The company that runs the snowmobile center is the same one that operates the cruising paddle wheelers MS *Dixie II* and *Tahoe Queen,* so ride-and-cruise packages are available for visitors who want to make a day of it. Other packages include dinner and/or an overnight stay in a cabin at Zephyr Cove.

Lake Tahoe Adventures (3071 Hwy. 50, South Lake Tahoe, 530/577-2940 or 800/865-4679, www.laketahoeadventures.com), located next to Lira's Supermarket and across from the agricultural check station in Meyers, specializes in introducing beginners to snowmobiling with their two-hour Summit Tour through Hope Valley, following the Carson River all the way to Blue Lakes. No more than seven machines go out in each group, so the experience is fairly intimate. Helmets, gloves, and boots are included in the price, as well as shuttle transportation from the tour center in Meyers to the snowmobile base camp in Hope Valley. Tours cost $110 for single riders or $150 for two double riders. Snowmobile suits are available to rent for $10. Drivers must be at least 16 years old and hold a driver's license. Children 5 and under are not permitted on public tours, but private tours can be arranged. More experienced riders can sign up for longer tours that leave the groomed trails behind and set out into fresh powder. Kids 8 years old and up can try snowmobiling on their own on a special groomed track.

Currently only one company on the South Shore allows self-guided snowmobile rentals. **Sierra Mountain Sports** (2500 Emerald Bay Rd. at the Lake Tahoe Golf Course, South Lake Tahoe, 530/542-3294, www.sierramountainsports.com) provides snowmobiles for one day or longer rentals (rates are generally around $250 per day) as well as safety tips, riding instruction, a helmet, and a map. If you have a towing vehicle, a trailer is included with your rental, so you can tow the machines to any of the designated snowmobile areas. The company also has a second rental location in Stateline at 100 Lake Parkway at the Edgewood Tahoe Golf Course.

Ice-Skating

November–March, weather permitting, Heavenly Village's outdoor **ice-skating rink** is open 10 A.M.–8 P.M. daily (530/542-4230, www.theshopsatheavenly.com). Where else can you practice your figure-eights while your non-skating friends browse through Heavenly Village's exclusive shops? The rink is on the small side, so you might not be able to execute a triple camel, but it's good fun for kids. Skate rentals are good for the entire day ($20 adults,

Skaters dress up in 1970s costumes at Heavenly Village's ice rink.

© ANN MARIE BROWN

$15 children 12 and under), so you can come, skate, go, and return to skate again as often as you please.

More serious skaters can be found at the indoor **South Lake Tahoe Ice Arena** (1176 Rufus Allen Blvd., South Lake Tahoe, 530/542-6262, www.tahoearena.com, public skating hours vary). This full-service ice-skating facility consists of a regulation National Hockey League–size ice arena, locker rooms, snack bar, retail store, arcade, and party rooms. Skating and hockey lessons are available, as well as public skate sessions. The rink used to be run by the City of South Lake Tahoe, but since August 2011, a private company has taken over its management. This has always been a great place to skate or play hockey, but it should get even better in coming years now that there is some money behind it.

Sleigh Rides

If the snow permits, every December–March the Borges family offers winter-wonderland-style sleigh rides in the big meadow across the road from **MontBleu** (U.S. 50 and Loop Rd., Stateline, 775/588-2953 or 800/726-7433, www.sleighride.com, $20 adults, $10 children 2–10, free for children under 2). Rides last about 30 minutes and take place in one of five handmade sleighs, including a romantic two-seater and a party-style 20-passenger sleigh. Blankets are provided for snuggling with loved ones, and hot chocolate and cookies are available for purchase. If you're planning to propose marriage to that special someone and don't want to make a public show of it, private rides are available ($50 adults, $25 children 3–10). The Borges's horses are celebrities—they frequently appear in Pasadena's Tournament of Roses parade.

On the opposite side of South Lake, the horses at **Camp Richardson's Corral** (Emerald Bay Rd. at Fallen Leaf Lake Rd., South Lake Tahoe, 530/541-3113, www.camprichardson. com, $28 per person) also carry passengers on sleigh rides through the snow-covered landscape. Reservations are required.

Entertainment and Shopping

CASINOS AND NIGHTLIFE

If you have wads of cash burning a hole in your pocket, you might as well donate some to the South Shore casinos. There are five to choose from on the Nevada side of the South Shore at Stateline, and all are within shouting range of each other: MontBleu Resort, Harrah's Lake Tahoe, Harveys Resort and Casino, Horizon Casino Resort, and Lakeside Inn and Casino. What's the difference between them? Not much, since most are owned by two large gaming conglomerates. The gaming giant Harrah's owns Harrah's Lake Tahoe and Harveys. Columbia Sussex Corporation owns Horizon Casino Resort and in 2006 purchased the old Caesars Lake Tahoe for a cool

$45 million and repackaged it as MontBleu Resort Casino and Spa. Only Lakeside Casino remains independent.

Blackjack, craps, keno, bingo, poker, slot machines, roulette wheels, and sports books are available everywhere, and in plentiful supply. Harveys has the largest amount of casino floor space (52,000 square feet) and the most slot machines (more than 2,000), with Harrah's coming in second.

Worth noting, for rock-and-roll buffs, is that **Horizon Casino Resort** (50 Hwy. 50, Stateline, 775/588-6211 or 800/648-3322, www.horizoncasino.com) can lay claim to an interesting piece of American history. It was originally known as the Sahara Tahoe, the resort where

SOUTH SHORE CASINO ROUNDUP

With a handful of casinos lined up side by side along U.S. 50 in Stateline, two owned by the same conglomerate (Harrah's and Harveys are owned by the Harrah's Corporation), how can the uninitiated tell them apart? From the outside, they look remarkably similar, but each has its own unique strengths. Here's a brief guide to which casino is best for which activities:

· **Best fine-dining restaurant:** Casinos are usually better known for quantity rather than quality of food, but one big exception is Ciera Steak and Chophouse at MontBleu. Tahoe's only four-star restaurant, Ciera wins high marks for its gourmet food, intimate curtained booths, and sophisticated ambience.

· **Best nightclub for dancing:** VEX at Harrah's. You've never seen anything quite like the VEX go-go dancers, whose gyrating antics will inspire you to new moves of your own. But to avoid the lines and the pricey cover charge, head to Opal at Montbleu.

· **Best nightclub for downing cocktails:** Opal Ultra Lounge at MontBleu, where the young and restless sit perched on overstuffed chairs and the fire dancers perform at midnight. While you're killing brain cells with neon-colored alcohol, you might as well try the hookahs.

· **Best rooms for an overnight stay:** Harrah's consistently gets the highest marks for its 500-square-foot and larger guest rooms, which have unusual luxuries like two bathrooms and multiple telephones.

· **Best place for live music:** Harveys Outdoor Arena in summer, Harrah's intimate South Shore Room the rest of the year.

· **Biggest gambling floor:** Harveys, at 52,000 square feet. It also has the most slot machines (more than 2,000).

· **Best for families:** Horizon, for its giant heated swimming pool, gaming arcade, and eight-plex movie theater.

· **Best spa:** Reflections at Harrah's. Get the 70-minute soothing stones massage or the enzymatic sea-mud wrap.

· **Best for cheap drinks:** Lakeside. The drinks are why they call themselves "the locals' favorite."

in the 1970s Elvis Presley often fired up the crowds. Today the Horizon is a bit lower key than the neighboring Harrah's-owned properties and attracts more families, in part because of its eight-screen movie theater and huge arcade room. In 2009, all gaming tables were removed from Horizon Casino, so now the only way to gamble here is at the slot machines.

The **Lakeside Inn and Casino** (168 Hwy. 50, Stateline, 775/588-7777 or 800/624-7980, www.lakesideinn.com) caters more to Tahoe locals. It is set off farther east from the larger casinos—it's the only one that is not quite within easy walking distance of the others, especially for older gamblers—so people who come here usually stay for the evening. Cheap drinks are standard fare at Lakeside, and their restaurant,

the Timber House, is well loved for its prime-rib dinners and inexpensive breakfasts.

For people who tire of gambling fairly quickly (or run out of cash), the casinos offer much more than roulette tables and one-armed bandits. Besides a huge selection of restaurants, there's also music, magic, cabaret, or comedy always happening at one or more of the casinos' nightclubs. Big-name performers usually appear on weekends only, but lesser-known singers, musicians, and dancers appear every night of the year.

King-of-the-strip **Harrah's** is home to the **South Shore Room** (15 Hwy. 50, South Lake Tahoe, 775/588-6611 or 800/648-3773, www.harrahs.com), which has hosted a long line of famous American entertainers since it first opened in the 1950s. A typical weekend night might see performers like Keb Mo', Los Lobos, or Tower of Power. For those who want to take part in the action as well as be entertained, Harrah's **VEX Nightclub** (775/586-6705, 10:30 P.M.–4 A.M. Fri.–Sat.) is the hot spot, where discounted drinks are a common occurrence, the high-energy techno music pumps at deafening volumes, and more than a dozen go-go dancers (female and male) do their hip-swinging acts in a variety of box, pole, and cage contraptions and while suspended above the dance floor on a series of catwalks and bridges. The bikini-clad gals dancing in the "shower boxes" always seem to rev up the crowd. And yes, it's true, the female dancers go topless on weekend nights. If you're not a drinker, you can always go take a hit at the oxygen bar.

MontBleu Resort Casino (55 Hwy. 50, Stateline, 775/586-2000, www.montbleuresort.com) has four nightclubs, the most popular being **Opal Ultra Lounge** (10 P.M.–close Wed.–Sun.), where the drinks are neon colored and the crowd is young, trendy, and usually from out of town. Opal has a seductive lounge ambience, with fire dancers performing at midnight and patrons lounging on overstuffed chairs while they smoke from hookahs (Turkish water pipes used to smoke flavored tobacco) and drink absinthe. Hotel guests receive free admission at Montbleu's clubs.

Harveys (30 Hwy. 50, Stateline, 775/588-2411 or 800/427-8397, www.harrahs.com) has two nightclubs: the **Hard Rock Café** (775/588-6200), where live bands play on weekends, and the tequila-obsessed **Cabo Wabo Cantina,** owned by none other than the Red Rocker himself, Sammy Hagar. If you're a real party animal, ask the bartender for a "body shot." If you aren't, order a Cabo Waborita and sip it very, very slowly. Harveys also sponsors an outdoor concert series at its 5,000-seat amphitheater in summer, with aging-but-still-famous headliners like Loggins and Messina, the Eagles, James Taylor, and, of course, Sammy Hagar.

Right next to the gondola in Heavenly Village, **Fire and Ice** (in Marriott Timber Lodge, 4100 Hwy. 50, South Lake Tahoe, 530/542-6650, www.fire-ice.com) offers an impressive array of cocktails that are huge, colorful, and generally overpriced. Their gigantic 48-ouncer is best shared with two or three friends. The customers are generally twentysomething out-of-towners, and the music is high energy. Best seats in the house are the ones outside by the fire pits.

If you prefer to get away from the casino part of town but still want to enjoy great entertainment, several other spots around the South Shore offer live music and nightlife. And because these places are located in California, not Nevada, you won't find yourself choking from cigarette smoke. The young and athletic flock to **Divided Sky** (3200 Hwy. 50, South Lake Tahoe, 530/577-0775, www.thedividedsky.com, happy hour 3–6 P.M. daily), located above the Downtown Café in Meyers. This popular hangout for rock climbers and snowboarders looks and feels a lot like a San Francisco South-of-Market dive, but without any suits.

Summertime brings live bands to **Whiskey Dick's** (2660 Hwy. 50, South Lake Tahoe, 530/544-3425, 1 P.M.–2 A.M. daily). The emphasis here is on rock and roll and heavy metal. The crowd is usually wearing leather, and the parking lot is filled with Harleys.

The beer-drinking, pool-playing set heads to **Turn 3 Sports Bar** (2227 Hwy. 50, South Lake Tahoe, 530/542-3199, noon–2 A.M. daily), a place where you can let your hair down, play a few games of pool or darts, and toss your peanut shells on the floor. Karaoke usually happens on Thursday nights; don't forget your earplugs.

Live music featuring local bands is a common occurrence at several South Lake bar/restaurants: Beacon Bar and Grill at Camp Richardson Resort (530/541-0630), Fresh Ketch in the Tahoe Keys Marina (530/541-5683), McP's Pub Tahoe (530/542-4435), and Rojo's Tavern (530/541-4960).

No discussion of South Lake Tahoe bars and nightlife would be complete without mentioning **Mount Tallac Brewery** (2060 Eloise Ave., South Lake Tahoe, 530/541-7405), which may well be the most low-profile brewery in the world. They don't even have a website. The small brewery has a tasting room at its shop, which is open only 5–7 P.M. daily (call ahead to confirm). If you have your heart set on visiting and can't make it during those hours, Jeff, the head brewer, will try to accommodate you. The brewery is a little hard for first-timers to find; it's on the corner of Eloise and Dunlap, right on the bike trail. An amber ale and pale ale are available year-round; other flavors like the Desolation Wilderness Wheat and Backcountry Blonde are brewed seasonally. Occasionally, live bands play here on summer evenings.

And if your idea of nightlife is snuggling up with your sweetie and a bag of popcorn at the **movie theater,** there are two on the South Shore: the eight-plex at Horizon Stadium Cinema inside Horizon Casino (775/589-6000) or Heavenly Village Cinema (530/544-1110, www.heavenlycinema.com).

SHOPPING

Seasoned factory outlet shoppers will want to head straight to the Y at South Lake Tahoe, where more than a dozen outlet stores are bunched together for easy browsing, and parking is free and plentiful. The **Factory Stores at the Y** (junction of U.S. 50 and Hwy. 89, www.shopthey.com) outlet center includes Bass Shoes, Izod, Adidas, Pearl Izumi, Van Heusen, Sunglass Hut, Fragrance Hut, Blue Willow Home, and other major brand names.

The **Village Center** at Stateline (corner of U.S. 50 and Park Ave.) features a huge variety of stores anchored by a large Raley's supermarket, plus standard mall stops like Jamba Juice, Baja Fresh, Subway, and Starbucks Coffee. A few art galleries, a ski-and-bike shop (Tahoe Sports Ltd.), a hardware store, a jewelry store, and a

few women's clothing boutiques fill out the rest of the lineup. Perhaps the nicest thing about this shopping center is that it is an easy walk from the Marriott and Heavenly Village complex next door, including the Heavenly gondola.

Next door at **Heavenly Village** (1001 Heavenly Village Way, South Lake Tahoe, www.theshopsatheavenlyvillage.com), 50-plus shops and art galleries and 14 restaurants cater more to tourists than locals. A half-dozen galleries and jewelry stores are mixed in with clothing stores, ski rental shops, and eateries such as Cold Stone Creamery, Wolfgang Puck Express, and a few that you won't find in every other mall in America (try breakfast at Driftwood Café). The Heavenly Village center also has a day spa, eight-plex cinema, a wine boutique, and other retail businesses that serve life's not-so-essential needs. The shopping village was creatively designed and features heated cobblestone sidewalks, covered walkways, open bonfire pits, and a clock tower. In the winter, a diminutive ice-skating rink provides an attraction for the kiddies, and in the summer, that same outdoor space is converted to a miniature golf course.

FESTIVALS AND EVENTS

A few annual events on the South Shore are worth planning your vacation around. Don't miss attending some part of the **Valhalla Arts and Music Festival** at the Tallac Historic Site, a series of concerts featuring jazz, bluegrass, New Age, folk, Latin, reggae, and classical artists. Concerts and theater performances are held inside the 200-seat Boathouse Theater and the Valhalla Grand Hall. The festival usually begins in late May and runs until late September. For program information, contact the Tahoe Tallac Association (530/541-4975 or 888/632-5859, www.valhallatahoe.com). Ticket prices for shows range from free to $30. Another wonderful event at the Tallac Historic Site is the **Great Gatsby Festival** (530/544-7383,

© ANN MARIE BROWN

The shops at Heavenly Village attract summertime strollers and browsers.

www.tahoeheritage.org, free), a celebration of the roaring 1920s at Lake Tahoe, which takes place in mid-August.

If you have a latent lusty Elizabethan peasant hiding inside you, don't miss the **Valhalla Renaissance Faire** (415/354-1773, www.valhallafaire.com, $17 adults, $12 teens, $7 children 12 and under) at Camp Richardson, usually held for two weekends in late May or early June. Costumed players offer arts and crafts demonstrations, cook and serve hearty English food, test their skills in games and races at the tournament field, hawk their wares, and generally make merry while speaking words like *forsooth*.

The city of South Lake Tahoe pulls out all the stops for its annual **Fourth of July** celebration. Each year, extravagant pyrotechnics burst into the air over the surface of Lake Tahoe. Watching the fireworks is free, but the difficult part is making your way through the crowds to a vantage point where you can see them, and

then—worse yet—getting back to your lodging after the show's over. Most people think it's worth the trouble, though. The fireworks show is amazing, and patriotic spirit runs high among all the partying. For information on special Fourth of July events, contact the Lake Tahoe Visitors Authority (530/544-5050, www.tahoesouth.com).

In mid-July, celebrities show up with their clubs and caddies for their chance at a purse of $600,000 and plenty of network television exposure at the **American Century Celebrity Golf Championship** (www.tahoecelebritygolf.com). Held at Edgewood Tahoe Golf Course near Stateline, this is the richest celebrity tournament in golf.

As fall approaches, prepare to celebrate the salmon at the annual **Kokanee Salmon Festival** at the Taylor Creek Visitor Center (530/543-2600 or 530/543-2674). The kokanee, a species of landlocked salmon and a popular Tahoe sport fish, performs its annual spawning rites in

Taylor Creek every October, when the adult fish travel upstream to spawn and die. (In spring, their offspring travel downstream back to Lake Tahoe.) From the trail alongside the creek, visitors can watch the female salmon lay her eggs and the male salmon fertilize them. During the course of this free two-day event, usually held on the first weekend in October, there are a wide variety of educational programs, nature walks, and informational tours related to the ecology of Lake Tahoe.

Wintertime isn't only about skiing and snow sports on the South Shore. Another eagerly awaited event is the **Tahoe Adventure Film Festival** (530/318-1688, www.laketahoefilmfestival.com), usually held at MontBleu Casino in mid-December, and then repeated in mid-January in Reno. Films cover adrenaline-pumping subjects like base jumping, white-water kayaking, skateboarding, and rock climbing, but in the most extreme versions you can imagine.

FAMILY FUN

The folks who run the Stateline casinos are no dummies; they quickly figured out that it was smart to provide the kids with something to do while Mom and Dad gamble away the family nest egg. Each of the big casinos has its own game arcade, or, as the casinos prefer to call it, Family Fun Center.

For some family fun that isn't attached to a casino, go play a few rounds of pee-wee golf at **Magic Carpet Golf** (2455 Hwy. 50, South Lake Tahoe, 530/541-3787, 10 A.M.–10 P.M. daily in summer, spring and fall hours vary, closed in winter, $8–11). Magic Carpet Golf also has an arcade for gaming.

If bowling is your bag, head to the lanes at **Tahoe Bowl** (1030 Fremont Ave., South Lake Tahoe, 530/544-3700, www.tahoebowl.com, 2–11 P.M. daily in summer, 11 A.M.–11 P.M. daily in winter) and teach your kids how to roll a few strikes or spares. With 16 lanes available, the wait isn't usually too long, and if it is, you can hang out in the sports bar, send the kids to the video arcade, or munch on some pizza.

In winter, spend a few hours on one of the local sledding or tubing hills with the kids, or take them on a horse-drawn sleigh ride. If the weather is poor, try indoor ice-skating at the **South Lake Tahoe Ice Arena** (1176 Rufus Allen Blvd., South Lake Tahoe, 530/542-6262, www.tahoearena.com, public skating hours vary).

Accommodations

CASINOS AND HEAVENLY GONDOLA AREA
Casino Hotels

If you want to gamble without a long commute from your bed, you have a half-dozen choices in Stateline. Far and away the best of the casino lodging choices is **C Harrah's** (15 Hwy. 50, Stateline, 775/588-6611 or 800/786-8208, www.harrahs.com, $109–299), which consistently scores high marks for its customer service. The resort has 525 rooms spread out over 18 stories, and key to enjoying your stay is to get the best lake view you can afford. That way when your wallet has been cleaned out at the casino, you will still be able to look out the window and enjoy the view. The large (500 square feet and up), tastefully decorated rooms have unusual luxuries like two bathrooms and multiple telephones. The intention is to make you feel like you are very rich, and for most people, it works. Sometime during your stay, make sure you have a meal at the Forest Buffet on the 18th floor, where the view will knock your socks off, even if the food is standard casino buffet fare.

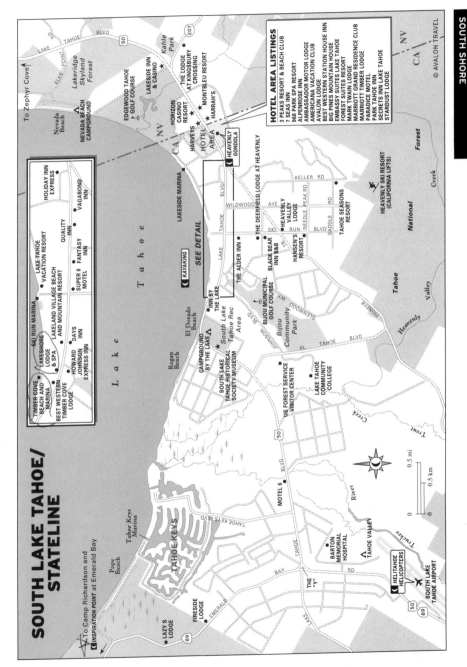

SOUTH SHORE

SOUTH LAKE TAHOE/ STATELINE

HOTEL AREA LISTINGS

3 PEAKS RESORT & BEACH CLUB
7 SEAS INN
968 PARK SPA RESORT
ALPENROSE INN
AMBASSADOR MOTOR LODGE
AMERICANA VACATION CLUB
AVALON LODGE
BEST WESTERN STATION HOUSE INN
BIG PINES MOUNTAIN HOUSE
EMBASSY SUITES LAKE TAHOE
FOREST SUITES RESORT
MARK TWAIN LODGE
MARRIOTT GRAND RESIDENCE CLUB
MARRIOTT TIMBER LODGE
PARADICE MOTEL
PARK TAHOE INN
SECRETS INN LAKE TAHOE
STARDUST LODGE

© AVALON TRAVEL

And if you want to feel like you are still young and restless, stay up late one night and head out to Harrah's VEX nightclub to see the amazing go-go dancers, both female and male.

It's all about excess at **Harveys** (18 Hwy. 50, Stateline, 775/588-2411 or 800/648-3361, www.harrahs.com, $79–399), which is right across the street from Harrah's and a great second choice if the former is full or out of your price range. This four-diamond resort hotel has eight restaurants and 10 cocktail lounges. In addition to 24-hour gaming, Harveys also has a health club, heated outdoor pool and hot tub, full-service wedding chapel, and sprawling video arcade. But aside from the 740 nicely appointed rooms, most with excellent lake views, Harveys's biggest attractions may be the 100-plus tequila varieties at the Cabo Wabo Cantina, the flambé table service at the Sage Room Steak House, and the grand lake views from the 19th floor at 19 Kitchen/Bar. Or maybe it's the fact that Harveys has a monumental 52,000 square feet of casino floor space. It's all about the numbers here.

Just a stone's throw away is the **MontBleu Resort Casino and Spa** (55 Hwy. 50, Stateline, 775/588-3515 or 888/829-7630, www.montbleuresort.com, $69–329). MontBleu is the old Caesars Tahoe, which was taken over by Columbia Sussex Corporation in 2006. The fallen Caesars's faux marble columns and toga-clad statues are ancient history, but sadly, some of the hotel rooms still have the dated look of the old ownership. The huge resort boasts 437 rooms and suites, many with desirable perks like jetted spa tubs. Although many guests' overall impression is that MontBleu is in need of a makeover, the resort's 40,000 square feet of casino space, two nightlife venues, half-dozen restaurants, and luxurious spa facility keep them coming back. Book a suite if you can afford it—they are far nicer than the "deluxe" rooms.

One of the Big 3 Hs on the South Shore (Horizon, Harveys, and Harrah's), the monolithic **Horizon Casino Resort** (50 Hwy. 50, Stateline, 775/588-6211 or 800/648-3322, www.horizoncasino.com, $59–199) has 539 hotel rooms in two separate towers, one reaching 15 stories high and the other merely 9. Be forewarned: The Horizon is often less expensive than the other Hs, but you get what you pay for. The majority of its rooms are very basic (think Best Western and you have the right picture), with televisions being the only amenity of note. Both the rooms and the casino itself seem to be aging gracelessly, with tired decor and worn furnishings. The best bets are the higher-priced rooms and suites located on the top floors of the highest tower; these feature floor-to-ceiling windows with views of Lake Tahoe. Otherwise, your room might have a view of the casino across the street, or if you are lucky, the Horizon's pool, which happens to be the largest outdoor heated pool on the South Shore. The best room in the place is the Elvis Suite; book it and you can sleep where "The King" slept in the 1970s when he was a regular performer at the Horizon (then called the Sahara Tahoe). The Horizon bills itself as being more "subdued" than other South Shore casinos. Its gaming floor was permanently closed in 2009 (no card or dice games), but the slot machines remain, as well as a game arcade for the kiddies and an eight-plex movie theater. If you feel like stuffing your gut like a true gourmand, the resort offers a big casino buffet as well as a separate restaurant, the Four Seasons.

The **Lakeside Inn and Casino** (168 Hwy. 50, Stateline, 775/588-7777 or 800/624-7980, www.lakesideinn.com, $69–299) is not the most glamorous casino resort at Lake Tahoe, but it's a good place to stay for easy access to gaming, skiing, and South Shore nightlife, without all the fanfare and crowds of Stateline's larger casinos. The Lakeside's 124 rooms are furnished in mountain-style decor (hickory furniture, wood paneling, and local

Tahoe artwork) and have convenient amenities like wireless Internet access and in-room ski racks. Famous for the huge portion sizes at the in-house Timber House Restaurant and Bar, the Lakeside attracts folks looking for a quick weekend getaway consisting of mindless gambling, wanton overeating, and imbibing $3 drinks. South Shore locals flock to the restaurant here, especially on prime rib nights. Room rates are surprisingly reasonable for the Stateline area, but the casino will get plenty more out of your wallet at the craps table.

Condominium-Style Resorts and Hotels

If you prefer a condominium stay to a hotel or motel for your vacation, the two Marriott properties in the Stateline/Heavenly/casino area of the South Shore are the premier options. **Marriott's Timber Lodge** (4100 Hwy. 50, South Lake Tahoe, 530/542-6600 or 800/465-4213, www.marriott.com, $129–799) has a location that can't be beat—right next to the Heavenly gondola and Harrah's casino, and an easy walk to shops and restaurants no matter what the weather. As you would expect at an upscale "condotel" resort, the Timber Lodge is loaded with amenities: an impressive fitness facility, two on-site spas providing all the latest treatments, the hip Fire and Ice restaurant (530/542-6650, www.fire-ice.com, 11:30 A.M.–9 P.M. Sun.–Thurs., 11:30 A.M.–10 P.M. Fri. and Sat.), a heated outdoor pool and three outdoor Jacuzzis, and plenty of activities for kids. The lobby lounge is a stunner, with a huge rock fireplace, massive timbers, and dark leather and log furniture. The 473 guest rooms and one-, two-, and three-bedroom "villas" also have mountain-style decor, plus all the comforts of home: full kitchens, washers and dryers, jetted tubs, and the like.

On the opposite side of the gondola, the **Marriott Grand Residence Club** (1001 Heavenly Village Way, South Lake Tahoe, 530/542-8400 or 800/627-7468, www.marriott.com, $129–799) offers studios and one-, two-, and three-bedroom condominiums, or "residences," as they call them. These are arguably the most luxurious condo rentals in South Lake, with spacious living areas, tasteful mountain-style decor, fully equipped kitchens, fireplaces, whirlpool tubs, and a host of extras, including a health club, ski storage area, valet parking, and concierge desk. But even if they were run-down shacks people would still flock here, because the Grand Residence is located right at the base of the Heavenly gondola and next to Heavenly Village's outdoor ice rink, shopping center, restaurants, and movie theater. Once you're here, you don't need your car at all.

Families enjoy the nine-story **Embassy Suites Lake Tahoe Hotel and Ski Resort** (4130 Hwy. 50, South Lake Tahoe, 530/544-5400 or 877/497-8483, www.embassytahoe.com, $159–399), which has all the amenities of a full-service hotel but no casino downstairs to pollute the little ones' minds. Each of the hotel's 400 units are two-room suites with one king or two queen beds in the bedroom, plus a pull-out couch in the living room for the kiddies, and a convenient kitchenette with a refrigerator, microwave oven, and coffeemaker, but no cooking facilities. Two televisions in separate rooms will keep the family from arguing over what to watch. Those who happen to be in Lake Tahoe on business will appreciate the large desk and work area, free wireless Internet access, and two telephones with voice mail. If you like having room to spread out, the spacious accommodations here will satisfy. The hotel sits right on the California/Nevada state line (but still on the no-gaming California side), so the Heavenly gondola and Village shops are a short walk away and the casinos are right next door. A stay here ensures you can be one of the first to ski on Heavenly's slopes in the morning. Rates include a full cooked-to-order breakfast in the morning and other nice touches, like a newspaper delivered to your door and an evening wine reception.

Also within a few steps of Heavenly Ski Resort's gondola, the **Forest Suites Resort** (1 Lake Pkwy., South Lake Tahoe, 530/541-6655 or 800/822-5950, www.forestsuites.com, $65–150 hotel rooms, $99–399 suites) is a great choice for serious skiers who want to be out on the slopes, not stuck driving the car. In addition to standard hotel rooms, the resort offers one- and two-bedroom suites with a living room, dining area, and kitchen, so you can fix your own coffee and be in the gondola line the moment it opens for business. A continental breakfast is offered daily, and ski rentals and a ski repair shop, a fitness center, heated outdoor pools, hot tubs and sauna, and a game room with pool and foosball tables are on-site. In summer, the resort offers access to a private stretch of Tahoe beach.

Located a few miles from the bustle of downtown Stateline, high up on Kingsbury Grade and immediately adjacent to Heavenly Ski Resort's Nevada side, **The Ridge Tahoe** (400 Ridge Club Dr., Stateline, 775/588-3553 or 800/334-1600, www.ridgetahoeresort.com, $85–265) is a full-amenity condominium resort set on 11 acres, with more than 300 units providing everything you'd expect when you rent a ski condo: health club, indoor/outdoor swimming pool, whirlpool spas and saunas, scheduled activities for kids and adults, the Hungry Bear restaurant and bar, full-service spa, on-site ski shop, and shuttle transportation to the casinos. One- and two-bedroom units are available with living rooms, full kitchens, and gas fireplaces. Hotel rooms and junior suites (without kitchens) are also available. Some of the units have awesome views of Nevada's Carson Valley, while others overlook the parking lot, so be sure to request what you want.

If you'd prefer something a little more low-key, the two-bedroom condos at **Tahoe Summit Village** (750 Wells Fargo La.,

Stateline, 775/588-8571 or 866/265-2041, www.tahoesummitvillage.com, $75–495) provide easy access to skiing, as they are right between the North Boulder and Stagecoach chairlifts on Heavenly's Nevada side, but you'll have to leave the condo complex for groceries, restaurants, and the like. The condos have wood-burning fireplaces, whirlpool tubs, fully equipped kitchens, washers and dryers, and plenty of room for 6–8 people.

Of a similar understated ilk is **The Lodge at Kingsbury Crossing** (133 Deer Run Ct., Stateline, 775/588-6247 or 800/854-2324, www.thelodgeatkc.com, $139–157), which offers one- and two-bedroom suites that sleep 4–6 people. These condos are configured hotel-style, with a long connecting hallway between them. The condos have everything you need for hanging out, including full kitchens for cooking your meals. As with the other condo complexes in the area, you'll need your car to get around town, as most restaurants and attractions are not within walking distance, although a Red Hut waffle shop is right next door.

Cabins

If you're the type who wants to stay busy on your Tahoe vacation and have lots of activities available right at your doorstep, book a stay at one of the 28 lakeside cabins or four lodge rooms at **Zephyr Cove Resort** (760 Hwy. 50, Zephyr Cove, 775/589-4906 or 800/238-2463, www.zephyrcove.com, $99–350 for accommodations for two; larger cabins higher). This old-style Tahoe resort has been in business since the 1900s, and despite the modern recreation offerings (Jet Skiing, beach volleyball, parasailing, personal watercraft rentals, snowmobiling, and much more), it still manages to retain its historic feel. If you have a big family, some cabins sleep up to 10 people. A few cabins are lakefront, while the others are lake view or no view at all, and, of course, the better the scenery, the higher the price. All your vacation needs can be served on-site. There is a restaurant, bar, coffeehouse, horseback riding, sportfishing, boat rentals, lake cruising on the MS *Dixie II,* and a sandy beach for swimming and sunning. The casinos of Stateline are only five miles away.

Motels and Lodges

Less than 100 yards from Heavenly's gondola lies an eco-friendly hotel that's unlike any other lodging property on the South Shore. The 58-room 🌑 **968 Park Spa Resort** (968 Park Ave., South Lake Tahoe, 877/544-0968, www.968parkhotel.com, $75–350) is the first truly eco-conscious lodging in the Tahoe basin, with "green" bragging rights that include energy-efficient lighting and appliances, trash cans made of recycled plastic, organic bath products, and wall insulation made from recycled blue jeans. The hotel opened in January 2009 after a yearlong reconstruction and remodel of what was once a Days Inn motel. The former building was stripped to the studs and completely redone. Despite 968 Park's ecofriendly bent, there's no shortage of luxuries here, from 42-inch plasma televisions in every room to dual-flush toilets with heated seats in every bathroom. Also on the premises are a pool, hot tub, sauna, and a day spa offering a full array of treatments. In 2011, 968 Park Spa Resort added an organic beer and wine bar in the lobby.

In the same neighborhood is the **Park Tahoe Inn** (4011 Hwy. 50, South Lake Tahoe, 530/544-6000 or 800/560-9800, www.parktahoe.com, $59–319), which many consider to be the "grown-up" place to stay in the casino area. The inn has amenities that appeal to adults: Tempur-pedic beds, quality bath products, concierge service, free wireless Internet, a year-round Jacuzzi and heated pool, free passes to a stretch of Tahoe beach, and discount vouchers to local attractions, restaurants, and nightclubs. The Park Tahoe was renovated in summer 2008, so everything is fresh and modern-looking, and it's pet-friendly, too. In

2011 the owners opened a second location a few miles west in South Lake Tahoe, called Park Tahoe Aspen Court (4003 Hwy. 50), which offers similar amenities except no pool.

Adjacent to the Stateline casinos are city blocks full of nondescript motels, lined up side by side, one after another. One that stands out (among many that don't) is the **Alpenrose Inn** (4074 Pine Blvd., South Lake Tahoe, 530/544-2985 or 800/370-4049, www.alpenroseinntahoe.com, $49–199), a charming place with only 18 rooms that reflects the European refinement of its owner, Hannelore Conrad. All the rooms at Alpenrose are nonsmoking and immaculately clean. Some have fireplaces, and all share access to an indoor whirlpool Jacuzzi. The inn has access to a small private beach. A complimentary continental breakfast is served each morning.

You might be skeptical of a casino-area lodging called the **Paradice Motel** (953 Park Ave., South Lake Tahoe, 530/544-6800, www.paradicemoteltahoe.com, $99–315), but only the name is cheesy at this nice motel. The Paradice has tastefully remodeled rooms (redone in 2006), comfy beds with crisp linens, and a caring management that provides guests with coffee and pastries in the morning and nightly turndown service. Since there are only 14 rooms available, be sure to book early.

Practically next door to the Paradice is the **Secrets Inn Lake Tahoe** (924 Park Ave., South Lake Tahoe, 530/544-6767 or 800/441-6610, www.secretsinn.com, $79–299), also freshly remodeled and with modern amenities like Jacuzzi tubs and 32-inch flat-panel televisions. All rooms have king beds and fireplaces, and since children aren't permitted, this is a great spot for a romantic getaway. Don't be put off by the bland exterior of this motel; its interior will surely impress, especially for the price. The best bargains are usually midweek, when you can often get your third night free by booking online.

The **Best Western Station House Inn** (901

Park Ave., South Lake Tahoe, 530/542-1101, www.stationhouseinn.com, $68–248) is located a few blocks off U.S. 50 (great for peace and quiet) and a short walk from a private beach (great for summer fun). The Stateline casinos are within easy walking distance. Most of its 98 rooms have one queen or king bed; larger suites with king beds and sofa-sleepers are also available. The inn offers summer and winter packages that include lake cruises, ski-lift tickets, and dinner coupons for the in-house restaurant, LewMarNel's Steaks and Spirits (5:30–9 P.M. daily, $20–45). If you really want to save money, visit during the low-season months of April, May, and November, when rates drop 30–40 percent.

If you like to travel with your dog, **3 Peaks Resort & Beach Club** (931 Park Ave., South Lake Tahoe, 800/331-3951, www.3peakshotel.com, $85–210 plus $25 for dogs) is your kind of place. The sign out front bears a Saint Bernard wearing bathing trunks, and 3 Peaks is indeed dog-friendly. The resort has a great location on Park Avenue a few blocks from Heavenly's gondola, but far enough off the noisy main drag. It's also only two blocks from a gated, members-only Tahoe beach, which human guests can use, but unfortunately, not their dogs. The resort has standard hotel rooms, plus one- and two-bedroom "cabin-style" suites with fully equipped kitchens and living rooms with fireplaces. If you and your sweetheart are celebrating a special occasion, book the Honeymoon Suite, with its heart-shaped Jacuzzi tub.

You'll recognize the **Mark Twain Lodge** (947 Park Ave., South Lake Tahoe, 888/544-1378 or 530/544-5733, www.marktwainlodge.com, $69–279) by the moose sculpture out front. What does a moose have to do with Lake Tahoe, or with Mark Twain? Nothing. But the lodge is a perennial favorite of budget travelers at South Shore. Its 10 guest rooms and four two-bedroom suites were beautifully renovated in 2004, and some have fireplaces, whirlpools,

and/or mini-kitchens. The suites can sleep up to eight people, although a maximum of six would be more comfortable. The lodge's heated outdoor pool is popular with guests in summer, as is the hot tub in winter. Room rates are based on the number of people and time of the year. Everything in Stateline is a short walk away.

The **7 Seas Inn** (4145 Manzanita Ave., South Lake Tahoe, 530/544-7031 or 800/800-7327, www.sevenseastahoe.com, $65–205) wins the prize for "Most Ridiculous South Shore Motel Name." Nothing about its moniker or its ocean-blue exterior tells you you're in the mountains, but that doesn't seem to bother the legions of repeat customers who love this no-nonsense, low-budget motel. The 7 Seas is only two blocks from the Heavenly gondola, but if you are too lazy to walk, you can catch the shuttle. A free continental breakfast is served in the morning, and the owner, Carolyn, loves pets and will welcome yours with open arms.

If you want the convenience and no frills of a motel but don't like staying at the big chains, you'll like the **Ambassador Motor Lodge** (4130 Manzanita Ave., South Lake Tahoe, 530/544-6461, www.laketahoeambassadorlodge.com, $49–149). Harveys and Horizon Casino are just a stone's throw away, but the motel is far enough off busy U.S. 50 to be quiet at night. The 57 units have all the basics, and a few even have kitchens. A large heated pool will keep the kids happy in summer. Dogs are permitted in some rooms with advance reservations.

From the outside, the **Avalon Lodge** (4075 Manzanita Ave., South Lake Tahoe, 530/544-2285 or 888/544-7829, www.avalonlodge.com, $129–199) looks like a typical South Shore motel. But inside, its rooms are more hotel-like than motel-like, with tasteful furnishings like canopy and four-poster beds, plush bedding, oversize bath towels, gas fireplaces, refrigerators, coffeemakers, and microwaves. It's worth the extra money to get a spa room if one is available. Heavenly's gondola and the Stateline casinos are just two blocks away, but it is peaceful and quiet here on Manzanita Avenue. A complimentary breakfast is served each morning, and pets are welcome here.

For those who want a budget-priced, pet-friendly motel near the casinos, the **Big Pines Mountain House** (4083 Cedar Ave., South Lake Tahoe, 530/541-5155 or 800/288-4083, www.thebigpines.com, $59–169) is a suitable option. Previously known as the Viking Motor Lodge, Big Pines Mountain House has 76 guest rooms, some with kitchenettes and/or electric fireplaces, which are comfortable enough without having the cookie-cutter feel of a Motel 6 or Super 8. A free continental breakfast is served (doughnuts, fruit, and coffee), and the swimming pool is popular with families on summer afternoons. The motel is within walking distance of the casinos and the Heavenly gondola, but its biggest draw is its short stretch of private Lake Tahoe beach, a few blocks away. One drawback: The walls are thin. If you're a light sleeper, book somewhere else.

A little farther from the casinos but just across the street from the Heavenly gondola is the **Stardust Lodge** (4061 Hwy. 50, South Lake Tahoe, 530/544-5211 or 800/262-5077, www.stardust-tahoe.com, $85–355). This is the place with the 1950s-era neon sign right on U.S. 50—you can't miss it. The Stardust and the associated **Americana Vacation Club** (3845 Pioneer Tr., South Lake Tahoe, 530/541-8022 or 800/822-5920, www.americana-tahoe.com, $85–355) are self-titled "resort motels"—lodgings that were converted from motels to time-share resorts 25-plus years ago. If you want to ski or ride at Heavenly and not pay an arm and a leg for lodging, the Stardust is a good bet. The suites are on the small side (288 square feet), but they are roomy enough for two and come equipped with a furnished kitchenette. The two outdoor hot tubs are a welcome sight after a long day on the slopes, and the two swimming pools see plenty of action in summer. Doughnuts and fruit are served in the morning. Guests receive passes to a private Tahoe beach located a few blocks away. If you want a slightly larger suite that would better suit a small family, book a stay at the Americana.

A perennial favorite of purse-string watchers, the **Holiday Inn Express** (3961 Hwy. 50, South Lake Tahoe, 530/544-5900 or 800/544-5288, www.hiexpress.com, $125–290) may well be the best deal in the vicinity of Stateline. The motel is set back far enough from U.S. 50 to make it blissfully quiet at night, but still close enough to all the South Shore action to make it convenient for skiing, restaurants, nightlife, and the like. The Heavenly gondola and casinos are within walking distance; the Heavenly Village shops and restaurants are right across the street. A pool and hot tub await you at the end of the day, and like at all Holiday Inns, wireless Internet and a continental breakfast are included in the rate. The 89 rooms are clean and comfortable, and the decor is a huge step up from similarly priced budget motels.

Campgrounds and RV Parks

The privately operated **Zephyr Cove RV Park and Campground** (760 Hwy. 50, Zephyr Cove, 775/589-4907, www.zephyrcove.com, $29–40 for tents, $39–79 for RVs) is part of the huge Zephyr Cove Resort complex, which includes cabins, a restaurant, general store, and marina, horse stables, and a host of vacation-oriented activities that make it a zoo on most summer days. Camping at Zephyr Cove is camping in style, with full hookup sites, a coin-operated laundry, showers, flush toilets, and the like. Set across the highway from the lake, the camp has 93 RV sites (some with lake views), 10 drive-in campsites, and 47 walk-in campsites. The walk-in sites are the farthest from the busy highway and by far the best bet.

Operated by the U.S. Forest Service, lovely **Nevada Beach Campground** (775/588-5562,

$32–38) is located just two miles northeast of the California/Nevada state line, off U.S. 50 at Elk Point Road. Nevada Beach is a popular day-use site with a long and wide stretch of precious sandy shoreline, which is perfect for sunbathers and swimmers. The adjacent campground is bare-bones (no showers or dump station), but it's well loved due to its lakeside location. Some of the 54 sites have lovely lake views; all have some shade from big Jeffrey pines. A short walk of about 100 yards gets you to the water's edge, and Nevada Beach is a spectacular spot for sunsets. RVs up to 45 feet long are permitted. Firewood is sold on-site; gas, groceries, and laundry are 0.5 mile away at the Round Hill Shopping Center on U.S. 50. Reserve in advance at 877/444-6777 or www.recreation.gov.

SOUTH LAKE TAHOE

Not every Tahoe traveler wants to be within walking distance of the casinos and/or the Heavenly Ski Resort gondola. If you're the type who is seeking lodging a little farther from the South Shore action, the following hotels, motels, condos, and bed-and-breakfasts serve that purpose. All are within the city limits of South Lake Tahoe, and many are within walking distance of restaurants and other businesses, but all are relatively isolated from the notorious casino/Heavenly/Stateline congestion. Nonetheless, everything on the South Shore is fairly close together, so if you feel like heading to the casinos for an evening out, you can still be there in about 10 minutes of driving.

Bed-and-Breakfasts

If you have wads of cash burning a hole in your pocket, book a stay at one of five rooms or three cabins at the **C Black Bear Inn Bed & Breakfast** (1202 Ski Run Blvd., South Lake Tahoe, 530/544-4451 or 877/232-7466, www.tahoeblackbear.com, $210–335, larger cabins $270–470), a luxurious B&B that was built

in the 1990s but has an old-style Tahoe look. The place was constructed to take advantage of Tahoe's beauty, with huge picture windows, river-rock fireplaces, exposed wood beams, and tasteful mountain-style decor and landscaping. The owners, Jerry and Kevin, are the most accommodating people you'd ever hope to meet; they take good care of their guests. Wine and cheese are served at sunset. Lavish breakfasts, served in the common dining room, are included in the room rate. If you stay in one of the cabins, breakfast is brought to your door each morning. Since 2010, the Black Bear also serves dinner six nights a week (closed Tues.), and you will definitely want to eat at least one meal here.

Right next door to the Black Bear Inn is **The Deerfield Lodge at Heavenly** (1200 Ski Run Blvd., South Lake Tahoe, 530/544-3337 or 888/757-3337, www.tahoedeerfieldlodge.com, $169–329), a 12-room luxury inn that specializes in weddings and small group events, but also accommodates regular overnight visitors. Everything is done to perfection here, from the elegantly decorated rooms and suites with fireplaces and Jacuzzi tubs to the lavish breakfast buffet and evening wine and cheese reception. Top-notch concierge service is The Deerfield's specialty.

For a more budget-minded B&B stay, it's hard to top the **C Alder Inn** (1072 Ski Run Blvd., South Lake Tahoe, 530/544-4485, www.thealderinn.com, $89–149) with its 24 artfully decorated rooms and friendly, people-pleasing owners, Chad and Layni Davis. The building's exterior is modest (this was once a 1950s motel), but set foot in a guest room and you find yourself pampered by hundreds of small details, from cozy bathrobes to luxurious bedding to a large flat-screen television. Try to score one of the upstairs rooms with their ornate ceiling fans. On weekends, a complimentary breakfast of breads, spreads, oatmeal, fruits, pastries, coffee, and juice is served. Each room also has its own refrigerator and microwave. For chilly winter evenings, there's an outdoor hot tub and fire pits. In summer, you can walk to the restaurants and activities at Ski Run Marina or swim in the inn's outdoor pool.

Previously known as the Inn at Heavenly, and before that as the St. Moritz Inn, this lodging was reincarnated in summer 2011 as **Heavenly Valley Lodge** (1261 Ski Run Blvd., South Lake Tahoe, 530/564-1500 or 855/697-5478, www.heavenlyvalleylodge.com, $95–295). If you love updated mountain-style decor (river rock, knotty pine, gas fireplaces, quilts), you'll love the 11 rooms here. A cross between a really nice motel and a bed-and-breakfast, the Heavenly Valley Lodge has a motel-like configuration (room doors open out to the parking lot) but all the luxuries of a B&B, including plush linens, a full hot breakfast each morning, afternoon wine and snacks, and gracious innkeepers who live on-site.

Condominium-Style Resorts

The **Inn by the Lake** (3300 Hwy. 50, South Lake Tahoe, 530/542-0330 or 800/877-1466, www.innbythelake.com, $130–328 for hotel rooms, $368 and up for two-bedroom suites and townhomes) is not right on the lakeshore, nor does it have any fabulous lake views, but what they do here, they do well enough. This 100-unit resort sits on six acres across U.S. 50 from Lake Tahoe and is well suited for vacations on the South Shore. Each room has its own private balcony, plus a small refrigerator and microwave; the deluxe suites have fully equipped kitchens. A continental breakfast is served each morning, and the inn boasts a state-of-the-art fitness center, 2,000-square-foot event or meeting space, and year-round heated pool and bi-level spa (the two levels are connected by a small waterfall). If you want to borrow a bicycle or a pair of snowshoes, they'll happily loan them to you. If you are traveling with your dog, Fido is welcome here for an extra $20 charge per night, and he or she will be treated like royalty with a silver bowl and doggy blanket.

One of the nicest lakefront condo resorts in South Lake Tahoe, **Lakeland Village Beach and Mountain Resort** (3535 Hwy. 50, South Lake Tahoe, 530/544-1685 or 800/822-5969, www.lakeland-village.com, $99–279 for studios and one-bedroom units) allows visitors the Tahoe vacation home experience at hotel prices. Set on 19 wooded acres including a quarter-mile stretch of sandy beach, each of the condos here has a fireplace, private balcony, and kitchen or kitchenette. The 210 units come in various configurations as small as studios and as large as five bedrooms. In summer, guests have use of two tennis courts, a small pier, a sand volleyball court, and two swimming pools and hot tubs. In winter, free shuttles run to Heavenly's gondola and all the South Lake Tahoe action. The place is run by Premier Resorts, a large conglomerate that also manages similar properties in resort destinations like Sun Valley, Idaho, and Hawaii.

Adjacent to Ski Run Marina is the Sunterra-owned **Lake Tahoe Vacation Resort** (901 Ski Run Blvd., South Lake Tahoe, 530/541-6122 or 800/438-2929, www.laketahoevacationresort.com, $189–279). Although many of the units are owner-occupied time-shares, dozens of studios and one- and two-bedroom condos are available for nightly or weekly rental. The six-story resort is right next to the marina, so summer visitors can rent boats or kayaks, and year-round visitors can go for a lake tour aboard the paddle wheeler *Tahoe Queen*. All the typical resort amenities are available: indoor and outdoor pools, whirlpools and sauna, lounge, and organized children's activities. All units have fully equipped kitchens, so you can cook your own meals if you so desire. If you don't, several restaurants are within walking distance.

Across from Heavenly (not the gondola, but the resort itself) lies **Tahoe Seasons Resort** (3901 Saddle Rd., South Lake Tahoe, 530/541-6700 or 800/540-4874, www.tahoeseasons.com, $150–270), a full-service resort offering one-bedroom suites with private whirlpool tubs, wet bars, fireplaces, coffeemakers, microwaves, and cable television. Not every unit has a fireplace; make sure you get one that does. In winter, you can rent or buy skis at the sports shop, eat at the Needles Restaurant, buy stuff at the general store, hang out at the fireside lounge and pub, and generally not leave the premises except to go skiing. In addition to a year-round pool and hot tub, the resort also has summer-season sport offerings, like rooftop tennis and volleyball courts.

Cabins

Long ago at Lake Tahoe, there were lots of places like **Hansen's Resort** (1360 Ski Run Blvd., South Lake Tahoe, 530/544-3361, www. hansensresort.com, $50–220 for one- and two-bedroom units, $240–350 for four-bedroom cabin), family-run cabin resorts that offered hospitality first and foremost without all the "bling." Now places like Hansen's are few, but many families will be happier here than at a noisy casino resort. Hansen's has nine old-style green-and-white cabins located about a half mile from U.S. 50, near Heavenly Ski Resort. The cabins are modest and simply furnished; all have cable television, and some have kitchens and fireplaces. In winter, guests can walk over to Hansen's Tube and Saucer Hill for some old-fashioned sledding fun (cabin guests get free use of the hill). If your kids aren't old enough to ski, tubing or sledding will get them hooked on snow.

Motels and Lodges

There's only a narrow strip of sandy beach between the lodge rooms and the lake at the ◖ **Tahoe Lakeshore Lodge and Spa** (930 Bal Bijou Rd., South Lake Tahoe, 530/541-2180 or 800/448-4577, www.tahoelakeshorelodge. com, $199–299 for lodge rooms, $199–499 for one- and two-bedroom condominiums), so every room boasts a fine lake view. The lodge's

offerings include 46 rooms with queen beds and gas fireplaces, plus 26 one- and two-bedroom condominiums with full kitchens and fireplaces. A year-round heated pool is right next to a 500-foot stretch of private Tahoe beach, so you can swim in warm or cold water. In addition, the lodge is home to Elements, a full-service day spa, which offers an intriguing assortment of massage therapies, body wraps, facials, and the like.

There are a couple of Best Westerns in South Lake Tahoe, and they are quite different in style and ambience. The **Best Western Station House Inn** (901 Park Ave., South Lake Tahoe, 530/542-1101, www.stationhouseinn.com, $98–198) is located near the casinos on Park Avenue and is a great choice for those who want to be close to the action. The **Best Western Timber Cove Lodge** (3411 Hwy. 50, South Lake Tahoe, 530/541-6722 or 800/972-8558, www.timbercovetahoe.com, $119–299) is located a couple miles west of Stateline and enjoys a prime lakefront location. The lodge is divided into town-house-style clusters of buildings, and when you reserve, it's worth paying the extra money for a unit right on the lakeshore, especially one with a fireplace. A small marina rents kayaks and pedal boats, and offers sportfishing, parasailing, and Emerald Bay tours. If your dog is traveling with you, he or she is welcome in some rooms for an extra $10 per night.

The ceiling mirrors might be considered in bad taste, and some rooms are starting to show their age, but most guests seem to have fun at the **Fantasy Inn** (3696 Hwy. 50, South Lake Tahoe, 530/541-4200 or 800/367-7736, www. fantasyinn.com, $99–299). The inn's 52 rooms are set up for romance, with oversize whirlpool tubs for two, king beds, and seductive lighting. If you want something really unique, pay the higher tariff for one of the 15 one-of-a-kind theme rooms, including Romeo and Juliet, Graceland, and Caesars Indulgence. No, this isn't a place to bring the kids, but fun-loving couples will have a good time here. The best deals are found midweek in winter with the inn's stay-and-ski packages.

The best thing about the **Howard Johnson Express Inn** (3489 Hwy. 50, South Lake Tahoe, 530/541-4000 or 800/221-5801, www. hojo.com, $39–139) is that a stay here won't break the bank. If you've stayed at a Howard Johnson's anywhere else in the United States, you'll know what to expect at the one in South Lake: clean but unremarkable rooms, cable television, in-room coffeemakers and refrigerators, a complimentary continental breakfast that will make your blood sugar soar, and a heated pool and spa.

For the price alone, you gotta love a place like the **Quality Inn** (3838 Hwy. 50, South Lake Tahoe, 530/541-5400 or 877/424-6423, www.qualityinn.com, $49–99), which often has rooms available on weekends when the fancier places are filled up. Sure, the 120 queen- and king-bed rooms have the all-too-familiar vanilla flavor of a chain motel, but at least you know what you are getting. A few suites with kitchenettes are available, and for skiers and riders on a budget, the motel is located only one mile from Heavenly's gondola. A high-sugar, high-carbohydrate continental breakfast is included in the rate. And if you happen to crave tandoori during your stay, you're in luck: The Taj Majal Indian restaurant is on-site and serves lunch and dinner.

Budget travelers will also be pleased with a stay at the **Vagabond Inn** (3892 Hwy. 50, South Lake Tahoe, 530/544-3642 or 800/522-1555, www.vagabondinn.com, $49–159), with 36 rooms in the heart of South Lake Tahoe. A few of the higher-priced rooms have fireplaces and whirlpool tubs. Muffins, juice, and coffee are provided in the morning. Families appreciate this place because children 18 and under stay free.

A unit of the **Days Inn** chain thrives in South Lake Tahoe, with a convenient location close to Heavenly (3530 Hwy. 50, South Lake Tahoe, 530/544-3445 or 800/329-7466, www.daysinn.com, $49–189). The motel offers a heated outdoor pool in summer and year-round hot tub. If you've stayed at a Days Inn elsewhere in America, you won't find too many surprises here.

Ask for a room in the back, away from U.S. 50, to ensure a good night's sleep at the **Motel 6 South Lake Tahoe** (2375 Hwy. 50, South Lake Tahoe, 530/542-1400 or 800/466-8356, www.motel6.com, $49–99). This ultrabasic motel has 143 rooms, a guest laundry, a small swimming pool, and budget rates year-round. And as most dog lovers know, all Motel 6 locations welcome dogs (one per room) at no extra charge, but you are not supposed to leave him or her unattended in your room. At this particular Motel 6, walking Rover is a snap, because the Upper Truckee River is only about 50 yards to the east. A paved trail that runs behind the motel heads right to it.

Much like the Motel 6, but with a different number, South Lake's **Super 8 Motel** (3600 Hwy. 50, South Lake Tahoe, 530/544-3476 or 800/237-8882, www.super8tahoe.com, $49–169) provides all the basics for a decent night's sleep and not much more. The 108 rooms here are clean and inexpensive, and have a king bed or two double beds. An on-site sports bar, Mo's Place, serves hamburgers and assorted pub food to accompany its pool tables and multiple TVs. An outdoor hot tub is popular year-round; a children's play area and swimming pool are available in summer. Dogs are permitted for an extra $10 per night charge.

Campgrounds and RV Parks

Operated by the City of South Lake Tahoe, the 170-site **Campground by the Lake** (1150 Rufus Allen Blvd., South Lake Tahoe, 530/542-6096, www.cityofslt.us, $26–36, open April–October) has almost everything a camper could ask for: space for RVs and trailers up to 45 feet long (but no hookups), water, restrooms, showers, a boat ramp, and access to Lake Tahoe for swimming and fishing. The camp's name is just a bit misleading: Lake Tahoe is across U.S. 50 from the camp, so your tent will not be right on the lakeshore. All sites are set among a forest of pines; to reduce the noise level, get one as far away from the highway as possible. If you don't have your own tent or RV, try to reserve one of the campground's half-dozen sleeping cabins or tent cabins, which sleep 4–6 people comfortably ($50 per night).

EMERALD BAY ROAD
Bed-and-Breakfasts

The pet-friendly **◖ Fireside Lodge** (515 Emerald Bay Rd., South Lake Tahoe, 530/544-5515, www.tahoefiresidelodge.com, $119–220) is an ideal choice for dogs and their people. The lodge looks like a motel, but it's a whole lot nicer and offers amenities you'd expect at a bed-and-breakfast inn: a large continental breakfast, wine and cheese in the afternoon, and river-rock gas fireplaces and kitchenettes in each of the nine rooms. There is a small additional charge for pets. In winter, you can snowshoe around the large field right behind the inn or roast marshmallows around the outdoor fire pit. The lodge owners are happy to provide their guests with free snowshoes in winter and bikes and kayaks in summer. A paved bike trail runs right by the lodge.

Cabins

It isn't easy to get summer reservations, but **◖ Camp Richardson Resort** (1900 Jameson Beach Rd., South Lake Tahoe, 530/541-1801 or 800/544-1801, www.camprichardson.com) is a great place for a taste of the "old" Lake Tahoe. Built in the 1920s, the family-style resort on 150 acres of private land has cozy cabins under the pines, plus a great restaurant and bar, The Beacon (530/541-0630, 11 A.M.–9 P.M. daily in summer, winter hours may vary, $9–37), alongside the beach. Some cabins are lakefront; most

have kitchens and woodstoves, fireplaces, or gas stoves. The cabins range in size from studios for two to larger units that will sleep up to eight people. In summer, they are rented by the week only ($1,200–2,650). In winter, you can rent them by the night ($95–265). The resort also has hotel rooms and beachside inn rooms for rent by the night year-round ($80–180). The Pope-Baldwin Bike Path runs right by the resort, a full-service marina is on-site, and horse stables are right across the highway. In winter, Camp Richardson has groomed cross-country ski trails. You'll never run out of activities here.

Motels and Lodges

Less than a half mile from the Pope-Baldwin Bike Path on Emerald Bay Road lies the **Lazy S Lodge** (609 Hwy. 89, South Lake Tahoe, 530/541-0230 or 800/862-8881, www.lazys-lodge.com, $69–199), a 20-unit cottage-style motel. Many of the studios and two-room accommodations come with fully equipped kitchenettes and fireplaces. All units share use of a large heated pool, hot tub, picnic tables, and barbecues. The Lazy S is just far enough from the hubbub of South Lake Tahoe to feel like a relaxed getaway, but it's still within five miles of Heavenly and the casinos. If you want to attend a musical event at Valhalla, it's practically right next door.

Campgrounds and RV Parks

A favorite of tent campers who want to hike right from their tent door, tiny **Bayview Campground** (530/544-5994, $15) has only 13 sites for tents and mini-RVs (up to 20 feet), and no reservations are accepted. Located at Highway 89 at Emerald Bay, right across the highway from Inspiration Point, the Forest Service–managed camp is the site of a major trailhead into the Desolation Wilderness. The camp has water and chemical toilets.

The **Eagle Point Campground at Emerald Bay State Park** (Hwy. 89 at Emerald Bay,

The spacious sites at Eagle Point Campground provide easy access to the Rubicon Trail and a convenient location near Emerald Bay.

South Lake Tahoe, 530/541-3030 or 530/525-7277, $35) is perched on a high point above Emerald Bay, and yes, some but not all the sites have remarkable lake views. Many of the 100 sites are quite spacious, too. Eagle Point Campground can accommodate small trailers and RVs (up to 21 feet long) and has restrooms, coin-operated showers, and water, but no hookups. Not surprisingly, this camp is quite popular during the short season that it is open (mid-June–Labor Day), so you must reserve far in advance at 800/444-7275 or www.reserveamerica.com. The best sites are 66–70 on the Emerald Bay side of the loop; a short trail leads from there down to the beach. Dogs can join you for camping but are not allowed on any of the park's trails.

If you have your own boat or kayak, you can stay at one of 22 sites at **Emerald Bay Boat-in Camp** (530/541-3030 or 530/525-7277, $35), on the northern shore of Emerald Bay. Each campsite has a mooring buoy. Boaters can either sleep on board their boat (a fine idea if you have a yacht but a bad idea if you have a kayak) or camp in a designated site on shore. Each campsite has a table, storage locker, and fire ring. Water is available in the campground, and there are chemical toilets. The boat camp is usually open Memorial Day–Labor Day, depending on weather conditions. Reserve in advance at 800/444-7275 or www.reserveamerica.com.

A colossal 332 campsites for tents and RVs up to 35 feet long are found at **Camp Richardson Resort** (1900 Jameson Beach Rd., South Lake Tahoe, 530/541-1801 or 800/544-1801, www.camprichardson.com, $35–55 for tents and RVs), in addition to its cabin rentals, general store, ice-cream shop, restaurant and bar, horse rentals, bike rentals, cross-country ski trails, and so much more. With all this going on, you won't feel like you are alone in nature when you camp here, but for many people, that's just fine.

The camp has all the full-service amenities: full RV hookups, a disposal site, water, showers, restrooms, and a boat ramp. One downer: No pets are allowed. Tent campers should be sure to reserve a site at Badger's Den Campground, which is on the lake side of the resort. The other sites are across the highway. Try to score one as far away from the road as possible.

The Forest Service–run **Fallen Leaf Lake Campground** (2165 Fallen Leaf Lake Rd., South Lake Tahoe, 530/544-0426, $32–34) has 206 sites for tents or RVs up to 40 feet long and a great location just a few hundred yards from Fallen Leaf Lake, three miles north of the Y intersection of U.S. 50 and Highway 89. As of 2011, the campground also has six yurts for rent for $80–82. These are circular, tent-like structures that can sleep five or six people. The yurts have sleeping platforms, an electric light, and a space heater; all you need to bring is a sleeping bag. The campground has water, flush toilets, and showers (bring a stack of quarters if you want hot water), but no RV hookups. An easy trail leads from the campground to the lake. Reserve in advance at 877/444-6777 or www.recreation.gov. The camp is usually open May 15–October 15, weather permitting.

SOUTH OF THE Y
Campgrounds and RV Parks
The **KOA Kampground of South Lake Tahoe** (760 Hwy. 50, South Lake Tahoe, 530/577-3693 or 800/562-3477, www.laketahoekoa.com, tent sites $39–49, RV sites $47–71, log cabins $185–250, open Apr.–Oct.) has what all KOAs have: spaces for RVs and trailers up to 40 feet long, full hookups (even cable TV hookups), a disposal station, restrooms, showers,

laundry, cable TV, a heated swimming pool, playground, and lots of things that should be spelled with a *C* but are spelled with a *K*, like the rental Kottages, which are small, cozy cabins. There are 60 sites in all, and this particular KOA has wireless Internet. The tent sites have picnic tables, campfire rings (or kampfire rings, if you prefer), and barbecue grills. If you forgot the ingredients for s'mores, you can buy them at the general store. Fishing in the Truckee River is possible just 100 yards from the door of your tent or RV.

Huge, private **Tahoe Valley Campground** (1175 Melba Dr., South Lake Tahoe, 530/541-2222, $30–70) boasts a staggering 415 sites and can accommodate supersize RVs up to 60 feet long. It has all the standard RV-park amenities: full hookups, a disposal station, restrooms, and showers, plus some luxuries you might not expect—a swimming pool, tennis courts, a small store, and laundry. The camp is open year-round, a rarity around Lake Tahoe.

Wrights Lake Campground (off U.S. 50, 17 miles west of South Lake Tahoe, $20–36) may be a long way from the shores of Lake Tahoe, but it is situated right on the southwest edge of the Desolation Wilderness at 7,000 feet in elevation. For day hikers and backpackers, this is an ideal location; a multitude of trails lead right from camp. For rock climbers, the spectacular Phantom Spires are nearby. For everybody else, there is easy access to swimming and fishing in Wrights Lake (great for fly-fishing in float tubes). The 76-site camp has water and vault toilets and is suitable for RVs or tents. Reserve in advance at 877/444-6777 or www.recreation.gov.

Food

SOUTH LAKE TAHOE
Breakfast and Lunch

For nostalgia-lovers who cherish 1950s-style diners, a meal at the Red Hut Café (2723 Hwy. 50, South Lake Tahoe, 530/541-9024, www. redhutcafe.com, 6 A.M.–2 P.M. daily, $7–12) will put you in your happy place. This 1950s-era diner has been wildly popular since, well, the 1950s. Locals and visitors alike head here for breakfast, where they usually have to fight for one of the dozen or so booths or settle for a counter stool. The place is so popular that in 1990 the owners opened a second location at 229 Kingsbury Grade in Stateline (775/588-7488), and in 2009 a third location at U.S. 50 and Ski Run Boulevard, not far from the Heavenly gondola. This third Red Hut (3660 Hwy. 50, 530/544-1595, 6 A.M.–8 P.M. daily), which is much larger than the others, stays open for dinner as well as breakfast and lunch. At all three Red Huts, waffles are a hot ticket, usually served with fresh or frozen fruit (depending on the season) and heaps of whipped cream. Pancakes, eggs, and four-egg omelets are also popular, as well as old-school biscuits and gravy; lunch consists of burgers and grilled sandwiches. Portions are large, and the cholesterol factor is generally very high.

South of the Y in South Lake Tahoe are two great breakfast places situated right across the street from each other. On the west side of U.S. 50 is Bert's (1146 Hwy. 50, South Lake Tahoe, 530/544-3434, 7 A.M.–2 P.M. daily, $7–14). On the east side is Ernie's (1207 Hwy. 50, South Lake Tahoe, 530/541-2161, www.erniescoffee-shop.com, 6 A.M.–2 P.M. daily, $7–14). It's only fair to mention them together because they are related so closely in geography, menu, and quality. Both restaurants serve dependably good food and offer all the standard coffee-shop fare: eggs, omelets, pancakes, French toast, biscuits

and gravy, and huevos rancheros. Ernie's has a few vegan choices, plus a health-oriented dish called Cassie's protein pancakes. Bert's also serves an outstanding corned beef hash, eggs Benedict, and California breakfast burrito. So how do you choose between the two? If you are eating with a large family or group, you'll do better at Ernie's, which is the larger of the two and has big booths that can accommodate a crowd. Tahoe locals tend to prefer Bert's because of its more intimate space and old-style-coffee-shop atmosphere. But really, you can't go wrong at either one.

You don't have to be a health-food nut to love the nutritious fare at Sprouts (3123 Harrison Ave. at U.S. 50, South Lake Tahoe, 530/541-6969, 8 A.M.–9 P.M. daily, $7–10). The food is so tasty that even junk-food devotees won't mind eating stuff that is good for them. Sprouts is run by a husband-and-wife team who have a creative flair with wholesome food. Try the breakfast bowl (brown rice, beans, steamed eggs, salsa, and avocado), "killer nachos," tempeh burgers, salads, or one of several choices of fresh-squeezed juices: carrot, orange, wheatgrass, beet, and so on. You will feel healthier just perusing the menu. Don't forget to bring cash—they don't take credit cards here.

Odd as it is for a ski resort town, there's a nautical theme to the decor at the Driftwood Café (1001 Heavenly Village Pkwy., 530/544-6545, 7 A.M.–3 P.M. daily, $8–12). Instead of antique skis and snowshoes adorning the walls, you'll find ocean-related items, but that doesn't stop hordes of snow lovers from eating here on their way to or from the Heavenly gondola. Located in the Heavenly Village Shopping Center, the café serves an array of omelets (made with whole eggs or eggs whites, your choice), scrambles, and old-school breakfast fare like biscuits and gravy and eggs Benedict.

Lunch consists of salads, soups, and sandwiches. Nothing is particularly fancy or gourmet, but it's a serious step up from Denny's, and the prices are very reasonable considering the Heavenly Village location. Weekend mornings can be packed, but weekdays are usually pretty quiet.

For a creative sandwich or inventive salad at lunch, or a breakfast burrito, smoothie, or super-healthy acai bowl at breakfast, stop in at the **Tahoe Keys Café** (2279 Hwy. 50, South Lake Tahoe, 530/542-3800, www.tahoekeyscafe.com, 7 A.M.–4 P.M. daily, $5–10). Free wireless Internet access and a friendly Tahoe vibe make this place a must-stop whether you are a local or a visitor. Whether you eat here or take your order to go, the sandwich choices are far from the ordinary. Try the one with baked sweet potato, fresh mozzarella, tomatoes, and marinated onions, or the wildly popular grilled cheese made with swiss, mozzarella, and homemade pesto. Breakfast burritos made with organic, free-range eggs are just the ticket if you are racing off for a hike in summer or a day on the slopes in winter. The place is a little hard to find; it's the little log cabin behind the thrift store near Tahoe Keys Boulevard and U.S. 50.

In the category of South Shore's surprising "strip-mall cafés" is **Tahoe Java** (2540 Hwy. 50, South Lake Tahoe, 530/542-1474, 6:30 A.M.–2:30 P.M. weekdays, 7 A.M.–2 P.M. weekends, $5–7), ingloriously set in the Swiss Chalet shopping center at U.S. 50 and Sierra Boulevard. Here you'll find a cozy ambience, friendly staff, and all the java you can drink, plus hot and cold breakfasts (bagels, burritos, oatmeal, fresh-baked muffins, and an acai bowl), lunches (wraps, paninis, soups, and salads), and free wireless Internet.

Another favored coffee shop for those who disdain the Starbuck's conglomerate is **Alpina Coffee Café** (822 Emerald Bay Rd./Hwy. 89, South Lake Tahoe, 530/541-7449, 7 A.M.–3 P.M. daily), contained in a charming cottage on the road to Emerald Bay. In the summer, coffee drinkers and their dogs sit out in the small garden. There isn't a whole lot on the menu here (although the upside-down bran muffins are a sellout every day), but that's just fine with the loyal patrons, who are more than satisfied with a bagel, a latte, and a chance to read the newspaper among friends, or get connected with free Internet service. The coffee is roasted locally by Alpen Sierra Roasters. Tea drinkers: You'll find more than two dozen choices here.

And lastly, those who believe breakfast should be comprised of a well-crafted sticky bun or a chunk of crusty baguette should check out **Sugar Pine Bakery** (3564 Hwy. 50, South Lake Tahoe, 530/542-7000, www.sugarpinebakery.net, 7 A.M.–6 P.M. Tues.–Sat.). Husband-and-wife chefs (and graduates from the Culinary Institute of America) run this upscale bakery boutique. Don't ask for doughnuts here. Instead, choose from a range of breads (ciabatta, foccacia, fougasse, challah, sourdough, baguette, nine-grain) or sweets (almond-filled croissants, cinnamon rolls, eclairs, chocolate chip cookies, red velvet cupcakes). Coffee and sandwiches are available, too.

Burger Joints

The South Shore loves its burgers. Old-school burger joints—the kind where you order at the window and then eat at a picnic table or in your car—are alive and well in South Lake Tahoe. At the head of the class is the **Burger Lounge** (717 Emerald Bay Rd., South Lake Tahoe, 530/542-4060, 11 A.M.–8 P.M. daily June–Sept., closed on Mondays Oct.–May, $9–12), where everyone can find a burger to suit their taste, even if that means it's a veggie burger or a turkey burger or a hamburger smothered in peanut butter (it's not as weird tasting as it sounds). All their burgers are half-pounders, so you won't be wondering where the meat is. Onion rings and french fries are a big deal here (get a half order unless you have the appetite of a sumo wrestler); especially popular are the pesto fries and Cajun fries. Sure, they are greasy, but isn't that the point? The limited inside seating leaves a lot to be desired, but in the summer, everyone wants a table outside anyway.

Another perennial favorite for burgers is **Izzy's Burger Spa** (2591 Hwy. 50, South Lake Tahoe, 530/544-5030, 11 A.M.–8 P.M. Sun.–Thurs., 11 A.M.–9 P.M. Fri.–Sat., $4–9). Despite the unusual name, you won't find massages or facials on the menu, just honest burgers with a variety of toppings, from plain old cheese and bacon to a teriyaki glaze with a pineapple ring. Pass on the fries and order the world-class onion rings instead. Like at the Burger Lounge, there is nothing appealing about sitting inside this place, so get a spot at one of the picnic tables under the pines.

Sure, the burgers are good enough at the **Sno-Flake Drive-In** (3059 Hwy. 50, South Lake Tahoe, 530/544-6377, 11 A.M.–8 P.M. daily, $5–10), but the real reasons people come here repeatedly are for the milk shakes and sweet potato fries. And perhaps also because when you eat here, you feel like you're reliving the 1960s, and there is something undeniably cool about that. If you aren't a fan of red meat, get the turkey burger, which is first-rate. In the summer, the Sno-Flake dispenses hundreds of soft-serve cones per day, and not just to little kids. The most seasoned customers order the vanilla cone dipped in chocolate. Craving a peanut butter shake? They have been making them here since 1962.

Casual American

Located near Heavenly's California Lodge, the **Blue Angel Café** (1132 Ski Run Blvd., South Lake Tahoe, 530/544-6544, www.theblueangelcafe.com, 11 A.M.–9 P.M. daily, $8–15) is a dependable choice for gourmet food to go or to eat in. This stylish little café looks like something you might find in San Francisco's

Marina District, with big arrangements of fresh flowers, pale yellow walls, and comfy couches around the fireplace. The menu changes often, but expect to find creative and international dishes such as pulled pork tacos, Thai curry, and a roasted vegetable napoleon. Sandwiches include veggie burgers, a salmon BLT, and the crowd-pleasing bacon cheeseburger. There's free Wi-Fi access for those who need to check email.

Located inside a 1960s-era strip mall, **Freshie's** (3330 Hwy. 50, South Lake Tahoe, 530/542-3630, 11:30 A.M.–9 P.M. daily, closed in November) wins the award for "most uninspiring restaurant location," but the owners have made the most out of what they had to work with. Beloved throughout the South Shore, Freshie's has a fun and creative atmosphere (a Hawaiian surfing theme) and outstanding Pacific Rim–style dishes, Hawaiian-style ribs, original salads, and a great selection of microbrews. The fish tacos are delectable. In the summer months, you can forgo the strip mall altogether and eat outside on the rooftop deck. Fun, casual, and surprising, Freshie's is a winner for dinner or lunch, and two can eat well here for about $30.

The Beacon at historic Camp Richardson Resort (1900 Jameson Beach Rd., South Lake Tahoe, 530/541-0630, www.camprichardson. com, 11 A.M.–9 P.M. daily, winter hours may vary, $9–37) is a Tahoe institution—the only "beach house"–style restaurant on the lake. In the warm months, diners covet the umbrella-shaded tables on the huge outdoor deck, which opens onto a sandy lakeshore beach. Summer lunches can be a bit of a zoo because of the multitudes of kids playing on the beach, but sunset dinners are a great experience. The fried calamari is wildly popular, as is the Rum Runner, the restaurant's signature rum-laced well drink. Entrées include everything from hamburgers to fancy seafood dishes. Live music is offered on summer weekends.

If you want to meet the South Tahoe locals,

go to **Steamers** (2236 Hwy. 50, South Lake Tahoe, 530/541-8818, www.steamersbar.com, 11 A.M.–10 P.M. daily, $7–14) around cocktail hour, say 5–7 P.M. This small tavern is well known for its affordable Friday-night steak dinners, Saturday-night tacos, and reasonably priced beer selection. There's no pretension here—it's all about the brews, the bar food, and the three big-screen TVs. The place is named after the mighty steamships that once ruled the waves of Lake Tahoe. If the bar area is too dark for your taste, in summer you can sit outside at the back patio tables.

Hearty appetites will achieve satisfaction— perhaps even heavenly delight—at the **Timber House Restaurant** (168 Hwy. 50, Stateline, 775/588-7777 or 800/624-7980, www.lakesideinn.com, open 24 hours daily), without breaking the bank. A favorite of locals and visitors alike, this restaurant at the Lakeside Inn and Casino is not exactly fine dining, but the sourdough bread is brought to your table hot and plentiful, and the huge slabs of prime rib won't leave you feeling hungry. The Timber House's $4.99 breakfast has filled the bellies of more than a few local construction workers, and the $10.99 prime rib comes in portions big enough to feed a crowd.

A great choice for casual dining in Zephyr Cove is the restaurant at the historic **Zephyr Cove Resort** (760 Hwy. 50, Zephyr Cove, 775/589-4968, www.zephyrcove.com, 7 A.M.–3 P.M. Mon.–Wed., 7 A.M.–9 P.M. Thurs.–Sun., $10–25). Housed in an 1860s-era building, the wood-paneled dining room and its menu have an "old Tahoe" slant: trout and eggs for breakfast, thick burgers for lunch, and an array of large-portioned entrées for dinner, like rainbow trout, New York strip steak, and Rubicon short ribs. The restaurant's milk shakes are legendary (try the banana chocolate). Their malt shake is "so thick it holds the straw up."

Equally popular with locals and visitors alike, the **Brewery at Lake Tahoe** (3542 Hwy.

50, South Lake Tahoe, 530/544-2739, www.brewerylaketahoe.com, 11 A.M.–11 P.M. daily, $10–24) is housed in a redbrick cottage right on U.S. 50. Serving handcrafted beers and tasty pub food since 1992, the Brewery has an extensive menu that ensures everyone will find something they want to eat. There' a wide array of salads, burgers, sandwiches, wraps, paninis, pastas, and pizzas. Best bet? Stick with the pizza, which has a delectable thin crust. Beer lovers will also appreciate the extensive list of microbrews that are brewed on-site, from the Bad Ass Ale (their signature brew, which has a higher-than-usual alcohol content) to the Paramount Porter. An extended happy hour is offered most weekdays (11 A.M.–5 P.M.), with discounted beer, wine, and food.

A new and welcome addition to the Stateline/ Heavenly gondola district is **Stateline Brewery and Restaurant** (4118 Hwy. 50, South Lake Tahoe, 530/542-9000, www.statelinebrewery.com, 11 A.M.–11 P.M. daily, $13–37), which is literally right at the state line (just barely on the California side). The main restaurant is in the basement near Cecil's Café, so in winter, there's nothing over-the-top about a meal here, but in summer, patrons can sit outside at the sidewalk picnic tables and watch the world go by on U.S. 50. As with the Brewery at Lake Tahoe, the Stateline Brewery's menu is huge and runs the gamut from salads and fish tacos to pizzas, Alaskan crab legs, ribs, filet mignon, and prime rib. You can spend a lot of money here or just a moderate amount. To keep the cost down, show up during happy hour (3–6 P.M.), when food and drinks are much more reasonably priced.

Seafood and Steak

When Tahoe locals want a seafood lunch or dinner, **The Fresh Ketch** (2435 Venice Dr., Tahoe Keys Marina, South Lake Tahoe, 530/541-5683, www.thefreshketch.com, 11:30 A.M.–9:30 P.M. daily, $10–28) is where

On summer evenings, diners eat at sidewalk tables at the Stateline Brewery.

© ANN MARIE BROWN

they go. It's far enough off the beaten U.S. 50 track (tucked into Tahoe's only inland marina, Tahoe Keys) that most casual tourists would never find it. The Fresh Ketch prides itself on a wide selection of fresh fish, from ahi tuna to smoked trout. On Thursday, Friday, and Saturday they serve sushi as well. Two separate dining areas are available: The upstairs is more formal; the downstairs opens earlier (at 11:30 A.M.) and is more casual and less expensive. Both have views of the boats in the Tahoe Keys Marina. Live music plays downstairs several nights a week. In summer, even the kids will be comfortable dining here at the patio tables outside on the grass.

Owned and operated by the same folks who run Gar Woods on the North Shore, **Riva Grill** (900 Ski Run Blvd., Ski Run Marina, South Lake Tahoe, 530/542-2600, www.rivagrill. com, noon–9:30 P.M. Mon.–Thurs., noon–10 P.M. Fri.–Sat., $23–40) offers fine dining at the Ski Run Marina. Just like at Gar Woods,

Riva Grill is known for its long list of well drinks with provocative, "wink-wink" names. The Wet Woody, a rum-and-fruit concoction, is their trademark elixir. Dinner may be a little expensive, but at least you don't have to add in the cost of valet parking; it's free. The menu includes several seafood dishes, plus free-range chicken, braised lamb shank, and filet mignon. The dining room is decorated with lots of stylish, polished mahogany, just like those fast wooden boats of days gone by. The outside deck has only a so-so view of the lake; the upstairs windows offer a more expansive view.

Located at the Best Western Station House Inn, **LewMarNel's** (901 Park Ave., South Lake Tahoe, 530/542-1101, www.stationhouse-inn.com, breakfast 7–9:30 A.M. and dinner 4:30–9 P.M. daily, $17–39) is a restaurant catering to big eaters whose appetite is more discriminating than that of the average casino buffet diner. If you are tired of having to order à la carte everywhere you go, you'll be happy here. Dinner begins with complimentary cheese fondue and fresh-baked sourdough bread, and all entrées come with soup or salad and potatoes or rice. Steaks are the main event here, but seafood, pasta, and poultry dishes are served as well. Amazingly, some diners save enough room to order apple pie à la mode for dessert. Wine lovers will be pleased with the extensive wine list, rated as "one of the greatest wine lists in the world" by *Wine Spectator Magazine*. Many first-time diners are surprised to see that the waiters are wearing tuxedos, and yes, that's real silverware on the table, not stainless steel.

Casinos and steakhouses go together like blackjack and an empty wallet. The three biggest casinos on the South Shore—Harrah's, Harveys, and MontBleu—all have their own version. Arguably the best of the lot is **Ciera Steak and Chophouse** at MontBleu (55 Hwy. 50, Stateline, 800/648-3353, www.montbleuresort.com, 5:30–10 P.M. Sun.–Thurs., 5:30–10:30 P.M. Fri.–Sat., $30–90). With a AAA four-star rating, Ciera's setting is classy and sophisticated—moody lighting, white tablecloths, candlelight, cushy booths lined with red velvet (politely demand a booth when you make reservations; a mere table simply won't do). The choice of steaks includes the popular 14-ounce New York strip, the diminutive 10-ounce filet mignon, and the humungous 32-ounce rib eye, which is aged for 28 days. Plenty of fish and seafood options keep the no-red-meat club happy, including an amazing macaroni and cheese dish. Side dishes are typical steakhouse fare—creamed spinach, sautéed mushrooms, scalloped potatoes, and the like. For dessert, your waiter will bring you a complimentary dish of chocolate-covered strawberries presented in a swirling fog of dry ice, or you can order something you'll have to pay for from the dessert menu. One more temptation: The wine list consists of more than 300 bottles, so bring your reading glasses.

The **Sage Room Steak House** at Harveys

(18 Hwy. 50, Stateline, 775/588-2411, www.harrahs.com, 6–9 P.M. Thurs. and Sun., 5:30–10 P.M. Fri.–Sat., $25–45) wins hands-down for longevity—it's been serving up steaks since 1947, in a wood-paneled dining room lined with the original art of Western painters Russell and Remington. Tableside service is the signature here, whether your waiter is tossing a Caesar salad for two or setting bananas Foster aflame. Sure, it's a little kitschy, but it's all part of the tradition. A wide range of steaks and seafood dominate the menu (filet mignon is a specialty), and there are also a few old-school entrées like veal scaloppine and leg of lamb. Take your mom or your grandma here; she'll love it.

On the 19th floor of Harveys, **19 Kitchen/Bar** (30 Hwy. 50, Stateline, 775/586-6777, www.harrahs.com, 5:30–9:30 P.M. Tues.–Sat., $25–40) offers what has to be one of the best sunset dinner seats on the lake. More than a few marriage proposals have taken place here, and when you gaze out the windows on a clear day, you, too, might be inspired to action. The menu is heavy with seafood selections, but with some eclectic, and maybe even eccentric, touches, like the lobster mashed potatoes side dish or the homemade doughnuts for dessert. Be adventurous and order lump crab cakes with green papaya salad, sea bass in a baby shrimp lobster broth, or "The Forks" (smoked salmon and caviar poppers, served on the tines of upright forks). Be careful not to poke your eye out with that one. If you get the chance, check out the men's bathroom, which features some interesting artwork above the urinals (can't reveal more without spoiling).

Yes, the **Chart House** (392 Kingsbury Grade, Stateline, 775/588-6276, www.charthouse.com, 5–9 P.M. Sun.–Fri., 5–10 P.M. Sat., $20–39) is a chain restaurant, but the views from this top-of-the-hill dining room on Kingsbury Grade make it feel anything but ordinary. A million-dollar renovation in 2004 made this Stateline standby even better than before, with tasteful, cozy decor. The food is basically the same as at all Chart Houses in resort towns across the United States—well-prepared seafood, prime rib, and steaks, and a salad bar that fills the length of the dining room—but it is the stunning lake view, framed by majestic pine trees and visible from almost every table, that keeps locals and visitors coming back for more. Sunsets are unforgettable.

California Cuisine

Affordable lakefront restaurants on the South Shore aren't easy to find, but the **(** **Bistro on the Pier** (3411 Hwy. 50, South Lake Tahoe, 530/541-6722, 11:30 A.M.–9 P.M. daily, $10–25) takes up the slack in fine style. At the Timber Cove Marina, on a boardwalk pier built over the water, you can gaze at the azure waters of Lake Tahoe as the sun sinks over the western mountains. Pick an inside seat in the upstairs dining room colorfully decorated with Picasso prints, or choose a table outside on the pier or on the small upstairs deck. The food is classic California cuisine, with several creative fish, chicken, and beef dishes on the often-changing menu. For lunch, you can choose from gourmet sandwiches, salads, or a variety of small plates ($10–16). The only tricky part is finding this place—you have to pull into the Best Western Timber Cove Lodge driveway and then go around the back to find it.

Speaking of lake views, the restaurant at **(** **Edgewood Golf Course** (180 Lake Pkwy., South Lake Tahoe, 775/588-2787, www.edgewoodtahoe.com, 5:30–9 P.M. daily, $26–35) has a vista that will knock your socks off. The restaurant's high, vaulted ceiling and big windows overlooking the lake will make it hard to focus your eyes on the upscale continental-style menu. Most golf courses serve up basic fare for hungry golfers, but since it costs about 200 bucks to golf at Edgewood, the quality of the food is on par with the green fees. Appetizers include crab cakes, sautéed scallops, and ostrich

medallions. Entrées are a variety of fresh seafood, plus elk chops, osso bucco, filet mignon, and aged rib eye. Whatever you do, time your reservation so that you won't miss the sunset. In the summer months, Edgewood's outdoor deck is open, with a lower-priced, more casual menu served at a collection of tables and chairs overlooking the lake. Year-round, the Brooks Bar is open adjacent to the restaurant.

You don't have to reserve a room at South Lake Tahoe's finest bed-and-breakfast, the **(** **Black Bear Inn** (1202 Ski Run Blvd., South Lake Tahoe, 530/544-4451, www.tahoeblackbear.com, 6–9:30 P.M. Wed.–Mon., $25–40) in order to enjoy its chef's splendid dinners. The inn welcomes guests and non-guests for an evening meal six nights a week, with a short menu of entrées that change frequently, but often include lobster ravioli, beef wellington, and rack of lamb. All fruits and vegetables are organic and purchased from the local farmers market whenever possible. Chef Alex is a whiz, and his creations are as gourmet as you'll find in South Lake Tahoe. On warm summer evenings, you'll want to dine outside amid the inn's beautiful gardens.

From the outside, this intimate fine-dining restaurant looks like somebody's cozy cottage in the pines. But **(** **Evan's** (536 Emerald Bay Rd., South Lake Tahoe, 530/542-1990, www.evanstahoe.com, 5:30 P.M.–close daily, $26–36) is a long-standing success story on Tahoe's southwest shore, serving up classic continental cuisine just at the edge of the city limits. It's far from the madding crowds of downtown, but close enough to be an easy drive from anywhere in South Lake. Entrées include roast venison with wild-rice cakes, veal sweetbreads, rack of lamb, and fresh seafood. The seared foie gras is a standout appetizer. *Zagat* gives it 27 points out of 30, and *Bon Appétit* magazine called this 11-table restaurant "a jewel." Its size is both an asset and a liability: The intimacy is lovely, but the dining room gets noisy when every table is filled.

When a restaurant has been written up by

magazines like *Bon Appétit* and *Wine Spectator* and newspapers like the *New York Times* and the *San Francisco Chronicle,* diners should expect great things. **◖Nepheles** (1169 Ski Run Blvd., South Lake Tahoe, 530/544-8130, www. nepheles.com, 5 P.M.–close daily, $20–32) will exceed your expectations. The restaurant has been serving California cuisine near Heavenly Ski Resort since 1977, before most chefs knew what California cuisine was. Memorable appetizers include the swordfish egg rolls and seafood cheesecake. Entrées are comprised of traditional fare like rack of lamb and filet mignon, and nontraditional fare like broiled elk, prepared in fresh, creative ways. (Nephele was the Greek goddess of epicurean delights.) As an unusual sideline, the restaurant also has three private hot tubs for rent by the hour, so you can finish out your meal with a soothing soak.

Irish and Scottish

If you're cruising north from the South Shore up Highway 89, you can't miss the **Rockwater Bar & Grill** and **Murphy's Pub** (787 Emerald Bay Rd., South Lake Tahoe, 530/544-8004, www.murphyspubtahoe.com, 11 A.M.–11 P.M. daily, $10–25), both housed in the same building just north of the Y. This is a great place to go after a day of skiing, when all you want is a dark beer and a chance to catch up on the sports scores. Five television sets, usually showing rugby or soccer matches, are located in the bar. If you need more entertainment, there's billiards and darts, plus live music a couple nights a week. The menu has a noticeable Irish accent—including the Guinness beer on tap—but the food is not the big draw here, unless you are clamoring for bangers and mash. The heated outdoor patio and bar are open year-round.

For high-quality food from the British Isles, pay a visit to **MacDuff's Pub** (1041 Fremont Ave., South Lake Tahoe, 530/542-8777, www.macduffspub.com, noon–11 P.M. daily,

$12–27), tucked away on a quiet street in the Bijou neighborhood, two blocks off U.S. 50 (near the bowling alley). The pub has a Scottish bent, but its menu is surprisingly international: Moroccan lamb burger, truffle macaroni and cheese, French onion soup, veggie burgers, wood-fired pizzas, and, of course, shepherd's pie. The upstairs bar is usually a bustling, noisy place; the downstairs dining room is more sedate.

French

Despite its strip-mall location, **Mirabelle** (290 Kingsbury Grade, Stateline, 775/586-1007, www.mirabelletahoe.com, 5:30–9:30 P.M. Tues.–Sun., $21–30) will make you feel like you're in a small café alongside the Seine. Chef/owner Camille Schwartz brings authentic *cuisine français* to the South Shore at this small dining room in a business park off Kingsbury Grade. All the classics are served, from lobster bisque and an escargots appetizer to a Grand Marnier dessert soufflé. In between are a multitude of entrées, from bouillabaisse to venison. Don't miss the onion tart if it's on the menu when you visit.

Swiss

What's not to like about any food covered in melted cheese? Exactly. That's a big reason the **Swiss Chalet** (2544 Hwy. 50, South Lake Tahoe, 530/544-3304, www.tahoeswisschalet. com, 4–10 P.M. Tues.–Sun., $21–30) has been in business in South Lake since 1957. Run by the same family, the Baumanns, for its entire existence, the Swiss Chalet is the oldest restaurant in town. The restaurant is set right along U.S. 50 at Sierra Boulevard, squeezed in so close to the road that it's apparent it was built before the highway was widened. The restaurant is filled with alpine kitsch such as cuckoo clocks and beer steins—this kind of decor only works in a ski town—but it also has a small and cheerful bar area where patrons can enjoy casual fare from the bar menu and live music a few nights a week. It's practically mandatory to order the cheese fondue for two, which is easily a meal in itself. But if you are more experienced with Swiss-German food, go for one of the schnitzels or spaetzles or the beef stroganoff. If you can possibly make it all the way to dessert, tackle the apfelstrudel and then prepare to spend the next week on the treadmill.

Italian

If your stomach is set on classic Italian food, **◖ Scusa** (2543 Hwy. 50, South Lake Tahoe, 530/542-0100, www.scusalaketahoe.com, 5–9 P.M. daily, $15–25) is the place on the South Shore. Since 1992, the restaurant has been doling out its famous cream of roasted garlic soup, plus pasta dishes served with 10 different sauces, and as of December 2010, the owners are enjoying a new, much larger location right in the center of South Lake Tahoe at U.S. 50 and Sierra Boulevard. The atmosphere is casual but classy; it's fine to show up in your ski parka, but you'll dine on white linen tablecloths. If you aren't in a pasta mood, the menu also includes fresh fish, veal, shrimp, chicken, and vegetarian entrées. The lobster ravioli appetizer is legendary, and a saxophonist plays on weekend evenings.

For celebrating a special occasion with your sweetie, the intimate **◖ Café Fiore** (1169 Ski Run Blvd., South Lake Tahoe, 530/541-2908, www.cafefiore.com, 5:30–10 P.M. daily, $18–34) is the spot, with its fabulous Italian/continental cuisine and meager seven tables. Don't imagine you will get in without reservations. The food at Café Fiore is miles away from the typical cannelloni and ravioli served at so many American Italian restaurants. Entrées include grilled lamb chops with shiitake mushrooms and pine nuts, grilled eggplant crepes stuffed with smoked salmon, and seafood linguine in a cognac, caper, and lemon butter sauce. Vegetarians always have a few interesting choices, and the garlic bread is to die for. The restaurant is located in a diminutive cottage behind Nephele's off Ski Run Boulevard and is easy to miss if you don't know it's there.

A few miles to the east in Zephyr Cove, **Capisce** (178 Hwy. 50, Zephyr Cove, 775/580-7500, www.capiscelaketahoe.com, 5–10 P.M. daily, $17–30) woos Italian-food-lovers to make the 15-minute drive from South Lake and Stateline. Homemade raviolis are a big draw here, but there are plenty of other first-rate choices on the menu, including risotto, shrimp scampi, and flank steak. This family-run restaurant is all about service and about making each customer feel welcome. Don't be surprised if the owners come to your table to introduce themselves; even Grandma likes to say hello. Nobody leaves here unhappy.

For simple Italian food that the whole family will enjoy (nothing too cutting-edge), **Passaretti's** (1181 Hwy. 89, South Lake Tahoe, 530/541-3433, www.passarettis.com, 11 A.M.–9 P.M. daily, $11–19) serves up steaming plates of pasta, pasta, and more pasta in a wide variety of shapes and flavors. Lasagna, manicotti, ravioli—all the carb-loading basics are done well here. A few seafood, steak, and veal dishes will satisfy high-protein dieters. All meals begin with a trip to the hearty salad-and-soup bar—a great start when you are starving after a day on the slopes. The restaurant is located just south of the Y at South Lake.

Pizza

There's something about pizza and skiing that just seems to go together. Not surprisingly, you'll find a pizza place at almost every major intersection on U.S. 50, but unfortunately, most of them are nothing to write home about. One winning entry is **Blue Dog Pizza** (next to Raley's in the Village Center at 4000 Hwy. 50, South Lake Tahoe, 530/541-0813 and inside Tahoe Bowl, 1030 Fremont Ave., South Lake Tahoe, 530/541-0886, www.

bluedogpizzatahoe.com, 11:30 A.M.–10 P.M. daily), with two successful locations that have been operating for more than a decade. All the usual topping combinations are available here, including a few specialties like the "Walk the Dog" with white sauce, chicken, spinach, and bacon; and "Hair of the Dog" with jalapeños, pepperoni, sausage, and green chilis ($22 large, $12 small). Calzones and oven-toasted sandwiches are also done well. Blue Dog has been so successful in South Lake Tahoe that they even sell their own T-shirts, and yes, local people wear them. Order your pizza online if you want to save yourself a wait.

South of the Y, **Lake Tahoe Pizza Company** (1168 Hwy. 50, South Lake Tahoe, 530/544-1919, www.laketahoepizzaco.com, 4–9:30 P.M. daily) also serves a decent version of the old dough, cheese, and tomato sauce gambit. Several gourmet-style toppings are available in addition to the classics like pepperoni and mushrooms. Their salad bar is a winner. The restaurant's friendly atmosphere and affordable prices attract a loyal following. For about $30, four people could eat well here.

Mediterranean

You can be transported to the Greek isles with just one meal at **Artemis Mediterranean Grill** (2229 Hwy. 50, South Lake Tahoe, 530/542-2500, www.artemismediterraneangrill.com, 11 A.M.–10 P.M. daily, $8–20). Despite its unpromising location on U.S. 50 in the King's Trading Post shopping center, this small restaurant is surprisingly cozy inside and serves decidedly un-Tahoe-like fare. Authentic Mediterranean gyros and pita sandwiches come in a variety of meats (lamb, chicken, venison, roast duck, etc.). The Artemis burger, made with ground venison, pomegranate barbecue sauce, and crumbled gorgonzola, will blow your mind. Vegetarians have a choice of some spectacular soups and salads as well as several vegetarian entrées, and Greek traditionalists can order the eggplant and lamb moussaka for dinner and house-made baklava for dessert. You can't go wrong with anything on the menu, but don't be in a hurry; because everything is made from scratch, you may have to wait awhile for your food.

Mexican

Everybody is always happy with a meal at **The Cantina** (765 Emerald Bay Rd., South Lake Tahoe, 530/544-1233, www.cantinatahoe.com, 11:30 A.M.–9 P.M. daily, $10–16). This "nontraditional" Mexican restaurant serves up smoked chicken polenta, Texas crab cakes, and a calamari relleno, as well as the more typical burritos, tacos, and fajitas. Wash it all down with one of the Cantina's salt-rimmed margaritas or one of their 30 different beer varieties. Drinks are a lot cheaper during the weekday happy hour, 3–6 P.M. The restaurant is always busy, but salsa and chips come to your table the moment you sit down. No wonder it's been voted "Best Mexican Restaurant" in South Lake each year since 1998.

On the other hand, if you want your Mexican food to be more on the authentic side, and if to you that means a place with a cracked linoleum floor, multiple TVs blaring soccer matches, an awesome salsa bar, and gigantic burritos, then make tracks for **Taqueria Jalisco** (3097 Harrison Ave., South Lake Tahoe, 530/541-6516, 11 A.M.–8 P.M. daily, $7). Be forewarned that this is not the place for people who like to eat at Chevy's or Baja Fresh. Also, know in advance that South Shore locals claim this as their own special place—mostly because it's darn near impossible for anybody else to find the front door. Here's the secret: Taqueria Jalisco is directly behind Rojo's and the veterinarian's office in the strip mall near the junction of San Francisco Street and U.S. 50. Jalisco's does not face the street; its door opens out to the back of the parking lot. Once inside, order a quesadilla or a super burrito, and you won't need to eat again for about 12 hours. And never, ever skip the salsa bar. That's like going to Disneyland and not seeing Mickey Mouse.

Asian

If you've just pulled into South Lake Tahoe from points west on U.S. 50, **Orchid's** (2180 Hwy. 50, South Lake Tahoe, 530/544-5541, 11 A.M.–10 P.M. daily, $6–16) is the first restaurant east of the Y. It's worth a stop here for a Thai dinner before heading downtown. Don't be discouraged by the restaurant's unappealing strip-mall location. Once you're inside, you'll be instantly transported to Southeast Asia. You can order all your favorites—lemongrass soup, pad Thai, basil chicken, papaya salad, and the chef's special Similan Island red curry—and tell the chef how spicy to make them. The menu includes more than 70 items. Orchid's also has a second location in Stateline at 177 Highway 50 (775/588-5888), which is much closer for people staying at the casinos.

Until 2010, Orchid's never had much competition in town, but that changed when **Thai Nakorn II** (2108 Hwy. 50, South Lake Tahoe, 530/544-3232, www.thainakorntruckee.com, $8–17, 11:30 A.M.–9 P.M. daily, $6–16) opened less than a half mile away from Orchid's. Thai Nakorn's owners have two other locations in the area, one in Truckee and another in Reno, so they are no strangers to the restaurant business. Their six-page-long menu will leave you scratching your head, but you might as well close your eyes and point, because everything is delicious. The restaurant's ambience is more "Tahoe cabin" than Thai, but when in Rome, do as the Romans.

Unlike Thai food, good Chinese food is hard to find in South Lake Tahoe, but your best bet is **Hunan Garden** (900 Emerald Bay Rd., South Lake Tahoe, 530/544-5868, www. hunangardentahoe.com, 11 A.M.–9:30 P.M. daily, lunch $7, dinner $12). If you're a fan of

chicken with black bean sauce, mu shu pork, Szechuan chicken, or kung pao seafood, you'll find it here. Most people go for the bargain-priced buffet that is usually offered at lunch and dinner, but you can also order from an extensive menu.

If you enjoy the Mongolian barbecue concept of dining, you might like **Fire and Ice** in the Marriott Timber Lodge at Heavenly (4100 Hwy. 50, South Lake Tahoe, 530/542-6650, www.fire-ice.com, 11:30 A.M.–10 P.M. daily, lunch $15, dinner $27). This is how a meal here works: You go to the food bar and select a bunch of raw items (chicken, fish, tofu, veggies, pasta, potatoes, etc.) and a choice of sauces. You hand over all your food to the "chef," and he or she proceeds to cook it in front of you on a huge grill while doing some tricks with knives and/or other utensils. Then you eat your concoction, and depending on how well your chosen items go together, you will either like it or you won't.

© ANN MARIE BROWN

The outdoor fire pits at Fire and Ice are a great spot for après-ski.

If you don't, no matter, because this is an all-you-can-eat deal, so you can go back and try again. If you're over 25 years old, you'll probably find this place a bit overhyped, but because Fire and Ice is located right at the Heavenly gondola, it's always packed. Far and away the best part of eating here is getting a seat by the outdoor fire pits on a sunny winter day.

Sushi

One of the best things about a vacation in Tahoe is that in terms of dining, it's not that different from a vacation in San Francisco. Think you can't get good sushi in the mountains? Think again. **The Naked Fish** (3940 Hwy. 50 #3, South Lake Tahoe, 530/541-3474, www.thenakedfish.com, 5–9:30 P.M. Mon.–Fri., noon–3 P.M. and 5–10 P.M. Sat.–Sun., $6–15) is located right on the main drag in South Lake Tahoe. From the outside, the setting doesn't look altogether promising. But step inside and you're in a blue-green world that shifts your mindset, and your appetite, to ocean-fresh fish in no time at all. Sushi, sashimi, teriyaki, tempura—they do it all here, and they do it well. Order a Big Kahuna roll and you'll be in heaven. In 2011, the restaurant expanded so that now it is nearly double its previous size—a good thing on Saturday nights when the wait for a table can be long. The additional space is called the Naked Fish Lounge, offering cocktail specials and sushi appetizers.

Farther away from the Heavenly/Stateline area, South Lake is blessed with two more excellent sushi restaurants. **Off The Hook** (2660 Hwy. 50, South Lake Tahoe, 530/544-5599, www.offthehooksushi.com, 11:30 A.M.–2:30 P.M. and 4:30–9 P.M. Mon.–Fri., 2–10 P.M. Sat.–Sun., $6–15) can also satisfy your cravings for wasabi and pickled ginger. A diverse menu includes more than 60 rolls, including some creative choices with macadamia nuts and other unusual ingredients. If you want something cooked, not raw, order the Dragon Balls,

which are spicy tuna with shrimp and crab in an inari pocket, deep fried and topped with eel sauce. Vegetarians and vegans will find plenty of options here.

Finally, there's **Samurai** (2588 Hwy. 50, South Lake Tahoe, 530/542-0300, www.sushi-tahoe.com, 5 P.M.–close daily, $6–20), which has been serving sushi at the lake since 1984. They were the first sushi bar in South Lake Tahoe. Have a seat around the 1960s-era circular fireplace or pull up a stool at the sushi bar and look forward to well-prepared fresh fish, an Asian-bistro menu of cooked fare, and a huge variety of chilled and warm sake. If you aren't well-versed in sake, order one of the four sake samplers and learn the finer points. Large groups (up to 12 people) can reserve the private Tatami room. Happy hour on weekdays (5–6:45 P.M.) offers a selection of discounted hand rolls and half-price beer or hot sake.

Hawaiian

Maybe Hawaiian isn't the type of food that comes to mind after a day of skiing at Heavenly, but sometimes it's worth thinking outside the box. **Kalani's** (shop #26 at Heavenly Village, 1001 Heavenly Village Way, South Lake Tahoe, 530/544-6100, www.kalanis.com, 11:30 A.M.–3 P.M. and 5–9:30 P.M. Sun.–Thurs., 11:30 A.M.–3 P.M. and 5–10 P.M. Fri.–Sat., $15–35) Pacific Rim fusion cuisine will put you in an aloha state of mind as fast as you can say "opakapaka." This award-winning restaurant features fresh fish flown in daily from Hawaii, a full-service sushi bar with a litany of signature rolls that change daily, and memorable Hawaiian-influenced entrées like blue crab–crusted onaga fillet or lomi lomi salmon-and-watercress platter laced with papaya-seed dressing. The restaurant is chic and stylish but still comfortable, and the food is elegantly presented. In addition to the hours listed above, Kalani's also has a happy hour (4–6 P.M. daily).

Practicalities

INFORMATION

Several visitors centers are located in and around the South Shore. At Heavenly Village, the **Explore Tahoe: An Urban Trailhead** (4114 Hwy. 50, South Lake Tahoe, 530/542-2908, www.cityofslt.us, call for hours) opened in 2007 as a joint project between the City of South Lake Tahoe, the U.S. Forest Service, and the California Tahoe Conservancy. There's plenty to interest kids and adults here, including a large plasma-screen television displaying continuous video about the Lake Tahoe basin, and a children's table with a wildlife guessing game. Forest Service personnel are on hand to answer all your questions about where to hike, bike, ski, and sightsee. The center is located at the Heavenly Village Transit Center, so you can easily ride the Nifty Fifty Trolley or BlueGo bus here.

Across the street from Lakeside Inn and Casino near Kahle Community Park is the **Lake Tahoe Visitor Authority**'s Nevada office (169 Hwy. 50, 3rd Fl., Stateline, 775/588-5900, www.tahoesouth.com). The California office of the **Lake Tahoe Visitors Authority** (3066 Hwy. 50, South Lake Tahoe, 530/544-5050 or 530/541-5255, www.tahoesouth.com) is next door to the Lake Tahoe Historical Society Museum near El Dorado Beach. These visitors centers are particularly helpful if you are looking for lodging, restaurants, tours, or businesses of any kind. The visitors centers on the South Shore keep fairly standard summer hours, usually 10 A.M.–5 P.M. daily, but winter hours vary, so call ahead.

The **U.S. Forest Service** also has two visitors centers in South Lake Tahoe. At the main office (35 College Dr., South Lake Tahoe, 530/543-2600, www.fs.fed.us/r5/ltbmu, 8 A.M.–4:30 P.M. Mon.–Fri.), you will find tons of information on hiking, biking, and other outdoor activities on Forest Service land. Books on Tahoe's natural history are for sale, as well as hiking maps and guides. A much smaller Forest Service visitors center (on Hwy. 89, 530/543-2674), three miles north of the Y, is located at Taylor Creek by the parking lot near the Stream Profile Chamber. Hours are 8 A.M.–5:30 P.M. daily mid-June–September, 8 A.M.–4:30 P.M. daily in October.

The **League to Save Lake Tahoe,** a nonprofit organization, has an interpretive center and bookstore located in downtown South Lake Tahoe (2608 Hwy. 50, South Lake Tahoe, 530/541-5388, www.keeptahoeblue.org, 9 A.M.–5 P.M. daily June–Aug., weekdays only Sept.–May).

SERVICES
Medical Care

South Lake Tahoe is served by **Barton Memorial Hospital** (2170 South Ave., South Lake Tahoe, 530/541-3420, www.bartonhealth.org) as well as two 24-hour emergency care centers: **Tahoe Urgent Care** (2130 Hwy. 50, South Lake Tahoe, 530/541-3277) and **Stateline Medical Center** (150 Hwy. 50, Stateline, 775/589-8900).

Post Offices

Several post offices are conveniently located along the South Shore, including one just south of the Y at 950 Emerald Bay Road and another in Meyers at 1285 Apache Avenue. The main **South Lake Tahoe post office** (1046 Al Tahoe Blvd., 530/544-5867) is located at the Rite Aid Shopping Center on U.S. 50. This is the only post office in town that has Saturday hours (noon to 2 P.M.). On the casino (Nevada) side of the South Shore, post offices are located at 223 Kingsbury Grade in Stateline and 212 Elks Point Road in Zephyr Cove.

Internet Access

Need to check your email or surf the Web? Do so at the South Shore's two public libraries: the **El Dorado County Library** (1000 Rufus Allen Blvd., South Lake Tahoe, 530/573-3185) or the **Douglas County Library** (233 Warrior Way, Zephyr Cove, 775/588-6411). Or buy a cup of java at one of a handful of local coffeehouses that allow free wireless Internet use for their customers: **Alpina Coffee Café** (822 Hwy. 89, South Lake Tahoe, 530/541-7449), **Tahoe Java** (2540 Hwy. 50, South Lake Tahoe, 530/542-1474), or **Tahoe Keys Café** (2279 Hwy. 50, South Lake Tahoe, 530/542-3800). You'll be supporting local businesses and also getting a taste of the homey South Shore vibe. Wireless users can also head to any of five Starbucks locations or two McDonald's locations on the South Shore to access Wi-Fi hot spots, but you won't find any homey vibes there.

If you're driving around town, you may find that much of the South Lake Tahoe/Stateline area has wireless access. The BlueGo public transportation system, with on-demand kiosks at locations throughout the South Shore, has created more than 30 Wi-Fi hot spots.

GETTING THERE
By Air

The **South Lake Tahoe Airport** (1841 Airport Rd., 530/541-2110, www.mountainwestaviation.com) is currently not operational for commercial flights, although plenty of private pilots enjoy the privilege of landing here. Those of us without private planes can fly into **Reno-Tahoe International Airport** (2001 E. Plumb La., 775/328-6400, www.renoairport.com) and then rent a car or take bus, shuttle, or limousine service to the South Shore. A shuttle service runs several times each day between the Reno-Tahoe International Airport and the South Shore's casinos and hotels. Contact South Tahoe Express (866/898-2463, www.southtahoeexpress.com). The cost is $27.50 per adult one-way or $49 round-trip. The fee for children under 12 riding with their parents is $15.50 one-way or $28 round-trip.

For a more private and also pricier ride, on-demand limousine service is offered by **Bell Limousine** (775/786-3700 or 800/235-5466, www.bell-limo.com), **Executive Limousine** (775/333-3300, www.exlimo.com), or **No Stress Express** (775/885-9832, www.nostressexpress.com).

Visitors can also fly into the Sacramento, Oakland, San Francisco, or San Jose airports, then rent a car to drive to Lake Tahoe. Sacramento Airport is 2 hours from the South Shore; the three other airports are about 3.5 hours away.

By Car

There are many possible driving routes to the South Shore of Lake Tahoe. From the San Francisco Bay Area or Sacramento, the primary route is to take U.S. 50 east through Placerville and over Echo Summit to South Lake Tahoe (about 2 hours or 100 miles from Sacramento and 3.5 hours or 200 miles from San Francisco).

From Reno-Tahoe International Airport, take U.S. 395 south through Carson City, then take U.S. 50 west to South Lake Tahoe (about one hour or 60 miles).

By Bus

Visitors can reach South Lake Tahoe by two major bus lines: **Greyhound Bus Lines** (800/231-2222, www.greyhound.com) or **Amtrak Bus** (800/872-7245, www.amtrak.com). The bus depot is located at the **South Y Transit Center** (1000 Hwy. 50, South Lake Tahoe). The Amtrak bus is the most convenient, as it travels daily to and from South Lake Tahoe and Sacramento, with a stop in Placerville.

By Train

The nearest Amtrak train depots are in

DRIVING SAFELY IN WINTER

Lake Tahoe in wintertime is a genuine snowy wonderland, but traveling in the white stuff presents its own unique challenges. It's important to be prepared before you go.

Before you head to the mountains, check your car to make sure your brakes, windshield wipers, exhaust system, and heater are in good working condition, and that your tires are inflated correctly and their treads are not worn. Make sure your radiator is filled with antifreeze. If you don't have chains that are sized properly for your car's tires, buy a set. Even if your vehicle is equipped with four-wheel drive, you are required by California law to carry snow chains when traveling over some mountain passes, including Carson Pass (Highway 88) and Echo Pass (U.S. 50). Although most of the time you will not need them, especially if your car has four-wheel drive or all-wheel drive, in the midst of big storms, the California Highway Patrol may stop you at the mountain passes and require that you install your chains—or turn you around if you don't have any with you.

Take a look at your snow chains before you set out, and check the links and fasteners to make sure they work. If you haven't used chains before, practice putting them on under sunny skies and dry conditions. Chains should go on your car's drive wheels, so you need to know whether your car has front- or rear-wheel drive.

In case roads are closed or an accident occurs and you get stranded, you should keep some emergency supplies in your car. At the minimum, carry one or two flashlights and extra batteries, warm blankets and clothing, water and snacks, an ice scraper, a shovel, and sand or kitty litter (to pour on the snow around your tires for extra traction if you get stuck). A clean towel is also useful for cleaning your hands after installing tire chains.

When you are ready to leave on your trip to Tahoe, allow yourself extra time in case the roads are icy. Make sure your gas tank is full, and keep it full (or close to it) for the duration of your trip. (If roads are closed, you may have to take a longer route than you planned.) As you drive, remember that shady areas of the road, bridge decks, and underpasses may be icy when the rest of the road is not, especially late at night and early in the morning. Allow plenty of stopping distance between you and the vehicles ahead. If you are driving an SUV, keep in mind that four-wheel-drive vehicles provide more power for traction but not for stopping. Go slow and avoid sudden stops and direction changes.

The best winter driving advice is always to check on road conditions before you go. California highway information is available at www.dot.ca.gov or 800/427-7623. Nevada highway information is available at www.safetravelusa.com/nv or 877/687-6237.

Truckee or Reno; both cities are a little more than an hour's drive from South Lake Tahoe. Amtrak buses and/or other bus services travel between Truckee and Reno and South Lake. The **Amtrak Thruway Station** is located at the **South Y Transit Center** (1000 Hwy. 50, South Lake Tahoe). For schedules and information, contact Amtrak (800/872-7245, www.amtrak.com).

GETTING AROUND

Public transportation services are easy to come by in South Lake Tahoe. Many casinos and ski resorts provide free shuttle service; low-cost buses, trolleys, and taxis are widely available. And with all the traffic in the downtown area, public transportation is a much better way to go than driving your own car.

By Shuttle or Bus

Public transportation is available by bus year-round from **BlueGo** (530/541-7149, www.bluego.org). Fixed bus routes between Stateline and the Y run 5:15 A.M.–12:45 A.M. daily. Additional fixed-route buses travel in winter only to the ski resorts. Tickets are $2 per person one-way or $5 for an all-day pass. You can also "order" door-to-door service on BlueGo through their on-demand shuttle service. Self-service touch-screen kiosks and phones are located at various locations throughout the South Shore from Meyers to Zephyr Cove, including Zephyr Cove Resort, Horizon Casino, South Lake Tahoe Chamber of Commerce, Super 8 Motel, the McDonald's at Ski Run and at the Y, Embassy Suites, Camp Richardson Resort, and many other spots. Order service by kiosk or phone, or on the Internet at www.bluego.org. Advance reservations are advised. If you order service and wish to get a ride as soon as possible, the reservation system will inform you of your estimated wait time.

The **Nifty Fifty Trolley,** operated by BlueGo, offers narrated tours combined with shuttle service (9:15 A.M.–7:15 P.M. summer only) throughout the length of the South Shore. The trolleys are open-sided buses—replicas of 19th-century streetcars with polished oak seats and brass poles—that allow riders to enjoy the fresh mountain air while they travel. Trolley

drivers provide passengers with tips on things to see and do, and give out information on Tahoe's history, flora, and fauna. (Some drivers are talkative and enthusiastic; others behave like they barely tolerate living at Lake Tahoe.) Two routes are available on the Nifty Fifty Trolley—one heading north from the South Y Transit Center to Emerald Bay and D. L. Bliss State Park, the other heading east to the casinos and Stateline (Kingsbury Transit Station). Riders can get on and off as often as they like with a $5 all-day pass, or ride one-way for $2. The Nifty Fifty pass is also good on BlueGo's fixed bus routes.

Cruise guests on the *Tahoe Queen* or MS *Dixie II* can take advantage of free shuttle service from the South Shore area to the boats' respective marinas at Zephyr Cove and Ski Run. In the winter months, Heavenly Resort and Sierra-at-Tahoe Resort offer free ski shuttles from various locations along U.S. 50 and the South Shore to the slopes. Contact the resorts for more information.

© ANN MARIE BROWN

a Nifty Fifty Trolley

Surprisingly, there's only one boat shuttle that runs along the south end of the lake, the **South Shore Water Shuttle,** which travels from Lakeside Marina (530/541-9800) near the casinos to Camp Richardson Marina (530/542-6570) to Timber Cove Marina (530/544-2942). The shuttle runs June–September; fares are $12 one-way or $18 round-trip for adults and $8 one-way or $12 round-trip for children 12 and under. The return-trip ticket can also be used on the Nifty Fifty Trolley. However, there is no public parking at any of these marinas, so you'll have to walk there or take the BlueGo bus. Or, if you are staying in the casino area, you can get a free shuttle to Lakeside Marina (530/541-9800 for reservations and information).

If you'd like to get from the South Shore to the North Shore in the summer months, the **Emerald Bay Shuttle** (775/323-3727, www.lake tahoetransit.com) travels from Emerald Bay northward to Tahoe City. The service usually runs late June–Labor Day only.

And if you need to go to or from Reno/Tahoe International Airport and the South Shore, your best bet is the **South Tahoe Express** (866/898-2463, www.southtahoeexpress.com), which offers 11 daily departures between the airport and the South Shore's major casinos and resorts. The cost is $27.50 per adult one-way or $49 round-trip. The fee for children under 12 riding with their parents is $15.50 one-way or $28 round-trip.

By Car

To get current updates on road conditions on the California side of the South Shore, phone 800/427-7623 or visit www.dot.ca.gov. To get current updates on Nevada road conditions, phone 877/687-6237 or visit www.safetravelusa.com.

For **car rentals** in South Lake Tahoe, try Enterprise Rent-a-Car (2281 Hwy. 50, South Lake Tahoe, 530/544-8844, www.enterprise. com) at U.S. 50 and Tahoe Keys Boulevard. Avis Rent-a-Car (775/588-4450) is located inside Harrah's Casino, and Hertz Rent-a-Car (775/586-0041 or 800/654-3131) is located inside Harveys Casino. All the major car-rental agencies are also available at Reno-Tahoe International Airport.

By Taxi

Yellow Cab Company (530/544-5555 or 775/588-1234) offers taxi service in South Lake Tahoe and Stateline.

NORTH AND WEST SHORES

While the South Shore is known as the high-energy, nightlife-and-action side of the lake, the North and West Shores have always been more sedate. A wealth of outdoor activities are available here, including skiing at 10 alpine resorts, hiking in Ed Z'berg Sugar Pine Point or D. L. Bliss State Parks, biking along a wealth of paved and dirt trails, or golfing at one of eight courses. Two good-size cities are found on the North Shore, Tahoe City and Truckee, both brimming with restaurants, shops, and lodgings. Beyond the towns are miles of river, forest, and lake shoreline—a bounty of open space—and the people who live here like it that way. Although there are ample tourism-related businesses, the region is more appropriately characterized by its abundance of public parkland, cozy knotty-pine cabins, and lakefront estates, including some of Tahoe's grandest mansions, both publicly and privately owned. The West Shore in particular has an "old-money" ambience. This is classic Tahoe, with giant conifers and massive timber-and-stone lodges, including Fleur du Lac, the estate of Henry Kaiser and the movie location for *The Godfather II*.

Still, the North Shore does experience crowding, especially in the summer months. The Y in Tahoe City, where the highways, bike paths, and Truckee River convene, is one of the busiest spots around the lake. Visitors rent rafts for a leisurely float down the river,

© ANN MARIE BROWN

HIGHLIGHTS

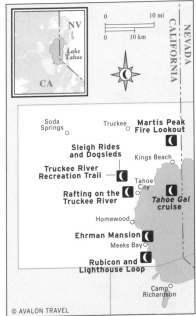

© AVALON TRAVEL

LOOK FOR ⟨ TO FIND RECOMMENDED SIGHTS, ACTIVITIES, DINING, AND LODGING.

⟨ *Tahoe Gal* **cruise:** The locals' favorite tour boat, this small paddle wheeler plies Tahoe's waters for a romantic sunset dinner cruise, a happy-hour cruise, and a scenic shoreline breakfast cruise (page 118).

⟨ **Ehrman Mansion:** There is something for everyone at the Ehrman Mansion property at Ed Z'berg Sugar Pine Point State Park: tours of the elegant, 11,000-square-foot, stone-and-timber lodge; a nature center; a few short interpretive trails; and a marvelous stretch of West Shore beach (page 119).

⟨ **Martis Peak Fire Lookout:** For a bird's-eye view of Lake Tahoe and points north, you can't do much better than the scene from Martis Peak Fire Lookout, where a U.S. Forest Service fire spotter will welcome you to his or her perch (page 124).

⟨ **Rubicon and Lighthouse Loop:** For a taste of Tahoe's spectacular shoreline scenery, take this easy two-mile loop hike at D. L. Bliss State Park. After only a short walk on the Rubicon Trail, you'll find yourself at dramatic Rubicon Point, where you can peer several hundred feet down into the lake's depths before looping back past a restored 1916 lighthouse (page 140).

⟨ **Truckee River Recreation Trail:** The most scenic of the multiple paved bike paths around Lake Tahoe, the Truckee River Recreation Trail runs 5.5 miles from Tahoe City to Squaw Valley USA, following within a few feet of the river's edge for its entire distance (page 141).

⟨ **Rafting on the Truckee River:** Take a mellow float down the Truckee River in a raft or inner tube from Tahoe City to River Ranch Lodge, where you can sit out on the deck and enjoy lunch (page 145).

⟨ **Sleigh Rides and Dogsleds:** The best way to enjoy the North and West Shores' winter wonderland, without putting out any effort of your own, is to dash through the snow in an open sleigh drawn by handsome horses or eager huskies (page 166).

a cluster of restaurants feed hungry tourists, sightseers lean over the railing of Fanny Bridge to watch the fish swim in the river below, history buffs tour the Gatekeeper's Museum, and bike riders pedal off on a network of trails. Some of Tahoe's best people-watching takes place near the Y, where Highways 28 and 89 meet, but head south or east and the throngs disappear. On the West Shore, communities like Tahoe Pines, Tahoma, and Meeks Bay are separated by scenic beaches offering opportunities for boating and swimming. To the east of Tahoe City, the charming hamlets of Kings Beach and Tahoe Vista boast a collection of restaurants and places to stay.

Frequently overlooked in favor of the towns on Lake Tahoe's shoreline, the quaint town of Truckee is worth a stop for railroad and history enthusiasts, browsers, and casual strollers. The town burgeoned during the construction of the transcontinental railroad through Donner Pass in 1868. In 1900, the Lake Tahoe Railway was completed between Truckee and Tahoe City, allowing tourists a much easier route to the lakeshore. The original train depot, now more than a century old, still serves railway passengers. But it's not just the lovingly restored buildings and gentrified hipness of Truckee that attract visitors. The region around Truckee and Donner Pass offers some of the best outdoor recreation of the entire Tahoe region, including world-class alpine ski resorts such as Squaw Valley USA and Northstar-at-Tahoe, North America's largest cross-country ski resort at Royal Gorge, and almost limitless rock-climbing and hiking opportunities.

PLANNING YOUR TIME

Many visitors spend a week or more in and around the North and West Shores, both in the winter and summer seasons. This is especially true if you are interested in outdoor recreation—skiing or other winter sports, hiking, rock climbing, mountain biking, golfing, and water sports. Just visiting some of the North or West Shore's sightseeing highlights, and dining at a few of its fine restaurants, will require a minimum of two days. In the summer months, be sure to visit the **Ehrman Mansion** at Ed Z'berg Sugar Pine Point State Park and take a walk on one of the park's short nature trails, or have a picnic on the mansion's beach. Stroll around the Tahoe City Y and stop in at the **Gatekeeper's Cabin Museum** to see its marvelous collection of Native American

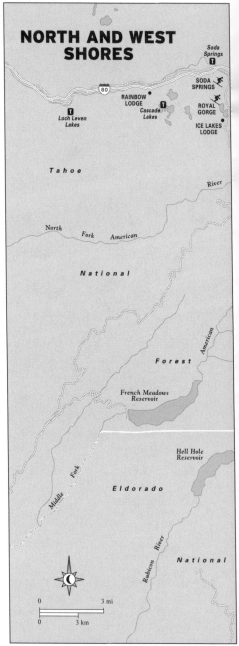

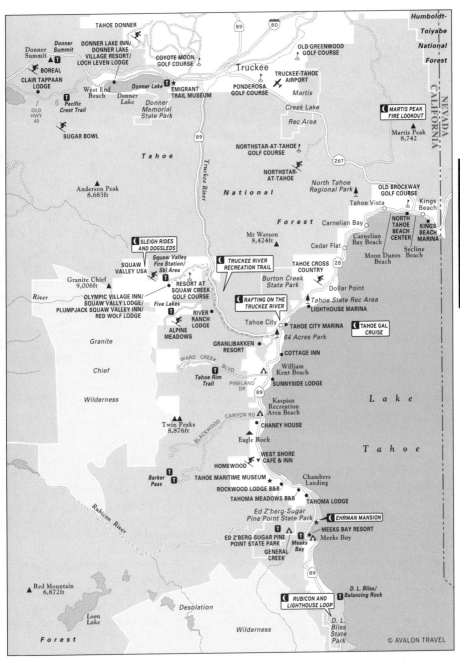

Humboldt-
Toiyabe
National
Forest

NEVADA
CALIFORNIA

TAHOE DONNER

DONNER LAKE INN/
DONNER LAKE
VILLAGE RESORT/
LOCH LEVEN LODGE

Donner
Summit

Donner
Summit

BOREAL

CLAIR TAPPAAN
LODGE

West End
Beach

Pacific
Crest Trail

OLD
HWY
40

SUGAR BOWL

COYOTE MOON
GOLF COURSE

OLD GREENWOOD
GOLF COURSE

Truckee

TRUCKEE-TAHOE
AIRPORT

PONDEROSA
GOLF COURSE

Martis

EMIGRANT
TRAIL MUSEUM

Donner Lake

Donner
Lake

Donner
Memorial
State Park

Creek Lake

Rec Area

MARTIS PEAK
FIRE LOOKOUT

Martis Peak
8,742

Tahoe

National

NORTHSTAR-AT-TAHOE
GOLF COURSE

NORTHSTAR-
AT-TAHOE

North Tahoe
Regional Park

OLD BROCKWAY
GOLF COURSE

Anderson Peak
8,683ft

Forest

Tahoe Vista

Kings
Beach

Mt Watson
8,424ft

Carnelian Bay

NORTH
TAHOE
BEACH
CENTER

KINGS
BEACH
MARINA

Cedar Flat

Carnelian
Bay Beach

Moon Dunes
Beach

Secline
Beach

SLEIGH RIDES
AND DOGSLEDS

SQUAW
VALLEY USA

Squaw Valley
Fire Station/
Ski Area

TRUCKEE RIVER
RECREATION TRAIL

TAHOE CROSS
COUNTRY

Granite Chief
9,006ft

River

OLYMPIC VILLAGE INN/
SQUAW VALLY LODGE/
PLUMPJACK SQUAW VALLEY INN/
RED WOLF LODGE

RESORT AT
SQUAW CREEK
GOLF COURSE

Five Lakes

Burton Creek
State Park

Dollar Point

RAFTING ON THE
TRUCKEE RIVER

Tahoe State Rec Area

LIGHTHOUSE MARINA

RIVER
RANCH
LODGE

ALPINE
MEADOWS

Tahoe City

TAHOE CITY MARINA

64 Acres Park

TAHOE GAL
CRUISE

Granite

GRANLIBAKKEN
RESORT

COTTAGE INN

Chief

WARD CREEK

BLVD

Tahoe Rim
Trail

PINELAND
DR

William
Kent Beach

SUNNYSIDE LODGE

Wilderness

Kaspian
Recreation
Area Beach

Lake

Twin Peaks
8,876ft

CANYON RD

BLACKWOOD

CHANEY HOUSE

Eagle Rock

Tahoe

WEST SHORE
CAFÉ & INN

HOMEWOOD

TAHOE MARITIME MUSEUM

Chambers
Landing

Barker
Pass

ROCKWOOD LODGE B&B

TAHOMA MEADOWS B&B

TAHOMA LODGE

Rubicon River

Ed Z'berg-Sugar
Pine Point State Park

EHRMAN MANSION

ED Z'BERG-SUGAR PINE
POINT STATE PARK

Meeks
Bay

MEEKS BAY RESORT

Meeks Bay

GENERAL
CREEK

Red Mountain
6,872ft

Desolation

D. L. Bliss/
Balancing Rock

RUBICON AND
LIGHTHOUSE LOOP

D. L.
Bliss
State
Park

Loon
Lake

Forest

Wilderness

© AVALON TRAVEL

© ANN MARIE BROWN

Sightseers line up along Fanny Bridge to see the trout swimming in the Truckee River.

baskets. Allow some time for a few hours of fun recreation, like a lazy float down the Truckee River in a raft or inner tube, or an easy bike ride along the paved **Truckee River Trail** followed by lunch at River Ranch Lodge. And don't miss the chance for a few meals at some of the North and West Shores' fine restaurants, especially those with big lake views.

TOUR BOATS AND CRUISES
◖ *Tahoe Gal* Cruise

For a romantic sunset dinner cruise, happy-hour cruise, or a scenic shoreline breakfast cruise, you can't go wrong with **North Tahoe Cruises** (952 N. Lake Blvd. in the Lighthouse Mall, Tahoe City, 800/218-2464, www.tahoe-gal.com, $20–40 adults, $10–19 children), which operates the paddle wheeler *Tahoe Gal*. Smaller than the paddle wheeler cruise boats on the South Shore, the *Tahoe Gal* provides a more intimate cruising experience with a

maximum of 150 people on board. Tours last between 90 minutes and three hours and depart from Lighthouse Shopping Center, at the dock behind the Safeway supermarket. For a special experience, book the full-moon cruise, which takes place only once a month.

Tahoe Sailing Charters

If you prefer wind power to paddle-wheel power, Tahoe Sailing Charters (700 N. Lake Blvd., Tahoe City, 530/583-6200, www.tahoesail.com, $50–80 adults, $30–40 children) offers daily two-hour afternoon and sunset cruises, as well as Sunday brunch cruises to Emerald Bay (May–Oct.). Tours depart from the Tahoe City Marina; passengers can elect to help with the hands-on sailing or just sit back and relax on the 50-foot sailboat *Tahoe Cruz*. Beer, wine, sodas, and bottled water are included, and tours are limited to 25 passengers.

Sights

❸ EHRMAN MANSION

Pay a visit to the Ehrman Mansion (7360 Hwy. 89/W. Lake Blvd., Tahoma, 530/525-7982, www.parks.ca.gov, $8 day-use fee per vehicle, tours $8 adults, $5 children 6–17, free for children under 6) at Ed Z'berg Sugar Pine Point State Park, 10 miles south of Tahoe City, to see how the Tahoe rich lived at the start of the 20th century. This three-story, timber-and-stone lodge was built in 1903 as the summer home for Isaias W. Hellman, a San Francisco financier. Over the course of his lifetime, Hellman acquired 2,000 acres of land around Lake Tahoe, much of which is now Sugar Pine Point State Park. His grand, 11,000-square-foot house, which he called "Pine Lodge," was equipped with three porches covered in Oriental rugs, a circular staircase, leaded-glass windows, and fine furnishings in each of its eight bedrooms. The grounds were carefully landscaped with trees, lawns, flower beds, and a Ehrman Mansion (vegetable garden. A pier and two boathouses were built for the family's speed-boats. Much of the construction materials for the estate had to be transported across the lake by steamship, as no road existed in the early 1900s between this site and Tahoe City.

The mansion was later inherited by Hellman's daughter, Florence Hellman Ehrman, who spent summers here with her husband, accompanied by an army of more than 30 servants, all of whom were housed in various buildings on the property. Tours of the mansion are offered 10 A.M.–3 P.M. daily in summer (530/525-7982 or 530/525-7232, www.sierrastateparks.org, $8 adults, $5 children 6–17, free for children under 6).

A nature center with bird and wildlife displays is housed in the mansion's old water tower. Also on the property, just north of the pier, is a hand-hewn, 19th-century log cabin that was the home of trapper and fisherman William "General" Phipps, the first permanent settler on Lake Tahoe's west shore. The entire estate enjoys a gorgeous setting on the shore of Lake Tahoe—an inviting spot for a picnic or a quick, cold swim.

GATEKEEPER'S CABIN MUSEUM

Located right next to the Truckee River outlet in William B. Layton Park at the Tahoe City Y is the Gatekeeper's Cabin Museum (130 Hwy. 89/W. Lake Blvd., Tahoe City, 530/583-8717 or 530/583-1762, www.northtahoemuseums.org, 11 A.M.–5 P.M. daily May–mid-Oct., Fri.–Sat. only in winter, $3 adults, $1 children 12 and under), which brings to life Tahoe's reign as the queen of the California resort destinations in the late 19th century. In those days, before roads were built along the lakeshore, travelers crisscrossed the lake by passenger steamships. Scale models of four of these ships are on display, along with other bits and pieces of Tahoe memorabilia, including period clothing and winter sports equipment. Serious historians will be interested in the Ellen Attardi research library, which includes books, oral histories, photographs, and newspapers from Tahoe's pioneer era to more modern times. The museum building itself is an authentic log cabin. The original cabin on this site, built in 1909, was the home of the first river gatekeeper, whose job was to measure and regulate Tahoe's water level. Five different men held this duty from 1910 to 1968. When the gatekeeper's cabin was destroyed by fire, the present-day museum was hand carved from lodge-pole-pine logs on the same foundation.

In an adjoining building is the **Marion Steinbach Indian Basket Museum,** exhibiting more than 800 Native American baskets made by more than 85 different tribes, including the

© ANN MARIE BROWN

One of the North Shore's most fascinating museums, the Gatekeeper's Cabin boasts a large display of Native American baskets.

local Washoes and Paiutes. The woven baskets are as large as three feet in diameter and as small as one-quarter inch. This world-class collection, which belonged to Marion Steinbach and was donated after her death in 1991, also includes Native American pottery, dolls, rattles, hats, and artifacts. The museum may be closed on Monday and Tuesday.

TRUCKEE RIVER OUTLET/ FANNY BRIDGE

Situated at Outlet Point, the only spot where the waters of Lake Tahoe find an escape from the lake's basin, tiny Truckee River Outlet State Park is comprised of the land surrounding the Lower Truckee River at Tahoe City. Here the river is crossed by a dam and Fanny Bridge, named for the posteriors of the tourists who lean over the bridge's railing to see the giant trout in the river below. The Donner Lumber Company built the first dam across the

Truckee River outlet in Tahoe City in 1872. Water released through the dam controlled the flow of logs to lumber mills downstream. This led to long-running conflicts and a court battle, known as the Tahoe Water War, over who had the right to regulate the flow of water—the lakeshore landowners or the downstream Truckee River water users. Today the water is controlled by the Federal Watermaster in Reno, Nevada, but the dam's 17 gates are still raised and lowered on this site using the same hand-turned winch system employed since 1913. The Gatekeeper's Cabin Museum is a few feet away, and the paved Tahoe City Lakeside Trail passes by and continues to the Commons Beach area.

WATSON CABIN

Perched on a bluff alongside busy North Lake Boulevard and above Commons Beach, the Watson Cabin (560 N. Lake Blvd./Hwy. 28, Tahoe City, 530/583-8717 or 530/583-1762, www.northtahoemuseums.org, noon–4 P.M. weekends Memorial Day–June 30, noon–4 P.M. Wed.–Mon. July–Labor Day, free) is the oldest log structure remaining in the North Tahoe area. The cabin was built in 1908 by Robert Montgomery Watson, Tahoe City's first policeman, and his youngest son, using local materials such as hand-hewn logs, native stone, and deer antlers. Part of the structure's claim to fame is that it had the area's first indoor bathroom. The cabin was given to the son, Robert, as a wedding present in 1909, and he and his wife, Stella, used it as a summer retreat and occasionally as a year-round home, although they found the Tahoe winters difficult. By the 1940s, the Watsons were dismayed by the traffic and noise of downtown Tahoe City, so they leased out the cabin. From the late 1940s until 1990, the building was used as a gift shop. Today at the Watson Cabin, docents from the North Lake Tahoe Historical Society dress in period costumes and tell stories of early-20th-century Tahoe life.

SQUAW VALLEY USA

Although the 1960 Winter Olympics are a long-vanished memory for most, the host of those games, Squaw Valley USA (1960 Squaw Valley Rd., Olympic Village, 530/583-6955 or 530/583-6985, www.squaw.com) has parlayed its Olympic glories into its raison d'être for being a year-round destination. Located five miles northwest of Tahoe City, and with the symbolic Olympic flame still greeting visitors at its entrance, Squaw boasts an extraordinary 3,600 acres of skiing terrain serviced by 30 chairlifts. As of 2011, Squaw and its neighboring resort, Alpine Meadows, are under the same ownership, which means a ticket at one resort gets you access to both. Technically, that means that Squaw ticket holders have access to 6,000 acres of ski terrain, 44 lifts, and 270 trails. During the ski season, shuttles run between the two resorts every 30 minutes.

Squaw offers plenty for nonskiers, too. In 2012, Squaw opened its SnoVenture Activity Zone in cooperation with Squaw Creek Resort. Perfect for nonskiers, SnoVenture has a kid-friendly day lodge, expanded snow-tubing course, and mini-snowmobiles for kids ages 6–12. An open-air **skating rink** is found at Squaw's High Camp, accessible via the aerial tram, for those who wish to do a few pirouettes (it's an ice-skating rink in winter and a roller-skating rink in summer). Also at High Camp is the **1960 VIII Olympic Winter Games Museum.** This room full of photographs and posters commemorates what was in 1960 the largest Olympics ever held, with 34 nations sending more than 1,000 athletes, all of whom were housed on-site in the first-ever Olympic Village. The 1960 Olympics were also the first winter games to be nationally televised, and the first to use electronic computers to tally scores.

Squaw Valley offers a wide range of summer activities, too. A cable car sails 2,000 feet above the ground to the **High Camp Bath and Tennis Club,** elevation 8,200 feet, where an artificial lagoon lures swimmers and bathers, and a café serves meals on an outdoor deck above the pool. Plenty of parents let their kids play in the water while they order a Blue Lagoon margarita, put on their dark shades, and enjoy the summer-pool-party atmosphere. At this elevation, sunscreen is a must—every summer day a few unprepared, oblivious sunbathers face an unpleasant red-skinned surprise at the end of the day.

Hiking trails lead from the tram station to surrounding high peaks, and outdoor concerts are held on weekends. Summer cable-car hours of operation are 9:40 A.M.–6 P.M. daily mid-June–Labor Day; open weekends only the rest of the year, except for ski season. Summer cable-car rates are $29 for adults, $22 for teens, $10 for children 12 and under; skate and/or swim passes are extra.

Down below at Squaw Valley and Squaw Creek, visitors can play 18 holes of golf, ride

NORTH AND WEST SHORES

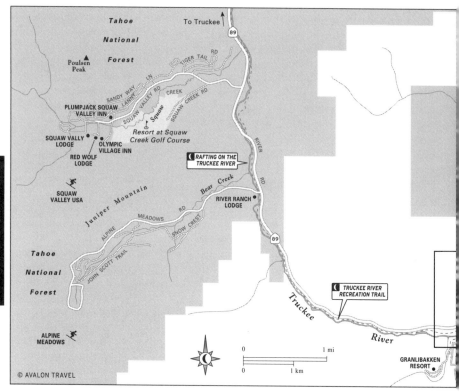

horseback, or browse the upscale shops at The Village at Squaw Valley. Then again, some visitors just take a look at this beautiful alpine valley and wonder what it would have been like if they hadn't altered the landscape for the sake of recreational sports.

TAHOE MARITIME MUSEUM

Lake Tahoe's colorful maritime history is memorialized at this West Shore museum located just south of Homewood ski area (5205 W. Lake Blvd./Hwy. 89, Homewood, 530/525-9253, www.tahoemaritimemuseum.org, 10 A.M.–5 P.M. Thurs.–Tues. in summer, 10 A.M.–4:30 P.M. Fri.–Sun. in winter, $5 adults, children 12 and under free). The collection includes eight antique watercraft,

including the *Shanghai,* an 1890s-era launch that was discovered on the bottom of Lake Tahoe in 2000, and a Gar Wood runabout. Several outboard engines on display date back to the early 20th century. Exhibits highlight the famous steam-powered vessel *Tahoe,* which plied the lake's waters in the late 19th century. A special children's room encourages kids to learn about boating with activities like line tying, boatbuilding, watercolor painting, and other arts and crafts.

EAGLE ROCK

This short walk offers such big payoffs that you can easily convince the nonhikers in your family to do it. A walk of less than a half mile with a 250-foot elevation gain leads to the top of

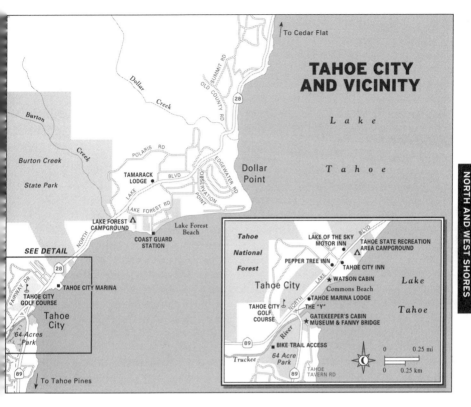

Eagle Rock and spectacular views over Lake Tahoe. Eagle Rock is the neck of an eroded volcanic plug, which dammed up the surrounding volcano like a cork. Because the massive rock juts out over Highway 89 and the West shore, it provides one of the most easily accessible viewpoints of the lake and a great spot for taking photographs. Eagle Rock's summit view scans the entire length of the lake from north to south. Although the Washoe Indians had been visiting Eagle Rock for centuries, Westerners started to climb the rock as early as 1881. At the start of the twentieth century, these early tourists built a gazebo on the summit. The trail begins at the signboard and pullout area along the west side of Highway 89, 6.5 miles south of Tahoe City (just south of Barker Pass Rd.).

Most people reach the top of Eagle Rock in about 15 minutes of walking.

EMIGRANT TRAIL MUSEUM

When Californians get hungry on a hiking trip, inevitably someone cracks a sorry joke about the Donner Party, an ill-fated group of emigrants who took what they thought was a shortcut while trying to make their way westward from Illinois in 1846. Caught in a series of early snowstorms at what is now known as Donner Lake, members of the wagon train were forced to eat the bodies of their deceased companions in order to survive the premature winter. The tragedy is remembered at the Emigrant Trail Museum at Donner Memorial State Park (12593 Donner Pass Rd. off I-80,

Truckee, 530/582-7892, www.parks.ca.gov, 10 A.M.–5 P.M. daily, $3 adults, $1 children). The museum highlights the mid-1800s emigrant movement with a collection of displays, including a fully loaded covered wagon and a slide show detailing the tragic Donner story. Exhibits also interpret the history of Donner Pass, including the building of the transcontinental railroad, the ice harvesting and lumber business, and the lifestyles of the local Native Americans. A few hundred feet away is the **Pioneer Monument,** an impressive bronze statue that honors the thousands of emigrants who attempted the arduous trek across the western mountains. Its 22-foot-high pedestal marks the depth of snow that trapped the Donner Party in this valley. The cabin site of the Murphy family, where 16 Donner Party members from three different families spent the winter of 1846–1847, is a short walk away. Built in haste as the snow fell, a large boulder was used as one wall of the earthen-floor cabin. A few miles away, the Donner Party is also remembered at the **Donner Historical Site,** four miles north of Truckee and I-80 on Highway 89. A short interpretive trail leads you to the tree where other members of the Donner Party pitched their tents and struggled through winter.

DONNER SUMMIT BRIDGE AND OLD HIGHWAY 40

For spectacular views of Donner Lake, Truckee, the surrounding mountains, and the magnificent rock cliffs for which Donner Pass is famous, drive Old Highway 40 and stop at McGlashan Point, an overlook adjacent to Donner Summit Bridge. The concrete arch bridge itself is a beautiful work of architecture. Often called the Rainbow Bridge, it was completed in 1926 and featured a unique curve and span for that time. Constructed for $40,000, it was revered as an engineering marvel, and it was a key link in the Lincoln Highway, the first transcontinental road in the United States. Today, the bridge and the old highway are a view-rich, quiet alternative to driving I-80. The historic route and the interstate run parallel for about 11 miles. From I-80 heading east, take the Soda Springs exit and follow it to Donner Pass. From I-80 heading west, take the Donner Lake exit to Donner Pass Road, then turn right.

DOWNTOWN TRUCKEE

The historic town of Truckee, 12 miles northwest of Tahoe City, was settled in 1863 and named for a Paiute Indian chief. It came into existence as a way station serving wagon traffic traveling over Donner Summit's emigrant routes, and thrived due to the construction of the transcontinental railroad. The first train passed through Truckee in 1868; Amtrak still travels through the town. An enjoyable historical walking tour of the downtown's wooden sidewalks will take most visitors an hour or two, although serious shoppers could easily spend a day browsing Commercial Row's many stores. Start by picking up the walking tour brochure at the Truckee visitors center (10065 Donner Pass Rd., Truckee, 530/587-2757 or 530/587-8808, www.truckee.com, 9 A.M.–5:45 P.M. daily), located at the century-old train depot. Among the town's many historic buildings, don't miss the two-story **Old Truckee Jail Museum** (10142 Jibboom St., 530/582-0893, www.truckeehistory.org, 11 A.M.–4 P.M. weekends in summer), one block north of Commercial Row. It showcases the longest operating jail in California, which incarcerated criminals during 1875–1964.

◖ MARTIS PEAK FIRE LOOKOUT

For a bird's-eye view of Lake Tahoe and points north, it's hard to do better than Martis Peak Fire Lookout. In summer and fall, drive your car or ride your bike to the lookout tower, elevation 8,650 feet. In winter and spring, you can get there on snowshoes or cross-country skis. No matter what time of year, the expansive view from the top will wow you. The tower is staffed by a U.S. Forest Service worker during daylight hours in summer and fall. When the lookout is not busy spotting fires, he or she will be happy to interpret for you the expansive high view of Lake Tahoe and Carnelian Bay to the south, Boca and Stampede Reservoirs to the north, Donner Lake, Mount Tallac, the Truckee airport, Twin Peaks, and dozens of other landmarks. On clear days you can even see Mount Lassen, 100 miles to the north.

From Highway 28 at Kings Beach, drive northwest on Highway 267 for 3.7 miles. Just beyond Brockway Summit, turn right on Martis Peak Fire Lookout Road and continue 4 miles to the lookout.

Recreation

HIKING

The following hikes are listed from west to east along the I-80 corridor, and from north to south along the Highway 89/Emerald Bay Road corridor.

For more information on the trails described in this section, contact Tahoe National Forest, Truckee Ranger District (10342 Hwy. 89, Truckee, 530/587-3558, www.fs.fed.us/r5/tahoe). Or contact Lake Tahoe Basin Management Unit (35 College Dr., South Lake Tahoe, 530/543-2600, www.fs.fed.us/r5/ltbmu). For trails in Ed Z'berg Sugar Pine Point State Park or D. L. Bliss State Park, contact California State Parks Sierra District (7360 W. Lake Blvd., Tahoma, 530/525-7277 or 530/525-7232, www.parks.ca.gov).

If you'd like to go on a guided hike, contact **Tahoe Trips and Trails** (10918 Brockway Rd., Truckee, 530/587-2251 or 800/581-4453, www.tahoetrips.com), a company that offers various day-hiking trips combined with overnight stays at area lodgings.

Loch Leven Lakes

- Distance: 7.8 miles round-trip
- Duration: 4 hours
- Effort: Moderate
- Elevation change: 1,100 feet
- Trailhead: Loch Leven Lakes

- Directions: From I-80 near Soda Springs, take the Big Bend/Rainbow Rd. exit and drive 1 mile west on Hampshire Rocks Rd. to the trailhead parking area, which is 0.2 mile east of the Big Bend Visitor Center and 0.5 mile west of Rainbow Lodge. The trail begins across the road from the parking area.

The Loch Leven Lakes are like a little slice of heaven on earth—three granite-backed bodies of water that can be reached by a moderate hike of only 3.9 miles one-way. If only the trailhead wasn't right off I-80, this hike truly would be heaven. Unfortunately, because of the too-easy trailhead access, this is one of the most heavily trampled destinations in the North Tahoe region. Another problem is that for the first mile or so, you can't escape the constantly annoying sound of I-80 traffic. But once you top the ridge, you leave all sounds of civilization behind and are able to focus on the gorgeous Sierra scenery. Trailhead elevation is 5,700 feet, and the path leads through a glaciated landscape of huge granite boulders scattered amid Jeffrey and lodgepole pines. After crossing a creek and a set of railroad tracks, the path climbs a steep 800 feet in only 1.3 miles, then reaches the ridgetop and descends slightly to the lowest of the three Loch Leven Lakes, 2.7 miles from the trailhead. A crowd is usually congregated here, so go left at the junction by the lake and continue another 0.5 mile to the middle Loch Leven Lake, or better still, another 1.2 miles to the upper lake, High Loch Leven, 3.9 miles from the start and the most beautiful of them all. Because much of the last stretch of trail traverses granite slabs, some hikers have difficulty locating the upper lake, but there is usually someone around who can show you the way. If not, keep your eyes peeled for trail cairns; they'll guide you right to the lakeshore. If you have the energy to add a fourth lake to your itinerary, you can follow a side trail leading right (west) from the lowest Loch Leven Lake to Salmon Lake, just under a mile away.

Lower Lola Montez Lake

- Distance: 6.6 miles round-trip
- Duration: 3 hours
- Effort: Moderate

© ANN MARIE BROWN

Trails in D. L. Bliss State Park run through the forest and along the shoreline.

- Elevation change: 500 feet
- Trailhead: Soda Springs
- Directions: From I-80 near Soda Springs, take the Soda Springs/Norden exit and cross over the overpass to the north side of the freeway. Follow the paved road east, past the fire station, for 0.3 mile to the trailhead parking area.

At 7,200 feet in elevation, Lola Montez Lake has all the scenic qualities of a high alpine lake, but without the frigid water. The lake is shallow enough that in most years it warms up enough for swimming by July, making it a favorite destination for vacationers and locals alike in the Soda Springs area. However, partly because the trail is so easy, partly because it is right off I-80, and partly because it is favored by mountain bikers, this path is a bad choice for a summer weekend afternoon. For hikers who enjoy peace and quiet, save this hike for the off-season (autumn is lovely), or in summer, stick to weekday mornings only. The first couple of miles of the route cut through a private housing development called Toll Mountain Estates on a mix of wide dirt road and single-track trail. In order to keep hikers and mountain bikers off private property, the path is well signed, so you're in no danger of getting lost. After about an hour of walking along alternating trail and dirt road, you come out to a meadow and a trail fork. Bear right for the lake, which is now only 0.25 mile ahead. Fishing in Lower Lola Montez Lake is decent, but swimming is the main event. Who was Lola Montez, anyway? One of the most colorful characters of the Old West, she operated a saloon in the 1850s in the mining town of Grass Valley.

Mount Judah Loop

- Distance: 5.2 miles round-trip
- Duration: 2.5 hours
- Effort: Moderate
- Elevation change: 1,200 feet

- Trailhead: Pacific Crest Trail/Sugar Bowl Academy
- Directions: From I-80 near Soda Springs, take the Soda Springs/Norden exit and follow Old Hwy. 40 east for 4 miles to just beyond Donner Ski Ranch. Turn right into the parking lot for Sugar Bowl Academy, then turn right on a dirt and gravel road and drive 100 yards to the Pacific Crest Trail on the left, at a gated road. (You can also access the trailhead by driving from Donner Lake west up to the original Donner Pass along Old Hwy. 40; the trailhead is just beyond the pass.)

If you don't mind the appearance of ski-lift operations marring your nature experience, the Mount Judah Loop is a fine hike that offers outstanding views of Lake Mary, Donner Lake, Martis Valley, Castle Peak, and Lake Van Norden, among other landmarks. The trail begins by following the Pacific Crest Trail from near Donner Summit off Old Highway 40, and it climbs gradually but steadily all the way to the top of Mount Judah. One mile from the trailhead, bear left on the Mount Judah Trail to start along the loop. A few spur trails lead off to the left, heading to high overlooks above the Donner basin, but just stay on the main path, which soon becomes an old dirt road. At 1.6 miles the climb tops out at a saddle below the multiple granite spires of Donner Peak, elevation 8,019 feet. Look just to the left of the trail to find an Emigrant Trail marker that designates Emigrant Pass, elevation 7,850 feet. Don't miss the chance to climb up and explore Donner Peak's odd collection of summit pinnacles, where you'll enjoy marvelous views, especially of Donner Lake far below. (The highest pinnacles require climbing equipment and experience to reach, but some of the lower ones are an easy walk up.) From the saddle, continue south along the trail for another mile to Mount Judah's 8,243-foot summit, a bald, windswept high point along a view-filled volcanic ridge. Beyond the summit, the loop trail switchbacks downhill and westward for 0.7 mile until meeting up with the Pacific Crest Trail, where you head right. You'll pass underneath the Sugar Bowl chairlift on your return, then walk through an impressive grove of big red firs on your way back to the trailhead.

Palisade Creek Trail to Heath Falls

- Distance: 10 miles round-trip
- Duration: 6 hours
- Effort: Moderate/strenuous
- Elevation change: 1,700 feet
- Trailhead: Cascade Lakes
- Directions: From I-80 near Soda Springs, take the Soda Springs/Norden exit and follow Old Hwy. 40 east for 0.8 mile to Soda Springs Rd. Turn right (south) and drive 0.8 mile to Pahatsi Rd. Turn right. Pahatsi Rd. turns to dirt in 0.2 mile, and its name changes to Kidd Lakes Rd. At 1.5 miles,

© ANN MARIE BROWN

Donner Peak is a worthy destination on the Mount Judah Loop.

FEELING THE ALTITUDE

Many hikers experience a shortness of breath when hiking only a few thousand feet higher than the elevation where they live. If you live on the coast, you may notice slightly labored breathing while hiking at an elevation as low as 4,000 feet. As you go higher, it may get worse, sometimes leading to headaches and nausea. Since the lakeshore of Tahoe is at 6,200 feet, and the mountains surrounding the lake top out above 10,000 feet, the high elevation can be problematic for some people. It takes a full 72 hours to acclimate to major elevation changes, although most people feel better after 24 to 48 hours.

The best preparation for hiking at high elevation is to sleep at that elevation, or as close to it as possible, the night before. If you are planning a strenuous hike at 7,000 feet or above, spend a day or two beforehand taking easier hikes at the same elevation. Get plenty of rest and drink lots of fluids. Lack of sleep, dehydration, and drinking alcohol can contribute to a susceptibility to "feeling the altitude."

When you get to the trailhead and start hiking, take it slower than you would at lower elevations. Give yourself a half hour of warm-up time so that your legs and lungs start working in sync. (Your legs will want to move at their usual swift pace, but your lungs may be lagging behind.) Keep drinking a lot of water during your hike—more than you think you need.

Serious altitude sickness typically occurs above 10,000 feet. It is generally preventable by simply allowing enough time for acclimation. Staying fully hydrated and fueled with food will also help. If you start to feel ill (nausea, throwing up, severe headache), you are experiencing altitude sickness. Some people can get by with taking aspirin and trudging onward, but if you are seriously ill, the only cure is to descend as quickly as possible. You'll feel better as soon as you get to a lower elevation.

you'll reach a fork. Continue straight for 2.3 more miles, then bear left at a fork and drive 0.5 mile farther. The trailhead is on the north side of the Cascade Lakes.

A hike to Heath Falls is like going on vacation on your credit card. You can have all the fun you want, but when you return home, you have to pay up. That's because the trip is downhill nearly all the way, dropping 1,700 feet over five miles through lovely alpine scenery. But alas, eventually it's time for the return trip—a long and steady climb over those same five miles.

The trail begins at the dam between the two Cascade Lakes, the first of many lakes you'll pass on this trip. Walk across the dam and spillway, then follow the trail through a lodgepole-pine forest, heading to your right at a sign for the North Fork American River. Prepare for a steady diet of granite, lakes, and vistas. You'll hike past 7,704-foot Devil's Peak and pretty Long Lake, as well as several smaller, unnamed lakes and ponds. At 2.2 miles, the trail leaves

this exposed, glaciated landscape behind and moves into a dense forest of cedars and firs, then switchbacks downhill for 2 miles to the Palisade Creek Bridge. Look for a junction 300 yards beyond the bridge where the Heath Falls Overlook Trail heads east. Follow it for 0.5 mile to the trail's end at a vista of Heath Falls on the North Fork American River. The overlook is a fair distance from the falls, which are sheltered deep in the canyon, but you can still hear and see the white water thundering over rock cliffs and into big pools. The land surrounding the waterfall is private property, so exploring any closer than the overlook is forbidden. After soaking in the scenery for as long as you wish, prepare yourself for the long uphill return trip.

Summit Lake

- Distance: 4.4 miles round-trip
- Duration: 2 hours
- Effort: Easy

- Elevation change: 400 feet
- Trailhead: Donner Summit/Pacific Crest Trail
- Directions: From I-80 west of Donner Summit, take the Boreal Ridge/Castle Peak exit. Drive to the frontage road on the south side of I-80, then continue 0.3 mile east to the road's end at the trailhead for the Pacific Crest Trail.

This easy hike is a perfect leg-stretcher for families who have grown weary of the drive to Tahoe and want to get out of the car before reaching their final destination. The trail begins at the Pacific Crest Trail (PCT) Trailhead at Donner Summit and ends 2.2 miles later at a pretty alpine lake at 7,395 feet. The numerous junctions along the way are clearly marked. A half mile from the start, turn left and follow the PCT Access Trail north (signed for Castle Pass and Peter Grubb Hut) through a tunnel underneath I-80. On the north side of the freeway is another junction; bear right for Summit and Warren Lakes. The trail climbs gently through a fir forest and occasionally breaks out of the trees to wide granite slabs that allow views to the south and east. At 1.7 miles you reach the start of the Warren Lake Trail; take the right fork for Summit Lake and travel the final 0.5 mile to the mostly forested lakeshore. Swimming, fishing, and picnicking are common activities here. The only thing that mars the scenery is the distant sound of car traffic moving along I-80. Those seeking a longer trip and a stiff climb can bear left instead at the 1.7-mile fork and follow the Warren Lake Trail to a high overlook atop the bald granite cliffs above Frog Lake, 1.8 miles farther (follow the 150-yard spur trail on the right to the best views). Or, for the truly hard-core, the trail continues another 3.5 miles beyond the overlook to Warren Lake, which is popular with backpackers but rarely visited by day hikers. The round-trip hike to Warren Lake is a full 15 miles with a butt-kicking 3,800 feet of elevation gain (1,900 feet in each direction).

Castle Peak

- Distance: 5.4–9.4 miles round-trip
- Duration: 3–5 hours
- Effort: Moderate/strenuous
- Elevation change: 2,100 feet
- Trailhead: Donner Summit/Pacific Crest Trail
- Directions: From I-80 west of Donner Summit, take the Boreal Ridge/Castle Peak exit. Drive to the frontage road on the south side of I-80, then continue 0.3 mile east to the road's end at the trailhead for the Pacific Crest Trail.

The turreted summit of 9,103-foot Castle Peak is a worthwhile destination for any crystal-clear day, when the peak's panorama can extend for 100 miles north to Lassen Peak and west to the Diablo Range. The throat of an ancient volcano, Castle Peak is a well-known destination for backcountry skiers and snow-shoers in winter, but an equally worthwhile summer trek. The trail is the same as that to Summit Lake for the first mile to the junction after the tunnel crossing underneath I-80. Here you'll leave the Summit Lake Trail behind and head left (west) for Castle Pass, staying on the Pacific Crest Trail (PCT). As the trail nears the Donner Summit Rest Area on I-80 (keep right at all junctions, still heading west), you'll pass a small pond and finally leave the highway behind as you hike northwest along the PCT to Castle Pass. The path crosses a dirt road at slightly more than 2 miles out, as well as several seasonal streams, causing potential wet feet as late as July. At Castle Pass, 3.5 miles from your start, look for an obvious use trail heading right (northeast) off the PCT, and follow it for 1.2 memorably steep miles to the west summit of Castle Peak. Use caution on the loose volcanic rock; the last 0.5 mile or so requires some scrambling, but the wide summit view is more than worth the effort. The eastern turret of the "castle" is the highest summit.

Note that many people cut 2 miles off the

length of this hike (or 4 miles round-trip) by parking on the north side of I-80 along Castle Valley Road, which turns to dirt and gets progressively rougher after the first 0.25 mile. Park alongside the road and then hike to Castle Pass via the dirt road/trail instead of the Pacific Crest Trail. The dirt road and PCT junction at the pass.

Donner Lakeshore Trail

- Distance: 2 miles round-trip
- Duration: 1 hour
- Effort: Easy
- Elevation change: 50 feet
- Trailhead: Donner Lake
- Directions: From I-80 near Donner Summit, drive 0.8 mile west on I-80 to the Donner Pass Rd. exit (not the Donner Lake exit). Turn left and cross over I-80, then continue along the frontage road for 0.5 mile to the Donner Memorial State Park entrance on the left ($8 day-use fee per vehicle). Once you pass through the entrance kiosk, take the right fork for the picnic and day-use area at China Cove. Park at the far end of the picnic area lot and walk to the lakeshore to pick up the trail.

The Donner Lakeshore Trail begins at the sandy swimming area at China Cove and parallels the southeast shoreline of three-mile-long Donner Lake. The path travels for a mile along the Jeffrey-pine-dotted shoreline and features more than a dozen interpretive plaques with information about the area's history, geography, and ecology. Among many other facts, you'll learn about the amphibians that reside in and around Donner Lake, how the lake was formed by the movement of glaciers, and why and how the train tracks were built on the steep slopes of Donner Summit. The hike is level and easy, and the lakeside scenery is lovely every step of the way; the only downer is that you never quite escape the sound of I-80 across the canyon. Every now and then, you'll even hear

the wail of a train churning up the tracks to Truckee or Reno. The trail ends by the lagoon on the east side of the lake, along the banks of Donner Creek. Before or after walking this pleasant trail, be sure to stop in at the Emigrant Trail Museum at the park; it offers some fascinating insights into this history-rich area.

Granite Chief Trail to Tinker Knob

- Distance: 15 miles round-trip
- Duration: 8 hours
- Effort: Strenuous
- Elevation change: 3,200 feet
- Trailhead: Squaw Valley Fire Station
- Directions: From Tahoe City, drive north on Hwy. 89 for 5 miles and then turn west on Squaw Valley Rd. Drive 2.2 miles to the Squaw Valley Fire Station on the right side of the road, just before the Olympic Village Inn. The trail begins on the east side of the fire station, but you must park your car in the large parking lot by the ski-lift buildings, then walk back to the trailhead.

Tinker Knob is not an easy summit to attain, but those who reach it always remember it. From the Squaw Valley Fire Station, it's a challenging 3.8-mile hike on the Granite Chief Trail to a junction with the Pacific Crest Trail (PCT), gaining 2,000 feet along the way. (You can "cheat" on this section of trail by riding the cable car at Squaw Valley uphill to the PCT, cutting your mileage nearly in half and knocking off three-quarters of the elevation gain.) Much of the ascent is forested, but occasional openings through the trees allow views of Squaw Valley, Lake Tahoe, and surrounding peaks. At just over 2 miles out, the trail crosses a massive granite slab divided into a series of wildflower-decorated benches; the path is marked by yellow paint.

When you reach the PCT, turn right (north) toward Tinker Knob. The next 3.5 miles follow an easier grade along the ridgetop, but with a cruel twist of fate the trail actually descends, losing 500 feet of hard-won elevation that will have to be regained later. The last stretch of trail follows a series of switchbacks up to Tinker Knob Saddle, where impressive views await and a trail on the right heads off to Coldstream Valley. Continuing another 0.25 mile northwest on the PCT leads to a high point from which you can leave the trail and climb 0.25 mile south to Tinker Knob's volcanic summit at 8,960 feet. A few rock cairns mark the top, where a head-swiveling vista—of Anderson Peak, Painted Rock, Silver Peak, Mount Rose, Granite Chief, the Royal Gorge of the American River Canyon, Donner Lake, and, of course, Lake Tahoe—awaits weary hikers.

Note that it is possible to shorten this hike by making a one-way shuttle trip. You'll need a second car waiting for you at the Coldstream Trailhead near Donner Memorial State Park. The Coldstream Trail meets the PCT just below the summit of Tinker Knob, so after gaining the summit via the route already described, you simply follow the Coldstream Trail 5.5 miles down to its trailhead. This makes a 13-mile one-way hike with a car shuttle. Some people also arrange a shuttle hike from the PCT Trailhead near Old Donner Pass (Old Highway 40), making a 15-mile one-way trip.

Granite Chief Trail to Granite Chief Summit

- Distance: 11 miles round-trip
- Duration: 6 hours
- Effort: Strenuous
- Elevation change: 2,800 feet
- Trailhead: Squaw Valley Fire Station
- Directions: From Tahoe City, drive north on Hwy. 89 for 5 miles and then turn west on Squaw Valley Rd. Drive 2.2 miles to the Squaw Valley Fire Station on the right side of the road, just before the Olympic Village Inn. The trail begins on the east side of the

fire station, but you must park your car in the large parking lot by the ski-lift buildings, then walk back to the trailhead.

As with the trail to Tinker Knob, it is possible to utilize a "hiker's handicap" by riding the Squaw Valley cable car to cut off more than 4 miles of hiking (each way), plus most of this trip's elevation gain. But if you decide to hike those miles instead, you'll know that you've truly earned the summit of 9,086-foot Granite Chief, one of the highest points in the Granite Chief Wilderness and the highest point in Placer County. From the Squaw Valley Fire Station, follow the Granite Chief Trail uphill for 3.8 miles, gaining a stiff 2,000 feet along the way as the trail alternates through dense forest and a series of exposed granite slabs. When you reach the Pacific Crest Trail (PCT), go left (south) toward Twin Peaks. The distant view of Lake Tahoe is stunning from here, but keep ascending, and more views will be your reward. (Try to ignore the ski-lift towers and other manufactured structures that mar the natural scenery.) After a sustained climb of about a mile, you reach the eastern flank of Granite Chief, and the PCT starts to descend. Leave the trail here and head right for 0.4 mile, following any of several use trails that lead to the summit of Granite Chief. On top of "the Chief" a banquet of peaks come into perspective, including Twin Peaks, Tinker Knob, Castle Peak, Needle Peak, and those of the jagged Crystal Range in the Desolation Wilderness. Some of Lake Tahoe can also be seen.

If you still have energy to burn after visiting Granite Chief, return to the PCT and hike southward for another 150 yards to a junction with the Emigrant Trail, leading 0.3 mile east to the Watson Monument on the saddle of Emigrant Peak. (This trail then continues to High Camp at Squaw Valley, so those who took the cable car instead of hiking up Granite Chief Trail will have already passed this way.) A short side trip to the stone Watson Monument provides a slightly different view of the North Tahoe basin, but don't expect much from the monument itself. Built by Bob Watson in 1931 to commemorate the pioneers who traveled this hazardous route through Emigrant Pass in the 1850s, the monument has deteriorated to the point where it is little more than a pile of rocks.

Loop lovers who wish to return to the base of Squaw Valley via a different route can continue to High Camp, get a meal or a snack if they so desire, and then follow the Shirley Lake/Shirley Canyon Trail back downhill.

Shirley Lake and Squaw Creek

- Distance: 2.5–5 miles round-trip
- Duration: 1–3 hours
- Effort: Moderate
- Elevation change: Varies
- Trailhead: Squaw Valley Ski Area
- Directions: From Tahoe City, drive north on Hwy. 89 for 5 miles and then turn west on Squaw Valley Rd. Drive 2.2 miles to where the road curves left into the main ski-area parking lot. Turn right on Squaw Peak Rd. and follow it past a condominium complex to its junction with Squaw Peak Way. Park alongside the road near this junction. Or, for a one-way downhill trip, park in the ski-area lot and ride the cable car to High Camp ($14–19 fee). Begin your hike there.

You have a couple of choices for this hike in lovely Shirley Canyon, which follows Squaw Creek past a series of waterfalls, cascades, and swimming holes. If you just want to take a short out-and-back hike and perhaps have a picnic or swim in Squaw Creek, you can start at the Squaw Peak Road/Squaw Peak Way junction and follow the trail as far as you like. Most people just go for a mile or so up this watery, flower-filled canyon, which is laced with a spiderweb of use trails. Some hikers travel as far as Shirley Lake, 2.5 miles up the trail and with 1,500 feet of elevation gain. Or, if you'd

like to enjoy a scenic gondola ride with your hike, you can take the Squaw Valley cable car to High Camp (your leashed dog is allowed to join you, at no charge), then head out the back of the station and follow the ski-lift maintenance road to the right and steeply downhill to Shirley Lake, 1.5 miles from High Camp. Although the ride on the aerial tramway is a winner, this is a somewhat forbidding stretch of trail—the dirt road is wide, exposed, and hot. Fortunately it is over with quickly since you are going downhill. Shirley Lake is small but pretty, with low granite cliffs on one side that invite jumping off. From the lake, continue 2.5 miles downhill through gorgeous Shirley Canyon, now on a narrow trail, eventually returning to the end of Squaw Peak Way, where you have an easy walk on the road back to your car. Note that although the trail is quite obvious in lower Shirley Canyon, it is a little harder to find in upper Shirley Canyon, especially in the first mile below the lake, where the trail traverses granite slabs and travels over and around rock boulders. Dabs of paint and trail cairns mark the way. Watch for them, and remember to keep the creek on your left.

Five Lakes

- Distance: 4.2 miles round-trip
- Duration: 2–3 hours
- Effort: Easy to moderate
- Elevation change: 1,000 feet
- Trailhead: Five Lakes
- Directions: From Tahoe City, drive north on Hwy. 89 for 3.6 miles and turn west on Alpine Meadows Rd. Drive 2.1 miles to the Five Lakes Trailhead on the right side of the road. Park alongside the road.

Some say that this trek into the Granite Chief Wilderness is so easy that it is actually *too* easy, and they may be right. Although the trail has a moderately steep grade, it is mercifully short, which makes it incredibly popular with casual weekend hikers. If possible, visit here in the off-season or on a weekday to experience the least amount of crowds along the trail. The trail takes off from Alpine Meadows Road, and the first 0.5 mile has the steepest grade. The next 0.75 mile continues uphill more gradually to the top of a granite ridge, completing a total 1,000-foot ascent. Switchbacks make the climb quite manageable, but welcome shade from occasional Jeffrey pines and white firs is in short supply along the route, so the trail can be hot. Views of the steep canyon below the ridge are impressive. At 1.8 miles, you reach the Granite Chief Wilderness boundary and enter a land of red fir and gray granite. A signed junction 0.25 mile farther points you left toward the lakes. The trail heads directly downhill to the largest of the five bodies of water at 7,500 feet in elevation. From there, you can follow side trails to the four other lakes, all east of the big one. Most people don't go any farther than the first big lake, where the swimming is nonpareil—the shallow water is clear and remarkably warm. A few white pines and hemlocks line the lakeshore, interspersed with stretches of grassy marsh and big, rounded boulders.

Brockway Spur View

- Distance: 2.8 miles round-trip
- Duration: 1 hour
- Effort: Easy
- Elevation change: 500 feet
- Trailhead: Tahoe Rim Trail/Brockway Summit East
- Directions: From Hwy. 28 on the North Shore, take Hwy. 267 north toward Brockway Summit, then turn right (east) at the sign for the Tahoe Rim Trail, 0.5 mile before the summit (Forest Service Rd. 16N56). Drive about 200 yards and park by the trail signboard.

An easy hike on the Brockway Spur View Trail leads to a big view of Lake Tahoe's North Shore.

For an easy, short hike with a spectacular view, it's hard to beat this short walk on the Tahoe Rim Trail. From the Brockway Summit Trailhead, follow the Tahoe Rim Trail north up the hill. After 0.5 mile of very gentle climbing, bear left on the clearly signed Spur View Trail. Continue uphill on a series of switchbacks, ascending more steeply, until you reach an obvious viewpoint lined with jagged volcanic boulders and sagebrush. This spot provides a commanding view of Lake Tahoe to the south. Taking this short leg-stretcher might easily inspire you to continue your travels along the Tahoe Rim Trail. This section from Brockway Summit East to Tahoe Meadows (18.9 miles of the total 165-mile trail) is well known for having some of the best views along the entire route. It was the last section of the long-distance trail to be completed.

Ward Creek to Twin Peaks

- Distance: 12 miles round-trip
- Duration: 6–7 hours
- Effort: Strenuous
- Elevation change: 2,400 feet
- Trailhead: Tahoe Rim Trail/Twin Peaks
- Directions: From Tahoe City, drive 2.5 miles south on Hwy. 89 to Pineland Dr., which is 0.2 mile south of William Kent Campground. Turn west on Pineland Dr. and drive 0.4 mile, then bear left on Twin Peaks Dr. Drive 1.6 miles (the road becomes Ward Creek Blvd., also signed as Twin Peaks Blvd.) to the Tahoe Rim Trail/Twin Peaks Trailhead on the left side of the road.

It's hard to believe, but during July and early August, the wildflower show along the trail to Twin Peaks often steals the show from the double peaks' spectacular summit view. Time your trip for the peak of the flower bloom and decide for yourself which feature is the most memorable aspect of this trip. Begin your hike by walking around the Twin Peaks Trailhead gate and following the old dirt road alongside coursing Ward Creek. The flower show is just beginning as you travel the pleasant first 2 miles of road/trail on a nearly level course. Shortly after crossing a small creek where old bridge foundations can be seen, the dirt road narrows to a trail, and at 2.3 miles from the start, you'll reach a crossing of Ward Creek. Hikers out for a casual stroll usually turn around here, but those heading for Twin Peaks must rock-hop their way across the stream, then begin a more noticeable ascent alongside Ward Creek. The flower gardens become increasingly showy over the next mile, as the trail sticks close to the creek's south side. During the peak bloom, more than two dozen species are in full color here.

After passing a boisterous waterfall at 3.3 miles, you leave the creek behind and begin a breathless climb through increasingly short and steep switchbacks. This is where much of the work lies on this trail. At 5.2 miles from the start, the trail gains the top of a ridge at 8,000 feet. Here, at a junction, a trail on the left leads 1 mile to Stanford Rock, a worthy destination in its own right with a view almost as fine as Twin Peaks. For Twin Peaks, go right instead and climb more gently for 1 mile to a junction with a narrow use trail on the right. Follow this trail northwest to the eastern summit of Twin Peaks, elevation 8,878 feet. Because of the loose talus rock and steep incline, the last stretch to the east summit requires careful scrambling using two hands and two feet. Those who feel uncomfortable with the risk factor may prefer to ascend the western summit of Twin Peaks. The view from either peak is no disappointment; both deliver a full panorama of easily identifiable landmarks covering the entire Tahoe basin. Be sure to bring a map with you so you can pick out Granite Chief, Tinker Knob, Mount Rose, Freel Peak, and Mount Tallac, amid a host of lesser-known peaks and precipices.

© ANN MARIE BROWN

The summit of Twin Peaks is a worthy hiking destination.

Barker Pass to Twin Peaks

- Distance: 10 miles round-trip
- Duration: 5–6 hours
- Effort: Moderate
- Elevation change: 1,600 feet
- Trailhead: Barker Pass
- Directions: From Tahoe City, drive 4 miles south on Hwy. 89 to Barker Pass Rd. (Forest Service Rd. 03), just south of the Kaspian Campground and picnic area. Turn right (west) and drive 7 miles to the end of the pavement, then continue on the dirt road for 0.3 mile to the Barker Pass/Pacific Crest Trail/Tahoe Rim Trail Trailhead. Begin hiking on the right (north) side of the road.

Although the Ward Creek route to Twin Peaks delivers the most scenic punch during the wildflower season, when the bloom is over you might want to choose a somewhat easier route to the 8,878-foot peaks and their world-class summit view. From Barker Pass, you can follow the Pacific Crest Trail/Tahoe Rim Trail north for 5 miles to Twin Peaks, enjoying a relatively mellow grade and views much of the way. Flower lovers will still be able to find some color on this trip, especially from the prolific mule's ears that favor the volcanic soils in this area.

The trail from Barker Pass begins with a climb up the slopes of 8,166-foot Barker Peak to a ridgeline with fine views of the surrounding volcanic landscape. It then descends into a dense forest of hemlock, white fir, and massive red firs. Over the next 1.5 miles, the trail loses almost 500 feet in elevation, which then must be gained back in a series of well-graded switchbacks that curve upward to a high point, 4.2 miles out. Here, you are rewarded with impressive vistas every way you look. Enjoy the view, and look forward to an even better one from the twin summits of Twin Peaks, now less than a mile away. Depart the Pacific Crest Trail at the right turnoff for the Tahoe Rim Trail; turn right and walk a short distance to the obvious use trail on the left heading up to Twin Peaks. The western summit is the closest and easiest to attain; both summits offer a classic Tahoe view, with dozens of easily recognizable peaks in sight.

Ellis Peak

- Distance: 8.2 miles round-trip
- Duration: 3–4 hours
- Effort: Strenuous
- Elevation change: 1,400 feet
- Trailhead: Barker Pass
- Directions: From Tahoe City, drive 4 miles south on Hwy. 89 to Barker Pass Rd. (Forest Service Rd. 03), just south of the Kaspian Campground and picnic area. Turn right (west) and drive 7 miles to the end of the pavement (0.3 mile before the Barker Pass/Pacific Crest Trail Trailhead). The trailhead and a dirt parking area are on the left (south) side of the road.

This short but memorably steep trip leads to

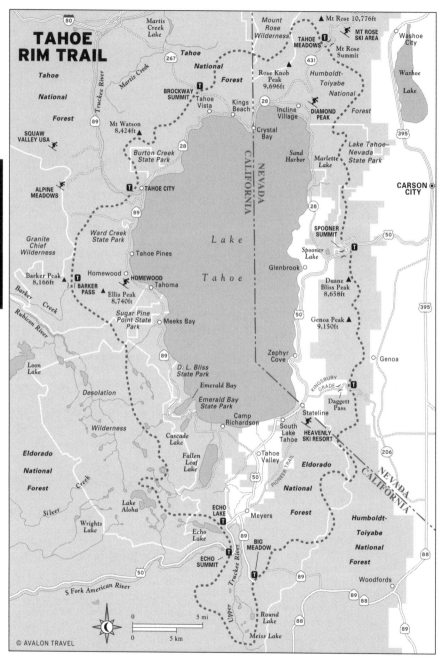

TAHOE RIM TRAIL

© AVALON TRAVEL

EXPLORING THE TAHOE RIM TRAIL

The Tahoe Rim Trail (TRT) is one of the greatest achievements in the history of trail building in California. Completed in 2001 after nearly 20 years of effort, the 165-mile trail makes a complete circuit around Lake Tahoe, ranging in elevation from 6,300 feet to 10,338 feet. Marked with light blue triangular TRT markers, the trail is accessible in most years mid-June–late October, depending on snow levels. Hiking and horseback riding are allowed on all portions of the trail, and mountain biking is permitted on much of it.

The trail is accessed by nine major trailheads. Starting at Tahoe City and going clockwise around the lake, they are: Truckee River Access/64 Acres Park in Tahoe City, Brockway Summit, Tahoe Meadows, Spooner Summit, Kingsbury Grade, Big Meadow, Echo Summit, Echo Lakes, and Barker Pass. A half dozen other trailheads also provide access to the trail. On much of the west side of the lake, the TRT and the long-distance Pacific Crest Trail, which travels from Canada to Mexico, are one and the same.

Although the vast majority of trail users hike or mountain bike on only short stretches of the Tahoe Rim Trail, it is possible to hike the entire thing, and many have accomplished that feat. Most people take about 10-20 days to hike the complete circuit. Camping is permitted on all parts of the trail except in Lake Tahoe Nevada State Park, where it is limited to two designated areas, and in the Desolation Wilderness portion of the trail, where overnight permits are required. In a few places, the trail passes right through a town (such as in Tahoe City), so it is relatively easy to restock your pack with food and supplies. At several points, the trail crosses roads or highways where you could arrange for friends or family to meet you with a food drop. The trail is subject to temporary closures due to weather conditions or trail work, so if you are planning a multiday trek, always check the website www.tahoerimtrail.org for the latest updates.

The Tahoe Rim Trail Association, which is headquartered in Incline Village, sponsors a wide variety of guided hikes and snowshoe tours along the 165-mile trail, as well as clinics on winter camping, map and GPS skills, wilderness first aid, and the like. Most events are free; check the website for a current schedule. The TRT is maintained mostly by volunteers, and the nonprofit Tahoe Rim Trail Association can always use additional volunteers and/or donations. Donors can become a member of the association for as little as $35 per person or $45 per family. For more information, go to www.tahoerimtrail.org or phone 775/298-0012.

the top of 8,740-foot Ellis Peak, where peakbaggers are rewarded with a fabulous view of Lake Tahoe, the Granite Chief and Desolation Wildernesses, and Hell Hole Reservoir. In fact, the hike is rewarding all the way, not just at the top, as the trail's wildflower displays rival its far-off views. The initial 0.7 mile of trail is the steepest part, but there is plentiful shade from big red firs along this stretch. When you reach the ridgetop, the vistas spread wide, with Lake Tahoe to the east and Hell Hole Reservoir to the west. Mule's ears and other wildflowers bloom in profusion on this sunny, windswept ridge. The trail continues climbing gently along the ridgeline for 0.5 mile, then heads abruptly downhill through a lodgepole-pine and fir forest, dropping 400 feet in elevation. At a junction with a wide dirt road, bear left to head for Ellis Peak, and prepare to face a confusing series of dirt road and trail junctions. In 0.25 mile, you'll note a left spur trail, but stay on the road until you reach a signed junction, 2.8 miles from your start. A left turn here will take you downhill to Ellis Lake in less than 0.5 mile, a worthwhile side trip. Staying straight at the junction, you'll follow a narrower trail steeply uphill and then shortly rejoin the dirt road, which continues its ascent to Ellis Peak. As you gain Knee Ridge, Ellis Peak's summit is clearly visible; a little more huffing and puffing, and you arrive at the top. The summit view extends from Pyramid Peak in the Desolation Wilderness to the eastern shores of Lake Tahoe, with a few close-up landmarks like nearby Twin Peaks adding dimension to the scene. Note that you may share this trail with mountain bikers or possibly even off-road-vehicle users.

General Creek to Lily Pond

- Distance: 6.6 miles round-trip
- Duration: 4 hours
- Effort: Moderate
- Elevation change: 400 feet
- Trailhead: Ed Z'berg Sugar Pine Point State Park
- Directions: From Tahoe City, drive 8 miles south on Hwy. 89 to the Sugar Pine Point State Park General Creek Campground entrance on the right. Park in one of the day-use lots near the entrance kiosk ($8 fee per vehicle), then follow the trail to the far end of the campground and site number 149.

Campers at Sugar Pine Point State Park who want to hike right from their tent flaps can do so on the General Creek Loop Trail (as can any noncampers who are willing to pay the state park day-use fee). The trail begins by site number 149 and forms a loop heading up one side of General Creek and back on the other. A wide and level dirt road, the loop is popular with cross-country skiers in winter. For this hike to Lily Pond, follow the north side of the General Creek Loop for 2.7 miles through a pleasant forest of white fir, incense cedar, and Jeffrey and sugar pines to its junction with a single-track trail on the right to Lily Pond. Leave the loop and follow the narrow trail uphill for 0.6 mile, through a dense and rocky forest, to small, tranquil Lily Pond, which is indeed covered with lilies. This peaceful spot is a good place to look for birds or amphibians. For your return, you can opt to take the south side

of the General Creek Loop for variety. Turn left on the bridge over General Creek to head back to the campground. Those looking for a much longer hike can continue on the main trail along General Creek for as long as they wish. The forested shore of lovely Lost Lake is a total of 6.5 miles from the campground and makes a fine destination for a long day hike. If you visit both Lily Pond and Lost Lake, you'll complete a round-trip of 14.2 miles.

Meeks Bay to Genevieve, Crag, and Stony Ridge Lakes

- Distance: 10–12.4 miles round-trip
- Duration: 5–6 hours
- Effort: Moderate
- Elevation change: 1,200–1,600 feet
- Trailhead: Meeks Bay
- Directions: From Tahoe City, drive 11 miles south on Hwy. 89 to the Meeks Bay Trailhead on the west side of the highway, across from the entrance to Meeks Bay Resort. Park in the small dirt parking lot. Day hikers must fill out a self-serve permit at the trailhead.

The Meeks Bay Trailhead offers one of the easiest entrances to the Desolation Wilderness, and the Meeks Creek Watershed contains half a dozen scenic lakes—two reasons why this trail is quite popular with day hikers and backpackers alike. The first 1.3 miles of the Meeks Creek Trail (also known as the Tahoe-Yosemite Trail) to the wilderness boundary follow an old dirt road that runs alongside Meeks Creek and is almost completely level. It's a perfect warm-up for hikers who have just driven to the trailhead and gotten out of their cars. At the Desolation boundary sign, the trail forks right off the dirt road and begins a gradual, forested climb. As you gain the ridge, the white fir and Jeffrey pine are replaced by higher-elevation red fir and western white pine. After crossing Meeks Creek on a footbridge at 3.2 miles, the trail climbs some more until the forest opens up to views of the surrounding glaciated landscape. You arrive at the pine-forested shore of shallow Lake Genevieve at 4.6 miles from the start. This small lake is worthy of a brief rest stop, then follow the trail to the left around its eastern shoreline to Crag Lake at 5 miles. As you might expect, a craggy peak looms behind it. Most day hikers make this scenic, swimmable lake their final destination, but those with extra energy can continue the ascent to lily-covered Shadow Lake at 5.3 miles or Stony Ridge Lake at 6.2 miles. The largest of the lakes in this basin, long and narrow Stony Ridge Lake, at 7,800 feet, is marked by reddish-colored granite and framed by Rubicon Peak and Jakes Peak.

Rubicon Trail

- Distance: 5.5 miles one-way
- Duration: 2.5 hours
- Effort: Moderate
- Elevation change: 500 feet
- Trailhead: D. L. Bliss
- Directions: From Tahoe City, drive 15.5 miles south on Hwy. 89 and turn left at the sign for D. L. Bliss State Park. Drive 0.5 mile to the entrance station ($8 day-use fee per vehicle), then continue for 0.7 mile to a fork. Bear right at the sign for Camps 141–168 and Beach Area, and drive 0.7 mile to the Calawee Cove Beach parking lot. The Rubicon Trail begins on the far side of the lot.

The Rubicon Trail is Tahoe's premier lakeshore hike. If you want to get the maximum dose of Lake Tahoe eye candy, with lots of postcard-perfect views of rocky inlets, sandy coves, and boats bobbing in the water, this is your trail. The hike runs 4.5 miles one-way from D. L. Bliss State Park to Vikingsholm Castle, and then an additional 1.6 miles from Vikingsholm to Eagle Point Campground at Emerald Bay State Park. Since there is no day-use parking at Eagle Point

NORTH AND WEST SHORES

© ANN MARIE BROWN

A hiker enjoys the view from the West Shore's Rubicon Trail.

Campground, most hikers just follow the stretch of trail between D. L. Bliss and Vikingsholm Castle, then hike up the Vikingsholm trail/road for 1 mile to its trailhead parking lot on Highway 89, making a total one-way hike of 5.5 miles. You'll need a shuttle car waiting to pick you up, or, in the summer months, check with the Tahoe Trolley (800/736-6365, www.laketahoetransit.com) to see if they are running bus shuttle service between the two trailheads. Of course, ambitious hikers can follow the trail out and back instead of one-way, completing a round-trip of up to 12 miles.

No matter how you do it, the path stays close to the lakeshore, although often high above it, and has a very relaxed grade. Highlights along the trail include Rubicon Point, Emerald Point, and Vikingsholm Castle, but really, the entire path is a highlight. Don't miss taking the short side trail that curves around the shoreline at Emerald Point, where the 1920s-era Emerald Bay Resort once stood, and allow some extra time so you can take the short tour of Vikingsholm Castle ($5 fee).

Not surprisingly, the trail is extremely crowded, especially in the peak season, so you might want to plan this trip for after Labor Day. The most jammed-up section occurs near the start of the trail in D. L. Bliss State Park by Rubicon Point, where the drop-offs into the lake are so steep that the trail is lined with chain-link fencing, and the path is so narrow that only one person can pass through at a time. Still, even on the busiest days, everybody is in high spirits as they enjoy this eye-popping, film-burning lakeside scenery.

◖ Rubicon and Lighthouse Loop

- Distance: 2 miles round-trip
- Duration: 1 hour
- Effort: Easy
- Elevation change: 500 feet
- Trailhead: D. L. Bliss
- Directions: From Tahoe City, drive 15.5 miles south on Hwy. 89 and turn left at the

sign for D. L. Bliss State Park. Drive 0.5 mile to the entrance station ($8 day-use fee per vehicle), then continue for 0.7 mile to a fork. Bear right at the sign for Camps 141–168 and Beach Area, and drive 0.7 mile to the Calawee Cove Beach parking lot. The Rubicon Trail begins on the far side of the lot.

This short and easy loop follows a scenic stretch of the Rubicon Trail, then visits an interesting piece of Lake Tahoe's history, the Rubicon Point Lighthouse. You can start this loop at one of two parking lots at D. L. Bliss State Park—the Calawee Cove Beach parking lot, which is the official start of the Rubicon Trail, or the lighthouse parking lot, at which the Lighthouse Trail begins. The route described here begins at Calawee Cove, but it really doesn't matter where you start.

Pick up the Rubicon Trail from the southeast end of the Calawee Cove parking lot. Scenic rewards are delivered almost immediately; from Rubicon Point, just 0.25 mile in from the parking lot, you can peer several hundred feet down into the lake's depths. The steep drop-offs from the trail to the lake are so vertical that the park has installed cables and chain-link fencing to keep hikers from inadvertently taking a tumble.

At 0.5 mile, you'll see a right spur trail to the old lighthouse. Ignore it; you'll visit the lighthouse on the return leg of your loop. Stay on Rubicon Trail for another 0.5 mile, enjoying nonstop lake views and the constant companionship of a bevy of chipmunks. At the next junction, 1 mile from your start, turn right and head for the Lighthouse Trailhead parking lot, where you walk a short distance through the lot (to your right), then pick up the Lighthouse Trail and head northeast to complete your loop. A half mile along this trail, you'll see a right spur leading down granite stair steps to the restored Rubicon Point Lighthouse. The Coast Guard built a gas-powered lighthouse on Rubicon Point in 1916, but keeping the light supplied with fuel proved too difficult. Even when lit, the lighthouse was so high above the shoreline that it just confused everybody. It was shut down in 1919 and replaced by a newer lighthouse, which still stands at Sugar Pine Point. The original Rubicon Point Lighthouse fell into ruins and wasn't much of a tourist attraction until 2001, when the short-but-stout structure was rebuilt. Pay a visit here and admire the site's spectacular lake view, then finish out the last 0.5 mile of your loop.

Balancing Rock Nature Trail

- Distance: 0.5 mile round-trip
- Duration: 30 minutes
- Effort: Easy
- Elevation change: 50 feet
- Trailhead: Balancing Rock
- Directions: From Tahoe City, drive 15.5 miles south on Hwy. 89 and turn left at the sign for D. L. Bliss State Park. Drive 0.5 mile to the entrance station ($8 day-use fee per vehicle), then continue for 0.7 mile to a fork. Bear left and drive 0.25 mile to the Balancing Rock parking lot on the left.

The Balancing Rock is a big hunk of granite that has been a curiosity at Lake Tahoe for centuries. It's a 130-ton rock that sits precariously balanced on a small rock pedestal, like a giant golf ball on an itty-bitty golf tee. Visitors to Lake Tahoe in the late 1800s took pleasure in having their photographs taken next to this geologic oddity, and today most people enjoy the same pastime. The trail's interpretive brochure explains that eventually erosion will wear away the pedestal and cause the Balancing Rock to lose its balance. But don't hold your breath, because it probably won't happen in our lifetime. In addition to Balancing Rock, the trail shows off many of the native plants and trees of the Tahoe area.

BIKING

Cyclists looking for an easy, pedal-spinning ride will want to explore the paved bike trails that travel the West and North Shores. A major hub for these trails is located at 64 Acres Park, also known as the Truckee River Access parking lot, 0.25 mile south of the Y off Highway 89. At this large parking lot, you'll find signboards that map out the various trails leading from this hub.

If you don't feel comfortable mountain biking around the North and West Shores on your own, guided trips are provided by the **Tahoe Adventure Company** (530/913-9212 or 866/830-6125, www.tahoeadventurecompany.com). All trips include a van shuttle to and from the trailheads, lunch, front-suspension bikes, and helmets. Rides are about 10–12 miles in length and are offered at various locations; the fee is $95–115 per rider.

Bike rentals are available at several locations on Tahoe's North and West Shores. The Back Country has a shop in Truckee (11400 Donner Pass Rd., 530/582-0909 or 888/625-8444, www.thebackcountry.net) and also rents bikes in the parking lot of Tahoe City Sushi, 690 N. Lake Blvd. in Tahoe City. Rentals are also available at Cycle Paths (10200 Donner Pass Rd., Truckee, 530/582-1890, www.cyclepaths.com) and Olympic Bike Shop (620 N. Lake Blvd., Tahoe City, 530/581-2500, www.olympicbikeshop.com). Farther to the east, you can rent bikes at Tahoe Bike and Ski in Kings Beach (8499 N. Lake Blvd., 530/546-7437, www.tahoebikeski.com). Typical bike rental rates are $8–12 per hour, $18–30 per half day, and $24–70 per day.

◖ Truckee River Recreation Trail

This is the most scenic trail of them all. It crosses a bridge by the trailhead, then continues alongside the Truckee River for 5.5 miles to the entrance road to Squaw Valley USA. Many bicyclists follow the trail only as far as River Ranch Lodge at Alpine Meadows Road, 4.5 miles out, where they enjoy lunch or dinner on the riverside deck, then ride back. But

© ANN MARIE BROWN

Families enjoy the Truckee River bike path in summer.

you could pedal farther by following the trail for another mile to Squaw Valley Road, crossing picturesque Midway Bridge along the way, then riding up Squaw Valley Road to meet up with its 2-mile-long paved bike path.

Another option from the same trailhead parking lot is to ride south along the **West Shore Bike Path,** which parallels Highway 89 for 9 miles to Ed Z'berg Sugar Pine Point State Park. Despite its terrific lakeshore views, the trail has one major drawback: It crosses Highway 89 dozens of times and occasionally is merely a bike lane on its shoulder, not a separate trail. Riders must exercise caution during heavy summer traffic. A third option from 64 Acres Park is to follow the **Tahoe City Lakeside Trail** around the Y (head east) and then connect to the 2.5-mile **Dollar Point Trail,** which travels from Tahoe State Recreation Area to Dollar Point. This is a great way to access some of Tahoe City's lovely shoreline without driving your car and fighting for parking. For

more information on Tahoe City's paved recreation trails, visit www.tcpud.org.

Barker Pass/ Blackwood Canyon Road

For a more challenging paved ride with an athletic hill climb, park near Kaspian Campground, 4.2 miles south of Tahoe City on Highway 89, and ride up Barker Pass/Blackwood Canyon Road. The route is smooth pavement all the way and gradually gains 1,400 feet in elevation over its 7-mile course to Barker Pass. Car traffic is generally very light. Streams, wildflowers, and aspen groves accompany you on the ascent, and when you reach the top, you have a 7-mile downhill cruise to look forward to.

Martis Peak Fire Lookout Road

The Martis Peak Fire Lookout Road, which takes off from Highway 267 just north of Brockway Summit, provides a similar solid hill workout, but on a much shorter ride—only 8

BIKING ESSENTIALS

1. A helmet. They don't call them "brain buckets" for nothing. Don't get on your bike without one. Make sure yours fits properly, and strap it on securely.

2. Food and water. Even if you aren't the least bit hungry or thirsty when you start, you will feel completely different after 30 minutes of riding. Always carry at least two water bottles on your bike, and make sure they are full of fresh, clean water. Add ice on hot days. For a ride of 2-3 hours, 100 ounces of water is not overkill, especially in the dry, high-elevation air at Lake Tahoe. Many riders prefer a bladder-style backpack hydration system, which has the extra advantage of providing room to carry a few snacks or car keys. Always bring some form of calories with you, even if it's just a couple of energy bars. If you carry extras to share, you'll be the hero or heroine when you give them to a rider in need.

3. Cycling gloves and cycling shorts. These make your trip a lot more comfortable. Cycling gloves have padded palms so the nerves in your hands are protected from extensive pressure when you lean your upper body weight on the handlebars. Cycling shorts have chamois or other padding in the saddle area.

4. Trail maps. Sometimes trails and roads are signed; sometimes they're not. Signs get knocked down or disappear with alarming frequency due to rain, wind, or souvenir hunters. Always carry a good map.

5. Bike repair kit. At the very least, if you're going to be farther than easy walking distance from your car, carry what you need to fix a flat tire. Great distances are covered quickly on a bike. This is never more apparent than when a tire goes flat 30 minutes into a ride and it takes two hours to walk back. So why walk? Carry a spare tube, a patch kit, tire levers, and a bike pump attached to your bike frame. Make sure you know how to use them. Many riders also carry a small set of metric wrenches,

Allen wrenches, and a couple of screwdrivers, or some type of all-in-one bike tool. These are good for adjusting derailleurs and the angle on your bike seat, making minor repairs, and fidgeting with brake and gear cables. If you're riding on dirt trails, carry extra chain lubricant with you or at least keep some in your car. Some riders carry a few additional tools, such as a spoke wrench for tightening loose spokes or a chain tool to fix a broken chain.

6. Extra clothing. At Lake Tahoe, weather and temperature conditions can change at any time. It may get windy or start to rain, or you can get too warm as you ride uphill in the sun and then too cold as you ride downhill in the shade. Wear layers. Bring a lightweight jacket and a rain poncho with you. Tie your extra clothes around your waist or put them in a small day pack.

7. Sunglasses and sunscreen. Because of the high elevation around Lake Tahoe, you need much more sun protection than you would at sea level. Put on a high-SPF sunscreen 30 minutes before you go outdoors, so it has time to take effect. Reapply if you are out for more than a couple hours.

8. First-aid kit. Like most of life, bicycling is a generally safe activity that in the mere bat of an eye can suddenly become unsafe. The unexpected occurs–a rock in the trail, a sudden change in road surface, a misjudgment or momentary lack of attention–and suddenly, you and your bike are sprawled on the ground. Usually you glance around nervously to see if anybody saw you, dust yourself off, and get back on your bike. But it's wise to carry a few emergency items just in case your accident is more serious: A few large and small bandages, antibiotic cream, and an elastic bandage can be valuable tools. A Swiss Army knife–one with several blades, a can opener, and scissors–can be used both for first aid and also for emergency bike repairs.

NORTH AND WEST SHORES

miles round-trip. From Highway 28 at Kings Beach, drive northwest on Highway 267 for 3.7 miles. Just beyond Brockway Summit, turn right on Martis Peak Fire Lookout Road

(Forest Service Rd. 18N02) and park in any pullout alongside the road. Route finding is easy, because you simply stay on the paved fire lookout road and ignore the numerous dirt road junctions. You climb, climb, and climb some more, and after gaining 1,500 feet in a mere 4 miles, you're at the fire lookout at elevation 8,750 feet. The view from here is one of the best on the North Shore, encompassing several distinct peaks—Lassen Peak, Castle Peak, and Round Top—and the Tahoe basin.

Old Donner Summit Road

Experienced road cyclists head for the Old Donner Summit Road, also known as Old Highway 40, for an out-and-back training ride of nearly 40 miles. The best place to start is at Donner Memorial State Park, pedaling alongside the north shore of Donner Lake for a warm-up. Then it's a strenuous climb up to Old Donner Pass (wave to the rock climbers as you spin by) and beyond to Sugar Bowl Ski Resort. The worst of the work is over now, and you'll enjoy a mostly downhill cruise along Old Highway 40 through Norden and Soda Springs to Rainbow Lodge. Most riders turn around at Cisco, then head back for a mellower climb up the west side of Donner Summit and a fast, twisting descent back to Donner Lake.

Hole in the Ground Trail

Mountain bikers have an untold wealth of trails to choose from on the North and West Shores. Fat tires are allowed, even welcomed, on an abundance of trails, including large sections of the Tahoe Rim Trail. The biggest problem for bikers is deciding which trail to ride. In the Donner Summit area, one that shouldn't be missed is the Hole in the Ground Trail, a 16.5-mile loop that begins and ends just off I-80. This incredibly popular trail was completed in 1998 to the cheers of mountain bikers everywhere. Today, more than 300 people ride it every summer weekend. The loop has a total 2,100-foot elevation gain, passes near two granite-bound swimming lakes (Sand Ridge and Lower Lola Montez), and doles out 10-plus miles of exciting single-track. To get

to the trailhead, take the Castle Peak/Boreal Ridge Road exit. Cross over to the north side of I-80 and follow the pavement to its end at a metal gate. One mile of riding on a rocky jeep road leads you to the official start of Hole in the Ground. Nine miles of single-track follow. The first stretch includes a heart-pumping climb up Andesite Ridge, with awe-inspiring views of Castle Peak and Squaw Valley. Next comes a long 2.5-mile descent on a knife-thin ridge; try to keep your eye on your front wheel and not the stunning Sierra scenery. After more ups and downs, plus two potential side trips to the lakes, the route joins Lower Lola Montez Lake Trail and cruises downhill to the Soda Springs fire station, then loops back on pavement to the starting point.

Stanford Rock Loop

Fat-tire riders seeking both a physical and technical challenge will enjoy the Stanford Rock Loop, a 14-mile ride with 2,200 feet of elevation gain that may require a good dose of bike-hiking, i.e., carrying your bike. The trailhead is at William Kent Campground on Highway 89, three miles south of Tahoe City and 0.2 mile north of Pineland Drive. The first 2.3 miles are a warm-up on paved roads as you head out to the Twin Peaks Trailhead; just follow Pineland Drive to Twin Peaks Drive to Ward Creek Boulevard. The next 3 miles are a gentle streamside ride on a smooth dirt road, which then narrows into single-track and begins to climb alongside Ward Creek. At mile 5.8, the trail moves away from Ward Creek, and the serious ascent begins. The next 1.5 miles are on the miserable side, unless you possess thighs of steel. When at last you reach a trail junction, bear left for Stanford Rock. You have one more climb and a ridgeline ramble to get there. When you do, you'll enjoy a well-earned vista of Lake Tahoe, the Desolation Wilderness, and Ward Creek Canyon. From the rock, you have 5 miles of mostly downhill cruising on wide trail to bring you back to Ward Creek Boulevard, which you then follow back to Highway 89.

General Creek Loop

If you want to get the kids interested in mountain biking, Ed Z'berg Sugar Pine Point State Park is a great place to do it. A five-mile loop on smooth dirt roads will bestow confidence in novice riders and leave them yearning for more. The General Creek Loop begins by campsite 149 in General Creek Campground. By heading straight past the first bridge, you'll ride the loop counterclockwise. The road/trail runs through a dense mixed conifer forest on the north side of General Creek and open meadows on the south side. One of the prettiest stretches is where the trail crosses over a marsh area and wooden bridge at mile 2.4; look for blooming corn lilies and wildflowers in spring. If after completing this short loop you want to keep on riding, it's simple to connect to Lake Tahoe's West Shore Bike Path (paved). Just follow the park road out to Highway 89 and pick up the trail heading north. Another place for kid-friendly mountain biking is at North Tahoe Regional Park in Tahoe Vista. Follow National Avenue uphill to where the road ends at the park. The bike trail begins at the far end of the parking lot.

Northstar-at-Tahoe Resort

Last but not least, for those who just want to coast downhill, not crank uphill, Northstar-at-Tahoe Resort (Hwy. 267 at Northstar Dr., 530/562-2268, www.northstarattahoe. com) operates a few of its chairlifts in summer (daily in July–August, Thurs.–Sun. only in early summer and fall) so that mountain bikers can be whisked to mid-mountain, then cruise downhill on two wheels. Remarkably, some even choose to ride uphill as well as down. The largest mountain-bike park in Northern California, with more than 100 miles of trails,

Northstar is usually open for biking late May–early October. A skills development area with log and ladder ties helps riders learn how to negotiate the technical stuff, and a mid-mountain "jump park" is designed for those who like to catch some air. One popular trail, Live Wire, is the resort's only irrigated trail, which means no dust clouds, even at the end of a dry summer. All-day lift tickets are $43 adults, $27 children 9–12. Afternoons are discounted ($29 adults, $15 children after 2 P.M.). Bike rentals, including a helmet and gloves, are also available for $99 per day or $79 per afternoon. If you are a beginner, try their "Rider 101 Mountain Bike Package" (starts at 1 P.M.), which includes access to the lower mountain trails via the Big Springs gondola, plus a rental bike ($80 weekdays, $139 weekends). Northstar lodging packages are also available, which allow you to stay overnight and bike free.

BOATING AND WATER SPORTS
◖ Rafting on the Truckee River

In terms of rafting opportunities, the Truckee River offers something for everyone, running the gamut from the mild to the wild. The most popular stretch, by far, is the 4.5 miles from Tahoe City to River Ranch, which can be navigated by almost any kind of boat, from inner tubes to kayaks to canoes, in midsummer. Because the river flow is controlled by the sluice gates of the dam at Fanny Bridge in Tahoe City, the ride is more like floating than rafting, but that's what makes it fun. There are sandy beaches and designated areas where you can pull up and have a picnic, and unlimited opportunities for jumping out of your boat for a swim. Portable toilets and picnic tables are available at points along the river.

This stretch of the Truckee is so tame that you don't need a guide. You can go when you want and where you want, and your dog can join you (as long as he or she likes the water). Several companies rent rafts, inner tubes, and other suitable floating devices. Drive up to the Y in Tahoe City, and you'll find them set up under big tents at the highway junction. **Truckee River Rafting/Mountain Air Sports** (55 W. Lake Blvd., 530/583-7238 or 888/584-7238) is the biggest of the lot and has the most obvious location, right at the Y. Another long-established company is the **Truckee River Raft Company** (185 Hwy. 89/River Rd., Tahoe City, 530/583-0123, www.truckeeriverraft.com), which is located about 150 yards farther north from the Y.

No matter which company you rent from, your float will end at River Ranch and a bus will pick you up and take you back to Tahoe City. Most people take two or three hours to float the 4.5 miles, but you could do it faster if you don't make any stops. Rafting rates are typically $35 adults and $30 children 12 and under. Reservations usually aren't needed unless it's a holiday weekend; most companies rent rafts 8:30 A.M.–3:30 P.M. daily in summer.

If you have your own raft or floating device, you can put in at the free **Public Raft Launching Facility,** which is located at the parking access for the Truckee River Recreation Trail in Tahoe City, otherwise known as 64 Acres Park (0.2 mile south of the Tahoe City Y). A concrete boat-launch pad is located right next to the bicycle bridge over the Truckee River. At the end of your float, you'll need to have a shuttle car waiting for you, or someone in your party will have to walk back four miles along the paved Truckee River Recreation Trail to get the car. A better choice is to plan carefully so that you arrive at River Ranch in perfect synchronization with the Tahoe Area Regional Transit (TART) bus (530/550-1212 or 800/736-6365, www.laketahoetransit.com), which makes the run from River Ranch to Tahoe City several times a day. One person in your party can ride the bus back to retrieve your car, then return to pick up the rest of the party and the raft.

Rafting is only permitted when the river flow is moderate enough to be safe, which is usually in the months of July and August. When the river is too high or fast, signs are posted to alert people to stay out of the water. And even when the river is safe to float, this adventure is not suitable for nonswimmers or very young children, as the river is deep in places and a few mini-rapids could tip your raft.

For something more adventurous, the lower Truckee River (below River Ranch) offers Class II and III rapids almost all summer long. Several tour companies offer **guided whitewater trips** on the lower Truckee. **Tahoe Whitewater Tours** (303 Alpine Meadows Rd., 530/581-2441 or 800/442-7238, www.gowhitewater.com, $68 adults and $58 children 7–12 for half-day trips) leads half-day and full-day trips mid-May–mid-September. Guided whitewater rafting trips are also available from **Tributary Whitewater Tours** (800/672-3846, www.whitewatertours.com) in Grass Valley.

Kayaking and Stand-Up Paddleboarding

As at other points along Lake Tahoe's massive shoreline, kayak tours and rentals are available in and around the North Shore in the summer months. **Kayak Tahoe** (at Patton Landing Beach in Carnelian Bay, 530/544-2011 or 530/546-7008, www.kayaktahoe.com) rents kayaks in the Carnelian Bay area, where the lakeshore is lined with fascinating boulder fields. No experience is necessary; beginners are outfitted with a sit-on-top kayak, and with only a few minutes of instruction can set out on their own. Kayaks can be rented for one or two hours ($15–25) or all day ($65–85).

Tahoe City Kayak (521 N. Lake Blvd., Tahoe City, 530/581-4336, www.tahoecitykayak.com) also offers tours, rentals, sales, and instruction. Tours are offered at eight different locations around the lake and are rated as easy, moderate, or difficult. Typical tour rates are $65–95 per person, often including a lunch. To the east at Kings Beach, **Tahoe Paddle & Oar** (North Tahoe Beach Center, 8299 N. Lake Blvd., Kings Beach, 530/581-3029, www.tahoepaddle.com, 9 A.M.–5 P.M. daily, tours $90–100 per person, rentals $20–30 per hour or $80–120 per day) rents kayaks and canoes, and provides guided kayak tours along the boulder-lined shores of Crystal Bay and Sand Harbor. In Crystal Bay, paddlers can visit the natural hot springs off Brockway Point.

In keeping with the latest trend in water sports, Tahoe Paddle & Oar also rents stand-up paddleboards of all kinds ($20 per hour, $80 all day), suitable for both paddling flat water or catching some waves. If you haven't tried it yet, stand-up paddleboarding is a sport in which the participant stands up on a large longboard and propels him- or herself with a modified canoe paddle. In the early 1960s, the sport entered the mainstream surfing culture when the local surfers of Waikiki would stand on their long-boards and paddle out with outrigger paddles to take pictures of the tourists learning to surf. Now it's the latest craze among water lovers as a new method of surfing, even in flat conditions. **Tahoe Adventure Company** (530/913-9212 or 866/830-6125, www.tahoeadventurecompany.com) also rents paddleboards right on the beach in Tahoe Vista Recreation Area. For first-timers, instruction is included.

To simply rent a kayak, not sign up for a tour, you may also try **North Tahoe Water Sports** (by the pier at Kings Beach State Recreation Area, 530/546-9253, www.northtahoewatersportsinc.com) or **Tahoe Eco-Sports** (8612 N. Lake Blvd., Tahoe Vista, 530/546-2780, www.tahoeecosports.com). In Truckee, go to **The Sports Exchange** (10095 W. River St., Truckee, 530/582-4510, www.truckeesportsexchange.com).

And if you brought your own kayak, you can put in at just about any public beach you can drive to. A popular area for beginner to intermediate kayakers to paddle is at **Rubicon Point** at D. L. Bliss State Park, one of the deepest parts of the lake at 1,200 feet. With a put-in at D. L. Bliss, you can paddle south into Emerald Bay and get a close-up look at Fannette Island. Other popular put-in spots include Meeks Bay, Hurricane Bay, or Sunnyside.

Kayakers with bigger ambitions should check out the **Lake Tahoe Water Trail** map (800/849-6589, www.adventuremaps.net), which shows available boat launches, campsites, lodging, dining, and more for all 72 miles of lake shoreline. And visit the website of the Lake Tahoe Water Trail Committee (www.laketahoewatertrail.org) for information on trip planning, Tahoe paddling events, and the local kayaking community.

Water Sports Outfitters and Marinas

Those interested in less natural but more thrill-oriented water sports should head for **North Tahoe Water Sports** (by the pier at Kings Beach State Recreation Area, 530/546-9253, www.northtahoewatersportsinc.com), where you can soar up to 1,400 feet above Lake Tahoe on a boat-driven parasail flight, rent aqua-cycles or Jet Skis, or just suffice with old-fashioned sailing or kayaking. The same company runs **Lake Tahoe Parasailing** (700 N. Lake Blvd., 530/583-7245) out of Tahoe City Marina. The parasailing contraption can hold two or three people at once, so you don't have to "fly" behind the boat alone, and with their stay-dry method, you don't have to worry about getting dunked in the icy waters of Tahoe. You are gently reeled out and back in to the deck of the parasail boat without ever getting your feet wet. Typical parasailing rates are $50–80 per person. The rate goes up the higher you choose to "fly," and the longer your flight is. A typical flight lasts about 8–15 minutes.

Another company in Kings Beach, **North Shore Parasail** (8290 N. Lake Blvd.,

530/546-7698 or 530/308-0985, www. parasailcatalina.com), offers a similar array of parasailing adventures and Jet Ski and kayak rentals. Find them behind Steamer's Restaurant. Personal watercraft can usually be rented for $65 per half hour or $100 per hour. If you want to parasail or rent personal watercraft, shop around. If business is slow on any given day, you can often get a deal by making a few phone calls.

More serious powerboats can be rented at the **North Tahoe Marina** (7360 N. Lake Blvd., Tahoe Vista, 530/546-8248 or 530/583-1039, www.northtahoemarina.com, $140–190 per hour). On the West Shore, **Action Watersports** at Meeks Bay Marina (530/525-5588, www.action-watersports.com) offers a full array of boat and water-toy rentals.

If you've always wanted to learn how to water-ski or wakeboard, Lake Tahoe is a great place to do it. The **High Sierra Water Ski School** (530/525-1214 or 530/583-7417, www. highsierrawaterskiing.com) has been teaching the sport for 25 years, and they also rent Jet Skis, Waverunners, small sailboats, powerboats, and the like. The school has two locations at two and seven miles south of Tahoe City, respectively: Sunnyside Marina (1850 W. Lake Blvd.) and Homewood Marina (5190 W. Lake Blvd.). On the North Shore, **Goldcrest Water Ski School** (8194 N. Lake Blvd., Kings Beach, 530/546-7412) also teaches waterskiing in July and August only.

If you brought your own boat or personal watercraft to Lake Tahoe and just need to find a boat ramp where you can put it in the water, you can do so on the West Shore at Homewood Marina (530/525-5966), Obexer's Marina (530/525-7962), or Sunnyside Marina (530/583-7201). On the North Shore, you can launch your craft at Kings Beach Recreation Area (530/546-7248), Lake Forest Boat Ramp (530/581-4017), North Tahoe Marina (530/546-8248), Sierra Boat Company

(530/546-2552), or Tahoe City Marina (530/583-1039).

And when it comes to water sports, don't forget that Lake Tahoe is not the only game in town. Over at Donner Lake, the marina at **Donner Lake Village Resort** (15695 Donner Pass Rd., Truckee, 530/587-6081 or 800/979-0402, www.donnerlakevillage.com) rents ski boats, fishing boats, personal watercraft, and canoes and kayaks. You can also launch your own boat here.

SWIMMING BEACHES

On the North Shore, beach lovers don't have to go far to find a strip of swimsuit-worthy sand. One of the nicest is just 1.5 miles east of town at **Lake Forest Beach Park** (Lake Forest Rd. and Hwy. 28, 530/581-4017, www.tahoecity-pud.com). The beach has picnic tables, fire pits, restrooms, barbecue grills, and a playground for the kiddies. Good news for Fido—dogs are permitted at this beach. When you and/or your four-legged friend get tired of swimming, it's great fun to laze around on the beach and watch the windsurfers and kiteboarders. **Tahoe State Recreation Area** (on the eastern edge of Tahoe City next to the Boatworks Mall) also has a nice beach, if you are lucky enough to get a parking spot ($8 parking fee). And **Commons Beach,** just a few steps from Fanny Bridge and the Tahoe City Y, was revitalized in 2004 with a grassy area; a playground for the kids, including a mini rock wall for junior rock climbers; barbecues; and a paved recreation trail. It's not a great swimming area because it's so rocky, but it's a fun beach for children. Almost every Sunday in summer, outdoor music concerts take place at the small amphitheater here.

In Tahoe Vista, the 600-foot-long sandy swimming beach at **Moon Dunes Beach** (across the highway from Rustic Cottages near Pino Grande) is a popular spot, with picnic tables and fire pits. There's no public parking lot, so you are on your own to find street parking.

© ANN MARIE BROWN

NORTH AND WEST SHORES

Kings Beach is a big beach party all summer long.

A short distance to the west lies **Tahoe Vista Recreation Area** (N. Lake Blvd. and National Ave.), another good place to take a dip.

In Kings Beach, the last town heading east on Highway 28 before California ends and Nevada begins, swimmers and beachgoers flock to the **Kings Beach State Recreation Area** (7360 W. Lake Blvd., 530/546-7248), a great place to take the kids because of the shallow, calm water. The beach has boat and Jet Ski rentals, a barbecue area, and a kids' playground ($8 parking fee). Also in Kings Beach is the **North Tahoe Beach Center,** directly across the street from the Safeway supermarket. The beach has grassy areas, a beach volleyball court, and picnic tables. **Secline Beach,** at the end of Secline Street in Kings Beach, is 50 yards off the highway and more secluded. The beach is rocky and blissfully free of development (no facilities here), but there isn't a lot of shoreline.

For those who want to bring their dog to the beach, **Carnelian Bay Beach** and neighboring **Patton Landing Beach** (on both the east and west sides of Sierra Boat Company, near Gar Woods Grill and across the street from Magic Carpet Golf) are two of the few "dog-legal" stretches of sand. (You may see dogs on other North Shore beaches, but that doesn't necessarily mean they are allowed.) A boardwalk marked with interpretive signs leads through restored wetlands to Carnelian Bay Beach. Its shoreline is rocky, but you can sun yourself on its smooth stones. Discerning eyes can search for semiprecious red and yellow carnelians. The water is shallow and inviting; retrievers will fetch darn near anything you throw into the water here.

Over on the West Shore, a few beaches make an obvious appearance along Highway 89, including **William Kent Beach** and **Kaspian Recreation Area,** both right next to the highway a few miles south of Tahoe City. If you don't want everybody driving by to see you in your bathing suit, head to **Ed Z'berg Sugar**

Pine Point State Park in Tahoma, where a lovely stretch of shoreline is found by the historic Ehrman Mansion ($8 parking fee). Adjacent to **Meeks Bay Campground,** 10 miles south of Tahoe City, is a white-sand beach with a boat launch, restrooms, and picnic facilities ($10 parking fee). Just south of Homewood is **Chambers Landing,** where a historic bar and restaurant are set within a few feet of a sandy, swimmable cove. And finally, what is arguably the West Shore's most beautiful public beach is found at Calawee Cove and Lester Beach at **D. L. Bliss State Park** (between Meeks Bay and Emerald Bay, $8 parking fee).

If you're in the Truckee area, pay a visit to **West End Beach at Donner Lake,** one of the few beaches near Tahoe that actually has a lifeguard ($4 adults, $3 children 17 and under). Or, if you prefer to have your swimming activities take place in a pool rather than a sandy cove, head over to Squaw Valley USA and ride the cable car to **High Camp Bath and Tennis Club** ($50–60 for cable-car fare and swimming pass), where a manufactured lagoon entices swimmers with its free-form shape and two islands landscaped with waterfalls and native boulders. There's also a 25-foot-diameter hot tub and, of course, a bartender mixing expensive cocktails.

FISHING

Lake Tahoe is open for fishing year-round, except for within 300 feet of its tributaries October 1–June 30. The best fishing for mackinaw trout is in spring and early summer, but they can be fished year-round. Brown and rainbow trout are also commonly caught in the lake. An excellent kokanee salmon fishery, with most action occurring around midsummer, is also on offer.

Because of the lake's massive size and depth, the best fishing is always done by boat and in the company of an experienced guide who knows the lake. Most **guide services** have a 90 percent or better catch rate; provide bait, tackle, and beverages; plus clean and bag your fish for you. Dozens of North Lake Tahoe guide services can take you out on the lake and greatly increase your chances of catching fish. Contact one of the following guides on the North or West Shores to learn more about their services: Kingfish Guide Service (5110 W. Lake Blvd., Homewood, 530/277-4851), Mickey's Big Mack Charters (at Sierra Boat Company, Carnelian Bay, 530/546-4444 or 800/877-1462, www.mickeysbigmack.com), or Chuck's Bait, Tackle, and Guide (8106 N. Lake Blvd, Kings Beach, 530/546-8425). Additionally, two guiding services operate out of Tahoe City Marina (700 N. Lake Blvd.) in the center of town: Reel Deal Sport Fishing (530/318-6272) and Captain Chris' Fishing Charter (530/583-4857).

The **Truckee River** and its environs is a world-famous fly-fishing area, but it, too, is not for the inexperienced. The river can be legally fished from the last Saturday in April to November 15, except for the section from the Tahoe City dam to 1,000 feet downstream, which is closed year-round. Streams in the area can be fished July 1–November 15, whereas lakes in the Truckee-Donner area, including Donner Lake, Boca Reservoir, Stampede Reservoir, and Prosser Creek Reservoir, can be fished year-round. Martis Creek Reservoir can also be fished year-round, but special rules apply: The lake is catch-and-release only, using artificial lures with single barbless hooks.

For expert local **fly-fishing** advice, contact one of these resources: California School of Flyfishing (Truckee, 530/470-0284), Randy Johnson's Tackle and Guide Service (Tahoma, 530/525-6575), Mountain Hardware and Sports (11320 Donner Pass Rd., Truckee, 530/587-4844), Thy Rod and Staff Fly Fishing (12611 Hillside Dr., Truckee, 530/587-7333), or Truckee River Outfitters (10200 Donner Pass Rd., Truckee, 775/853-7368).

Those who just want to stand on the shore of a scenic lake and drop in a line and some Power Bait or salmon eggs can do so at **Donner Lake,** near the boat ramp or the west end of the beach; **Boca Reservoir,** near the rocky sections of the stream inlet; and **Prosser Creek Reservoir** and **Stampede Reservoir.** The usual catch in these lakes is brown or rainbow trout and occasionally kokanee salmon. Donner Lake has big mackinaw and kokanee salmon, but you have to go out in a boat and go deep to find them. Boat rentals are available at each of these lakes for those who prefer trolling.

Stream anglers using spinners or Power Bait can set out for Coldstream Creek, a half-mile hike from Donner Memorial State Park; the section of the Little Truckee River between Boca and Stampede Reservoirs; or the main Truckee River between Tahoe City and Truckee along Highway 89.

If you need to buy a fishing license or bait or tackle supplies, head to Swigard's True Value Hardware (200 N. Lake Blvd., Tahoe City, 530/583-3738).

HORSEBACK RIDING

A handful of stables on the North Shore will let you borrow (okay, rent) Trigger or Seabiscuit for a few hours to ride across the open plains (okay, mountains and valleys). Just outside of Truckee, **Tahoe Donner Equestrian** (15275 Alder Creek Rd., Truckee, 530/587-9470, www.tahoedonner.com) provides a wide array of guided trail rides and equestrian activities, plus Friday-night barbecue rides and wagon rides. Guided trail rides are $40 per hour per person; pony rides are $25 per half hour. The barbecue ride is $60 for adults and $40 for children, and includes dinner. For the more serious rider, the equestrian center has five-day horsemanship camps in Western and English riding for children and adults.

Alpine Meadows Stables (2600 Alpine Meadows Rd., Alpine Meadows, 530/583-3905,

9 A.M.–6 P.M. daily), located 0.5 mile up Alpine Meadows Road, offers pony rides, guided trail rides, and multiday pack charters. Guided two-hour trail rides are $60 per person; one-hour rides are $35 per person.

Northstar Stables (910 Northstar Dr., Truckee, 530/562-2480, www.northstarattahoe.com) offers an array of trail rides ranging from one to three hours ($70–150) as well as breakfast and dinner rides ($80–90). Children must be 10 years or older to ride, but younger children can take part in "pony camp" ($40 per child, 1–4 P.M. Tues.–Sat. in summer only).

ROCK CLIMBING

The clean granite cracks and faces of **Donner Summit,** located off Old Highway 40 west of Truckee, are by far the most popular climbing spots on the North Shore. With about 400 different possible routes on a multitude of cliffs, the Summit has amazing variety, from easy scrambles to expert climbs. Donner doles out everything from bouldering to multipitch crack climbing. Plus, access is a snap; you can drive right up the old Donner Pass Road and find climbers scaling the rocks all around you, just a few feet from the pavement.

Coming in a close second for popularity is the **Big Chief** area, located between Squaw Valley and Truckee high above the river canyon. The rock here is volcanic, not granite, so it provides steep sport climbing over more than 100 bolted routes, none suitable for beginners. Instead, novice climbers head to **Twin Crags,** just north of Tahoe City on Highway 89. Beginners use topropes to sharpen their skills and gain some confidence on the rock. The south-facing crags are usually snow-free early in the year.

Climbers who just want to solve a few boulder problems head to Grouse Slabs at Donner Summit, Split Rock at the west end of Donner Memorial State Park (more than 25 routes possible here), or the house-size boulders near

Balancing Rock at D. L. Bliss State Park. Another good bouldering site is at the end of Old County Road, just east of Tahoe City off Highway 28.

For **climbing instruction** and/or guide service, contact **Alpine Skills International** (11400 Donner Pass Rd., Truckee, 530/582-9170, www.alpineskills.com). Their office is located upstairs at The Back Country outdoor store, but they conduct climbing classes at Donner Pass. Their one-day beginner's lesson costs $140 (June–September). Two-day beginner classes and more advanced courses are also offered, as well as a climbing clinic for women only. Or contact the **Tahoe Adventure Company** (530/913-9212 or 866/830-6125, www.tahoeadventurecompany.com), which offers a five-hour beginner's lesson for $130. Tahoe Adventure's North Shore courses are taught at Donner Summit.

If you are heading out on your own and forgot your chalk bag at home, several stores sell **rock-climbing equipment**: Alpenglow Sports (415 N. Lake Blvd., Tahoe City, 530/583-6917), The Back Country (11400 Donner Pass Rd., Truckee, 530/581-5861), and The Sports Exchange (10095 W. River St., Truckee, 530/582-4510).

And lastly, if a summer thunderstorm hits and there's no place outdoors where you can climb, you can always head to the 30-foot-high indoor climbing wall inside the cable-car building at **Squaw Valley USA** (530/386-1375 or 530/583-7673, www.squawadventure.com). A day of climbing is $15, including a harness, or $19 with a harness and climbing shoes.

GOLF

Golfers have almost as many options as skiers in the North Tahoe region, with a total of eight courses located within a 30-mile radius. For those who just want to hit a few balls without a lot of fanfare, the area has three nine-hole courses with green fees of $50 or less—the Old Brockway, Ponderosa, and Tahoe City Golf Courses.

Even nongolfers will enjoy a trip to the historic **Old Brockway Golf Course** (7900 N. Lake Blvd., Kings Beach, 530/546-9909, www.oldbrockway.com), a par 36 course with an outstanding course restaurant, the Blue Onion. Old Brockway has been rated as one of the top 10 nine-hole golf courses in Northern California by *Golf Today* magazine. Its scenic, Jeffrey pine–studded layout covers more than 3,200 yards with tight fairways, postage-stamp greens, and views of Lake Tahoe. Built in 1924 by Harry Comstock, owner of the Brockway Hotel, the course retains much of its historic character and charm. In 1934, Old Brockway was home to the first "unofficial" Bing Crosby Golf Tournament, when Bing would invite his friends to Lake Tahoe to play golf while he was entertaining at the nearby Cal-Neva Resort. The course's Blue Onion restaurant serves three meals a day during the golfing season, which is usually April–early November. Green fees are $40–50 for nine holes.

The nine-hole **Ponderosa Golf Course** (10040 Reynold Way, Truckee, 530/587-3501) is a par 35 regulation course set amid the ponderosa pines. The course was designed by Robert Balbach. The layout is fairly open and typical of a municipal course, but the greens are fast and sloping. Afternoon winds can make the greens even tougher. Green fees are $30–35 for nine holes, and no reservations are required.

Closed in 2011, but expected to reopen under new ownership in summer 2012, the **Tahoe City Golf Course** (251 N. Lake Blvd., Tahoe City, 530/583-1516, www.tahoecity-golf.com) is a par 33 course with views of Lake Tahoe and a long history on the North Shore. The course was built in 1917 by a female golf pro, May "Queenie" Dunn Hupfel, and was intended to be used by guests at the nearby Tahoe Tavern. In the 1950s, a host of celebrities played this course, including Bing Crosby, Bob Hope, Frank Sinatra, Dean Martin, Sammy Davis Jr., and Andy Williams. Tahoe City Golf Course

NORTH AND WEST SHORES

has fast and true greens that "break toward the lake," and with green fees of $40–50 for nine holes, a round of golf here won't break the bank. The course's bar and café serves a casual breakfast and lunch.

For golfing with more glitz, the North Shore's big resorts have world-class courses designed for the serious golfer. The tree-lined course at **Northstar-at-Tahoe** (168 Basque Dr. off Northstar Dr., Truckee, 530/562-3290, www.northstarattahoe.com) is a par 72, 18-hole beauty designed by Robert Muir Graves. The 6,897-yard course has water on 14 holes and gorgeous mountain and meadow views. It's a course for accurate hitters, especially on the back nine. Green fees are $80 (cart included) in summer, but substantially less mid-May–mid-June and mid-September–mid-October. The resort also boasts the earliest twilight rate hours around the lake; reduced fees start at 1 P.M. ($60). If you'd like to improve your game but don't want to pay for private instruction, free lessons are offered on Wednesday afternoons June–September; call for reservations.

Designed by the legendary Jack Nicklaus, the scenic course at **Old Greenwood** (12915 Fairway Dr., Truckee, 530/550-7010 or 800/754-3070, www.oldgreenwood.com) winds through 600 acres of stately Jeffrey pines and sagebrush, and has received an Audubon International certification for its environmental friendliness. The par 72, 7,518-yard course comes with a big price tag—18 holes of golf will cost you $140–190, cart included. Twilight rates drop to $75–100. Also in Truckee, the **Tahoe Donner Golf Course** (12850 Northwoods Blvd., Truckee, 530/587-9443, www.tahoedonner.com) offers similar beautiful scenery. Designed by Roy Williams and Bill Bell Jr., this semiprivate course has green fees of $75–150, cart included.

Over at Squaw Valley, the **Resort at Squaw Creek** (400 Squaw Creek Rd., Olympic Valley, 530/583-6300 or 800/327-3353, www.squawcreek.com) boasts an exceptionally challenging 18-hole championship course designed by Robert Trent Jones Jr. Rated as "one of the top ten courses you can play" by *Golf Magazine,* the par 72 links meander for 6,815 yards along the valley floor amid a wealth of wetlands. If you're not the world's most accurate hitter, bring a bag full of extra balls. The course has received Audubon International status as a certified co-operative wildlife sanctuary. Resort guests pay $85–115 to play (cart included); nonguests pay slightly more.

Last but certainly not least is the **Coyote Moon Championship Golf Course** (10685 Northwoods Blvd., Truckee, 530/587-0886, www.coyotemoongolf.com), which opened in 2000 and sits on 250 acres of undeveloped pine- and boulder-covered hills. The resort brags of having not a single house or structure to spoil its mountain and forest views, an exceptional rarity around Lake Tahoe. Golf great Brad Bell was the creative force behind the 7,117-yard, par 72 course, which meanders around and across Trout Creek. Green fees are $120–160 with cart ($95 twilight). The resort's restaurant serves three meals a day.

WINTER SPORTS
Downhill Skiing and Snowboarding

North Lake Tahoe is home to the largest concentration of alpine ski resorts in North America, including three giant, full-service megaresorts—Northstar-at-Tahoe, Squaw Valley, and Alpine Meadows (the latter two are now under the same ownership, so a lift ticket for one lets you ski at both)—and five smaller, more manageable ones—Homewood, Boreal, Sugar Bowl, Tahoe Donner, and Soda Springs. Add it all up, and you have a whole lot of snow-covered slopes within very few miles. Whether you choose to ski or ride, there is an abundance of choices here, from beginner-level bunny hills to near vertical runs that give envelope pushers a place to push themselves.

Bargain hunters should understand that if you choose not to, you hardly ever need to pay full price for lift tickets. You will have to do a little strategizing, though, which includes regularly scanning the resorts' websites for special deals, including discounted weekday skiing, stay-and-ski-free packages, or packages with lessons and/or rentals included. A great website to keep your eye on is **Snowbomb** (www.snowbomb.com), which offers vouchers for discounted tickets for most of the major resorts, plus discounts at local lodgings, ski shops, and restaurants. If you have a Costco store near your hometown, you can usually buy discounted lift tickets there for certain resorts, or visit www.costco.com. SaveMart and Lucky stores in California also sometimes carry discounted lift tickets.

If you need to rent ski or snowboarding equipment and you don't want to do so at the resorts (it's usually more expensive there), several shops in Tahoe City, Kings Beach, and Truckee can accommodate you. **Tahoe Dave's Skis and Boards** (800/398-8915 or 530/583-6415, www.tahoedaves.com) has a whopping five locations in the Tahoe City and Truckee area. Typical rental rates are about $28 per day for a basic alpine ski package (skis, boots, poles) and $29 per day for a snowboarding package (board and boots). If you want high-performance equipment, expect to pay more.

If you are looking to rent and/or buy, **Porter's Sports** (www.porterstahoe.com) is the place, with an online store and three North Shore locations open 9 A.M.–6 P.M. daily: Tahoe City (501 N. Lake Blvd., 530/583-2314), Truckee (11391 Deerfield Dr., 530/562-4079), and its Tahoe City outlet store (100 N. Lake Blvd., 640/583-0292). A toll-free number connects you to all three locations: 866/967-6783.

SQUAW VALLEY USA

The undisputed king of the North and West Shore resorts is Squaw Valley USA (1960 Squaw Valley Rd., Olympic Valley, 530/583-6955 or 530/452-4000, www.squaw.com, 9 A.M.–9 P.M. daily). Located 7 miles north of Tahoe City and 12 miles south of Truckee off Highway 89, Squaw's claim to fame is that it was the site of the 1960 Winter Olympics. Today it is one of the largest ski resorts in North America—and was made even larger by joining forces with Alpine Meadows at the end of 2011—and it's also one of the most expensive places to ski around Lake Tahoe. Lift tickets are $92–96 for adults 23–64, and $76–78 for seniors 65–75 and young adults 13–22. Tickets for kids 5–12 and seniors 76-plus are $49–51; kids 4 and under ski free. Half-day tickets (after 12:30 P.M.) are $68. But the high price comes with a lot of value: Now that Squaw and Alpine Meadows have joined as one, a ticket at one resort gets you access to both. Technically, that means that Squaw ticket holders have access to 6,000 acres of ski terrain, 44 lifts, and 270 trails. During ski season, shuttles run between the two resorts every 30 minutes (it's about a 10-minute ride from one resort to the other).

Night skiing at Squaw (3–9 P.M.) is a relative bargain at $39 for all ages. Skiers and riders have access to one trail: the brightly lit, 3.2-mile Mountain Run (an intermediate-level run), from High Camp to the village floor. The run is lit up by a 1000-watt, color-corrected floodlight system, designed to make easier vision on the snow. Skiers access the Mountain Run via the cable car to High Camp, where a bartender serves drinks right on the spot where you disembark. (Drinking may not help your skiing ability.)

Squaw's summit elevation is 9,050 feet at Granite Chief, and it features more than 170 possible runs spread out over 3,600 acres of terrain. Six mountain peaks are accessed by 34 lifts, including an aerial cable car and North America's only high-speed Funitel. Riders have a wide choice of places to play, with three terrain parks, two standard half-pipes, and two

SKI RESORT ROUNDUP

BEST SNOW
Kirkwood has, on average, the deepest snowpack anywhere in California, with an annual snowfall of more than 500 inches. Add in a base elevation of 7,800 feet (much higher than most other Tahoe resorts), plus 2,300 acres of terrain, and there is plenty of skiing to be done here.

BEST LAKE VIEWS
On the northeast shore, it's **Diamond Peak.** On the west shore, it's **Homewood.** On the south shore, it's **Heavenly.** At any of these three resorts, bring your camera and plan to take a lot of pictures.

BEST PLACE FOR LEARNING
Tahoe Donner Ski Area has wide-open bowls, uncrowded slopes, excellent grooming, and a friendly, courteous staff just waiting to get you hooked on skiing. The terrain is perfect for learning; trails are 40 percent beginner and 60 percent intermediate, with absolutely no black diamonds. A special award goes to **Diamond Peak** for specializing in teaching kids to ski and snowboard at a very reasonable price.

BEST RESORTS TO TAKE THE KIDS
At **Squaw Valley,** kids 4 and under ski free and kids 5–12 ski for about $40. Even better, Squaw has the new SnoVenture Activity Zone, with a kid-friendly day lodge, expanded snow-tubing course, and mini-snowmobiles for kids. **Sierra at Tahoe** gets an honorable mention for its abundance of family-friendly "extras"—great food and drink, snow-tubing hills, snow bikes, child care, and a friendly staff.

BEST FOR VARIETY
Opinions vary widely on this subject, but most will agree that **Alpine Meadows** has it all—steep chutes, cliffs, tree skiing, and wide-open bowls. **Sugar Bowl** is similarly blessed.

BEST OVERNIGHT STAY
Sugar Bowl wins for its slopeside Lodge at Sugarbowl, located at the top of the resort's one-mile-long gondola. With only 27 rooms and an excellent restaurant, this 1930s-era resort has a decidedly European feel. You can't drive your car to the inn; you and your luggage enjoy a magical gondola ride up the snow-covered slopes to access your ski-in, ski-out guest room.

BEST BARGAINS
Mount Rose and **Homewood** on midweek days, when skiers and riders can take advantage of screamin' deals.

BEST FOR NIGHT SKIING
Boreal, for having the most lighted terrain and because a daytime lift ticket allows you to ski or ride until 9 P.M. for one price (or skip the day skiing and just buy the cheaper night ticket). Second prize goes to **Squaw Valley.** Even though it has only one lighted run, it's the wonderfully long 3.2-mile Mountain Run.

BEST FOR INTERMEDIATES
A full 60 percent of **Northstar**'s runs are marked with blue squares—more than any other resort around Tahoe. Add in the new Village at Northstar's huge selection of shops and restaurants, plus an ice rink and great cross-country skiing trails, and Northstar has it all for intermediate skiers who want a well-rounded day in the snow.

BEST FOR SNOWBOARDING
Boreal is the Tahoe region's first and only all-mountain terrain park. Always a hit with legions of riders, Boreal's four terrain parks boast more than 100 features, including a superpipe. Youngsters can get their shred on at the Mini-Shred Park.

BEST ACTIVITIES FOR NONSKIERS
Heavenly wins for its gondola, which provides amazing views of Lake Tahoe, a sightseeing attraction that is tough to top. **Squaw Valley**'s aerial tram is also a winner for nonskiers who just want to enjoy the scenery, and its High Camp ice-skating rink is fun for everybody. For shopaholics, Northstar has the best selection of restaurants and shops in its Village, plus an ice-skating rink surrounded by cabana bars.

LONGEST RUN
Squaw Valley, at 3.2 miles. Second place goes to **Sugar Bowl,** at 3 miles.

superpipes. Even with all this, Squaw is not a place for skiers and riders who don't like crowds; on winter weekends, it is always the busiest resort on the North Shore. It helps if you know where to go. Beginners should head to the lifts at High Camp, with its large, open bowl and great views of Lake Tahoe. Lower on the mountain, the Papoose Learning Area is also a good place for novices to get a feel for the mountain. On the other end of the skills spectrum, the slopes of KT-22, Granite Chief, and Broken Arrow offer only expert terrain. Intermediates will do well in the Snow King, Shirley Lake, and Emigrant Peak areas, although these tend to be a bit crowded.

The reason for Squaw's success is not just the size and variety of its terrain (although that certainly helps), nor is it the fact that there is almost always abundant snow (an average 450 inches fall here per year, plus the resort has an advanced snowmaking system). It's the fact that the resort is an entire industry in and of itself, providing plenty of activities that have nothing to do with skiing. Squaw's High Camp offers mountaintop ice-skating and roller skating, snow tubing, and a summer swimming lagoon and spa. On the lower mountain, The Village at Squaw Valley includes dozens of shops and restaurants, plus a host of winter sports and other activities: snowshoeing, cross-country skiing, sleigh rides, dogsled tours, an indoor climbing wall, and so on. In 2012, Squaw opened its SnoVenture Activity Zone in cooperation with Squaw Creek Resort. Perfect for nonskiing families, SnoVenture has a kid-friendly day lodge, expanded snow-tubing course, and mini-snowmobiles for kids 6–12.Winter visitors who come to Squaw for a week's vacation could easily fill their time without ever leaving the valley.

Technologically, Squaw is often ahead of the pack; one example is its "Smart Gates" ticketing system. Skiers and riders leave their tickets in their pockets; they are scanned automatically as they pass by sensors on their way to the lifts.

ALPINE MEADOWS SKI RESORT

Just a few miles down the road from Squaw is its mellower neighbor, Alpine Meadows Ski Resort (2600 Alpine Meadows Rd., Tahoe City, 530/583-4232 or 530/581-8374, www.skialpine.com, 9 A.M.–4 P.M. daily). As of 2011, Alpine Meadows and Squaw Valley are not just neighbors; they are also business partners with the same ownership. This can only result in huge profits for both resorts. Now skiers and riders can buy one ticket and ski at both mountains in one day; shuttles run between the two resorts every 30 minutes. Ticket prices are identical at both resorts: $92–96 for adults 23–64, $76–78 for seniors 65–75 and young adults 13–22, $49–51 for kids 5–12 and seniors 76-plus; kids 4 and under ski free.

Located 6 miles north of Tahoe City and 13 miles south of Truckee off Highway 89, Alpine Meadows features 2,400 patrolled acres with more than 100 possible runs. Its summit elevation is 8,637 feet (base is 6,835). There is no shortage of snow here; the resort receives an average of 365 inches annually. Alpine Meadows' snowmaking capacity also covers a large network of runs.

Alpine Meadows has a total of 14 lifts, including one high-speed six-passenger chair and two high-speed express quads (you can get to the summit in six minutes). Except for the busiest holiday weekends, lift lines are generally not an issue. All the expected services are offered at the resort, including ski and snowboard instruction for adults and children, ski and snowboard rental and repair, guided out-of-bounds tours for skiers craving powder stashes and slopes less traveled, special clinics for those inclined toward moguls, a telemark ski camp, and plenty of on-mountain food service. Don't miss the chance to eat at least one hamburger on the large sundeck at the day lodge. Riders and tricksters will enjoy the variety in the resort's three terrain parks, including "The Shreadows," which features jumps,

spins, flat rails, down rails, half-pipes, and ta-
bletops; there is even a separate terrain park
just for kids. Expert skiers like the amount of
backcountry terrain that is accessible via the
lifts. Beginners and intermediates can sharpen
their skills on miles of scenic, groomed terrain.
With all this, it's no wonder Alpine Meadows
was rated one of America's top 25 winter resorts
by *Skiing Magazine.*

HOMEWOOD MOUNTAIN RESORT

On the West Shore, just five miles south of Tahoe
City, is the locals' favorite, Homewood Mountain
Resort (5145 W. Lake Blvd., Homewood,
530/525-2992, www.skihomewood.com,
9 A.M.–4 P.M. daily). Because of its proximity to
Lake Tahoe, Homewood is known for its unob-
structed lake views from almost every run, and for
its wind-protected location. Unlike at other Tahoe
resorts, Homewood skiers and riders are never
subject to "wind hold," when the resort closes
down the lifts due to high winds. Homewood
hasn't had such a closure in more than a decade.

Very little of the resort is visible from the
highway (only one ski run), so first-timers are
always surprised at how large Homewood is.
The resort has 1,260 acres of diverse terrain,
with 60 runs served by eight lifts, including
a high-speed chairlift that was installed in
2007 and whisks riders to the resort's north
side in just four minutes. The longest run is
two miles, with a 1,650-foot drop. Powder is
king here; Homewood sees an average snowfall of 482 inches, even though its summit elevation is only 7,880 feet. If you are training
for the X Games, two terrain parks are available. Weekend (Fri.–Sun.) and holiday ticket
prices are $59–63 adults, $45–52 half day, $39
teens 13–18 and seniors 62–69, $15 seniors 70-
plus, and $10 children 5–12. Children 4 and
under ski free. But weekdays (Mon.–Thurs.)
are amazing bargain days, when prices drop to
$33–39 for teens and adults and $25 for seniors 62–69.

Over the next 5–10 years, expect big changes
at Homewood. A planned village complex with
lodging and restaurants is in the works, with
the intention to change Homewood from a
"commuter's" ski resort to one where people stay and ski for a few days, in the style of
Squaw, Alpine Meadows, and Northstar.

NORTHSTAR-AT-TAHOE SKI RESORT

Midway between Kings Beach and Truckee
off Highway 267, Northstar-at-Tahoe Ski
Resort (Hwy. 267 and Northstar Dr., Truckee,
530/562-1010, www.northstarattahoe.com,
8:30 A.M.–4 P.M. daily) has undergone a renaissance in the last decade. A megamillion-dollar
redevelopment project, completed in 2007, re-
sulted in the construction of an impressive village complex with luxurious condominiums
and hotel-style rooms, an outdoor ice rink,
and a variety of upscale restaurants and shops.
Sound familiar? Right. It's a lot like Squaw
Valley now, only bigger and better, and with an
emphasis on the family, not the twenty-some-
thing single skier. Even very wealthy families
will feel right at home at Northstar, thanks to
the $300 million Ritz-Carlton, complete with
its own gondola connecting it to the Village.
Completed in 2010, this is Lake Tahoe's first
five-star hotel.

For skiers and riders of all abilities, fairly easy
runs still travel all the way from the top of the
mountain to the bottom, so even beginners can
ride the lifts all the way to the top. But advanced
skiers can have more fun here now since the 2007
opening of a passel of black-diamond runs on the
northwestern side of Mount Pluto and a high-
speed express quad lift on Lookout Mountain.

Northstar has 20 lifts and two gondolas serving 3,170 skiable acres. Average annual snowfall
is 350 inches. Of 97 possible runs, its longest
is the Logger's Loop, at 1.4 miles and a vertical drop of 2,280 feet. A full 60 percent of the
trails here are designed for intermediates. Seven
terrain parks, including one superpipe and

© ANN MARIE BROWN

Skiers and riders at Northstar enjoy long runs.

one half-pipe, keep the jibbers busy. In 2008, *Transworld Snowboarding* magazine ranked Northstar as third best overall snowboarding resort, and third best for parks and pipes.

And there is plenty at Northstar for non-skiers and nonriders to do, too: geocaching on snowshoes, a tubing hill, ice-skating, a bungee trampoline for kids and adults, and, of course, shopping and dining.

Lift tickets are $88–91 adults 19–64, $81–88 seniors 65 and up and teens 13–18, and $52–58 children 5–12. Half-day tickets are $5–15 less than full-day tickets for all age groups.

BOREAL MOUNTAIN RESORT

Farther to the west, Boreal Mountain Resort (19455 Boreal Ridge Rd., Soda Springs, 530/426-3666, www.borealski.com or www. rideboreal.com, 9 a.m.–4 p.m. daily and 3:30–9 p.m. for night skiing) is a well-known snowboarder's paradise. Usually the first ski resort near Lake Tahoe to open each year, Boreal

is located at the Castle Peak exit off I-80, three miles west of Donner Lake. Often Boreal starts making snow well before Thanksgiving. To encourage business throughout the ski season, ticket prices are kept relatively low: adults 19–59 are $49–56, teens 13–18 are $40–42, seniors 60–69 are $40, and seniors 70-plus and children 5–12 are $16. Kids 4 and under ski for just $5 a day. College students and active military can ski for $15 every Friday except for holiday blackout days (bring your ID).

If you really want to save money, try night skiing at Boreal, when adult, teen, and senior tickets are just $26 and kids 5–12 are $16. Boreal also offers a Parent Shared Ticket, allowing two adults to share a single pass, so parents can balance time with their toddlers.

Boreal's size is small (380 acres), and its terrain is covered by only 41 trails spanning 500 feet in elevation (7,700 feet at the summit and 7,200 feet at the base), but the resort makes the most of it by offering multiple terrain parks.

In fact, Boreal lays claim to having the first and only all-mountain terrain park in Northern California. Every run at Boreal has something dedicated just to snowboarders. For young riders, a kids' terrain park has smaller curves and rollers designed for the little shredders. Park and pipe lessons for all ability levels are offered all weekends and holidays for just $30.

Because of Boreal's location far to the west of Tahoe's lakeshore, it's the place where thousands of Sacramento and San Francisco Bay Area kids have learned to ski and/or ride. The resort brags that more than 400,000 people have taken their first run on skis or boards here. For many urban and suburban families, Boreal is an easy day trip from home, and the resort capitalizes on its location by catering to young beginners with its innovative learning center. The Nugget Chair Lift operates at a slower pace, taking the pressure off beginners who are just figuring out how to get on and off the lift. The Boreal Kids Club offers skiing lessons for kids 4–12, and snowboarding lessons for kids 8 and up. After the day's lessons are over, children are permitted to keep their equipment for the rest of the day, so they can show off what they have learned.

Boreal is also home to the **Western Ski Sport Museum,** which portrays the history of skiing from the 1850s to today. Old ski movies play in a small theater.

SUGAR BOWL

Not far from Boreal are three ski resorts located off Old Highway 40, the road that carried travelers across Donner Summit before I-80 was constructed. The most developed of the three is historic Sugar Bowl (629 Sugar Bowl Rd., Norden, 530/426-9000, www.sugarbowl.com, 9 A.M.–4 P.M. daily, $67–82 adults 23–59, $55–70 teens 13–22 and seniors 60–69, $25–30 kids 6–12 and seniors 70 and up; children 5 and under are free), considered to be the grand old dame of Tahoe resorts. Sugar Bowl can boast of having the first chairlift in operation in California, which started transporting skiers in 1936. Due in part to the secluded Lodge at Sugar Bowl, with guest rooms and a view-filled dining room located at the top of the mile-long gondola, this 1930s-era resort has a decidedly European feel. Most years, it can boast of having the most snow of any resort on the North Shore. Because of its high base elevation (6,883 feet), average snowfall a whopping 500 inches, and the resort is known for deep powder and steep chutes. Nearly 100 trails on four mountain peaks are serviced by 13 lifts, including the first gondola built in the United States and five high-speed quads. The longest run, Crowley's off Mount Lincoln, is three miles long with a 1,500-foot vertical drop. All this, and the resort is only two miles east of I-80 (Norden/Soda Springs exit), so getting here from Sacramento or the San Francisco Bay Area is a piece of cake.

If you experience a sense of déjà vu while skiing at Sugar Bowl, it might be because one of its founders was Walt Disney. Matterhorn-esque touches can be seen around the resort. Of all the Tahoe ski resorts, this one exhibits the most alpine charm. But the quaintness of the place doesn't mean it isn't right for snowboarders who just want to carve some turns. Sugar Bowl's Mount Judah features several terrain parks, including a half-pipe. And if you are thinking of bringing the kids for their first snow-sport lessons, the 7,000-square-foot Mountain Sports Learning Center has ticketing, lessons, and rentals under one roof. Child care is available for children 4–6 through the Sugar Bears program, which includes a non-intensive ski lesson.

SODA SPRINGS WINTER RESORT

Also at Donner Summit, Soda Springs Winter Resort (Old Hwy. 40/Donner Pass Rd., Norden, 530/426-3901, www.skisodasprings.com, 9 A.M.–4 P.M. Thurs.–Mon., adults $36, youths 17 and under $25) is a great beginner

© ANN MARIE BROWN

Sugar Bowl ski resort

hill, with gentle, wide-open runs. Located just one mile off I-80 at Donner Summit, the resort is easy to reach, but you'll never find big crowds here. You won't find high-priced lift tickets, either. Ticket prices include access to all lifts, snow-tubing tows, snowshoeing trails, and a sledding area. This place is all about family fun, with just as much emphasis placed on their tubing run as on skiing and riding. The resort has only four lifts—two for skiing, which access 16 runs, and two for tubing. Note that Soda Springs is usually closed on Tuesday and Wednesday, except during major holidays. And if you care about being an eco-friendly skier or rider, you'll be happy to know that Soda Springs operates on 100 percent green power.

DONNER SKI RANCH
The last of the three resorts on the old Donner Pass Road is Donner Ski Ranch (19320 Old Hwy. 40/Donner Pass Rd., Norden, 530/426-3635, www.donnerskiranch.com, 9 A.M.–4 P.M.

daily, $45 adults 18–69, $36 teens 13–17, $15 children 7–12 and seniors 70-plus, $5 children 6 and under), another historic, family-owned resort that believes staying small is a good thing. The resort has six chairlifts that service 52 runs spread out over 500 acres. The longest run is 1.5 miles with a 750-foot vertical drop. Like at nearby Soda Springs Resort, ticket prices are a real bargain. Uncrowded slopes and lots of beginner runs (25 percent) give novice skiers and riders a chance to gain confidence. Midweek, beginners can get an all-day lift ticket, equipment rentals, and a 90-minute lesson for $40. But intermediates can still have fun here; 50 percent of the trails are devoted to them.

TAHOE DONNER DOWNHILL SKI AREA
One additional low-key beginner area is located just north of Truckee. Tahoe Donner Downhill Ski Area (11603 Snowpeak Way, Truckee, 530/587-9400, www.tahoedonner.

com, 9 A.M.–4 P.M. daily, $41 adults, $21 children 7–12 and seniors 60–69, free for children 6 and under and seniors 70-plus) has gentle, wide-open bowls with almost no obstacles to intimidate novice skiers and riders. Three lifts service 14 runs on 120 skiable acres. There are no black-diamond runs here; 40 percent of the runs are for beginners, and the other 60 percent are intermediate.

GRANLIBAKKEN

Smallest of all the ski hills and the most subdued is Granlibakken (725 Granlibakken Rd., Tahoe City, 530/583-4242 or 877/552-0187, www.granlibakken.com, Fri.–Sun., daily during Christmas and New Year's holidays, $24 adults, $14 children 12 and under), a few miles south of Tahoe City. The oldest and least expensive ski "resort" at Lake Tahoe, Granlibakken was founded in 1931 as a training hill for Olympic ski jumpers. With only one run possible, skiers don't have to study the trail map before hitting the slope. Plus, if you are prone to falling, the vertical drop is only 300 feet. Learn-to-ski or learn-to-snowboard packages, including rentals, are only $50–70, so there isn't any place less expensive to take your first ski or snowboard lesson. Stay-and-ski packages are a popular option for parents who want to teach their kids how to ski or snowboard. The ski hill, ski school, and snack bar are open Friday–Sunday only, except for holiday periods, when they are open daily. So what's a *granlibakken?* It is Norwegian for "hill sheltered by fir trees."

Helicopter Skiing

Thanks to **Pacific Crest Heli-Guides** (P.O. Box 7402, Tahoe City, 530/544-3020, www.pacificcrestheliguides.com, $900 per person for a full day), you don't have to go all the way to Idaho or Montana to achieve the thrill of face shots in untracked snow. Groups of four guests are paired with guides to access over 100,000 acres of backcountry terrain consisting of gladed trees, open bowls, steep chutes, and classic couloirs. Full-day trips also include safety gear and lunch. Trips begin at 8 A.M. with an informational meeting at the Cedar House Sport Hotel in Truckee; the helicopters take off from Truckee-Tahoe Airport.

Cross-Country Skiing

Although some of the aforementioned downhill ski areas offer a smattering of Nordic ski trails as well, they don't hold a candle to a few North Shore resorts that specialize in it. For serious cross-country skiers and skate skiers, the only resorts worth considering are Royal Gorge and Tahoe Donner in the Truckee area, and Tahoe Cross-Country in Tahoe City. Northstar-at-Tahoe receives an honorable mention. All of these resorts have groomed trails for both skate skiing and traditional Nordic skiing (striding, or classic), as well as lessons, rentals, and beginner packages.

It's all about the numbers at **Royal Gorge** (9411 Hillside Dr., Soda Springs, 530/426-3871 or 800/500-3871, www.royalgorge.com, 9 A.M.–4:30 P.M. Thurs.–Mon., daily during holiday periods), which lays claim to being North America's largest cross-country ski resort. One hundred different trails (32 novice, 50 intermediate, and 18 advanced) crisscross 9,000 acres of terrain. The resort boasts 330 kilometers of wide, machine-groomed track, a snowmaking system, four surface lifts for practicing downhill technique, three trailside cafés, an overnight lodge, and eight warming huts sprinkled around the mountain. With a base elevation of 7,000 feet, the resort sees an annual snowfall that exceeds 600 inches. Additionally, because the resort is less than one mile from the Soda Springs/Norden exit off I-80, it is easily accessible.

Unfortunately, Royal Gorge has fallen into tough times financially and often the trail grooming is not as good as it should be. Since the resort's cross-country trail passes are the most expensive on the North Shore, call ahead and check to make sure the trails were groomed the night before you want to ski, and find out how many trails are open. Also, plan your trip with an eye on the calendar: Royal Gorge is closed on Tuesday and Wednesday. All-day trail passes are $29–34 adults, $20 teens 13–17, $8 kids 6–12, free for children 5 and under and seniors 75-plus. Adult half-day passes (after 12:30 P.M.) are $25–29.

A few miles farther east, **Tahoe Donner Cross Country** (15275 Alder Creek Rd., Truckee, 530/587-9484, www.tahoedonner. com, 8:30 A.M.–5 P.M., $25 adults and teens, $19 seniors 60–69, free for seniors 70-plus and kids 12 and under) has 51 trails covering 100 kilometers and 4,800 acres of terrain. The vast majority is suited to beginners and intermediates. Tahoe Donner is a very community-oriented resort; you'll see lots of local school kids training for races. If you want to learn skate skiing or traditional cross-country skiing (striding, or classic), the resort's instructors are top-notch. Private and group lessons are offered a few times daily. Five trailside warming huts give you a place to catch your breath; the Tahoe Donner Day Lodge offers terrific hot meals plus ski rentals and the like. On Wednesday nights in January and February, the resort lights up a 2.5-kilometer loop for night skiing (5–7 P.M.).

Closer to the lake, **Tahoe Cross Country** (925 Country Club Dr., Tahoe City, 530/583-5475, www.tahoexc.org, 8:30 A.M.–4:30 P.M., $23 adults, $19 youths 10–17 and seniors 60–69, free for seniors 70-plus and kids under 10, dogs $4) is located three miles north of downtown Tahoe City. You can kick-and-glide or skate on 19 groomed trails that cover 65 kilometers. Plenty of locals show up in the early morning and knock out a quick aerobic workout before they go to work. A huge draw at Tahoe Cross Country is that dogs are welcome

on a handful of trails—a rarity at cross-country ski areas. (Dogs are permitted only on weekdays 8:30 A.M.–5 P.M. and weekends and holidays 2–5 P.M.) Three trailside warming huts provide shelter or a meeting point for a midday lunch. A very cozy day lodge has games for the kids, hot food and drinks, and a warm fire. For the best bargain, show up on Tuesday (nonholiday), when trail passes are only $12.

Of the big downhill resorts that offer cross-country skiing, **Northstar-at-Tahoe** (Hwy. 267 and Northstar Dr., Truckee, 530/562-2475 or 530/562-2218, www.northstarattahoe.com, 9 A.M.–4 P.M. Mon.–Thurs., 8:30 A.M. –4 P.M. Fri.–Sun. and holidays,$26 adults and teens, $14 children 5–12 and seniors 65 and up, free for children under 5) has the most extensive trail system (38 trails covering 35 kilometers), plus equipment rentals, lessons, and warming huts. From Northstar Village, you have to ride the gondola (or take the express chairlift) to reach mid-mountain and the cross-country skiing day lodge. This means that even if you don't need to rent equipment, it will take you about 25–30 minutes from the time you park your car until you can actually start skiing. You must walk from the parking lot though the Village, board the gondola and ride uphill, and then walk the short distance to the cross-country lodge to access the ski trails.

Northstar's trail fees provide access to the machine-packed trail system (for skate skiing, cross-country skiing, and snowshoeing), plus use of the Big Springs Express Gondola and the Village Express Quad chairlift. Half-day and full-day telemarking clinics are offered. For beginners, a downer at Northstar (and if you're aerobically fit, it's not much of a downer) is that from the day lodge where you rent equipment and get your trail pass, you have to ski uphill for about a mile to reach the main trail system. Some people get pretty discouraged on that first uphill mile.

The **Resort at Squaw Creek Nordic Center**

(400 Squaw Creek Rd., Olympic Valley, 530/583-6300, ext. 6631, www.squawcreek.com, 9 A.M.–5 P.M. daily, adults $20, children $18) has 18 kilometers of groomed trails spread out over 400 acres, plus an on-site rental and repair shop. These trails are 70 percent beginner level, so it's a good place to learn how to kick and glide, but not so great if you already have some experience. All trails begin at the Squaw Creek parking lot.

Do-it-yourselfers can get their glide on at one of the state-run **Sno-Parks** in the vicinity. Sno-Parks, which are basically plowed parking lots alongside or near the highway, are marked by distinctive brown signs. Here, for the price of a $5 daily permit or $25 annual permit, you can ski on marked and unmarked trails. Sno-Park permits are sold at sporting-goods stores, businesses located near Sno-Parks, and many other locations. The Sno-Park program hotline (916/324-1222) has information on where to buy permits and where Sno-Parks are located.

At **Donner Lake Sno-Park** (by the Emigrant Trail Museum at Donner Memorial State Park, Donner Lake exit off I-80, 530/582-7892), marked ski trails lead along the shore of Donner Lake and to the Donner Party historic sites. At **Donner Summit Sno-Park** (Castle Peak exit off I-80, just past the Boreal Inn, 530/587-3558), parking is on the south side of the highway, but the skiing trails are on the north side (ski underneath the freeway on the frontage road). This is a very popular area, with many skiers heading up to Castle Peak.

On the West Shore, three miles south of Tahoe City, **Blackwood Canyon Sno-Park** (Lake Tahoe Basin Management Unit, 530/543-2600) is open for cross-country skiing and snowmobiling. Blackwood Canyon Road, which is popular for biking and driving in summer, is gated off and unplowed, so it makes a perfect spot for kicking and gliding, or striding on snowshoes. The first 2.5 miles are flat and suitable for beginners; the road/trail continues

for another 7 miles and gets more and more steep all the way to the summit of Barker Pass.

Another good area for beginning to intermediate skiers are the 15 kilometers of ski trails at **Ed Z'berg Sugar Pine Point State Park.** The park's campground remains open in winter for intrepid snow campers, and the General Creek Loop makes a perfect easy ski trail, as does the lakeshore near the Ehrman Mansion. Skiing at Sugar Pine Point is like taking part in history; the Nordic skiing and biathlon races of the 1960 Winter Olympics were held on these same trails. Skiing is free, but you do need to pay a parking fee of $8. A great source of information on the West Shore's cross-country ski trails (Sugar Pine Point, Blackwood Canyon, Paige Meadows, McKinney-Rubicon Road, and Meeks Creek, among others) is **West Shore Sports** (5395 W. Lake Blvd., Homewood, 530/525-9920, www.westshoresports.com, 8 A.M.–5 P.M. daily). They also rent cross-country skis and snowshoes for $15–25 per day.

And finally, it's not much to brag about, but it's free: **North Tahoe Regional Park** (875 National Ave., Tahoe Vista, 530/546-0605) also has 11 kilometers of groomed cross-country skiing trails. For an hour or so of exercise at no cost, this place works just fine.

Snowshoeing

Although most snowshoers prefer to set off on their own on backcountry trails, beginners and those seeking a tamer experience can head to one of Tahoe's big resorts to get some experience. At **Alpine Meadows** (2600 Alpine Meadows Rd., Tahoe City, 530/583-4232, www.skialpine.com), marked snowshoe trails begin near the lodge and meander through the forests around the base of the mountain. At **Northstar-at-Tahoe** (Hwy. 267 and Northstar Dr., Truckee, 530/562-1010, www.northstarattahoe.com), snowshoers can travel on all 60 kilometers of the cross-country ski trail system, and the resort holds frequent snowshoe clinics and races. Snowshoers can also access the 18 kilometers of cross-country trails at the **Resort at Squaw Creek** (400 Squaw Creek Rd., Olympic Valley, 530/581-6637). And at **Royal Gorge** (9411 Hillside Dr., Soda Springs, 530/426-3871, www.royalgorge.com), North America's largest cross-country ski resort, snowshoers can take their pick from 90 groomed trails that travel a total distance of 330 kilometers. At all sites, snowshoe rentals are available. Rates are typically $15–20 for a half day or $22–30 for a full day.

Some of the big ski resorts offer guided snowshoe tours. Sign up for one of the guided full-moon snowshoe tours at **Squaw Valley** (530/583-6983, www.squaw.com), held a few nights each month in winter. Cost for the cable-car ride, snowshoe rentals, and tour is $40 per person. **Northstar-at-Tahoe** offers a wide range of snowshoe tours, from easy, family-oriented afternoon tours to moonlight tours and stargazing tours complete with telescope viewing ($40–50 adults, $25 children, dogs on leash permitted on evening tours). Snowshoes can be rented for an additional charge. Evening tours are very popular, so advance reservations are required.

On the West Shore, the rangers at **Ed Z'berg Sugar Pine Point State Park** hold guided snowshoe walks on occasional winter/spring weekends and full-moon nights. Phone the park at 530/525-7982 or visit www.parks.ca.gov for a current schedule.

Sledding and Tubing

Sometimes the most fun in the snow comes from using the simplest equipment, and that's why tubing parks and sledding hills are a big hit around Lake Tahoe. Several ski resorts have gotten in on the tubing action, including

Boreal, which has its own tubing playground, Playland Tube Park (19455 Boreal Ridge Rd., Soda Springs, 530/426-3666, www.borealski.com or www.rideboreal.com, 10 A.M.–4 P.M. Sun.–Fri., 10 A.M.–8 P.M. Sat., $25 for two hours).

The **Soda Springs** ski resort (Old Hwy. 40/Donner Pass Rd., Norden, 530/426-3901, www.skisodasprings.com) has Tube Town, with tubing offered daily 10 A.M.–4 P.M. ($25 for all ages all day). If you think tubing is mere child's play, get on the Tube Express and be prepared to have your socks knocked off. Soda Springs also has the Little Dipper and Planet Kids, geared for ages 8 and under (under 42 inches tall), with a "moving carpet" to help kids get up the slope. Kids 6–12 can hop on their very own pint-size snowmobiles and try out the sport of snowmobiling on a circular track ($10 for 10 laps).

On the West Shore, **Granlibakken Resort** (625 Granlibakken Rd., Tahoe City, 530/583-4242 or 877/552-0187, www.granlibakken.com) has a saucer hill; the cost is a mere $10 per person, including saucer rental. No sleds or tubes are allowed.

Squaw Valley USA (1960 Squaw Valley Rd., Olympic Valley, 530/583-6955 or 530/583-6985, www.squaw.com) has three snow-tubing lanes, open to tubers ages four and up. Rates are $20 per hour. **Northstar-at-Tahoe** has snow-tubing lanes at mid-mountain. Rates are $23 for the first hour and $14 per hour thereafter.

The locals' favorite is the family snow play area at **North Tahoe Regional Park** (at the end of National Ave., Tahoe Vista, 530/546-0605 or 530/546-4212). For only $5 per person, families can play in the snow all day (saucers, tubes, or sleds provided; you can't bring your own equipment). The park also has a snack bar, bonfire pit, heated restrooms, and picnic area, plus panoramic lake views. Or bring your own equipment to the **Tahoe City Snow Play Area,** just a few hundred feet south of the Tahoe City Y, and the sledding is free.

Snowmobiling

Because of the proximity of miles of Tahoe National Forest lands, snowmobiling opportunities abound on the North and West Shores.

© ANN MARIE BROWN

Snowmobiling is a popular winter activity on the North Shore.

For those who have their own machines, two popular snowmobile trailheads are at Brockway Summit on Highway 267 (3 miles north of Kings Beach) and Little Truckee Summit on Highway 89 (16 miles north of the I-80/Hwy. 89 junction in Truckee). Contact the Forest Service (530/994-3401) for more information. On the West Shore, three miles south of Tahoe City, **Blackwood Canyon Sno-Park** (530/543-2600) is also open for snowmobiling.

Beginners and others who would like to take a snowmobile tour have several options. **Lake Tahoe Snowmobile Tours** (530/546-4280, www.laketahoesnowmobilingtours.com, $140–310 for one person on a single-rider machine, $170–380 for two on a double-rider machine) operates from their base camp one mile south of Northstar-at-Tahoe off Highway 267. They offer a 90-minute lake-view tour and a two-hour summit tour several times daily, plus private tours by special arrangement. Helmets are

included; snowsuits, gloves, and boots can be rented for $10 (a really good idea). Advance reservations are recommended.

Several other companies offer similar snowmobile tours on the North Shore. Typical rates for a two-hour tour are $140 for a single rider or $170 for two riders on a double machine. **Eagle Ridge Snowmobile Outfitters** (530/546-8667, www.tahoesnowmobiling.com) operates on Tahoe National Forest land 14 miles north of Truckee. The company has 200 miles of groomed trails for beginners, and cross-country riding on untracked powder for more advanced riders. Tours of various lengths are available, from two hours to two days. Moonlight rides are also offered. **Coldstream Adventures** (530/582-9090, www.coldstreamadventures. com) also provides snowmobile tours in Tahoe National Forest. Those who don't want to sign up for an organized tour but would still like to experience the cheap thrill of revving up a snowmobile can head for North Tahoe Regional Park in Tahoe Vista (at the end of National Ave.), where **North Tahoe Winter Adventures** (530/546-0605) will rent you a machine to drive around their groomed track ($70 for one hour, $40 for 30 minutes).

Ice-Skating

For the graceful, several skating rinks operate around the North Shore. In the Squaw Valley area, the outdoor **Olympic Ice Pavilion** (1960 Squaw Valley Rd., Olympic Valley, 530/581-7246 or 530/583-6985, www.squaw.com, 11 A.M.–4 P.M. daily Nov.–Apr., 11 A.M.–8 P.M. during winter holidays) offers winter skating at its Olympic-size rink (100 by 200 feet), but you must pay to ride the cable car to High Camp to skate there. Cable-car rates are $22–29 for adults and $10–15 for children 12 and under. Add to that the skating fee: adults $12 per hour and children $6 per hour, including rentals. The rink used to be open for ice-skating year-round, but it was too difficult to maintain the

© ANN MARIE BROWN

Ice-skating at Northstar Village is a fun activity for families who don't want to ski.

ice in summer. Now it is converted to a roller-skating rink in the warmer months.

Down in the valley below, the **Resort at Squaw Creek** (400 Squaw Creek Rd., Squaw Valley, 530/583-6300, www.squawcreek.com, 10 A.M.–10 P.M. daily Nov.–Apr., $15 adults, $12 children 5–15, $8 kids under 5, including skate rental) has its own ice-skating rink, but it is sized more for beginning skaters and children. Mom and Dad can watch the action from a large sunny deck by the rink.

Northstar-at-Tahoe (Hwy. 267 and Northstar Dr., Truckee, 530/562-3689, www.northstarattahoe.com, noon–8 P.M. Sun.–Thurs., until 9 P.M. Fri.–Sat., skate rentals $10) has a 9,000-square-foot ice rink at the center of the Village at Northstar, complete with live music on weekends, cabana bars, outdoor fire pits, and a s'mores kiosk. Skating is free, but all skaters must sign a waiver. If you don't know how to skate, lessons are available.

If you'd rather skate with the North Shore locals, head to the **Truckee River Regional Park** ice-skating rink (10500 Brockway Rd., 530/582-7720 or 530/587-6172, www.tdrpd.com, Wed.–Sun. late Nov.–mid-March, hours vary each day so call ahead, adults $6, children $3, skate rentals $2). Located 0.5 mile south of downtown Truckee off Highway 267, the ice rink features public skating, skate rentals, a snack bar, and group and private lessons for all age groups taught by experienced instructors. The outdoor rink is set amid tall pines, and there's usually a bonfire burning (bring your marshmallows), overhead lights in the evening, and music to skate by.

◖ Sleigh Rides and Dogsleds

There's nothing like dashing through the snow in a horse-drawn open sleigh to make you feel like winter is the greatest season of them all. Snuggle up with your sweetie under a warm woolen blanket while Trigger and his friends, or Rover and her friends, trot through the white stuff. Watching the animals at work is as much fun as enjoying the scenery; the horses and dogs seem to enjoy the trip as much as their human passengers. Depending on snow conditions, horse-drawn sleigh rides are often available at the **Resort at Squaw Creek** (530/583-6300 or 800/327-3353, www.squawcreek.com, $50 adults, $25 kids 2–10). If you have your heart set on this activity, call ahead to make sure the horses are available and the snow is deep enough.

If you'd rather have your sleigh pulled by a group of 8–10 strong and friendly Alaskan huskies, contact **Wilderness Adventures** (530/550-8133, www.tahoedogsledtours.com, $110–125 per person weighing more than 60 pounds, $55–75 for children weighing less than 60 pounds). The panting dogs travel at an average speed of about 13–14 miles per hour, so this is a great way to see the countryside. Dogsleds can accommodate two adults and two children, with a maximum weight of 500 pounds per sled. If you have more people in your party, the company can run two or more sleds simultaneously. One-hour tours are offered daily at the Resort at Squaw Creek, weather permitting. Reservations are required.

Entertainment and Shopping

NIGHTLIFE

Since the North and West Shores are on the California side of the lake, gambling casinos are nonexistent in this area. But there's still some nightlife to be found. In Truckee, live music happens almost every night at the ultrahip **Moody's Bistro** (10007 Bridge St., 530/587-8688, www.moodysbistro.com). Even ex-Beatle Paul McCartney has shown up here and sung a few bars. Live music, lots of beer, and a dance floor are found a block away at the **Bar of America** (10042 Donner Pass Rd., 530/587-3110). More sedate nightlife happens at Truckee's **Cottonwood Restaurant** (10142 Rue Hilltop at Brockway Rd., 530/587-5711, www.cottonwoodrestaurant.com). Live acoustic music is usually featured on weekend nights.

At Squaw Valley, the après-ski action is at **Bar One** (530/583-6985), upstairs in the Olympic House next to the Sundeck Tavern, with live music on Saturday afternoons and evenings. The bar has pool tables and multiple TVs showing ski and snowboard movies or sporting events.

Among the fairly sedate towns that line the North Shore, your best bet for nighttime action is probably found at **Lakeside** (850 N. Lake Blvd., Tahoe City, 530/583-2000, www.lakesidetahoecity.com, 11 A.M.–2 A.M. daily), where there are pool and foosball tables, live music and a dance floor, 14 beers on tap, and 17 blaring high-definition TVs for sports fans. It's located behind the Safeway store, on the lake side. Or head to Kings Beach and **Caliente!** (8791 N. Lake Blvd., Kings Beach, 530/546-1000, www.calientetahoe.com, 4 P.M.–2 A.M. daily), where the young and beautiful can be found drinking cocktails on the roof deck in summer. With 100-plus varieties of tequila on the menu, plus drinks with names like Calientini and Chupacabra, you can't go wrong here.

And if your idea of nightlife is snuggling up with your sweetie and a bag of popcorn at the **movie theater,** there are two within a few miles of each other on the North Shore: Brockway Twin Theatre (8707 N. Lake Blvd., Kings Beach, 530/546-5951) and Cobblestone Cinema (475 N. Lake Blvd., Tahoe City, 530/546-5951). If nothing is playing that interests you, check out the offerings at the associated Incline Village Theater (901 Tahoe Blvd., Incline Village, 530/546-5951).

NORTH AND WEST SHORES

NORTH AND WEST SHORES

SHOPPING

A few good shopping options are found in Tahoe City. The **Boatworks Mall** (760 N. Lake Blvd., www.boatworksmall.com) has a dozen specialty shops, including a yoga and massage studio, a hair studio, a half-dozen clothing and home accessory boutiques, plus a great restaurant, Jake's on the Lake. **Cobblestone Center** (475 N. Lake Blvd., www.cobblestonetahoe.com), a Bavarian-style shopping village in the center of town, has a variety of unique retail shops situated below its quaint clock tower, including Bluestone Jewelry, Tahoe Rug Studio, Kalifornia Jean Bar (women's apparel), and the Bookshelf bookstore. Cap off a day of shopping with dinner in one of the local restaurants, a glass of wine at the wine bar Uncorked, or by watching a movie at the Cobblestone Cinema (530/546-5951).

Over at Squaw Valley, dozens of shops and restaurants are found at **The Village at Squaw Valley** (530/584-6266, www.thevillageatsquaw.com). All the things you don't need but you really want can be found here, at shops like First Street Leather (fur and leather outerwear), Granite Chief (skis and accessories), Sierra Shades (sunglasses), Tails by the Lake (a pet boutique), and Mind Play (games and toys). There's also a full-service day spa, Trilogy, where you can get a massage or have your nails done. If you are feeling a bit worn down from all the shopping, an espresso at Starbucks or a milk shake from Ben & Jerry's will perk you right up.

You can also shop till you drop at the **Village at Northstar** (866/369-0215, www.northstarattahoe.com). Buy outdoor gear at Helly Hansen, Oakley, The North Face, True North, or Butterbox, or indoor fashion at boutiques like Shoe, Gloss, and Spirits in Stone. Make your own candles at the Villager Candle Shop. Create your own jewelry at Farrah Ralé Bead Design Studio. Take a yoga or tai chi class, or get a massage at Balance Holistic Health. Shop for handmade soap and bubble bath at Lather and Fizz, or

kids' games at Ambassador Toys. If you haven't been to Northstar since the Village was completed in 2007, this place will boggle your mind.

Shopping in **Truckee's Commercial Row** (530/587-2757, www.historictruckee.com) is fun even for those who don't like to shop. The historic Victorian-era buildings on Truckee's main street are fascinating to look at, and the row is lined with restaurants, bars, and art galleries as well as upscale boutiques. For the hard-core shopper looking for serious bargains, there's the **Tahoe Truckee Factory Outlet Stores** (12047 Donner Pass Rd., Truckee) near the I-80 Donner Lake exit.

FESTIVALS AND EVENTS

Summer is festival season around Lake Tahoe, with special events happening almost every weekend, especially at the big resorts like Northstar and Squaw Valley. Boat lovers won't want to miss won't want to miss **Wooden Boat Week** (530/581-4700, www.laketahoeconcours.com, free) and associated **Concours d'Elegance** in Carnelian Bay, usually held in June at the Tahoe Yacht Club and Sierra Boat Company. This boat show features the largest gathering of antique wooden boats in North America.

Squaw Valley and its shopping village (www.thevillageatsquaw.com) find a litany of excuses to hold summer events each year. The Celtic Solstice Celebration takes place in June, followed by a big Fourth of July celebration, followed by the late-July Squaw Valley Art, Wine, and Music Festival. Somewhere in the middle of summer they usually throw in a kite festival and a blues festival, too.

While summer festivals at Lake Tahoe tend to be about art, music, and culture, the 10-day winter **Snow Festival** (530/583-7167, www.tahoesnowfestival.com, free) is all about making merry. North Tahoe's Snow Festival, usually held in early March, includes a lot of silliness, like grown-ups racing on tricycles, a "polar bear" swimming race in Lake Tahoe,

TAHOE IN THE MOVIES

Since the 1920s, more than 50 movies have been filmed along the shores of Lake Tahoe. The mountain scenery, glitzy casinos, and cobalt waters of the lake just seem to lend themselves to the Hollywood imagination.

Probably the most famous of the films shot on location at Tahoe were the early-1970s *Godfather* and *Godfather II*, the saga of the immigrant Corleone family's life in crime. While the first film was shot partly in Stateline and Crystal Bay, the West Shore was used as the location for the second *Godfather*, in particular the timber-and-stone lakeside estate known as **Fleur du Lac** near Tahoe Pines, which once belonged to the cement magnate Henry Kaiser. The first film won an Academy Award for Best Picture (1973). Director Francis Ford Coppola as well as actors Marlon Brando and James Caan also won Oscars. The second *Godfather* again won Best Picture (1975), and Coppola again won Best Director. Robert DeNiro was awarded an Oscar for Best Supporting Actor. Many fans insist that Al Pacino was the real star of the film, however. He was nominated for an award but didn't win.

Another Academy Award winner filmed near Lake Tahoe was the 1990 thriller *Misery,* in which Kathy Bates won Best Actress for her role as a psychotic fan who rescues a romance novelist (James Caan again) from a car crash in a freezing blizzard. The movie was filmed near Donner Pass, a place where there is usually a reliable supply of freezing blizzards. However, it didn't snow when the movie crew was there, so they had to make snow to film the scene.

Some movies go down in history as classics, but many more don't, and that is certainly the case for a slew of other filmed-at-Tahoe movies, like the forgettable Chuck Norris film *Good Guys Wear Black* (1978), which was filmed on the South Shore at Squaw Valley; or the hysterically campy (but not intentionally so) *Showgirls* (1995), filmed at Horizon Casino. Sometimes it's the actors who wish they could forget the film, and that is probably the case for Kevin Costner in *The Bodyguard* (1992), a sappy love story that also starred Whitney Houston. Parts of the movie were filmed at Fallen Leaf Lake.

and people trying to keep their heads warm by wearing funny hats.

FAMILY FUN

Squaw Valley USA may be the exclusive domain of skiers and riders in winter, but in the summer months, it becomes Familyville. The resort offers a multitude of activities that appeal to kids, from ice-skating and swimming at High Camp Bath and Tennis Club to climbing walls and a ropes course at the **Squaw Valley Adventure Center** (530/386-1044, www. squawadventure.com). A 30-foot wall indoors and a 45-footer outdoors attract kids of all ages (including adults). This is basically rock climbing in an artificial, gym-type environment, with the climbers on belay. An all-day pass is $15 per person. The ropes course consists of a mammoth-size jungle gym that is built on and around 50-foot-high towers. A session on the course is $48 for kids 7–15 or $52 adults. As if that isn't enough to give Mom a heart attack, there's the Skyjump Bungee Trampoline, where kids can do somersaults and flips while hanging tethered in midair. The cost is $12 for a five-minute session.

The **Village at Northstar** (866/369-0215, www.northstarattahoe.com) is giving Squaw a run for its money in terms of attracting visiting families, especially in the summer months. In addition to its mountain-bike park, which appeals more to older kids and adults, the resort offers free scenic chairlift rides for sightseeing and hiking, roller skating in summer and ice-skating in winter, and a bungee trampoline for kids. Adults will also enjoy the two dozen boutique shops and multiple dining options.

For an activity that measures zero on the adrenaline level, you can always take the kids to play a round of miniature golf (in summer only, of course). On the North Shore, two putt-putt golf courses are open Easter–Thanksgiving, weather permitting: **Kings Beach Miniature Golf** (8693 N. Lake Blvd., Kings Beach, 530/546-3196) and **Magic Carpet Golf** (5167 N. Lake Blvd., Carnelian Bay, 530/546-4279). Magic Carpet has several different courses, including one with a Tahoe theme: waterfall, bears, etc. There's also a video arcade where kids can play all the latest games. Rates average $7–10 per person for a round of minigolf.

If you are looking for a place to take the kids to get their ya-yas out without having to visit the local automated teller machine, try **Commons Beach** (at Fanny Bridge and the Tahoe City Y) in Tahoe City, where a playground area includes a mini-boulder for junior "rock climbers" ages six and older, plus swings and other playground equipment for kids of all ages.

For something more educational, young children are sure to enjoy the **Kid Zone Museum** (11711 Donner Pass Rd., Truckee, 530/587-5437, www.kidzonemuseum.org, 10 A.M.–5 P.M. Tues.–Sun., call to check on reduced winter hours, children under 18 $7, adults $5), which has hands-on educational exhibits designed for the little ones, plus an art center and computer corner. Or head over to Sierra Nevada College in Incline Village and visit their **Tahoe Environmental Research Center** (291 Country Club Dr., Incline Village, 775/881-7566, www.terc.ucdavis.edu, 1–5 P.M. Tues.–Fri., occasionally open on Sat., free).

In winter, don't forget to spend a few hours on one of the local sledding or tubing hills with the kids, or take them on a horse-drawn carriage ride or a dogsled ride. And for a summertime family-bonding activity, be sure to rent a raft in Tahoe City and float lazily down the Truckee River, or take the whole family on a bike ride on the paved Truckee River Recreation Trail.

Accommodations

TAHOE CITY
Bed-and-Breakfasts

One of the most unusual B&Bs in North Tahoe is the four-room **Chaney House** (4725 W. Lake Blvd., Tahoe City, 530/525-7333, www.chaney-house.com, $180–275), which was built in the 1920s by an Italian stonemason. The lakefront home of Gary and Lori Chaney, this mini-castle has 18-inch-thick stone walls, gothic arches, and many other old-world touches. If you want maximum privacy, reserve the Honeymoon Hideaway, the only room that is completely separate from the main house.

Condominium-Style Resorts

If you want to pretend you own a condo on the lakeshore in Tahoe City, book a stay at the **Tahoe Marina Lodge** (270 N. Lake Blvd., Tahoe City, 530/583-2365 or 800/748-5650, www.tahoeml.com, $208–315). Located within a stone's throw of the Tahoe City Y, the complex has one- and two-bedroom condominiums for rent, with a six-person maximum in the largest units. Everything in Tahoe City is within walking distance, and the complex has its own tennis courts, heated pool, and sandy Tahoe beach. The units are completely furnished with everything you would need for a multiple-night stay, so all you need to bring are your clothes. The largest lakefront units are the most expensive (up to $500 per night), but for many, the view and the extra space are worth it.

Motels and Lodges

The 19 river-view rooms at the 🄲 **River Ranch Lodge** (Alpine Meadows Rd. at Hwy. 89, Tahoe City, 530/583-4264 or 866/991-9912, www.riverranchlodge.com, $125–189) are hard to come by but worth every penny. Located just three miles outside Tahoe City and on the road to Alpine Meadows ski area, the River Ranch Lodge exudes an "old Tahoe" feel that you won't find at any in-town lodgings. Most rooms have one king bed furnished with a down comforter or quilt. Some rooms have private balconies that overlook the river. Be sure to eat a few meals at the lodge's restaurant, and in summer, get a table outside on the river-view deck. Rates are generous and include a continental breakfast each morning. An additional bonus: Well-behaved dogs are allowed in some rooms in the summer months, but only if you make prior arrangements.

The **Pepper Tree Inn** (645 N. Lake Blvd., Tahoe City, 530/583-3711 or 800/624-8590, www.peppertreetahoe.com, $89–212) has one big advantage over all the other downtown motels in Tahoe City: It's seven stories high. So even though it's across the busy highway from the lake, rooms on the third story and higher have wonderful lake views. The motel was completely renovated in 2003, so you won't find any 1950s decor here. Each room comes with a king or two queen beds and has a microwave, small refrigerator, television, and coffeemaker with a bean grinder. You don't have to drink your freshly ground coffee out of Styrofoam cups, either; each guest is provided with a ceramic mug. If you can afford it, book one of the tower suites, which have whirlpool tubs for two.

If you book a stay at **Tamarack Lodge** (2311 N. Lake Blvd., Tahoe City, 530/583-3350 or 888/824-6323, www.tamarackattahoe.com, $85–170), make sure you ask for a room away from busy North Lake Boulevard. This wonderful old-style lodge is located about a mile east of Tahoe City, freeing it from the bustle of downtown, but it's also a bit close to the highway, so room selection is key. Most rooms are lined with knotty pine and have queen beds; some rooms have two queen beds and/or kitchens. Four cabins are also available. Except for holidays, rates for two people are often under $100, which is why legions of Tahoe travelers return to this place year after year.

The 23 rooms at the **Lake of the Sky Motor Inn** (955 N. Lake Blvd., Tahoe City, 530/583-3305, www.lakeoftheskyinn.com, $89–150) have either a forest view or a parking-lot view, so make sure you ask for the best view you can afford. This single-story motel is nothing extraordinary, but the rates are very reasonable, and the rooms have vaulted, open-beam ceilings and decent furnishings. Rooms have one king bed or two queen beds. A complimentary continental breakfast is available, and in summer, you can swim in the outdoor pool.

The two-story **Tahoe City Inn** (790 N. Lake Blvd., Tahoe City, 530/581-3333 or 800/800-8246, www.tahoecityinn.com, $59–199) offers a choice of room types: deluxe spa rooms with one king bed or two double beds, family suites that will sleep up to six people in two separate bedrooms, and standard rooms, which are, well, standard. Romantics will like the heart-shaped spa in the king-bed rooms. Room rates vary widely depending on the season and day of the week, so phone ahead and work the best angle you can. Fido and Fifi will be pleased to know that they are welcome here.

Campgrounds and RV Parks

Tahoe State Recreation Area (530/583-3074, www.parks.ca.gov, $35) is set in the middle of Tahoe City and has 34 sites for tents or RVs up to 24 feet long and all the critical campground amenities: water, flush toilets, and showers. But what really matters is its beachside location, just a few steps from Tahoe's blue waters. And a bonus: If you get tired of grilling your own hamburgers, you can take a short walk and eat at McDonald's. The campground also has its own fishing and boating pier. Given their lakeside location, these sites are coveted, so reserve way in advance at 800/444-7275 or www.reserveamerica.com. Weather permitting, the camp is open from the last week in May until the end of September.

Just down the road, the Tahoe City Public Utility District runs **Lake Forest Campground** (Hwy. 28 and Lake Forest Rd., 530/583-3796, www.tahoecitypud.com, $20), which enjoys a peaceful location 1.5 miles east of town and has 20 tent or RV sites, a boat ramp, and public fishing access. No reservations are accepted; it's first come, first served.

Between two and four miles south of Tahoe City are two Forest Service–run campgrounds,

William Kent and **Kaspian.** William Kent is an 86-site camp that can accommodate tents or RVs up to 40 feet long ($27–29). Kaspian is a tiny 9-site camp that is better suited for tents; the sites are walk-in, meaning you can't park your car right next to your site ($19–21). Unfortunately, both camps are right next to Highway 89, but that also gives campers easy lake access (right across the road). Reserve in advance at 877/444-6777 or www.recreation.gov; open approximately mid-May–mid-October.

TAHOE VISTA AND KINGS BEACH
Bed-and-Breakfasts
If you must have lakefront lodging, stay at the **Shore House** (7170 N. Lake Blvd., Tahoe

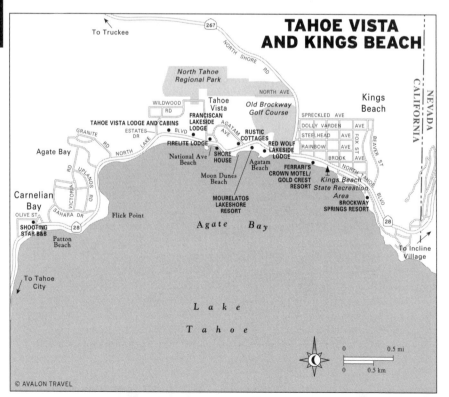

Vista, 800/207-5160, www.shorehouselaketahoe.com, $140–325), which, unlike a traditional bed-and-breakfast, has guest rooms with private outdoor entrances, more in the style of a motel or lodge. Most of the inn's nine rooms have fabulous lake views, decks or balconies, gas fireplaces, private bathrooms, and feather beds. The decor is mountain style, which means walls covered in knotty pine and handmade log furniture. The exterior gardens and hot-tub area adjoin a sandy beach and pier on Carnelian Bay. This B&B is famous for its gourmet breakfasts cooked by the innkeeper, an award-winning chef. In summer, the food is served alfresco on the lawn next to the lakeshore.

There are only a handful of bed-and-breakfasts in the North Shore area, but **Shooting Star** (315 Olive St., Carnelian Bay, 888/985-7827 or 530/546-8903, www.shootingstarbandb.com, $199–399) takes up the slack in fine style. From the front door of this contemporary home, you can stroll to the lake or drive a few short miles for skiing or snowboarding. Three rooms are available for rent, one with a king bed and two with queens. Everything is done with an emphasis on quality: down comforters, lavish bathrooms, and a gourmet breakfast. Many people who stay here come back again.

Condominium-Style Resorts

If you want to stay in a condo that is as appealing in summer as it is in winter, **Brockway Springs Resort** (9200 Brockway Springs Dr., Kings Beach, 530/546-4201, www.brockwaysprings.com, $239–299 for a one-bedroom unit) has the ideal all-season location. It's right on the lake in Kings Beach, and the resort owns a full half mile of shoreline. The year-round swimming pool is heated by natural hot springs and is set just a few feet from the lake. Brockway Springs has tons of amenities: tennis courts, saunas, clubhouse, boat dock, and more. The condos and town houses come in

configurations from one to four bedrooms, so you can bring your aunts and uncles. All units are completely furnished with everything you'd expect: fully equipped kitchens, televisions, patio furniture, and barbecues. Most units have fireplaces. Brockway Springs brags of having the best lakefront rates on the North Shore, and it may be true. The price goes down if you stay for more than two nights.

The same company that runs the attractive Red Wolf Lodge at Squaw Valley also manages **Red Wolf Lakeside Lodge** (7630 N. Lake Blvd., Tahoe Vista, 877/681-4171, www.redwolflakesidelodge.com, $139–329 for two people). The lodgelike condominiums come in studio and one- and two-bedroom configurations, each with a private patio or balcony, Jacuzzi tub, fireplace, and fully equipped kitchen. The front desk has kayaks, sleds, snowshoes, and the like available for loan at no extra charge. Perhaps best of all, because Red Wolf is located on the lake side of the highway, the condos offer great sunset views over the water.

Cabins

When the owners of a cabin resort are thoughtful enough to set out cookies and iced tea for their guests in the evening, you can bet it's a nice place. **Rustic Cottages** (7449 N. Lake Blvd., Tahoe Vista, 530/546-3523 or 888/778-7842, www.rusticcottages.com, $74–189 for two people) is a delightful place, with adorable cottages that were built in 1925 as the labor camp for the Brockway Lumber Company. Each of the freestanding cottages is different; some have kitchens or fireplaces, or both. The place is popular for family reunions and small groups, but it's equally nice for couples. A continental breakfast is provided each morning, and guests can borrow sleds and snowshoes in the winter. Cottages sleep 2–6 people; the larger units are priced at $200–400 per night. Dogs are permitted in some cottages for an extra fee of $20 per night.

The same nice folks run **Tahoe Vista Lodge and Cabins** about a mile away (6631 N. Lake Blvd., Tahoe Vista, 530/546-3523 or 888/778-7842, www.rusticcottages.com, $89–109 for two people), which was known as the Burrough's Resort when it was first opened in the 1940s. The current owners saved the resort from demolition in 2002 and completely restored it to its original grandeur. In addition to cabins, Tahoe Vista also has rooms in a main lodge, suites, and duplexes, plus an outdoor swimming pool and beach access (across the highway). A family of five can often find accommodations here for about $180. Dogs are permitted in some cottages for an extra fee of $20 per night.

For lakefront accommodations, book a cottage at the **Franciscan Lakeside Lodge** (6944 N. Lake Blvd., Tahoe Vista, 530/546-6300 or 800/564-6754, www.franciscanlodge.com, $85–185 for two people). Perched a few feet from the lapping waters of Lake Tahoe, this cute red-roofed cottage resort has everything you want for a summer vacation: sun, sand, and water. One rule is strictly enforced: Don't feed the Canada geese that flock to the beach (or they might follow you back home to Poughkeepsie). The lodge has a private sandy beach and pier on the lake, and a heated swimming pool. Note that some units are across the highway from the lake (they are priced lower), so be sure to request what you want. A few units are large enough to sleep eight people ($250–350).

Motels and Lodges

Located across the highway from the lake, the **Firelite Lodge** (7035 N. Lake Blvd., Tahoe Vista, 530/546-7222 or 800/934-7222, www.tahoelodge.com, $79–149) is an affordable choice for an overnight stay. The motel has all the usual amenities—heated pool and spa, guest laundry, free continental breakfast, free wireless Internet—and its rooms are equipped with microwaves, refrigerators, coffeemakers, and a choice of bed configurations: one or two queens or doubles, or one king. A few units have lake views and/or fireplaces, and those are your best bet.

If you can get past the blinking neon crown out front, **Ferrari's Crown Motel** (8200 N. Lake Blvd., Kings Beach, 530/546-3388 or 800/645-2260, www.tahoecrown.com, $99–239) is a good bet for a North Tahoe summer vacation. The 1950s-style motel has location, location, location, as in right on the lakeshore in Kings Beach. Some rooms have lake views, kitchenettes, spas, or gas fireplaces; the most expensive rooms are lakefront, meaning right on the water. A family-oriented place, the motel's swimming pool is always busy on summer days, as is their stretch of private beach. The owners also own the neighboring **Gold Crest Resort** (8194 N. Lake Blvd., 530/546-3388 or 800/645-2260, $99–239), a similar lakefront property.

If you don't mind paying a higher tariff, excellent lakefront accommodations are also available at **Mourelatos Lakeshore Resort** (6834 N. Lake Blvd., Tahoe Vista, 530/546-9500 or 800/824-6381, www.mirtahoe.com, $150–300 for two people), a small motel-style lodge that sits right on the Tahoe sand. All studio suites are either lake view or lakefront, and you can guess which costs more. Each has a semiprivate deck and comes with either a wet bar or full kitchen.

WEST SHORE
Bed-and-Breakfasts

An ever-reliable bet for West Shore lodging, **Tahoma Meadows Bed and Breakfast** (6821 W. Lake Blvd., Tahoma, 530/525-1553 or 866/525-1553, www.tahomameadows.com, $109–199 for two people) gets plenty of repeat business from satisfied customers who enjoy its 15 cottages and common breakfast room. This place offers all the comforts of a

SIERRA CLUB SKI HUTS

For an overnight winter backcountry experience without the hassle of snow camping, skiers, snowboarders, and snowshoers can spend the night at one of four Sierra Club ski huts on Tahoe's North and West Shores. The huts are between three and five miles from the nearest respective trailhead, so they can be reached in about a half day of skiing or snowshoeing by those of intermediate ability or better, assuming that the weather cooperates. About 2,000 people stay at these huts each winter, so advance reservations are a must (800/679-6775, www.sierraclub.org), especially for weekend nights. A hut stay is an amazing bargain—$15 per person per night. All of the huts are maintained entirely by Sierra Club volunteers.

Of the four huts, the Peter Grubb Hut is the oldest, most popular, and easiest to reach. Built in 1938, it is situated below 8,325-foot Castle Peak and just east of the Pacific Crest Trail. The hut has a main room with a wood-burning stove, tables, and a kitchen area. An upstairs sleeping loft accommodates 15 people, and an outhouse is located about 75 feet from the cabin. Hut travelers leave their cars at the California Sno-Park near Donner Summit, then ski or snowshoe just under three miles to the hut. The Peter Grubb Hut makes a great base camp for exploring Sand Ridge Lake and Castle and Basin Peaks.

The Ludlow Hut, built in 1958, is located south of Homewood at Richardson Lake, on the northern edge of the Desolation Wilderness, requiring a ski or snowshoe of about five miles. The hut has a main room with a wood-burning stove, tables, and a kitchen area. An upstairs sleeping loft accommodates 15; an outhouse is about 100 feet away. Skiers start this trip at either Sugar Pine Point State Park or the McKinney Creek Trailhead farther north. While staying at the hut, intrepid backcountry skiers and snowboarders can explore Rubicon Peak and the General Creek area.

The newest of the huts is the Bradley Hut, which was reconstructed in 1998 in Pole Creek near Squaw Valley. Its original 1957 location was in the Five Lakes Basin near Alpine Meadows Ski Resort, but after Five Lakes became part of the Granite Chief Wilderness, the Sierra Club moved the hut. From the Pole Creek Trailhead on Highway 89 (7.5 miles north of Tahoe City), a steady ascent over about 4.5 miles gets you to the Bradley Hut, which seems posh and modern compared to the other, older huts. Many skiers combine a trip to the Bradley Hut with a trip to the Benson Hut, which is four miles distant.

The Benson Hut, built in 1948, is situated below the north face of Anderson Peak, five miles south of the Sugar Bowl ski resort. It is well known for its outstanding views and fierce winds. The hut is a popular overnight stop for skiers traveling from the Donner area to Squaw Valley or simply making a loop around Donner Summit. The main room on the ground floor has a wood-burning stove, table, and kitchen. The upstairs sleeping loft can accommodate 12 people; an outhouse is about 100 feet away. Most Benson Hut visitors begin their trip at Sugar Bowl, which sometimes will sell one-way lift tickets to ease the start of the trek—a 1,500-foot climb to reach Mount Lincoln. Some hut-goers claim that the Benson Hut is haunted, which adds to its allure.

traditional B&B, including evening snacks and a full, hearty breakfast in the morning, but because the guest rooms are individual cottages, you have more privacy. A few cottages are dog-friendly; request one in advance if you want to bring your four-legged friend ($20 per night additional charge). A few larger "family cottages" have kitchens; those go for $175–375. The owners offer some screamin' midweek deals for stay-and-ski packages at Alpine Meadows, Squaw, and Homewood.

If you prefer a more traditional B&B in which guests share the owner's home, the **Rockwood Lodge Bed and Breakfast** (5295 W. Lake Blvd., Homewood, 530/525-5273 or 800/538-2463, www.rockwoodlodge.com, $150–225) fits the bill. This is the kind of "old Tahoe" home we all wish we owned, built of

NORTH AND WEST SHORES

native stone, hand-hewn beams, and knotty pine. The inn has five rooms, all with queen beds, down comforters, and sitting areas. Breakfast is served outside on the patio in summer. On winter evenings, you'll want to hang out by the huge fireplace.

Condominium-Style Resorts

You don't have to host a corporate meeting or a huge wedding party to book a stay at **Granlibakken Resort and Conference Center** (725 Granlibakken Rd., Tahoe City, 877/552-6301 or 800/543-3221, www.granlibakken. com, $150–195 for two people), although that's how most people get introduced to the place. The resort, which is set on 74 beautiful acres, also welcomes families, couples, and single travelers with condo-style studios, suites, and one- to five-bedroom town houses. Certain features come standard with every visit, like Granlibakken's well-loved hot breakfast buffet, so you won't have to flip pancakes and fry eggs on your vacation. Some units have kitchens, fireplaces, decks, and/or separate dining areas. The complex has a heated outdoor pool, hot tub, and tennis courts. Many visitors take advantage of stay-and-ski packages with lift passes for Homewood and other ski resorts (Homewood is just a few miles away). You can cross-country ski or snowshoe right from the property. And in summer, the emphasis switches from skiing to tennis, with an array of tennis camps and lessons for adults and teens.

Cabins

The woodsy **Cottage Inn** (1690 W. Lake Blvd., Tahoe City, 530/581-4073 or 800/581-4073, www.thecottageinn.com, $150–340 for two people) is downright adorable. The moment you drive in, your eyes glimpse immaculate, storybook gardens and cozy wood cottages with bear-clad exteriors. Bear-clad? That's right. Wooden bears carved by Jonathan "the Bear Man" of Wyoming are all over this place—hanging from the rafters, peeking in the windows, and clinging to the walls. The original 1938 cottage buildings were completely remodeled in the 1990s. Pick your theme: fishing, hunting, skiing, sailing, and so on—and the Cottage Inn probably has a room or suite to match. The price tag comes with a lot of extras (in addition to the hand-carved bears): private beach access, a sauna, a full breakfast, fresh-baked cookies, and afternoon wine and cheese. Tahoe City is just a couple of miles away, and you can walk to the restaurant and bar at Sunnyside Lodge.

For summer vacationers who want to be right on the beach, **Meeks Bay Resort** (7941 Emerald Bay Rd./Hwy. 89, Meeks Bay, 530/525-6946 or 877/326-3357, www.meeks-bayresort.com, $125–375) has some world-class real estate along a sandy stretch of calm and shallow Meeks Bay. Owned and operated by the Washoe Tribe, the resort has a variety of accommodations—from log cabins to motel rooms to a grand "mansion" that rents for $1,000 per night—but they all have one thing in common: a location just a few steps from the lakeshore. The resort also has a marina on-site with water-sport rentals (kayaks, canoes, paddleboats, and the like), or you can bring your own boat and dock it here. The resort is open in summer only, usually May–October.

Dog owners rejoice: For an extra $10, Fido is welcome in the cabins at **Tahoma Lodge** (7018 W. Lake Blvd., Tahoma, 866/819-2226, www. tahomalodge.com, $120–185). The 1940s-era cabins are nothing fancy, but they provide all the vacation basics: kitchens, private baths, fireplaces or woodstoves, and cable television. As the owners describe it, this is a "jeans-and-sneakers" kind of place. Cabins can accommodate 2–5 people; the larger cabins are more expensive.

Lodges and Inns

For lakefront accommodations on the West Shore, a perennial favorite is **Sunnyside**

Lodge (1850 W. Lake Blvd., 530/583-7200 or 800/822-2754, www.sunnysidetahoe.com, $155–330). Just two miles south of Tahoe City, but far enough from the hustle and bustle, Sunnyside's 23 lakeside rooms are perfectly suited for a night of romance. Some rooms have river-rock fireplaces; others have wet bars. All are decorated in an elegant mountain-lodge style. Guests enjoy a gourmet-style continental breakfast in the morning (the pastries are baked fresh daily by their in-house chef, not wrapped in plastic and shipped from a factory in Des Moines) and afternoon snacks 3–5 P.M. Basically, this is a bed-and-breakfast disguised as a lodge. For dinner, guests don't have to travel far; the wonderful Sunnyside Restaurant is on the property. Like most places at Lake Tahoe, rates vary greatly depending on the season and day of the week. Discounted midweek ski packages are available in winter.

If you aren't afraid to part with some serious cash, book a stay at the marvelous **C West Shore Café and Inn** (5160 W. Lake Blvd., 530/525-5200, www.westshorecafe. com, $249–649). Opened in 2006, this place defines sophisticated mountain-style lodging. The inn offers four two-room suites and two single rooms, each with a gas fireplace and private balcony. The rooms and suites are huge, averaging 500 square feet. Leather furniture, 46-inch flat-screen televisions, fine linens, and slate-tiled bathrooms make up the carefully planned decor. The higher-priced suites have the best views, of course, with the blue waters of Lake Tahoe expanding outward as far as you can see. While staying here, you must eat at least one dinner at the inn's restaurant (noon–9 P.M. daily in summer, Friday–Monday only in winter, dinner $20–45, lunch $13–30).

Campgrounds and RV Parks

One of the few campgrounds around the lake that is open for year-round camping, **General**

Creek Campground at Ed Z'berg Sugar Pine Point State Park (530/525-7982, www.parks. ca.gov, $35) is located 10 miles south of Tahoe City off Highway 89 in Tahoma. The camp has 175 sites for tents, trailers up to 24 feet, and RVs up to 30 feet, as well as restrooms with flush toilets, showers, and a dump station. There are also 10 group sites that can accommodate up to 40 people each. In winter, you can cross-country ski right from your tent, and in summer, you can hike or mountain bike through hundreds of acres of conifer forest, or swim at the beach by the park's historic Ehrman Mansion. General Creek flows near the camp and is open to fishing mid-July–mid-September. Reserve sites in advance at 800/444-7275 or www.reserveamerica.com.

Just a mile south of Ed Z'berg Sugar Pine Point State Park is the privately operated campground at **Meeks Bay Resort** (7941 W. Lake Blvd., Tahoma, 530/525-6946 or 877/326-3357, www.meeksbayresort.com, $25–45) and the Forest Service–run **Meeks Bay Campground** (530/583-3642, $23–25), both on the lake side of the highway. Beach lovers will be happy at either one. Meeks Bay Resort's camp has 28 sites for tents or RVs up to 60 feet long and all the developed-resort amenities: showers, flush toilets, full hookups, general store, and marina. The Forest Service's Meeks Bay Campground has 36 sites suitable for tents or small RVs (20 feet or less). Some sites are for tents only. Flush toilets are the only luxury besides a wonderful stretch of Meeks Bay shoreline, complete with a boat ramp. Arrive early in the morning to nab a site far from the highway and closer to the lake. Reserve in advance at 877/444-6777 or www.recreation.gov.

Six miles farther south toward Emerald Bay, **D. L. Bliss State Park** (530/525-7277, www. parks.ca.gov, $35–45) has 168 campsites on the lake side of the highway. Most are tent sites, but small RVs or trailers up to 18 feet are welcome (there are no hookups). The camp has restrooms with flush toilets and showers. The main activities here are swimming in Lake Tahoe, hanging out at the park's beautiful beaches, and hiking the Rubicon Trail, which begins a short distance from camp. Reserve sites in advance at 800/444-7275 or www.reserveamerica.com.

TRUCKEE, NORTHSTAR, AND SQUAW VALLEY
Inns and Bed-and-Breakfasts

If you want to stay in a modern, environmentally conscious hotel, your best bet near Truckee is the **❰ Cedar House Sport Hotel** (10918 Brockway Rd., Truckee, 530/582-5655, www.cedarhousesporthotel.com, $170–370). Innovative architecture and contemporary furnishings (leather platform beds, bent plywood chairs, stainless-steel bar stools, flatscreen TVs) in the 42 rooms and suites give this hotel a hip feel. The "European" continental breakfast includes fresh breads, pastries, yogurt, fresh fruit, cold cuts, and cheese. Dogs are allowed in some rooms for an extra $50 per night; dog beds and bowls are provided.

Built in 1885 in the heart of downtown Truckee, the **River Street Inn** (10009 E. River St., Truckee, 530/550-9290, www.riverstreetinntruckee.com, $115–195) is steeped in history. In its multiple past lives, it has served as a jail, a restaurant, a boardinghouse for workers in the ice-harvesting business, and a bordello. Restored and remodeled in 1999, the inn is now a cozy B&B with 11 guest rooms, each with a private bath, color television, and a comforter-covered queen bed. Rates include a continental-style breakfast. A large family suite is also available for $260–390 per night.

It may not be the best place for light sleepers, but the Victorian landmark **Truckee Hotel** (10007 Bridge St., Truckee, 530/587-4444 or 800/659-6921, www.thetruckeehotel.com, $49–169) is a pleasant and historic lodging choice in Truckee. Located a bit close to the train station in downtown Truckee, this grand

The woodsy Cedar House Sport Hotel blends naturally into its surroundings.

© ANN MARIE BROWN

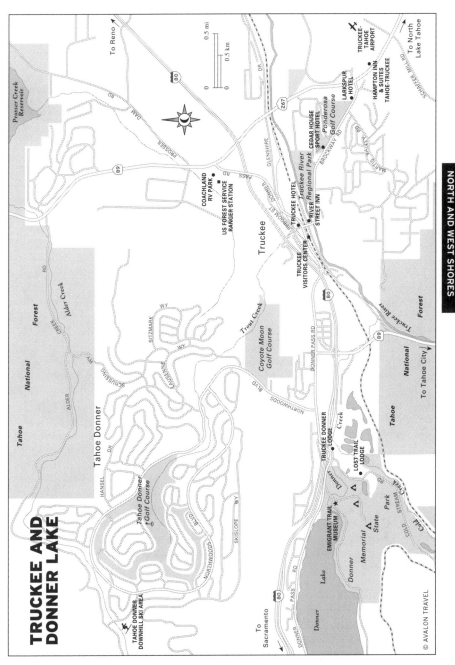

TRUCKEE AND DONNER LAKE

© AVALON TRAVEL

old hotel was built in 1873 and remodeled in the early 1990s. With rates including a continental breakfast, it's the most affordable lodging around. Eight rooms with private baths and claw-foot tubs cost a bit more than the 29 rooms with shared baths, so make sure you know what you are getting. On weekends, afternoon refreshments are served in the parlor. Moody's Bistro, a wonderful restaurant and jazz club, is located on the first floor.

Hotels and Condominium-Style Resorts

If you are coming to play at Squaw Valley, stay at the European-style **Olympic Village Inn** (1909 Chamonix Pl., Olympic Valley, 530/581-6000 or 800/845-5243, www.olympicvillage-inn.com, $149–299 in winter, $119–179 rest of year). The Tyrolean-esque structure is lovely to look at, inside and out, and offers 80 luxurious suites for the discriminating traveler (or for nondiscriminating travelers with sizable bank accounts). Most rooms have balconies with mountain views; some have fireplaces. All rooms include custom furnishings, well-equipped mini-kitchens, color televisions, down comforters, plush terry robes, morning newspapers, and overnight ski check. After wearing yourself out skiing all day, you can soak in one of five outdoor hot tubs or swim in the year-round heated outdoor pool.

Another excellent lodging option at Squaw Valley is the **Squaw Valley Lodge** (201 Squaw Peak Rd., Olympic Valley, 530/583-5500 or 800/549-6742, www.squawvalleylodge.com), which is equally as upscale as the Olympic Village Inn, but less subtle about it. The lodge has a concierge, health club, sauna, and three spas, and its guest suites come in sizes from studios (560 square feet) to three bedrooms (1,700 square feet). Each unit features a gourmet kitchenette, designer furnishings, and lots of other amenities that spell "expensive." The rate for a studio suite on winter holiday

weekends is $450, versus $250 for non-holiday winter days. Summer rates are typically $200–300. The nicer one-bedroom suites go as high as $600 on winter holidays, and two-bedroom suites are even higher. Bring your personal banker with you.

In its 60 rooms and suites, **PlumpJack Squaw Valley Inn** (1920 Squaw Valley Rd., Olympic Valley, 530/583-1576 or 800/323-7666, www.plumpjack.com, $269–399) offers much the same type of pampering as the Olympic Village Inn and Squaw Valley Lodge, and with the same easy access to the slopes. Each guest room has an honor bar, terry-cloth robes and slippers, complimentary wireless Internet access, a flat-screen TV and DVD player, and beautiful mountain views. A gourmet breakfast buffet for two is included in the rate, as is use of the resort's fitness facility, pool, and hot tubs. If your party is larger than two, family suites or one-bedroom suites are available. If you really want to break the bank, rent the PlumpJack penthouse for up to $745 a night.

Another fine lodging option at Squaw Valley is the **Red Wolf Lodge** (2000 Squaw Loop Rd., Olympic Valley, 530/583-7226 or 800/791-0081, www.redwolfsquaw.com, $209–329), a condominium complex with a ski-in, ski-out location at the base of Squaw (it's walking distance to the tram, shops, and restaurants). The studio and one-bedroom condos have living rooms with sleeper sofas, gas fireplaces, whirlpool bathtubs, and full kitchens; larger units are also available.

A bit separate from the rest of Squaw Valley, but still with ski-in and ski-out access, is the **Resort at Squaw Creek** (400 Squaw Creek Rd., Olympic Valley, 530/583-6300, www.squawcreek.com, $169–399), a place that most travelers discover when they are attending a business conference. Along with 23,000 square feet of indoor meeting space, the resort boasts a Robert Trent Jones Jr. championship golf course. More than 400 guest rooms and suites, including some two-story penthouses, are situated around the grounds, as well as five restaurants, a spa, and an outdoor ice-skating rink (winter only). The mountain view from the lobby is a stunner.

Since its renovation completion in 2007, **Northstar-at-Tahoe Resort** (530/562-1010 or 800/466-6784, www.northstarattahoe.com, $249–405) now boasts Tahoe's most impressive village complex of shops, restaurants, and condominiums. The resort rents guest rooms and "lofts" that can accommodate 2–4 people, as well as larger condominiums and mountain homes with as many as six bedrooms. The standard guest rooms have ski-in, ski-out privileges and are just steps away from shops and restaurants. The "loft" units boast the same convenient location but are larger, with a full kitchen, gas fireplace, and deck. Most people who stay here purchase the affordable stay-and-ski packages, or in summer, "stay-and-play" packages that include golf, tennis, mountain biking, or hiking.

Northstar can also boast of having Lake Tahoe's only five-star hotel, the $300 million **Ritz-Carlton** (13031 Ritz-Carlton Highlands Ct., Truckee, 530/562-3000, www.ritzcarlton. com), which opened at mid-mountain in 2010. The Ritz has 170 rooms and a 17,000-square-foot spa, plus its own gondola connecting it to Northstar Village. Like every other Ritz-Carlton in the world, this is a top-quality hotel with luxury appointments everywhere you look—a clear example of the principle of "getting what you pay for." Room rates change daily based on occupancy levels, so the only time to find a "bargain" is in the off-season (usually October, November, or May). The "basic" rooms go as low as $269 on weeknights in the off-season, but as high as $800 on holiday nights. In general, expect to pay about $500 for two people, unless you want to splurge on one of the much larger one- or two-bedroom suites. Then your rate could easily run into the realm of four digits.

Chain Motels and Hotels

The 100 rooms at the **Larkspur Hotel** (11331 Brockway Rd., Truckee, 530/587-4525 or 800/824-6385, www.larkspurhotels.com, $159–299) provide a pleasant lodging experience in rooms with modern, updated decor. The hotel is located outside the town of Truckee, so you'll have to drive to visit the shops and restaurants, but it's only one mile from Ponderosa Golf Course. If you feel like staying in for the evening and watching a little HBO, the motel has the Mountain Burrito Company downstairs, where you can order barbecued meats, giant burritos, and beers. A bonus: The complimentary continental breakfast has more than just the usual Danish and coffee; the food is actually hot and reasonably nutritious. Dogs are welcome here for an additional nightly fee, and in winter, the hotel offers ski packages with lift tickets to several resorts.

The **Hampton Inn and Suites Tahoe-Truckee** (11951 Hwy. 267, Truckee, 530/587-1197 or 888/587-1197, www.hamptoninntruckee.com, $154–249) also fits the bill for clean, dependable, vanilla-style lodgings. More than 100 rooms and 36 studio and one-bedroom suites are available with various configurations of king and queen beds. Some of the suites have whirlpool spas. A hot breakfast and free wireless Internet are included in the rate. The ski slopes at Northstar are just four miles away.

Another safe bet in the chain motel category is the **Truckee Donner Lodge** (10527 Coldstream Rd., Truckee, 530/582-9999 or 888/878-2533, www.truckeedonnerlodge. com, $129–249). The motel is right off I-80 at the Donner Pass Road exit, which makes it a great choice for travelers driving up from Sacramento or the Bay Area for the weekend. The Coldstream Trailhead for Donner Memorial State Park is just a few yards from the front door.

Hike-In Cabins

You have to earn your stay at **C Lost Trail Lodge** (8600 Coldstream Tr., Truckee, 530/320-9268, www.losttraillodge.com, $89 per person with a two-night minimum). In the summer that means a walk of a half mile to reach the lodge; in the winter it means snowshoeing or skiing four miles. But that's part of the appeal of a stay here—no cars and no road noise. Once you arrive, you may be surprised at the luxuries available: private Jacuzzis in three out of four cabin rooms (and showers in all of them), a cozy common area with a fire blazing in the huge riverstone hearth, and a kitchen with a six-burner Wolf range and double oven where you can cook your own gourmet meals (you must pack in your groceries). In winter, backcountry skiers enjoy the fact that they can access all different types of terrain from the lodge: steep chutes, mellow tree skiing through the forest, powder stashes, and a variety of south-facing and north-facing slopes. In summer, guests can hike to their hearts' content; the Pacific Crest Trail is just a few miles away. On weekend nights the lodge owner and any willing guests gather in the living room to sing or play music on the lodge's numerous instruments, which include several guitars, an upright piano, a stand-up bass, and a banjo. There are a few caveats to staying at Lost Trail Lodge: Your dog is allowed in your cabin with you, but not in the lodge common areas or kitchen. Because of the lodge's remote location, parents are discouraged from bringing their children. And if you're the kind of person who has to stay connected, you may be uncomfortable with the fact that there is no Internet connection or landline phone, but your cell phone might possibly work.

Campgrounds and RV Parks

Between two and eight miles south of Truckee are three Forest Service–run campgrounds (530/587-3558, $17–40) on Highway 89:

Granite Flat, Goose Meadow, and **Silver Creek.** Granite Flat is the largest with 75 sites, including 7 walk-in tent sites; Goose Meadow has 25 sites; Silver Creek has 23. All three camps are situated along the Truckee River, but unfortunately that also means they are close to Highway 89. To get away from the sight and sound of cars, Silver Creek is the best option, with seven riverfront sites that are located far from the road. All of the camps are on the primitive side: no hookups, showers, drinking water, or flush toilets (pit toilets only), but there is piped water. For anglers, rafters, or kayakers, camping doesn't get much better than this. Reserve in advance at 877/444-6777 or www.recreation.gov.

RVers who want amenities will do better at one of the 131 sites at privately operated **Coachland RV Park** (10100 Pioneer Tr., Truckee, 530/587-3071, www.coachland-rvpark.com, $44 for two adults). The park offers all the necessities: full hookups including cable TV, water, restrooms, showers, laundry, and a general store. It has a pleasant 55-acre setting in a pine forest at 6,000 feet, just off Highway 89 and I-80. Weekly and monthly rates, which are cheaper than the nightly rate, are available.

Fly-fishing anglers enjoy 25-site **Alpine Meadows Campground** at Martis Creek Lake (on Hwy. 267, one mile south of the Truckee airport, 530/587-8113, open May 15–Oct. 15, $18), which has water, restrooms, and catch-and-release fishing for Lahontan cutthroat, rainbow, and brown trout in Martis Creek Reservoir. No reservations; the camp is first-come, first-served.

Another great spot for anglers is **Prosser Family Campground** (10342 Hwy. 89, 530/587-9281, $17–19), located five miles north of Truckee off Highway 89. This camp has 29 sites and potable water and is within walking distance of Prosser Reservoir. Reserve in advance at 877/444-6777 or www.recreation.gov.

And for those who just want to be left alone, 10-site **Sagehen Creek Campground** (off Hwy. 89, nine miles north of Truckee, 530/587-3558) is found at the end of a rough access road (passenger cars okay). The best thing about this camp is that it's free, and fishing in Sagehen Creek is not too shabby. You'll need to bring your own water and pack out your garbage. To get there from Truckee: Drive nine miles north on Highway 89. Turn left at the Sagehen Summit turnoff and drive two miles.

DONNER LAKE AND SODA SPRINGS
Motels, Lodges, and Inns

Even travelers who don't consider themselves "B&B people" will enjoy a stay at the **Donner Lake Inn** (10070 Gregory Pl., Truckee, 530/587-5574, www.donnerlakeinn.com, $159–179), where five guest rooms, all with gas fireplaces, are situated across the street from the west end of Donner Lake. After a good night's sleep and a big home-cooked breakfast to start your morning, you can spend your days swimming, sailing, waterskiing, and fishing to your heart's content. In the winter months, Sugar Bowl and Northstar are only a few miles away.

Many California families have made Serene Lakes, near Donner Lake and Soda Springs, their summer or winter vacation destination for generations. Now those of us who don't own a vacation home in the area can stay at Serene Lakes, too, at the **Ice Lakes Lodge** (1111 Soda Springs Rd., Soda Springs, 530/426-3871, www.theicelakeslodge.com, $175–240, open Thurs.–Mon. year-round). Constructed in 2000, the large chalet-style lodge has 23 lake-view rooms, each simply and rather sparsely decorated with one king or two queen beds, plus a spectacular restaurant that looks out on Dulzura and Serena Lakes. In the lounge in winter, logs are always burning bright in the huge granite fireplace. A continental breakfast buffet is served each morning in the dining room. Nordic skiers can access the Royal Gorge cross-country trail system from the Ice Lakes Lodge Trailhead, located just a few steps from the lodge. Since the lodge is owned by the same folks who run Royal Gorge, guests can often take advantage of discounts on trail passes and other perks for cross-country skiers. If you're more of an alpine skier than a Nordic skier, the lodge is less than five miles from Sugar Bowl's downhill slopes. The only negative here is that the guest room walls are on the thin side, so earplugs might be a good idea. And just like Royal Gorge, the lodge is almost always closed on Tuesday and Wednesday.

Also owned and operated by Royal Gorge Ski Resort, the historic **Rainbow Lodge** (50080 Hampshire Rocks Rd., Soda Springs, 800/426-3871 or 530/426-3661, www.therainbowlodge.com) has been welcoming visitors to its 32 rooms, cozy bar, and delightful restaurant since the 1920s. Set at a bend in the Yuba River, constructed of hand-hewn timbers and natural stone, and decorated in classic ski-chalet style, this place has "historic mountain lodge" written all over it. Many of the rooms are on the small side, and they have their quirks (remember, this is a historic building), but because of the scenic riverside location, people love it here. In recent decades the lodge has become almost as popular in summer as it is in winter, due to the number of hiking, biking, and rafting options nearby. In winter, of course, skiing is the main event, particularly cross-country skiing at Royal Gorge, five miles away. Rates are $171–214 per night for rooms with private baths (breakfast included), but you can save money by reserving a room with a shared bath ($117–139).

Most visitors to Donner Lake are fortunate enough to own their own vacation homes, but those who aren't so lucky can stay at the **Donner Lake Village Resort** (15695 Donner Pass Rd., Truckee, 530/587-6081 or 800/979-0402, www.donnerlakevillage.com, $90–190

The Lodge at Sugar Bowl overlooks the ski slopes.

© ANN MARIE BROWN

for two people, higher for lakefront and lakeview units and on weekends and holidays, $229–425 for two-bedroom townhomes), on the west end of the lake. This two-story motelstyle resort offers "lodgettes" and studios, onebedroom suites, and townhomes, most with kitchens and fireplaces. The resort has a private beach and a marina that rents ski boats, fishing boats, and personal watercraft, so you won't have to wonder what to do with your time. If you have your own boat, you can tie it up here. In winter, Royal Gorge is just a few miles away.

Just down the road is **Loch Leven Lodge** (13855 Donner Pass Rd., Truckee, 530/587-3773 or 877/663-6637, www.lochlevenlodge.com, $120–140 for two in a room, suite, or studio, $240 and up for two in a townhouse), which has a similar setup on the shores of Donner Lake, except that all of its rooms are lakefront. The old-style lodge has been a popular vacation spot for more than 50 years. The lodge's bestloved feature is its 5,000-square-foot deck that overlooks the lake. Bring a book and settle into your favorite beach chair.

For a European-style stay-and-ski experience, consider the 70-year-old ◖ **Lodge at Sugar Bowl** (629 Sugar Bowl Rd., Norden, 530/426-6742 or 866/843-2695, www.sugarbowl.com), located at the top of the resort's one-mile-long gondola. You won't be able to drive your car here, but you and your luggage will enjoy a magical ride up the snow-covered slopes to the inn's 27 guest rooms and beautiful dining room. All rooms have their own private bathroom, TV/DVD, coffeemaker, and complimentary wireless Internet. Over the years, numerous celebrities have stayed here. Mountain-view rooms are $219–329 for two people; rooms without views are less. But plan a midweek stay, and you can save some serious bucks; rates are often as low as $169 Sunday–Thursday on nonholiday weeknights.

On the opposite end of the ski-lodging spectrum, there's the no-nonsense **Boreal**

Inn (19455 Boreal Ridge Rd., Soda Springs, 530/426-1012, www.rideboreal.com, $109–160), a basic three-story motel that is located 200 yards from the Boreal off-ramp at I-80, and about the same distance from Boreal's ski lifts, so skiers and riders can do their thing with the greatest of ease. Rooms can accommodate up to four people, so all your rider friends can pack in together to save money. A free continental breakfast is offered; children four and under stay free.

Hostels

You don't have to be a Sierra Club member to stay at the rustic but much-loved **Clair Tappaan Lodge** (19940 Donner Pass Rd., Norden, 530/426-3632 or 800/679-6775, www.sierraclub.org/outings/lodges, $60–65 adults, $30–35 children 4–13), but you do have to be willing to do a few chores. Sierra Club members save a few bucks off the rates, but everyone is welcome here (although children under four years of age are discouraged because of the close, dorm-like quarters). Built by Sierra Club volunteers in the 1930s, the lodge makes an affordable home base for a Donner Pass–area vacation, complete with three family-style meals included in the nightly rate. You'll have to make a few concessions, of course, like bringing your own sleeping bag or linens and blankets, or renting them for an additional $8 per day. You'll be sleeping in bunk beds equipped with mattresses, and sharing the communal restroom and shower facilities. And guests are expected to perform a brief chore in keeping with the communal nature of the lodge experience; this usually means about 20 minutes out of your day to set the table or wash a few dishes. Location is key here: You can snowshoe and cross-country ski on the lodge's own trails, or head to Royal Gorge, Sugar Bowl, Boreal, Soda Springs, and other nearby ski resorts. Even Squaw Valley and Alpine Meadows are only about 20 minutes away. Don't forget your bathing suit so you can spend some time in the hot tub.

Campgrounds and RV Parks

Campers who want to be near three-mile-long Donner Lake stay at **Donner Memorial State Park** (12593 Donner Pass Rd., Donner Lake exit off I-80, west of Truckee, 530/582-7892, $35). This popular state park campground has 170 sites that can accommodate RVs and trailers up to 28 feet. Camp amenities include water, restrooms, and showers, plus all the swimming and fishing you could ask for in Donner Lake. Reserve in advance at 800/444-7275 or www.reserveamerica.com.

Food

TAHOE CITY
Breakfast and Lunch

Breakfast is worth the wait at the **◖ Fire Sign Café** (1785 W. Lake Blvd., Tahoe City, 530/583-0871, 7 A.M.–3 P.M. daily, $10), a cozy place known for its creative home-style cooking. Every morning they serve up a special baked treat, like muffins or coffee cake. Omelets and crepes are huge and filled with creative concoctions. A stack of buckwheat pancakes or a whole-grain pecan waffle will leave your belly full all day. And if it's your first time, go ahead and order the eggs Benedict with salmon and spinach, and then you'll understand why you had to wait so long in the line trailing out the door.

One of the more famous and most long-running restaurants in Tahoe City, **Rosie's Café** (571 N. Lake Blvd., Tahoe City, 530/583-8504, www.rosiescafe.com, 7:30 A.M.–9:30 P.M. daily,

$7–15) is known as much for its decor as for its traditional American food. Check out the elk antler chandelier, moose head above the fireplace, antique skiing and sledding equipment, vintage bicycles, and assorted Tahoe memorabilia. Rosie's is open for three meals a day, but breakfast and lunch are the best bets. Nothing is too gourmet here—the menu consists of diner-style comfort food—but they do brag that their smoked salmon omelet was featured in *Bon Appétit* magazine. Families like the extensive children's menu. And just like at Fire Sign Café, plan to wait awhile if you show up midmorning, especially on weekends. But it's no problem; just order a Bloody Mary at the bar, and the time will fly by.

If you can't stand to wait but you still want a big breakfast, then head to the much-larger **Sawtooth Ridge Café** (877 N. Lake Blvd., Tahoe City, 530/583-2880, 7 A.M.–3 P.M. daily, $10), across the street from Tahoe City's Safeway, which serves the morning repast until 2 P.M., plus salads, soups, and sandwiches for lunch. The lengthy breakfast menu includes egg burritos, veggie eggs Benedict, latkes and eggs, corned-beef hash and eggs, biscuits and gravy, quiche of the day, a bunch of omelets, and buckwheat pancakes.

For those who don't want a sit-down breakfast—just a quick pit stop before heading off to the slopes or the trails—**Tahoe Dam Café** (55 W. Lake Blvd., Tahoe City, 530/581-0278, 6 A.M.–3 P.M. Mon.–Sat., 7 A.M.–3 P.M. Sun., open till 5 P.M. in summer, $5–8) fits the bill. The café has a killer location just a few steps from the Truckee River and offers locally roasted coffee and espresso, fresh pastries, and the like. The breakfast burritos are the hot ticket, but the bagel sandwiches with veggie sausage and smoked gouda score a close second. The emphasis is on organic ingredients. Come back in the afternoon for sandwiches, salads, smoothies, or frozen yogurt. Early birds will like that the café opens at 6 A.M. almost daily.

Another great place for a quick-stop breakfast is just down the road at the **Tahoe House Bakery** (625 W. Lake Blvd., Tahoe City, 530/583-1377 or 877/367-8246, www.tahoe-house.com, 6 A.M.–4 P.M. Sun.–Thurs., 6 A.M.–6 P.M. Fri.–Sat. and daily in summer, $5–10). Run by a Swiss family, Tahoe House's European-style breads, pastries, scones, coffee cakes, muffins, and bagels make the perfect breakfast to go. But the cozy gas fireplace, free Internet access, and cool Tahoe vibe may encourage you to stay awhile and order another cup of coffee. Everything is made on-site, including an extensive line of gourmet sauces, cheeses, jams, wine, and takeout dinners.

Burger Joints

A Tahoe City institution, the **Bridgetender Tavern** (65 W. Lake Blvd., Tahoe City, 530/583-3342, www.tahoebridgetender.com, 11 A.M.–11 P.M. Sun.–Thurs., 11 A.M.–midnight Fri.–Sat., $8–12) moved across the street from its historic location next to Fanny Bridge in 2002, but the casual bar/café still doles out the same delectable half-pound burgers, tacos, soups, wraps, and salads that it has since 1977. If you'd rather have a turkey burger or a veggie burger than a hamburger, they can do that. The fish-and-chips are popular, too, but what everybody orders is something from the huge selection of draft beers, and a plate of waffle fries with ranch dressing on the side. Diners can sit outside at wooden tables alongside the beautiful Truckee River or inside in the cozy log-cabin dining room.

Casual American

Located in the Boatworks Mall, **Jake's on the Lake** (780 N. Lake Blvd., Tahoe City, 530/583-0188, www.jakestahoe.com, 11:30 A.M.–9 P.M. daily in summer, 4:30–9 P.M. daily in winter, $17–38) has peaceful marina and lake views, and outdoor deck dining in summer. Jake's is well known for its weekday happy hour, when appetizers are half price and you can order a mai tai or an Alpine Sunset and watch the sun go down. The attractive bar area is large and airy enough to host a live band every Friday night. The menu leans heavily on pasta and seafood, including Idaho trout, lobster tail, giant scampi, and daily choices flown in from Hawaii, but meat lovers will appreciate the filet mignon, New York steak, and rack of lamb. You can save money by ordering from the café menu (burgers and salads). There's something for everyone here, even light eaters. And save room for the Hula Pie dessert, which is much like the Hula Pie served at the West Shore's Sunnyside Resort—a massive slice of ice cream pie.

In the Cobblestone Center in Tahoe City, **Evergreen** (475 N. Lake Blvd., Tahoe City, 530/581-1401, www.evergreentahoe.com, 11:30 A.M.–9 P.M. Tues.–Sun., $9–20) provides diners with an array of choices for both big and small appetites, and fat and thin wallets. Seasonal soups (try the carrot-ginger if it's available) and house-made pastas are the house specialties, but there are plenty of seafood entrées, salads, and standards like New York steak and grilled chicken breast. There's even a kids' menu.

Located a few miles north of Tahoe City near Alpine Meadows, the historic **River Ranch Lodge** (Hwy. 89 and Alpine Meadows Rd., Tahoe City, 530/583-4264, www.riverranchlodge.com, 5:30–9 P.M. daily year-round, 11:30 A.M.–9 P.M. in summer, $20–32) is a good place for a classic Tahoe dining experience. In the summer, diners can choose between indoor seating or a spot outside on the patio alongside the rushing waters of the Truckee River. The menu includes scallop risotto, buffalo steak, Idaho red trout, filet mignon, and lamb shank, and the riverside scenery can't be beat. In addition to the formal dinner menu, a café menu is offered, with sandwiches and the like going for $10–15.

A relative newcomer to Tahoe City, the ◖ **Dockside 700 Wine Bar and Grill** (700 N.

Lake Blvd., Tahoe City, 530/581-0303, www.dockside700.com, 11 A.M.–8 P.M. daily, $10–25) has garnered rave reviews because it offers a lakefront view and serves what most vacationers want to eat: barbecued meats, half-pound burgers, huge salads, pizzas, and the like—all at very reasonable prices. Think of it as extremely well-prepared pub food. Situated on the water in the Tahoe City Marina, the view from this restaurant is of boats—lots of them—and open water beyond. Sunsets are spectacular. In the summer, patrons dine on the covered porch to take advantage of the views; in the cooler months, the indoor dining room features a floor-to-ceiling river-rock fireplace. If you don't have time to sit down and eat, you can grab takeout food at the associated Double Dog Deli; almost everything on the restaurant menu is available there to go.

At Sunnyside's charming **Spoon** (1785 W. Lake Blvd., Tahoe City, 530/581-5400, www.spoontakeout.com, 3–9 P.M. daily in summer, closed Tues. and Wed. in winter, $9–14), you can eat in or take out from a short menu of American comfort food, including chicken penne alfredo, a tri-tip sandwich, or black bean and corn chili. If you are a soup lover, Spoon offers three choices every day (hence the name), but if you want beer or wine with your food, stop at the store before you come here (you can bring your own bottle at no charge). This is largely a one-woman operation, with the owner often serving as chef, hostess, and waitress. Set in a small cottage, the restaurant's seating is limited (nab a table upstairs or a table outside), but since many customers take out their food, there isn't usually much of a wait. In summer, Spoon's soft-serve ice cream is wildly popular.

California Cuisine

In the center of Tahoe City, ◖ **Christy Hill** (115 Grove St., Tahoe City, 530/583-8551, www.christyhill.com, dinner 5:30–9:30 P.M. daily, lunch noon–3 P.M. daily in summer only,

© ANN MARIE BROWN

Housed in a cozy cabin, Spoon serves delicious home-cooked meals.

$15–35) has been satisfying hungry diners for nearly a quarter of a century. Lauded by the *San Francisco Chronicle, Los Angeles Times, Wall Street Journal,* and *Bon Appétit* magazine, the food here is worthy of its reputation. A mix of California and French cuisine, the menu changes often, but certain favorites appear regularly: ahi sashimi, foie gras with chanterelle mushrooms, wild king salmon, and filet mignon with roasted shallots. It's not just the food that's worthy of laurels; it's also the eye-candy view. The restaurant sits 100 feet above Tahoe's shoreline, offering a panoramic blue-water vista. Not surprisingly, sunsets are sublime. In summer, the restaurant is open for lunch as well as dinner, so you have more chances to take in the lake view.

Savvy diners might normally steer away from a restaurant that boasts of having a "cuisine unique," but **Wolfdale's** (640 N. Lake Blvd., Tahoe City, 530/583-5700, www.wolfdales.com, 5:30–9:30 P.M. daily, $22–42) has

been successfully serving up mouthwatering dishes, accompanied by first-rate service and a nice lake view, for nearly 30 years. The menu is California cuisine with a distinct Asian influence, as chef/owner Doug Wolfdale studied under master Japanese chefs. Try the roasted quail stuffed with fennel sausage, or the green Thai curry seafood stew. One thing comes standard on every plate: gorgeous presentation. The food looks so artistic, it's a pity to eat it. On warm summer days, make a reservation for the outdoor dining area, and don't miss the trio of fresh sorbets for dessert.

A choice spot for riverfront dining is the aptly named **River Grill** (55 W. Lake Blvd., Tahoe City, 530/581-2644, www.rivergrilltahoe.com, 5–9:30 P.M. daily, $16–30), which serves fresh seasonal entrées alongside the banks of the Truckee (adjacent to the Bridgetender Tavern). Well-prepared classics are on the menu, including braised beef short ribs, grilled wild salmon, prawn raviolis, and a vegetarian lasagna, but a few surprises await, like an appetizer of macaroni and cheese with bacon. In summer, you can dine outside on the terraced riverside deck, or in the knotty-pine-paneled dining room.

Italian

For Italian food on the North Shore, **Zia Lina** (521 N. Lake Blvd., Tahoe City, 530/581-0100, 5–10 P.M. daily, $14–25) is a moderately priced choice. This neighborhood trattoria, in the same space where the popular Fiamma used to be, serves up northern Italian country cuisine. The wood-fired oven is constantly in use preparing thin-crust pizzas. Happy-hour specials are a great deal.

If it's summertime and you like your pizza with a river view, head over to **Front Street Station Pizza Company** (205 River Rd., Tahoe City, 530/583-3770, 11 A.M.–10 P.M. daily), which sits right alongside the Truckee River just northwest of Tahoe City's Y. This tiny little café makes pizzas, salads, and Italian sandwiches. A family of four can eat here for less than $50. The pizza is thin crust, New York–style, and in addition to the traditional toppings, there are a few creative choices, like the Steamer, which is a mix of jalapeños, onions, and pepperoni. Everything tastes better when you are sitting outside on the riverside deck, watching the rafters float by.

Mexican

At the **Blue Agave** (425 N. Lake Blvd., Tahoe City, 530/583-8113, www.tahoeblueagave.com, 11:30 A.M.–9:30 P.M. daily, $9–16), they serve about a billion different kinds of tequila. Okay, it's actually only 180, but regardless, it would take a very long time to try them all. The authentic Mexican and Southwest cuisine is prepared on the health-conscious side (no lard here). Specialties include shrimp fajitas, fruit-marinated carnitas, and seafood quesadillas.

TAHOE VISTA AND KINGS BEACH
Breakfast and Lunch

Yes, the **Old Post Office Café** (5245 N. Lake Blvd., Carnelian Bay, 530/546-3205, 6:30 A.M.–2 P.M. daily, $7–12) really used to be the post office in Kings Beach, for three decades beginning in 1942. That history is commemorated in the restaurant's wallpaper, which looks like stamps. It's been a breakfast-and-lunch joint since the 1970s, and on summer mornings, there is often a crowd waiting for a table. The menu is huge and includes all the morning favorites—eggs Benedict, huevos rancheros, breakfast burritos, omelets, biscuits and gravy, potato creations, even oatmeal—plus more than 30 varieties of sandwiches for lunch.

The **Log Cabin Caffe** (8692 N. Lake Blvd., Kings Beach, 530/546-7109, 7 A.M.–2 P.M. daily, $10–14) is another favorite for breakfast, and it's easy to see why. Instead of the same old same old, the Log Cabin serves up whole wheat griddle cakes, lobster eggs Benedict, a trout egg scramble, and cranberry orange waffles. The lunch menu is equally tempting: a half dozen salads including a seared ahi tuna on baby greens, several grilled panini sandwiches, and traditional and nontraditional burgers (beef, chicken, veggie, crab, and more). Figure on spending about $10 no matter what you order. It's all good.

You don't have to play golf to enjoy breakfast or lunch at the **Blue Onion** (400 Brassie Ave., Kings Beach, 530/546-3915, www.blueonion.com, 7 A.M.–4 P.M. daily, $5–14), you just have to like good food. The restaurant is situated in the clubhouse of Old Brockway, North Lake Tahoe's oldest golf course. For breakfast, try the Belgian waffles or a variety of sweet and savory crepes or egg scrambles. For lunch, choose from burgers, sandwiches, and salads. It's all delicious and moderately priced. In summer, you can sit outside on the redwood deck. The Blue

Onion is also occasionally open for dinner, but they mostly cater to private parties.

American

Situated right next to the North Tahoe sands at Kings Beach State Recreation Area, **Jason's Beachside Grille** (8338 N. Lake Blvd., Kings Beach, 530/546-3315, www.jasonsbeachside-grille.com, 11 A.M.–10 P.M. daily, $11–27) is the kind of place where you'll feel comfortable wearing your flip-flops in summer or Ugg boots in winter. The menu is classic American (salmon, pastas, prime rib, baby back ribs, flatiron steak). For lighter eaters, there is also a café menu with all kinds of burgers and appetizer-type foods ($7–12), and an overflowing salad bar. The restaurant's big deck is adjacent to the beach parking lot and 50 yards from the lakeshore, so the view of the beach action is usually quite entertaining. Live acoustic music is offered on weekend evenings at the adjacent Sand Bar. If you like fruity drinks, try the Huckleberry Finn, a frozen mudslide with huckleberries.

At **Gar Woods Grill** (5000 N. Lake Blvd., Carnelian Bay, 530/546-3366, www.gar-woods.com, 5:30–9:30 P.M. Sun.–Thurs., 5:30–10 P.M. Fri.–Sat., regular menu $24–39, bar menu $8–14), their claim to fame is the Wet Woody, a rum concoction that could easily inspire you to jump in the lake. It's run by the same folks who own Riva Grill in South Lake Tahoe, and the menu includes several seafood dishes, plus free-range chicken, braised lamb shank, and filet mignon, but there is also a much lower-priced bar menu. The lake view from the outdoor deck is divine, which is one reason why Sunday brunch is wildly popular in the summer months. In case you've missed the boat, so to speak, Gar Woods were the watercraft of choice for the Tahoe elite in the early part of the 20th century. Both Riva Grill and Gar Woods capitalize on that fact with heavy merchandising. A wealth of boating-related gifts, clothing, and gear are for sale.

Red-meat eaters will be right at home at the **Old Range Steak House** (7081 N. Lake Blvd., Kings Beach, 530/553-4020, www.steakhouse-tahoe.com, 5 P.M.–close daily, $16–36), which cooks up a huge variety of steaks—porterhouse, filet mignon, rib eye, New York strip—plus a few token poultry items. Bring your appetite, because all entrées include Caesar salad and red-skin potatoes. If you decide to order veggies on the side (not that your stomach will have any space), they are served in family-style portions, enough for the whole table. The house specialty is salt-roasted prime rib, and for dessert, it's cheesecake, of course. Don't tell your cardiologist that you ate here.

California Cuisine

Once a members-only restaurant, now, thankfully, reopened to the dining public (as of 2010), ◪ **Wild Goose** (7320 N. Lake Blvd., Tahoe Vista, 530/546-3640, www.wildgoose-tahoe.com, 5 P.M.–close daily in summer only, $22–39) may be the perfect date spot on the North Shore. First off, there's the Lake Tahoe view, which is hard to beat. There is no way to get closer to the water without going barefoot on the sand. Whether you sit indoors looking out the huge windows or outside on the tiered deck, you'll be wowed by the scenery. Then there's the outstanding food, amazing wine selection, and superior service. The menu changes often, but typical entrées include leek and goat cheese ravioli, rack of lamb, and Alaskan salmon. Dessert is worth saving room for, especially the chocolate fondue. While you are dining here, it may increase your appreciation to know that Wild Goose is set in a LEED-certified green building, designed using recycled materials: milk jugs on the wall panels, denim for insulation, car windshield glass in the tiles, and industrial scrap in its stainless steel kitchen equipment.

The atmosphere at **Spindleshanks** (6873 N. Lake Blvd., Tahoe Vista, 530/546-2191, www.spindleshankstahoe.com, 5:30 P.M.–close daily, $12–29) is best described as "upscale rustic." That means a cozy, woodsy interior and an array of comfort food, including a wonderful Caesar salad, baby back ribs, salmon Wellington, and oysters bienzo, all served in portions that fit the bill for the après-ski crowd. The food, while excellent, plays second fiddle to the wine at this bistro/wine bar. Spindleshanks offers a great happy-hour deal from 5–7 P.M. with wine flights at discounted prices. In the summer months, sit outside on the patio.

Italian

Nothing tastes better after a day of skiing than some basic, hearty Italian food, and that's what they do best at **Lanza's** (7739 N. Lake Blvd., Kings Beach, 530/546-2434, www.lanzastahoe.com, 5–10 P.M. daily, $14–22), an always-packed restaurant that is a great place for families and friends with big appetites. Choose a pasta from the menu and a sauce to put on it (marinara, pesto, and lots more), then add extras like Italian sausage or meatballs. Or go with rich, hearty Italian dishes like chicken or eggplant parmesan, baked penne, or lasagna. Lanza's has been packing in customers eager for homemade Italian dinners since 1973.

Mexican

Caliente! (8791 N. Lake Blvd., Kings Beach, 530/546-1000, www.calientetahoe.com, 4 P.M.–2 A.M. daily, $10–26) serves innovative Southwestern food—a far cry from basic bean-and-meat burritos. From the decor to the menu, you may think you are in Sante Fe. Caliente's specialties include grilled and batter-fried fish tacos, sweet corn polenta, grilled skirt steak, and braised beef rib flautas, but everything on the menu is worth a try. In the summer, everyone wants a seat on the rooftop deck, but the interior of the restaurant is also inviting, although it can be loud if the place is packed. With 100-plus varieties of tequila on the menu

and a bar that stays open late, cocktails are a big deal here. If it is your first visit, order a chupacabra. Lightweights should start with the smaller, 16-ounce size, and designate a non-drinking driver.

WEST SHORE
American

The lakefront restaurant at **Sunnyside** (1850 W. Lake Blvd., Tahoe City, 530/583-7200 or 800/822-2754, www.sunnysidetahoe.com, 4:30–10 P.M. daily year-round, 11:30 A.M.–10 P.M. daily in summer) features an expansive outdoor deck, which the owners claim is the largest lakeside deck in all of Tahoe. Regardless of its boasting rights, Sunnyside's deck is the happening, go-to place for lunch on a sunny summer day. The restaurant offers several different menus: a casual grill menu with burgers, salads, and the like ($11–17), a full array of more formal lunch and dinner entrées ($15–27), and a separate children's menu. The menus offer no surprises, with steaks, seafood, and a Kobe burger as the mainstays, but the food isn't the big attraction here—it's the lake view and the party atmosphere. If you've ever eaten at a Duke's or Hula Grill restaurant in Hawaii, you'll recognize Sunnyside's Hula Pie dessert, which is basically an enormous slice of ice cream pie. Sunnyside is a member of the same chain. Many Tahoe boaters cruise up to Sunnyside's dock and tie up, then enjoy lunch, dinner, or a rum-filled cocktail on the deck. Those without boats must resort to driving their cars or riding their bikes—Sunnyside sits right on the bike path.

Just down the road a short distance, the **West Shore Café** (5160 W. Lake Blvd., 530/525-5200, www.westshorecafe.com, 11:30 A.M.–9 P.M. daily in summer, noon–9 P.M. Fri.–Mon. in winter, dinner $20–45, lunch $13–30) is worth a look just for its elegant architecture (dark wood, high ceilings, big windows) and perfect lakefront setting. Under new

The deck at Sunnyside is a popular spot for lunch in summer.

and improved ownership as of 2011, this restaurant is a great choice for a special evening
out, but you will enjoy your meal more in the
daylight, when you can sit outside and enjoy
the truly amazing view. Whether you sit inside
or out on the deck, Lake Tahoe is practically in
your lap. The dinner menu consists of a laundry
list of standards (king salmon, Alaskan halibut,
Niman Ranch pork chop, New York strip steak,
rack of lamb) prepared very well and beautifully
presented. In summer, the West Shore Café offers valet boat service, just in case you arrived
in your private yacht. Although the restaurant
is typically only open Friday–Monday in winter, they offer a great happy hour from 3–5 P.M.
to entice the skiing crowd from Homewood,
located right across the street. During happy
hour, a selection of drinks and appetizers are
half price, making this high-end place very affordable. And once you've sampled the seared
ahi or the barbecued pork "wings," you'll be
clamoring to come back.

California Cuisine

Situated at the end of a narrow access road
off Highway 89, **C** **Chambers Landing
Restaurant** (6400 W. Lake Blvd., Homewood,
530/525-9190, www.chamberslandingbaran-
drestaurant.com, 11:30 A.M.–11 P.M. daily in
summer, closed in winter, $23–32) has the feel
of a "secret spot," when in fact it is anything
but. The main restaurant, a charming pavilion built of river rock and wood beams, enjoys a parklike setting a few feet from Tahoe's
shoreline. Its folding French doors allow it to
be completely open-air on warm days. The
building at the end of the pier is one of the
most photogenic spots on the West Shore. This
quaint structure is Lake Tahoe' oldest bar and
also its oldest boathouse, built in 1875 by John
Washington McKinney, who opened a hunting
and fishing camp on this site. Today, Chambers
is owned by West Shore locals Rick and Betty
Brown, who offer a simple menu that includes
hamburgers, grilled chicken sandwiches,

© ANN MARIE BROWN

The historic boathouse at Chambers Landing attracts boaters and non-boaters to its rustic bar.

bratwurst, and an array of salads. But the big draw is the infamous Chambers Punch, which is concocted of several different kinds of rum and orange and pineapple juice. Boaters tie up at Chambers' dock just to slurp one down. Drink two or three, and you will not be able to drive your boat (or drive your car, if that's how you arrived).

The oldest continually operating restaurant in Tahoe, **Swiss Lakewood Lodge** (5055 W. Lake Blvd., Homewood, 530/525-5211, 5:30–10:30 P.M. daily in summer, closed in winter, $22–35) is *très* European. With its faux painting of a wine cellar, a huge wine cask mounted into the wall, and old-world decor, you'll be convinced you are somewhere in western Europe, not California. This is the kind of place where beef Wellington and roast duck are standard issue, as well as Swiss-style fondue, rack of lamb, weinerschnitzel, veal, and venison. Vegetarians may not be happy here, especially when they see the mounted goat head

that hangs over the stone fireplace in the bar. If you are dining with a group, reserve the private dining room. In 2009, locals Rick and Betty Brown took over Swiss Lakewood (they also run Chambers Landing), and they are doing a great job with this classic, old-style Tahoe restaurant.

TRUCKEE AND SQUAW VALLEY
Breakfast and Lunch

Breakfast aficionados make haste for the dozens of omelet varieties at the diminutive and appropriately named **Squeeze In** (10060 Donner Pass Rd., Truckee, 530/587-9814, www.squeezein.com, 7 A.M.–2 P.M. daily, $10–16). Dozens of omelets? Yup, there are no fewer than 64 omelet choices on the menu, and the folks at Squeeze In claim that all of them are "the best on the planet." The tiny Truckee location, open since 1974, is decorated in charming Tahoe kitsch, including ski photos, bikes

A LIQUID TOUR OF LAKE TAHOE

Mai tais in Maui, margaritas in Mexico, hurricanes in New Orleans.... Seasoned travelers know you can judge a destination by the quality of its cocktails, and by that measure, Tahoe scores high marks. Whether it's après-ski or après-boating, there's something about sipping a liquid elixir lakeside that makes it clear you're on vacation. Here's a brief tour of some of Tahoe's great spots for signature cocktails:

· **North Shore: Gar Woods Grill** claims they have sold more than two million **Wet Woodys** (a trio of specialty rums, peach schnapps, and fruit juices). When you order one, you join a large and convivial club. Not a rum fan? At nearby **Caliente** in Kings Beach, have a seat at the bar and sip a tequila-laced **chupacabra.**

· **West Shore:** One mixed drink reigns supreme in the Tahoe cocktail echelon, and it can be acquired only in summer at **Chambers Landing**. Imbibing in a **Chambers Punch** (a top-secret concoction of rums and fruit juices) is a lakeside summertime tradition—no, make that requirement. The rest of the year,

when Chambers is closed, head to the **West Shore Café** and order a **martini.**

· **South Shore:** On Saturdays in winter, sign up for the **snowshoe cocktail races** at Camp Richardson. Run around the snow-covered course wearing snowshoes and carrying a cocktail on a tray. Don't spill a drop and you win a prize. Camp Rich's signature drink is the **Rum Runner** (spiced rum, light rum, still more rum, plus fruit juice), but other bars around the lake also serve them. In summer, order one at the lakefront tiki bar at **Round Hill Pines Beach.**

· **East Shore:** Skiing is fun. Skiing combined with wine-tasting is a lot more fun. Make a reservation for **Last Tracks Wine Tasting** at Diamond Peak Ski Resort, held on Sunday afternoons from February to mid-April. Enjoy wine and appetizers at the mid-mountain lodge, then ski down the hill at sunset. Don't ski? Then head to nearby **Bite** in Incline Village for a **pomegranate diablo** (tequila, pomegranate puree, Cointreau, and fresh lime juice). It's always five o'clock in Tahoe.

hanging from the ceiling, and customers' graffiti scribbled on the walls. Two more Squeeze Ins are located in Reno, Nevada. In 2010, the restaurant was featured on the Food Network television show *Throwdown with Bobby Flay,* in which owner Misty Young made her popular Spanish tortilla omelet. Now she's an even bigger Truckee celebrity.

Wild Cherries (11429 Donner Pass Rd., Truckee, 530/582-5602, 6 A.M.–6 P.M. daily, $5–12) is wildly popular, and for good reason. This is not your average coffeehouse, although the coffee is delicious; it's a combination bistro-café-gathering place that is always packed with people, despite its roomy interior and abundance of seating. For visitors, the free wireless Internet is a draw, and for locals, it's all about getting your breakfast or lunch in a place

where everybody knows your name. On weekend mornings, there's always a line-up at the counter for the large variety of bagels, muffins, pastries, and cookies (including some gluten-free choices). For those who want "real" food, a full menu offers choices: breakfast burritos, turkey pesto panini sandwich, vegan hummus wrap, big salads, freshly made soups and chili, and fruit smoothies. Skiers, you'll be among your people here. Wild Cherries is owned by ski racer Kristin Krone, who competed in the 1988 and 1992 Olympics.

And if you are looking for coffee in the quaint downtown area of Truckee, make a beeline for **Coffeebar** (10120 Jibboom St., Truckee, 530/587-2000, www.coffeebar-truckee.com, 6 A.M.–8 P.M. daily, $5–12), which looks and feels like a true Italian coffee

Be sure to try the Spanish tortilla omelet at Squeeze In.

bar, with an eco-friendly, sustainable twist. They are all about recycling and organics here. Coffeebar's baristas are artists, creating original designs on top of lattes and cappuccinos. Want something different? Try a lemon chiffon latte. There's regional Italian food, too, including paninis, salads, sweet and savory crepes, and a wealth of pastries. The strudels, which are stuffed with fillings running the gamut from red velvet to spinach and mashed potatoes, are local favorites.

Burger Joints

When a well-known chef and restaurateur opens up a burger joint, you just have to give it a try. **C Burger Me!** (10418 Donner Pass Rd., Truckee, 530/587-8852, 11 A.M.–9 P.M. daily, $7–12) is the creation of Mark Estee of the upscale Moody's Bistro. Like at his other restaurants, Estee doesn't skimp on ingredients. At Burger Me!, the burgers are made from beef

from Five Dot Ranch that is 100 percent all natural—no antibiotics or hormones. Milk shakes are made with Ben & Jerry's ice cream and organic milk. A basic hamburger comes on a white or wheat bun with any or all of the following: caramelized onions, lettuce, tomato, pickle, and special sauce. You can add cheddar, swiss, blue cheese, avocado, bacon, mushrooms, sauerkraut, or even a fried egg for 50 cents more. Turkey and veggie burgers are also available, and sometimes buffalo and ahi tuna, too. Whatever you order, you must get a side of the sweet potato fries.

Casual American

With an impressive view that overlooks downtown Truckee and the river canyon beyond, summer outdoor dining, and romantic candlelight in winter, **C Cottonwood** (10142 Rue Hilltop at Brockway Rd., Truckee, 530/587-5711, www.cottonwoodrestaurant.com, 4:30–10 P.M. daily, entrées $17–38, salads $7–15) is a winner for dinner in all four Tahoe seasons. The restaurant somehow manages to be rustic and sophisticated at the same time, as in "Truckee meets San Francisco." The decor (wooden skis, antique sleds, old Truckee photographs, candlelight chandeliers) creates an inviting setting for the creative and tasty food, which includes an eclectic variety of salads—try the garlic-laden Caesar, which should be eaten with your fingers—plus entrées like Thai red curry prawns, rabbit cassoulet, tofu stir-fry, and a memorable seafood stew. In summer, be sure to sit outside on the deck and order one of their incredible French martinis. If you are wondering about the history of this wooden hilltop structure, Cottonwood is housed in one of the nation's oldest ski lodges. In the late 1920s, a ski area was located here, complete with rope tows and a Poma lift that rose 700 vertical feet. The resort operated until 1969.

Casual diners who enjoy well-prepared food

© ANN MARIE BROWN

The vintage stainless-steel-and-glass JAX Truckee Diner is a hit with kids and adults.

will like the **Pacific Crest Restaurant,** a hip, friendly bistro located adjacent to the Bar of America in downtown Truckee (10042 Donner Pass Rd., Truckee, 530/587-2626, 11 A.M.– 9:30 P.M. daily, $9–28). A selection of creative wood-fired pizzas, sandwiches, and pastas is served for lunch and dinner, without any accompanying hype. Be sure to try the roasted portobello mushroom appetizer, or the cassoulet entrée. Weekend brunches are popular.

The populace mourned when the nostalgia-loving Truckee Diner closed in 2006, but it was reincarnated by restaurateur Bud Haley in 2009 as **JAX Truckee Diner** (10144 W. River St., Truckee, 530/550-7450, www.jax-truckee.com, 7 A.M.–10 P.M. daily, $10–17). The diner serves three squares a day in a vintage 1940s stainless-steel-and-glass structure next to Truckee's railroad tracks. Featured in the Food Network's television show *Diners, Drive-Ins, and Dives,* the cuisine here is best described as gourmet comfort food. Breakfast

and lunch are a complete array of everything you'd expect at a diner, but served with a lot more panache than at your average Denny's. Dinner has all the classics plus a few surprises, like Maryland blue crab cakes and Kobe beef meatloaf. There are plenty of burgers, pastas, and salads as well. Kids love this place, and not just because of the extensive kids' menu. Your server will also give them Etch-a-Sketches to play with until the meal arrives. The entire experience is a bit kitschy and on the pricey side, but if you are a fan of classic diners, you'll love this place.

The traveling public loves a good local brewery, and they'll find it at **Fifty Fifty Brewing** (11197 Brockway Rd., Truckee, 530/587-2337, www.fiftyfiftybrewing.com, 11:30 A.M.– 9:30 P.M. Mon.–Thurs., 11:30 A.M.–10 P.M. Fri., 10 A.M.–10 P.M. Sat.–Sun., $8–26). As at most breweries, Fifty Fifty offers an expansive selection of house brews and a diverse menu of pub-style food. Try the green chili soup, the

© ANN MARIE BROWN

Pub grub and a big selection of house brews are available at Fifty Fifty Brewing.

ahi BLT, or any one of the burgers and you'll go home happy. There are plenty of vegetarian choices, too. During dinner hours, this place is always packed, so if you are looking for a place for a quiet, romantic meal, this isn't it. But for après-ski with your buddies, you can't go wrong.

Open for three meals a day, **Smokey's Kitchen** (12036 Donner Pass Rd., Truckee, 530/582-4535, www.smokeyskitchen.com, 7 A.M.–9 P.M. daily, $5–24) is a dependable choice for family-style, casual American food, with an emphasis on barbecue. Lunch and dinner consist of hamburgers, veggie burgers, and barbecued meats in every possible configuration: pork ribs, beef ribs, pulled pork, pulled chicken, smoked links, beef brisket, and even barbecued salmon. If you order any kind of barbecue, you'll get to choose from a selection of classic side dishes, like corn bread, cowboy beans, onion rings, and more. Smokey's breakfast menu offers omelets, pancakes, and burritos ($5–13).

California Cuisine

If money is no object, you must have dinner at **Manzanita** at the Ritz-Carlton Hotel at Northstar-at-Tahoe (13031 Ritz-Carlton Highlands Ct., Truckee, 530/562-3000, www.manzanitalaketahoe.com, breakfast 7–11 A.M. daily, lunch 11 A.M.–2:30 P.M. daily, dinner 5:30–9:30 P.M. Sun.–Tues. and 5:30–10 P.M. Wed.–Sat., dinner entrées $34–43). There's a famous chef at the helm (Traci Des Jardins of San Francisco's Jardiniere) and a dark wood decor that clearly cost lots of money. Check out the bar's frozen "ice rail," on which drinks are set. Nothing on the dinner menu will surprise you (filet mignon, short ribs, seared sea bass), but everything is prepared with the best ingredients and the utmost care. Desserts are worth saving room for—especially the fresh sorbet. If dinner is too rich for your budget, show up for lunch for a $20 burger or $15 personal pizza. Really, it's worth it.

Situated right next to the Christy Lodge,

NORTH AND WEST SHORES

Graham's (1650 Squaw Valley Rd., Olympic Valley, 530/581-0454, www.dinewine.com, 5:30–10 P.M. Tues.–Sun. in winter, Wed.–Sun. in summer, $14–32) is a top pick for Squaw Valley diners. Housed in the first home constructed in Squaw Valley, which was built for the original owners of the ski resort, Graham's intimate dining room has a high pine ceiling and rock fireplace. Owner and chef Graham Rock is big on grilling things; a major portion of the brief menu consists of grilled meats—elk, veal, salmon, tuna, and lamb chops. A few appetizers shouldn't be passed by: the grilled quail over polenta and the potato leek soup. With more than 800 wines on its wine list, the restaurant has won the *Wine Spectator* Award of Excellence several times, as well as many other accolades.

Like its sibling restaurant in San Francisco, **PlumpJack Restaurant and Bar** at Squaw Valley (1920 Squaw Valley Rd., Olympic Village, 530/583-1578 or 800/323-7666, www.plumpjack.com, 7:30–10:30 A.M. and 6–10 P.M. daily, dinner $23–33) serves elegant, seasonal cuisine in a chic setting. The restaurant has received high marks from the *San Francisco Chronicle* as well as numerous travel magazines. The menu changes frequently, but count on creative dishes like almond-crusted halibut, bison short ribs, and Niman Ranch pork tenderloin. If you can't afford dinner here, try breakfast ($15 for the buffet) or lunch, or order from the bar/café menu (11:30 A.M.–10 P.M. daily, $9–19). The Balboa burger, made with ground chuck, will fill you up for about 10 hours. Since the restaurant is part of the PlumpJack Squaw Valley Inn, which hosts lots of skiing families, it even has a kids' menu.

Located in the Truckee Hotel, **Moody's Bistro and Lounge** (10007 Bridge St., Truckee, 530/587-8688, www.moodysbistro.com, 11:30 A.M.–9:30 P.M. weekdays, until 10 P.M. Sat.–Sun., lunch $10–15, dinner $19–29) has a swank feel that you wouldn't expect to find in downtown Truckee. The scene here is almost as much about jazz as it is about food; live music is offered several nights a week with no cover charge. Dinner entrées include Idaho trout, beef short ribs, Niman Ranch pork chop, lamb shank, and venison. Vegetarians always have a few excellent selections, too, like an eggplant and coconut red curry. Lunch is mostly soups, salads, and burgers, and the Sunday brunch is a winner. Chef and co-owner Mark Estee prides himself on a fresh, season-specific menu that changes daily.

Located in the Cedar House Sport Hotel, the restaurant **Stella** (10918 Brockway Rd., Truckee, 530/582-5655, www.cedarhousesporthotel.com, 5:30–8:30 P.M. Thurs.–Sun., $24–33) is a pleasant surprise for Cedar House hotel guests and others who happen to wander in, drawn by the aroma of fresh bread baking in wood-fired ovens. Stella's cozy, environmentally friendly space is the ideal setting for its uber-fresh, California-style cuisine. The menu changes at the whim of the chef, but a four-course tasting menu is often offered ($55). Entrées that appear frequently are roasted salmon, rack of lamb, and a duck confit cassoulet.

Italian

When you are craving Italian food, nothing else will do, so head straight to **Pianeta Cucina Italiana** (10096 Donner Pass Rd., Truckee, 530/587-4694, 5:30–9:30 P.M. daily, $19–35) and sate your need for melt-in-your-mouth pasta and fragrant sauces. This split-level restaurant with brick and stone walls and a dark wood interior is just the place for a romantic dinner after a day on the slopes. An interesting variety of raviolis and pastas are featured daily, but meat and seafood lovers can find plenty of options, too. The wine list is extensive and well priced, and don't forget to save room for tiramisu or one of the daily house-made desserts. As for the restaurant's name, *pianeta* means planet in Italian.

If you like your pizza truly New York–style,

with a crust so thin it's easiest to eat each slice by folding it in half, you'll love **Best Pies Pizzeria** (10068 Donner Pass Rd., Truckee, 530/582-1111, www.bestpiesco.com, 4–9 P.M. Mon., 11 A.M.–10 P.M. Tues.–Thurs., 11 A.M.– midnight Fri.–Sat., 11 A.M.–9 P.M. Sun., $16– 23 for a whole pizza). And if you like being able to order just a slice instead of a whole pizza, you will also be happy. All the usual toppings are available, but for something different, try the fried eggplant and sun-dried tomato pie, or the pizzadilla with chicken, jalapeños, onions, ranch, and wing sauce. The garlic knots appetizer—pieces of pizza dough tied into knots and baked, served swimming in a garlic-and-herb butter sauce—is a winner ($3).

Mexican

The best choice for Mexican food in Truckee, and possibly anywhere around the lake, is **Tacos Jalisco** (11400 Donner Pass Rd., Truckee, 530/587-1131, 8 A.M.–9:30 P.M. daily, $5–15), tucked away behind the 7-Eleven on Truckee's main drag. Get your taco fix here once, and you'll never want to go anywhere else. The house specialty is the Armadillo, which is cactus, beef, pork, shrimp, and peppers simmered in a spicy sauce, served steaming in a *molcajete* (lava rock bowl). In keeping with true Mexican tradition, on Sunday they serve menudo, a soup made from tripe (don't ask what that is), hominy, and chile peppers. No need to dress up here; this is a hole-in-the-wall place and nothing more, but the food is fantastic and cheap. There's often a line out the door and no place left to sit.

Located on the far west end of Commercial Row in Truckee, **El Toro Bravo** (10186 Donner Pass Rd., Truckee, 530/587-3557, 11:30 A.M.– 9:30 P.M. Sun.–Thurs., until 10 P.M. Fri.–Sat., $5–25) is housed in a small historic cottage. In addition to many traditional Mexican entrées (steak or chicken fajitas, chimichangas, enchiladas, chili rellenos, and the like), the restaurant serves a number of seafood specialties, like seviche, snapper Santa Cruz, grilled prawns, and oysters. Happy hour, 4–6 P.M., is popular with Truckee locals. If you've ever been to Santa Cruz, you may have eaten at El Toro Bravo's sister restaurant in Capitola.

Asian

You won't find chow mein on the menu at Asian-influenced **Dragonfly** (10118 Donner Pass Rd., Truckee, 530/587-0557, www.dragonflycuisine.com, 11 A.M.–2:30 P.M. and 5:30–9:30 P.M. daily, appetizers $11–14, lunch $9–13, dinner $23–28), but you will find Chinese five-spice pork tenderloin, Asian-style cioppino, and seared unagi. The menu may seem a bit trendy for downtown Truckee, but its fusion of Thai, Japanese, Vietnamese, and Indian cuisine is ingenious, and the Zen-like ambience of this place is sure to lower your blood pressure by a few points. Lots of diners favor the seafood noodle bowls, but if green curry is your thing, order it here. The sushi bar is also a winner. In summer, sit outside on the upstairs deck and watch the action on the street in downtown Truckee.

Don't think that just because you are 250 miles from the ocean, you can't get good sushi. All your raw favorites are available at **Mamasake** (The Village at Squaw Valley, 530/584-0110, www.mamasake.com, 11:30 A.M.–9:30 P.M. Mon.–Thurs., until 10 P.M. Fri.–Sun., $10–20). True to its name, Mamasake has a sake bar (be sure to order a sake martini), plus lots of unusual roll combinations and tapas-style small plates that will keep non-fish-eaters happy. One of the most popular menu items is Mama's Balls, which are fried inari pockets filled with seafood salad and tofu. A double-sided movie theater divides the dining room, and not surprisingly, skiing films are usually what's on the bill.

Not to be outdone by Squaw, the Village at Northstar also has its own sushi bar, **Mikuni**

(5001 Northstar Dr., Ste. 5101, 530/562-2188, www.mikunisushi.com, noon–9 P.M. Sun.–Thurs., noon–9:30 P.M. Fri.–Sat., $7–18), located right next to the skating rink. Yes, this is part of the Sacramento-based sushi chain by the same name, and yes, most of the rolls are the newfangled kind, featuring trendy combinations and eclectic sauces. The Truckee Train Wreck is their most popular roll and costs nearly 20 bucks, but you gotta try it.

Located near the Truckee airport, in the same shopping complex as Fifty Fifty Brewing Company, **Drunken Monkey** (11253 Brockway Rd., Truckee, 530/582-9755, www.drunkenmonkeysushi.com, 11:30 A.M.–9 P.M. Tues.–Sun., 5–9 P.M. Mon., $5–15) is a welcome addition to the sushi offerings in the Truckee area. The sushi is high quality and well prepared; you won't find any of the dreaded "imitation crab" here. But this is not just a sushi restaurant; it's also a place to order Asian-style tapas and noodle dishes, or sit at the Sake Bar and taste a huge selection of hot and cold sakes. For a special experience, order the "shabu shabu" hot-pot dinner for two (best to call ahead and reserve). It's a little bit like a meat-in-broth fondue.

For a taste of Bangkok in Thailand, make a beeline to **Thai Nakorn** (10770 Donner Pass Rd., Truckee, 530/550-0503, www.thainakorntruckee.com, 11 A.M.–9 P.M. Mon.–Fri., 4–9:30 P.M. Sat., $6–16), where you can order all your Thai favorites: lemongrass soup, pad Thai, pineapple fried rice, thom kai gai, and several flavors and colors of curry (try the pumpkin). Thai Nakorn's owners have two other locations in the area, one in South Lake Tahoe and another in Reno, so they are no strangers to the restaurant business.

DONNER LAKE AND SODA SPRINGS
California Cuisine
Just 15 minutes west of Truckee off I-80 lies

a special restaurant worthy of a special trip—the dining room at **Rainbow Lodge** (50080 Hampshire Rocks Rd., Soda Springs, 530/426-3661, www.therainbowlodge.com, breakfast and lunch 10 A.M.–2:30 P.M. and dinner 5:30–8:30 P.M., Thurs.–Mon., hours vary seasonally, $22–33). Start off with a drink in the historic lodge's lounge, which is decorated with photographs of early-1900s life at Donner Summit. Then, in summer, enjoy dinner on the patio overlooking the Yuba River, or in winter, by the river-rock fireplace in the dining room. Dinner entrées have a French country influence and include grilled duck breast, artichoke chicken, steak Diane, venison medallions, and a vegetable cassoulet. Don't miss the wild mushroom strudel appetizer. You can also order from the bar menu, where burgers and bar food are in the $8–14 range.

If a lake view appeals to you more than a river view, head over to the **Ice Lakes Lodge** at Serene Lakes (1111 Soda Springs Rd., Soda Springs, 530/426-7660, www.theicelakeslodge.com, noon–8 P.M. Fri.–Sat., noon–3 P.M. Sun., 5:30–8 P.M. Thurs., hours vary seasonally, $12–28). This restaurant also has well-deserved bragging rights for lovely alpine scenery—its huge windows overlook Serena and Dulzura Lakes—and memorable meals. Dinner entrées include a layered vegetable napoleon, baby back ribs, grilled Alaskan halibut, and house-made chicken potpie. The restaurant is usually closed on Tuesday and Wednesday.

American
If you've just come off the slopes at Sugar Bowl, Royal Gorge, or any of the Donner-area resorts, you probably want to eat ASAP. The **Summit Restaurant and Bar** (22002 Donner Pass Rd., Soda Springs, 530/426-3904, www.summitrestaurantandbar.com, 8 A.M.–8:30 P.M. Sat.–Sun., 4–8:30 P.M. weekdays, $8–22) comes to the rescue with a variety of sandwiches, including a half-pound sirloin

burger or a big breast of chicken, plus a few salads and lots of calorie-replenishing foods like onion rings and ice cream. Think of it as a Denny's restaurant in the mountains. There's no ambience to speak of, but your belly will be full when you leave.

Practicalities

INFORMATION

The following visitors centers are particularly helpful if you are looking for lodging, restaurants, tours, or businesses of any kind: **The Truckee Donner Chamber of Commerce** (10065 Donner Pass Rd., Truckee, 530/587-8808, www.truckee.com, 9 A.M.–5:30 P.M. daily) and **Tahoe City Visitors Center** (380 N. Lake Blvd., Tahoe City, 530/581-6900 or 888/434-1262, www.gotahoenorth.com, 9 A.M.–5 P.M. daily).

The **U.S. Forest Service** has a visitors center near Truckee (10342 Hwy. 89, Truckee, 530/587-3558, 8 A.M.–4:30 P.M. weekdays) and another at Big Bend (49685 Hampshire Rocks Rd., Soda Springs, take the Big Bend or Rainbow Rd. exit off I-80, 530/426-3609, hours vary). Here you will find tons of information on hiking, biking, and other outdoor activities on Tahoe National Forest land. There are books on Tahoe's natural history for sale, as well as hiking maps and guides. Information on Tahoe National Forest can also be found on the Web at www.fs.fed.us/r5/tahoe.

SERVICES
Medical Care

The North and West Shores are served by two hospitals under the same ownership: **Tahoe Forest Hospital** (10121 Pine Ave. at Donner Pass Rd., Truckee, 530/587-6011 or 800/733-9953, www.tfhd.com) and **Incline Village Community Hospital** (880 Alder Ave., Incline Village, 775/833-4100, www.tfhd.com).

Post Offices

Several post offices are conveniently located along the North and West Shores: the **Truckee post office** (10050 Bridge St. at Jibboom St., 800/275-8777), the **Tahoe City post office** (Lighthouse Shopping Center, 950 N. Lake Blvd., 800/275-8777), and the **West Shore post office** (5375 W. Lake Blvd., Homewood, 530/525-6777). Smaller post offices are located in Tahoma, Kings Beach, Carnelian Bay, Tahoe Vista, Olympic Valley, and Soda Springs.

Internet Access

Need to check your email or surf the Web? The North Shore's two public libraries have access: **Kings Beach Branch** (301 Secline St., Kings Beach, 530/546-2021) or **Tahoe City Branch** (740 N. Lake Blvd., Tahoe City, 530/583-3382). In Truckee, go to the Truckee Branch of the **Nevada County Library** (10031 Levon Ave., Truckee, 530/582-7846). You can also get Internet access at the **North Lake Tahoe Chamber of Commerce** office (245 N. Lake Blvd., Tahoe City, 530/581-6900).

If you are traveling with your laptop and it is enabled for wireless Internet, many businesses on the North Shore have wireless access. The Village at Squaw Valley, the Village at Northstar, most of downtown Truckee, many Tahoe City establishments, and the Truckee-Tahoe Airport are all Wi-Fi enabled. On the West Shore, Ed Z'berg Sugar Pine Point State Park has Wi-Fi access (within 200 feet of the Carriage House).

GETTING THERE
By Air

The **Truckee-Tahoe Airport** (10356 Truckee Airport Rd., 530/587-4119 or 800/359-2875, www.truckeetahoeairport.com) is currently not operational for commercial flights. But visitors can fly into the **Reno-Tahoe International Airport** (2001 E. Plumb La., 775/328-6400, www.renoairport.com) and then rent a car or take shuttle or limousine service. North Lake Tahoe Express (866/216-5222, www.northlaketahoeexpress.com, $40 per person one-way, $75 round-trip, discounts for multiple people in your party) has scheduled service from the airport to various points on the North Shore 3:30 A.M.–midnight daily. For a private ride, reserve with Bell Limousine (800/235-5466 or 775/786-3700, www.bell-limo.com).

Visitors can also fly into the Sacramento, Oakland, San Francisco, or San Jose airports and drive from there. Sacramento Airport is 2 hours from the North and West Shores; the three other airports are about 3.5 hours away.

By Car

From the San Francisco Bay Area or Sacramento, the primary driving route to the North and West Shores of Lake Tahoe is to take I-80 east to Truckee and then Highway 89 south to Tahoe City (about 2 hours or 100 miles from Sacramento and 3.5 hours or 200 miles from San Francisco).

From Reno-Tahoe International Airport, take I-80 west for 32 miles to Truckee. In Truckee, connect to Highway 267 to travel south to the lakeshore at Tahoe Vista or Kings Beach (12 miles), or Highway 89 to travel south to Tahoe City (15 miles).

By Bus

Visitors can access Truckee by two major bus lines: **Greyhound Bus Lines** (800/231-2222, www.greyhound.com) or **Amtrak Bus** (800/872-7245, www.amtrak.com). Tahoe Area Regional Transit (TART) (530/550-1212 or 800/736-6365, www.laketahoetransit.com) system buses connect with these bus lines at

the Truckee Depot to take passengers to points along the West and North Shores. A brand-new bus depot is under construction at the 64 Acres recreational park near the Tahoe City Y and will be completed in summer 2012. The $7 million facility will have 130 parking spaces, making it much easier for visitors to connect with TART buses to get around the North and West Shores.

By Train

The nearest Amtrak train depots are in Truckee or Reno. For schedules and information, contact **Amtrak** (800/872-7245, www.amtrak.com). Tahoe Area Regional Transit system buses connect with Amtrak at the Truckee Depot to take passengers to points along the West and North Shores.

GETTING AROUND
Shuttles and Buses

Tahoe Area Regional Transit (TART) (530/550-1212 or 800/736-6365, www.laketahoetransit.com) buses run a regular schedule from Meeks Bay north to Sugar Pine Point, Homewood, and Tahoe City (6 A.M.–7 P.M. daily). From Tahoe City, TART buses run north to Truckee and north and then west to Squaw Valley. TART buses also run east from Tahoe City to Tahoe Vista, Kings Beach, and Incline Village. Call or check the website for schedules and information. One-way fares are $1.75 for adults, $0.85 for children 6–12 and seniors 60-plus, and free for children 5 and under. All-day passes are $3.50 adults, $1.75 children and seniors. Most of the year, free buses also run in the evening hours; check the website for details.

TART also runs the free **Tahoe Trolley** June 30–early September, with service in and around Tahoe City, and in between Tahoe City and Squaw Valley, Tahoe Vista, Crystal Bay, and Incline Village, as well as the free **Emerald**

Bay Shuttle between Tahoe City and Emerald Bay late May–early October.

In winter, TART offers a free "Night Rider" service along the North Shore. Rides are free approximately 6:30 P.M.–midnight; scheduled stops are in Tahoe City, Squaw Valley, Northstar Resort, Homewood, Sunnyside Resort, Granlibakken, the Tahoe Biltmore, and more.

The town of Truckee operates **Truckee Transit** (530/587-7451), a year-round service that offers both fixed route and Dial-A-Ride bus service in the greater Truckee area. Fixed routes vary by the season, but in winter (mid-Dec.–mid-Apr.), a free ski shuttle service is offered daily between Henness Flats, downtown Truckee, Sugar Bowl, Donner Ski Ranch, and Soda Springs ski resorts, approximately 6:15 A.M.–noon and 2–7 P.M.

North Lake Tahoe Express (866/216-5222, www.northlaketahoeexpress.com, $40 one-way, $75 round-trip) offers service from North Lake Tahoe and Truckee to the Reno-Tahoe International Airport 3:30 A.M.–midnight. Reservations are required 24 hours in advance.

By Car

To get current updates on road conditions in California, phone 800/427-7623 or go to www. dot.ca.gov. To get current updates on Nevada road conditions, phone 877/687-6237 or go to www.safetravelusa.com.

For **car rentals,** contact Enterprise Rent-a-Car (11375 Deerfield Dr., Truckee, 530/550-1550) or Hertz (10266 Truckee Airport Rd., Truckee, 530/550-9191). All the major car-rental agencies are also available at Reno-Tahoe International Airport.

By Taxi

Several private cab services can get you where you want to go on the North Shore, or pick you up or drop you off at the Reno-Tahoe airport. Contact any of the following services: Truckee Tahoe Transportation (530/582-5828, www. truckeetahoetransportation.com), All-Star Taxi (530/448-2552, www.taxitahoe.com), Anytime Taxi (877/808-8294 or 530/414-4187, www. anytimetaxi.net), North Tahoe Checker Cab (866/420-8294 or 530/587-0666), or Lake Tahoe Taxi (530/577-7000).

EAST SHORE

The sunny East Shore of Lake Tahoe has two decidedly different personalities, embodied by the wealthy ski-and-golf town of Incline Village and the casino town of Crystal Bay to the north, and the miles of seemingly endless white sand that caresses the Nevada shoreline to the south. In Incline Village and Crystal Bay, you'll find some of the highest-income residents and most architecturally extravagant homes on the lake. Traveling southward, you'll find thousands of acres of undeveloped land—managed by the U.S. Forest Service and Lake Tahoe Nevada State Park—including the longest stretch of uninterrupted public shoreline on the entire lake.

The two biggest towns, Crystal Bay and Incline Village, are separated by a five-minute drive. Crystal Bay is marked by its four casinos—Crystal Bay Club, Cal-Neva Resort, Tahoe Biltmore, and Jim Kelly's Nugget—which, unlike their more modern South Shore counterparts, are a throwback to the gaming spirit of the 1950s and 1960s. The well-heeled town of Incline Village received its name not from its two nearby ski resorts but from the 1860s-era Incline Tramway, a 4,000-foot hydraulic tramway that hauled lumber 1,400 feet in elevation to the top of the ridge. The lumber then traveled in a water flume to the Virginia and Truckee Railroad yard near Carson City for use in the Virginia City silver mines.

By the late 1800s, Incline Village was

© ANN MARIE BROWN

HIGHLIGHTS

© AVALON TRAVEL

LOOK FOR ◖ TO FIND RECOMMENDED SIGHTS, ACTIVITIES, DINING, AND LODGING.

◖ *Sierra Cloud* **cruise:** Board this 55-foot catamaran from the Hyatt Regency's "floating bar" on its pier, then ply the waters of Tahoe while enjoying beer, wine, and appetizers (page 206).

◖ **Memorial Point:** This easy-access lake vista is located just a few miles south of Incline Village and provides a scenic introduction to the boulder-lined beauty of the East Shore (page 209).

◖ **Thunderbird Lodge:** Sign up for a guided tour of Thunderbird Lodge, and you can marvel at the eccentricities of fabulously wealthy real estate magnate George Whittell Jr., who built the 16,500-square-foot mansion on Tahoe's shoreline and kept exotic pets (page 209).

◖ **Virginia City:** A short drive from the lake into the interior of Nevada will bring you to Virginia City, the town made infamous by the Comstock silver-mining boom of 1857-1877, and at that time the second-biggest city in the West (page 211).

◖ **Chimney Beach and Secret Harbor:** This easy hike follows a wide trail that descends a little more than a half mile to Tahoe's east shoreline. From there, a path runs north and south to a series of rocky coves and secluded beaches, where there is plenty of room for swimmers and sunbathers to claim their own private stretch of sand (page 217).

◖ **Flume Trail:** If you're in good shape and have some experience on a mountain bike, don't miss the chance to ride one of the West's most famous trails, which runs high above Lake Tahoe's East Shore, providing outstanding lake views and nerve-wracking drop-offs (page 220).

◖ **Sand Harbor:** One of the East Shore's most beautiful beaches, Sand Harbor is a long white stretch of sand dotted with rounded boulders. It's a fine place to while away a summer's day (page 224).

completely deforested, and it remained a mere blip on the map until the late 1950s, when it was developed as a vacation resort as part of the Tahoe growth spurt instigated by the 1960 Winter Olympics at Squaw Valley. Even though the town is clearly well-to-do, its ambience is understated. The main landmark that defines the area is 10,778-foot Mount Rose, which

offers some of Lake Tahoe's best skiing in winter and highest-elevation hiking in summer.

A drive along the East Shore in the 20-mile stretch from Incline Village south to Zephyr Cove is pure eye candy. Although much of Highway 28 is lined by densely forested slopes, where the groves of conifers part, stunning vistas of the boulder-strewn shoreline and cobalt blue waters are visible. You won't find any commercial enterprises here except for the Spooner Lake Outdoor Company, which in summer operates a shuttle for mountain bikers riding the famous Flume Trail. Otherwise, there is nothing but public shoreline, and little for visitors to do except wander along the sand at one of a half dozen beaches with intriguing names, like Hidden, Sand Harbor, and Secret. More than anywhere else on Tahoe's shores, this is the place to go when you want to feel sand between your toes, wade into the lake, bask on warm granite boulders, and get lost in your own thoughts.

PLANNING YOUR TIME

Except for the towns of Incline Village and Crystal Bay, there is little in the way of visitor services on the East Shore. While mountain bikers and hikers could easily spend a week or more exploring the area's trails in summer, most visitors will be satisfied with two or three days here, whether for a skiing vacation in winter or a swimming and sunning vacation in summer. Be sure to allow enough time to drive the length of the East Shore and spend some time at one or more of its scenic beaches, such as **Sand Harbor.** A sailboat cruise on the catamaran *Sierra Cloud* out of the Incline Village Hyatt Regency is a fine way to spend an afternoon. In the summer months, a tour of the **Thunderbird Lodge** is a must, and year-round you'll want to spend a half day or longer at **Virginia City.**

TOUR BOATS AND CRUISES
◖ *Sierra Cloud* Cruise

Board the 55-foot catamaran **Sierra Cloud** from the Hyatt Regency's "floating bar" on its pier (on the beach behind the Hyatt's Lone Eagle Grille, 967 Lakeshore Blvd., Incline Village, 775/831-4386, www.awsincline.com, 11 A.M., 1:30 P.M., and 4 P.M. daily, also 6:30 P.M. Fri., $60 adults, $30

the Hyatt Regency's pier

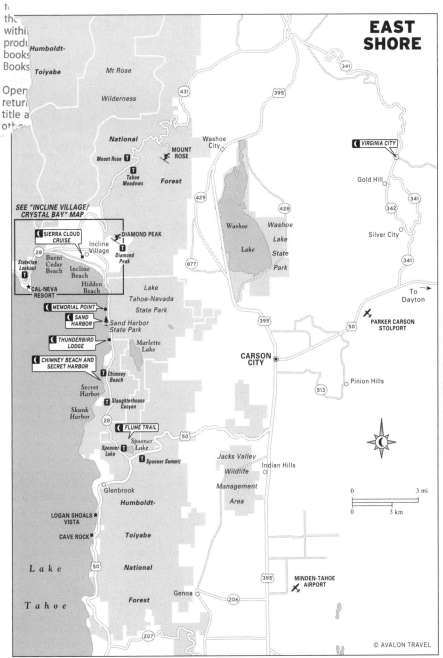

EAST SHORE

SEE "INCLINE VILLAGE/
CRYSTAL BAY" MAP

Humboldt-
Toiyabe

Mt Rose

Wilderness

National

Mount Rose

MOUNT
ROSE

Tahoe Meadows

Forest

SIERRA CLOUD
CRUISE

DIAMOND PEAK

Incline
Village

Diamond
Peak

Stateline
Lookout

Burnt
Cedar
Beach

Incline
Beach

Hidden
Beach

CAL-NEVA
RESORT

MEMORIAL POINT

SAND
HARBOR

Sand Harbor
State Park

Lake
Tahoe-Nevada
State Park

THUNDERBIRD
LODGE

Marlette
Lake

CHIMNEY BEACH AND
SECRET HARBOR

Chimney
Beach

Secret
Harbor

Slaughterhouse
Canyon

Skunk
Harbor

FLUME TRAIL

Spooner
Lake

Spooner Summit

Glenbrook

LOGAN SHOALS
VISTA

Humboldt-

CAVE ROCK

Toiyabe

National

Lake

Forest

Genoa

Tahoe

Washoe
City

VIRGINIA CITY

Gold Hill

Silver City

Washoe
Lake

Washoe
Lake
State
Park

To
Dayton

PARKER CARSON
STOLPORT

CARSON
CITY

Pinion Hills

Jacks Valley
Wildlife
Management
Area

Indian Hills

MINDEN-TAHOE
AIRPORT

0   3 mi
0   3 km

EAST SHORE

© AVALON TRAVEL

© ANN MARIE BROWN

A cruise on the *Sierra Cloud* catamaran is a fine way to spend an afternoon.

children), then ply the waters of Tahoe while enjoying beer, wine, and appetizers. Three cruises are offered daily, plus a Friday evening cruise with live music, each lasting about two hours. A nice assortment of wine, beer, cheese, and crackers are served by the young and friendly crew. With only 45 passengers on board, this cruise feels like a party with a bunch of good friends. For the best chance of having a strong wind in the sails, sign up for the 4 P.M. daily cruise or the Friday evening sunset cruise (late afternoons are more often breezy). When you return to the Hyatt Regency, you may want to cap off this great experience with dinner at the Lone Eagle Grille.

Sights

CAL-NEVA RESORT

Even if you aren't a gambler, Cal-Neva Resort casino (2 Tahoe Blvd./Hwy. 28, Crystal Bay, 775/832-4000 or 800/225-6382, www.cal-nevaresort.com) is worth a look. The casino, which was once owned by crooner Frank Sinatra, has a fascinating collection of photographs and artifacts of the Washoe Indian tribe housed in its Indian Room. The room's famous fireplace straddles the state line, as does the outdoor swimming pool. Like most casinos, this one is open 24 hours a day, so stop in anytime. Tours of the resort's underground tunnels are offered to the public.

TAHOE ENVIRONMENTAL RESEARCH CENTER

The scientifically inclined will enjoy a trip to Sierra Nevada College (291 Country Club Dr., Incline Village, 775/881-7566, http://terc.

ucdavis.edu, 1–5 P.M. Tues.–Fri., occasionally open on Sat., free) to see its three-story Tahoe Environmental Research Center, which was constructed with the latest green-building technology. Visitors can step aboard the virtual-reality deck of the U.C. Davis research vessel to see the instruments used to study the clarity of Lake Tahoe, or don 3-D glasses and "dive" under Lake Tahoe's surface, fly around the basin's watersheds, and see inside planet Earth to learn where earthquakes originate.

◖ MEMORIAL POINT

Located just two miles south of Incline Village on Highway 28, Memorial Point Overlook features one of the best and easiest-to-access lake vistas. Short trails lead to the edge of the lake, and there are lots of big boulders to climb around on (but no sand). Pack along a picnic, and you could easily while away an hour or two here, especially at sunset. Even in the winter

End the day with a picnic on the boulders at Memorial Point.

months, when much of the lakeshore is covered with snow, this sunny spot is usually warm and accessible. Best of all, there's no fee.

SAND HARBOR STATE PARK

Part of the Lake Tahoe Nevada State Park system, Sand Harbor (2005 Hwy. 28, 775/831-0494, www.parks.nv.gov, 8 A.M.–9 P.M. daily in summer, parking $12 per car, $1 fee for walk-ins) offers a rocky shoreline for fishing, a cove for snorkeling and scuba diving, a boat launch, sandy beaches for swimming and sunning, a stunning visitors center, a café and concession stand, and a self-guided, wheelchair-accessible nature trail along Sand Point. The 5,000-square-foot visitors center, which was completed in 2005 at a price tag of $5.1 million, features displays about Lake Tahoe's cultural and natural history, and an interactive map of the Tahoe basin. Food is available at the park's **Harbor House Bistro** (775/832-5115, open daily late May–early Sept.). Sand Harbor's gentle turquoise coves backed by giant granite boulders are a favorite spot for sunbathers, swimmers, and photographers. The crescent-shaped beach boasts soft, fine-grained, white sand, not the coarse gravelly stuff that is found on most of the East Shore's beaches. Kayak rentals and tours are available by advance reservation through Tahoe Adventure Company (530/913-9212, www.tahoeadventurecompany.com). Every summer Sand Harbor hosts an annual Lake Tahoe Shakespeare Festival (800/747-4697, www.laketahoeshakespeare.com) and other cultural events at its lakeside outdoor amphitheater. Sand Harbor is located three miles south of Incline Village. During July and August, it is best to arrive before 11 A.M. or after 4 P.M., as the parking lot fills up during peak afternoon hours.

◖ THUNDERBIRD LODGE

Eight miles south of Incline Village is the Thunderbird Lodge (5000 Hwy. 28,

EAST SHORE

© ANN MARIE BROWN

Exquisite stone masonry and wrought-iron craftsmanship are some of the architectural highlights of Thunderbird Lodge.

775/832-8750, www.thunderbirdlodge.org, tours $39 adults, $19 children 6–12, children under 6 are not permitted), an extravagant stone mansion that is Lake Tahoe's answer to Hearst Castle in San Simeon, California. The Thunderbird was built in the late 1930s by eccentric San Francisco real estate magnate George Whittell Jr., who kept a lion named Bill and a small elephant as pets, erected a lighthouse on his 140 acres of lake frontage, and built a 600-foot-long underground tunnel to connect his boathouse (the largest one on Lake Tahoe) to the main house. The estate was later purchased and added to by financier Jack Dreyfus in the 1980s.

Comprised of a 16,500-square-foot main lodge and a series of Tudor-revival cottages and outbuildings connected by winding pathways, bridges, staircases, and waterfall- and fountain-laden patios, the estate is a masterpiece of fine craftsmanship, with exquisite stone masonry and wrought-iron work. Docents lead 75-minute tours around the property, which will leave you with a whole new definition of "rich."

Tours are available May–October by reservation only. Visitors must be shuttled by bus to the lodge from the Incline Village/Crystal Bay Visitors Bureau (969 Tahoe Blvd./ Hwy. 28, Incline Village, 775/832-1606 or 800/468-2463, www.gotahoenorth.com). For a more special experience, the property can also be visited from the Hyatt Regency in Incline Village by boarding the 45-passenger catamaran *Sierra Cloud* (775/831-4386 or 800/553-3288, www.awsincline. com, $110 adults, $80 children 6–12). The boat trip includes coffee, tea, pastries, and fresh fruit, a narrated tour of the historic East Shore, and a guided walking tour of Thunderbird Lodge.

If you are staying on the South Shore, you can board the 40-foot wooden yacht *Tahoe* at Tahoe Keys Marina (Woodwind Cruises, 888/867-6394, www.tahoeboatcruises.com) for a tour of Thunderbird Lodge, although it is a very long boat trip from the South Shore. Tahoe City Kayaks (530/581-4336, www.tahoecitykayak.com) occasionally offers guided kayak tours to Thunderbird Lodge.

LOGAN SHOALS VISTA

Located on the lake side of Highway 28, one mile north of the Cave Rock tunnels, this vista point (free) is a fine spot to take a break from the highway and enjoy a view of Lake Tahoe and a banquet of peaks—Echo, Tallac, the twin Maggies, Rubicon, Ellis, Barker, Twin, Ward, Squaw, and Watson, among others. Directly across the lake is the broad U-shaped valley of Emerald Bay, which was carved out by receding glaciers. Peering through a cluster of pines, you also can get a fair view of Cave Rock to the south.

CAVE ROCK

Formed about three million years ago by a volcanic eruption, the rugged face of Cave Rock is the most notable geologic feature of the East Shore. The rock, which rises 360 feet above the lake's surface, was named not for the manufactured U.S. 50 tunnels that pass through it, but for the small caves on its southwest side that were cut by waves during the ice age when the lake was 200 feet higher than it is today. Cave Rock is actually not a rock at all, but an andesite plug that was the neck of an old volcano.

Washoe Indians, who lived at Lake Tahoe for more than 10,000 years, have always believed that Cave Rock is a sacred place. Only the Washoe shaman was allowed to enter its cave, to seek guidance for aiding the tribe. Today much of the cave has been altered by development, but Washoes still visit here to pay tribute to their past.

Also of great significance to white miners in the mid-1800s, Cave Rock was a major landmark on the Lake Bigler Toll Road, which the gold diggers used to travel back and forth to the Comstock mines in Nevada. The current tunnels in the rock were blasted for the construction of U.S. 50—the first in 1931 and the second in 1958.

Just south of Cave Rock is a small Nevada state park with a boat launch and day-use area ($6 fee per vehicle). The park is popular with anglers. Picnickers will enjoy a spectacular view of the West Shore with a 12-mile-wide expanse of Tahoe in between.

◖ VIRGINIA CITY

If you are curious about the West's mining history, don't miss a chance to visit the "living ghost town" of Virginia City, about a 50-minute drive from the lake, just east of U.S. 395 in Nevada (25 miles southeast of Reno and 15 miles northeast of Carson City). This once-thriving metropolis was the centerpiece of the

Virginia City looks much the same as it did during the silver mining boom of 1857-1877.

© ANN MARIE BROWN

EAST SHORE

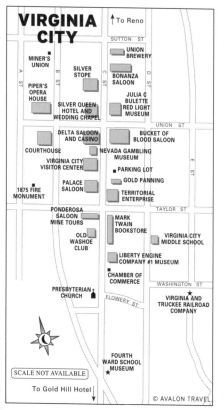

VIRGINIA CITY

↑ To Reno

SUTTON ST

MINER'S UNION
SILVER STOPE
UNION BREWERY
BONANZA SALOON
PIPER'S OPERA HOUSE
SILVER QUEEN HOTEL AND WEDDING CHAPEL
JULIA C BULETTE RED LIGHT MUSEUM

A ST
B ST
C ST
D ST

UNION ST

DELTA SALOON AND CASINO
BUCKET OF BLOOD SALOON
COURTHOUSE
NEVADA GAMBLING MUSEUM
VIRGINIA CITY VISITOR CENTER
PARKING LOT
1875 FIRE MONUMENT
PALACE SALOON
GOLD PANNING
TERRITORIAL ENTERPRISE

E ST

TAYLOR ST

PONDEROSA SALOON MINE TOURS
MARK TWAIN BOOKSTORE
OLD WASHOE CLUB
VIRGINIA CITY MIDDLE SCHOOL
LIBERTY ENGINE COMPANY #1 MUSEUM
CHAMBER OF COMMERCE
PRESBYTERIAN CHURCH
FLOWERY ST
WASHINGTON ST
VIRGINIA AND TRUCKEE RAILROAD COMPANY

FOURTH WARD SCHOOL MUSEUM

SCALE NOT AVAILABLE

To Gold Hill Hotel ↓

© AVALON TRAVEL

but fascinating nonetheless, the nation's largest National Historic Landmark is visited by more than 1.5 million people per year. Visitors can ride an old steam train past abandoned mining sites, tour Victorian mansions, cruise through town on a horse-drawn stagecoach, drink sarsaparilla, gamble, or tour an underground mine inside the Ponderosa Saloon. Not surprisingly, T-shirts, candy, and assorted other souvenirs are available for purchase in almost every shop on C Street, the town's main drag.

A few highlights not to be missed include the Silver Queen Hotel and Wedding Chapel, which has a wall-size painting made up of more than 3,000 silver dollars; and the Delta Saloon and Casino, famous for its "Suicide Table," where three of the casino's previous owners reputedly killed themselves over debts incurred from lopsided poker games. The Fourth Ward School, erected in 1876, is now a museum. The historic Piper's Opera House was built in 1885 and is still used for concerts and performances. May–October, be sure to take a ride on the restored **Virginia and Truckee Railroad** (775/847-0380, www.virginiatruckee. com, $10 adults, $5 children under 12) from Virginia City to Gold Hill. Passengers can sit in open-air cars or in an enclosed caboose. During the 35-minute ride, the conductor tells stories about the history of the area and the bonanza of the Comstock mines. Trains depart Virginia City eight times a day 10:30 A.M.–5 P.M.

Practicalities

Most visitors can see and do Virginia City in less than a day, but if you'd like to spend the night, several intriguing lodging options are available. The **Cobb Mansion Bed and Breakfast** (18 South A St., Virginia City, 877/847-9006, www.cobbmansion.com, $99–199) is an elegantly restored, three-story Victorian mansion (circa 1876) in the heart of town. It has six guest rooms, all with private baths, and each one is decked out to the nines

Comstock Lode silver strike in 1859, which served as the main catalyst for the early development of the Lake Tahoe basin. In a period of just under two decades, the Comstock Lode produced roughly $400 million in silver and gold, which made it the biggest ore-producing area in the nation during that time. Many men became millionaires in Virginia City. Money from the mines helped to finance the Civil War and paid to build old San Francisco. Partly because of these great riches, Nevada was granted statehood in 1864.

Today, Virginia City, with its false-front buildings and wooden sidewalks, looks much like the Old West towns featured in a multitude of Hollywood movies. A bit of a tourist trap in Victorian period furnishings. Every morning, a formal breakfast is served in the dining room. A few blocks away, the **B Street House Bed and Breakfast** (58 North B St., Virginia City, 775/847-7231, www.bstreethouse.com, $99–159) is another great option for lovers of Victoriana. Three guest rooms are located upstairs in this 1875 Victorian, which had fallen to ruins until the current owners spent four years restoring it. In 2011, the building received a listing on the National Register of Historic Places. Breakfast at B Street is a lavish affair, and innkeeper Carolyn's home-baked cookies are made fresh every afternoon.

Nevada's oldest hotel, the 1859 **Gold Hill Hotel** (Hwy. 342, 775/847-0111, www.goldhillhotel.net, $60–225) is still in operation after a century and a half. It offers 20 rooms and guesthouses, plus a bookstore, saloon, and wonderful restaurant. Most Virginia City establishments are open for business 10 A.M.–5 P.M. daily year-round; the saloons stay open later.

From Spooner Summit, take U.S. 50 east to Carson City, then continue east for another seven miles to the Highway 341 turnoff. Turn north and drive seven miles to Virginia City. For more information, contact the Virginia City Chamber of Commerce (www.virginia-city-nv.org) or Virginia City Convention and Tourism Authority (775/847-4386 or 800/718-7587, www.visitvirginiacitynv.com).

GENOA

Nevada's oldest permanent settlement, the town of Genoa was originally established in 1851 as the trading post Mormon Station. Today the tiny hamlet is home to a handful of antiques shops, art galleries, and bed-and-breakfast inns, plus Nevada's oldest "thirst parlor" (the Genoa Bar has been in business since 1853; 775/782-3870, www.genoabarandsaloon.com). Stopping for a drink in this marvelous historic bar is a must. History lovers should snoop through the cemetery where Snowshoe Thompson, the man who carried the mail across the Sierra Nevada on skis, was laid to rest. A small museum is housed in the historic Genoa Courthouse. For more information about Genoa's past and present, visit www.genoanv.com. From Spooner Summit, take U.S. 50 east to Carson City, then turn right at the third stoplight on Jack's Valley Road.

EAST SHORE

Recreation

HIKING

One of the most popular activities at Lake Tahoe is going for a hike, as the spectacular Sierra scenery quite naturally inspires the urge to explore. Before you set out on the trail, make sure you are prepared with a few essentials, such as bottled water (or some sort of water-filtering device), food, and a trail map. Because many of Tahoe's trails have rocky, uneven surfaces, hiking boots are highly recommended. Sunscreen and/or a sun hat are musts at this high elevation, and you don't want to be without mosquito repellent if the bugs are biting. And keep in mind that weather in the Sierra can change dramatically in a short period of time, so it's always wise to carry a lightweight rain poncho or jacket and other clothing for layering.

For more information on the trails described below, contact the Carson Ranger District of Humboldt-Toiyabe National Forest (1536 Carson St., Carson City, 775/882-2766, www.fs.fed.us/htnf). Or contact Lake Tahoe Nevada State Park (2005 Hwy. 28, Incline Village, 775/831-0494, www.parks.nv.gov).

The following hikes are listed from north to south along the east side of the lake.

Mount Rose

- Distance: 10 miles round-trip
- Duration: 3–4 hours
- Effort: Strenuous
- Elevation change: 2,300 feet
- Trailhead: Mount Rose
- Directions: From Incline Village, take Hwy. 431 (Mount Rose Hwy.) north for 8 miles to the highway summit and the large trailhead parking area on the left, signed as Mount Rose Summit Welcome Plaza. The trail begins behind the restrooms.

Hikers accustomed to exploring Yosemite and points farther south in the Sierra Nevada are always somewhat surprised at the lower elevations of the "big peaks" in the Tahoe area. Despite the magnitude of Lake Tahoe and its grand mountain scenery, only a few hikeable summits in the area top the 10,000-foot mark. Mount Rose is one of them, and at 10,778 feet, it is the undisputed monolith of Tahoe's northeast shore. A good trail leads all the way to the top, making it a must on every Tahoe hiker's itinerary. Mount Rose is a volcanic peak, and much of the route to the summit is treeless, waterless, and exposed, so be sure to pack along lots of extra water and sunscreen.

The trail begins at the large parking area just below the summit of the Mount Rose Highway. Take the trail from behind the restrooms and begin a moderate ascent on a shadeless slope carpeted with sagebrush, lupine, and mule's ears. Views of Tahoe Meadows, far below, will inspire you to visit that spot on another day. After a mellow ascent of 1.5 miles, the trail descends through a hemlock forest, where evidence of long-ago logging operations can be seen, to a lush meadow highlighted by Galena Creek's waterfall coursing down to its edge. In peak season, this meadow is filled with larkspur, paintbrush, lupine, and many other colorful flowers.

© ANN MARIE BROWN

Near the summit, the slopes of Mount Rose are dry and barren.

From the edge of the meadow, Mount Rose looks so close that you might assume you'll be on top in no time. However, the majority of this hike's 2,300 feet of elevation gain takes place in the next 2.6 miles, so the grade will surely rein in your ambitions. The trail makes its way steeply to a saddle west of the summit, where you go right for Mount Rose and another trail continues straight toward Big Meadows. You may be feeling a bit breathless, but you still have another 1.5 miles to the top, skirting along the broad shoulder of the peak. At first, low-growing whitebark pines provide a modicum of shade, but soon these disappear. Keep your eyes on the ground alongside the trail, and you may spot the wood-fruited evening primrose, a rare alpine plant with big yellow flowers on low-lying stems that grows only on the upper slopes of Mount Rose. The final 0.5 mile is a real butt-kicker, partly because of the high-elevation air and partly because the volcanic terrain is so open and exposed. But the view from the top is well worth the effort. On clear days, it is easy to pick out Mount Lassen nearly 100 miles to the north. The Sierra Buttes in Plumas National Forest can also be seen, as well as the desert lands surrounding Reno and Sparks, plus three major reservoirs—Prosser, Boca, and Stampede—and, of course, mighty Lake Tahoe. Low rock walls have been built on the summit to give hikers shelter from the frequent wind.

Tahoe Meadows

- Distance: 1.3 miles round-trip
- Duration: 1 hour
- Effort: Easy
- Elevation change: 40 feet
- Trailhead: Tahoe Meadows/Tahoe Rim Trail
- Directions: From Incline Village, take Hwy. 431 (Mount Rose Hwy.) north for 7.5 miles

EAST SHORE

© ANN MARIE BROWN

Trails run in all directions from the major trailhead at Tahoe Meadows.

to the large parking area on the right (southeast) side of the highway. The trail begins behind the visitors center.

The Tahoe Meadows Whole Access Trail was designed for wheelchair users, but hikers using two feet will find it equally enjoyable. This wide, high-desert meadow is set at 8,870 feet in elevation, with Mount Rose towering 2,000 feet above to the north. The loop trail's surface is smooth dirt, with nearly a dozen footbridges that were constructed to protect the multiple tiny creeks meandering through the wetlands. In early summer, wildflowers abound, including the pink tufts of pussypaws, bright yellow buttercups and marsh marigolds, and a variety of penstemon species. In August, pink and white elephant heads make an appearance. Although this trail is bordered by the busy Mount Rose Highway and the road noise never goes away, Tahoe Meadows somehow manages to retain a tranquil ambience that keeps visitors and locals alike coming back for more.

Ophir Creek

- Distance: 4 miles round-trip
- Duration: 2 hours
- Effort: Moderate
- Elevation change: 800 feet
- Trailhead: Tahoe Meadows/Tahoe Rim Trail
- Directions: From Incline Village, take Hwy. 431 (Mount Rose Hwy.) north for 7.5 miles to the large parking area on the right (southeast) side of the highway.

During the Tahoe wildflower season, which generally peaks in mid-July (although the timing varies greatly from year to year), there may be no better trail on the Nevada side of the lake than this one for admiring the blossoms. Some of the showiest flower species that thrive here are crimson columbine, mountain penstemon, and Sierra evening primrose. The Ophir Creek Trail begins at Tahoe Meadows just below the summit of the Mount Rose Highway, then

descends over the course of six miles to Davis Creek Park. Most people don't travel the entire length of the trail, as it makes a daunting descent of 3,300 feet, requiring a strenuous return trip unless a car shuttle is arranged. Instead, a satisfying walk can be had just by hiking out and back for a couple of miles each way. Begin by starting at the Tahoe Meadows Trailhead on the northeast end of Tahoe Meadows, hiking southwest across the meadow, then entering a lodgepole-pine forest. You'll pick up Ophir Creek Trail just beyond a crossing of Ophir Creek, 0.7 mile from the start. The Tahoe Rim Trail heads right; you'll go left. Once you are officially on the trail, which is the remains of an old road, you never stray far from the lovely creek's side. If you hike about 2 miles, you will be treated to a superb overlook of Wahoe Valley and its lake, thousands of feet below. On warm summer days, hikers will often spot paragliders and hang gliders riding the thermal breezes over the valley. Note that this trail is also popular with mountain bikers, although many only travel it in one direction—downhill.

Snowflake Lodge

- Distance: 2.6 miles round-trip
- Duration: 1.5 hours
- Effort: Moderate
- Elevation change: 700 feet
- Trailhead: Diamond Peak Ski Resort
- Directions: From Hwy. 28 at Incline Village, turn north on Country Club Dr. and drive 1 mile to Ski Way. Turn right and follow Ski Way to its end at Diamond Peak Ski Resort.

The mid-mountain Snowflake Lodge is the destination of this short, view-filled hike from the base of Diamond Peak Ski Resort (775/832-1177, www.diamondpeak.com). Although the route to get there follows a ski-lift maintenance road, not a real hiking trail, it's worth suffering through the exposed, 700-foot climb to reach Snowflake Lodge's 4,000-square-foot sundeck

© ANN MARIE BROWN

The lake views from Stateline Lookout are spectacular.

gate is locked and you must park in the small pullouts alongside Lakeview Dr., then walk up the fire road.

You can't beat the Stateline Lookout Trail for an early-morning or sunset walk. Located at the site where an old fire lookout tower once stood, this 0.5-mile interpretive loop trail sits smack on the California/Nevada border at an elevation of 7,017 feet, offering a bird's-eye view of Tahoe's North and East Shores. The fire road that leads to the lookout site and its trail is most often closed, so the road is usually part of the hike, making this 0.5-mile hike a 2-mile hike. But no matter; it's a pleasant walk up a fir- and pine-forested hillside. When you reach the parking area for the interpretive trail, located by a large signboard, head out in either direction and start enjoying gorgeous high lake views from Lookout Point. A dozen interpretive panels explain about the North Shore's logging history, the 1870s conflict over where in Lake Tahoe to set the California/Nevada boundary line, and the onset of the gambling and resort era on the North Shore. At one time, a Forest Service lookout person was stationed up here to spot fires. The small lookout building was known as "Hotel de Chipmunk."

◖ Chimney Beach and Secret Harbor

- Distance: 3 miles round-trip
- Duration: 1.5 hours
- Effort: Easy
- Elevation change: 300 feet
- Trailhead: Hwy. 28
- Directions: From Incline Village, drive 6 miles south on Hwy. 28 to a large paved parking lot on the right (lake) side of the highway (2.9 miles south of the Sand Harbor turnoff).

If you've become accustomed to all the private property that lines the North, West, and South Shores of Lake Tahoe, the amount of public land on Tahoe's East Shore comes as a

and its horizon-stretching view of Lake Tahoe. The deck is covered with picnic tables, so don't forget to pack your lunch. The road/trail starts at the ski resort's base lodge and follows the dirt and gravel road alongside the Lodgepole quad chair.

Stateline Lookout (Lookout Point)

- Distance: 2 miles round-trip
- Duration: 1 hour
- Effort: Easy/moderate
- Elevation change: 500 feet
- Trailhead: Rd. 1601
- Directions: From Hwy. 28 at Crystal Bay, turn north on Reservoir Dr. (just east of the Tahoe Biltmore Casino). Drive 0.2 mile and turn right on Lakeview Dr. Continue 0.5 mile to the gated fire road on the left (Rd. 1601). If the gate is open, you can drive uphill 1 mile to the parking lot. Often the

welcome surprise. Much of the East Shore's sparkling shoreline and sandy beaches are accessible to anyone who is willing to walk, and no day-use or parking fees are required. From the large Forest Service–managed parking lot, a wide trail descends just over a half mile (dropping 350 feet in elevation) to just above the water's edge, then runs north and south along the shoreline. Heading right will take you to Chimney Beach, where the remains of an old stone chimney can be seen. Heading left will take you to Secret Harbor, with its numerous rocky coves. Despite the fact that hordes of visitors descend to this shoreline on warm summer days, there is plenty of room for everyone to spread out and find their own stretch of sand. Don't forget your beach towel, and don't be shocked if you pass by an occasional nude sunbather. Bathing trunks are optional here.

Prey Meadows and Skunk Harbor

- Distance: 3 miles round-trip
- Duration: 1.5 hours
- Effort: Easy/moderate
- Elevation change: 600 feet
- Trailhead: Slaughterhouse Canyon
- Directions: From the junction of U.S. 50 and Hwy. 28, drive 2.4 miles north on Hwy. 28 to a pullout by a green metal gate on the left (lake) side of the highway. Park safely off the highway in the pullout.

Since Skunk Harbor is one of Lake Tahoe's most picturesque coves, it's hard to understand why its trailhead isn't signed and visitor parking is so limited. But that's reality at the Slaughterhouse Canyon Trailhead along Highway 28, and those factors, combined with the fact that the beach is a 1.5-mile hike from the highway, keep the crowd factor to a minimum. The trail is an easy-to-follow dirt road that starts at the highway and heads downhill through a Jeffrey pine and fir forest. You'll reach a junction 0.7 mile down the trail; the left

fork heads to wildflower-filled Prey Meadows in Slaughterhouse Canyon, a must-see during the peak of the bloom. The right fork continues to Skunk Harbor on the shore of Lake Tahoe, a secluded beach where George Newhall built a stone house in 1923 as a wedding gift for his wife, Caroline. The Newhall House was used not as an actual home, but as their private family picnic site. George and Caroline lived across the lake at Rubicon Bay and would cruise by boat to Skunk Harbor for afternoon outings. Later the house became the property of George Whittell, the eccentric owner of Thunderbird Lodge, who used it as a guesthouse. Although the house is now boarded up and in disrepair, it's a fascinating reminder of the glory days at Lake Tahoe. Meanwhile, just a few yards distant, the Skunk Harbor beach is a mix of coarse sand and rocks, and the shallow waters along the shore warm up quite nicely for swimming on summer days.

Spooner Lake Loop

- Distance: 2.1 miles round-trip
- Duration: 1 hour
- Effort: Easy
- Elevation change: 50 feet
- Trailhead: Spooner Lake
- Directions: From the junction of U.S. 50 and Hwy. 28, drive 0.6 mile north on Hwy. 28 to the Spooner Lake/Lake Tahoe Nevada State Park entrance. A $6 day-use fee is charged.

Spooner Lake is an artificial water body on the Nevada side of the lake that played an important role in the Comstock gold- and silver-mining boom. The lake served as a millpond and was part of a system of reservoirs, flumes, and pipelines that supplied lumber and water to the Virginia City and Gold Hill mines. Interpretive displays at the parking area detail this fascinating period in Tahoe's history. At 7,000 feet in elevation, the 1.6-mile trail that circles Spooner Lake's perimeter is snow-free much of the year, and when it is snow covered, it makes a fine track for snowshoeing or cross-country skiing. From the day-use parking area, follow the trail near the restrooms downhill to the tranquil lake's dam, 0.2 mile away. Cross the dam to start the loop, and you'll wander amid aspens and Jeffrey pines. Watch for large granite boulders that are marked by Native American *morteros,* or grinding holes. As you curve around the lakeshore, keep on the lookout for osprey (often seen diving into the lake for fish), killdeer, and even bald eagles. Binoculars are a handy accessory for this hike; several benches are conveniently placed in good spots for bird- and wildlife-watching. On the southeast side of the lake, a spur trail leads to the parking area at Spooner Summit. (Some people prefer to hike in 0.75 mile from this trailhead to avoid paying the state park day-use fee.) Fishing is permitted in Spooner Lake, but it is catch-and-release only. Because of the presence of leeches, swimming is a bad idea.

Marlette Lake

- Distance: 9 miles round-trip
- Duration: 5 hours
- Effort: Moderate
- Elevation change: 700 feet
- Trailhead: Spooner Lake
- Directions: From the junction of U.S. 50 and Hwy. 28, drive 0.6 mile north on Hwy. 28 to the Spooner Lake/Lake Tahoe Nevada State Park entrance. A $6 day-use fee is charged.

The North Canyon Road to Marlette Lake is a favorite path of mountain bikers making their way to the start of the infamous Flume Trail, but now hikers have their own trail to the beautiful lake—the North Canyon Trail, completed in 2005, which takes off from North Canyon Road and travels 4 miles to the lake. Bikers stay on one trail, hikers stay on another trail—everybody is happy. It's a toss-up whether it is better to hike this trail in early summer (for wildflowers) or mid-autumn (for the quaking aspen fall color show). Both seasons are winners. Begin the trip by following the wide path from near the parking lot restrooms toward Spooner Lake's dam. Before reaching the dam, you'll turn left (north) on North Canyon Road. Soon you'll pass the right turnoff for Spooner Lake cabin, which is available for overnight rental, and the historic Spencer Cabin, which is sometimes used as a warming hut for skiers in the winter. At 0.7 mile from your start, you'll meet up with the North Canyon Trail. Here you leave the dirt road and follow the narrower, hikers-only trail. The well-built path stays along the west bank of North Canyon Creek and is a gentle climb almost all the way until the last 0.5 mile, where it junctions with a trail coming up on the left from Chimney Beach, then drops steeply to the lake's southern shore. The closer you get to the lake, the denser the stands of aspens. Once you arrive, you can wander along the shoreline to find the best spots for picnicking and swimming. Those with extra energy to burn can take the 1.2-mile trail along the lake's east shore to Marlette Overlook, which provides breathtaking views looking west over Marlette Lake and Lake Tahoe. Note that fishing is not permitted in the lake because it serves as a fish hatchery for the state of Nevada. Given that the lake also supplies drinking water via a flume to Carson City and Virginia City, it's surprising that swimming is permitted here, but it is.

South Camp Peak

- Distance: 10.6 miles round-trip
- Duration: 5–6 hours
- Effort: Moderate/strenuous
- Elevation change: 2,200 feet
- Trailhead: Spooner Summit/Tahoe Rim Trail
- Directions: From the junction of U.S. 50 and Hwy. 28, drive 0.8 mile east on U.S. 50 to

Spooner Summit and the parking area on the right (south) side.

This hike on a portion of the Tahoe Rim Trail takes you to one of the most view-filled peaks in the Carson Range. Before you go, remember that this trail is in dry Nevada, not the much-wetter mountains on the California side of Lake Tahoe, so you need to carry plenty of water with you (there are no streams or springs along the trail). For early-season hikers, this is good news—South Camp Peak will be snow-free a month earlier than other summits around the lake. It is usually accessible by June.

The trail begins with an ascent over open slopes, then delves into a mixed conifer forest and delivers you to your first wide views at 1.5 miles, where a short spur trail leads to a high knoll. Snap a few pictures here, then continue onward. Much of the trail is smooth, hard-packed sand, making it a favorite area for mountain bikers. Two miles farther, the trail crosses Genoa Peak Road amid a heavily logged area. Catch your breath here before attacking the final 1.5-mile, 800-foot ascent to the top of South Camp Peak, mostly over densely forested slopes. The 8,818-foot peak has a broad, flat summit that seems to go on forever. You'll arrive on the northwest edge of it; which spot you decide to call the tippy-top is up to you. Views are excellent from just about everywhere along the nearly level, open plateau. Dozens of landmarks are easy to spot, including nearby Genoa Peak with its telltale radio towers, Mount Rose, Fallen Leaf Lake, Emerald Bay, Pyramid Peak, Freel Peak, Mount Tallac, and the tall buildings of the Stateline casinos.

BIKING

Skinny-tire riders who want to rack up some road mileage have a wealth of routes to choose from in the Carson City/Carson Valley area, including a 50-mile loop tour that cruises through Virginia City. A great source for information on Nevada road biking is www.

bicyclenevada.com. **Bike rentals** and equipment are available in Incline Village at Village Ski Loft and Bicycles (800 Tahoe Blvd./Hwy. 28, 775/831-3537).

Lakeshore Bike Path

Those seeking an easy, scenic ride on the East Shore should head for the Lakeshore Bike Path in Incline Village. This mostly level, paved trail connects with Highway 28 on both ends, and its entire one-way length is only three miles, but there are numerous mega-mansions to ogle along the way. Parking is easiest at the west end of the trail at the junction of Highway 28 and Lakeshore Drive (0.5 mile west of the Hwy. 431/Hwy. 28 junction). The trail parallels Lakeshore Drive, crossing it only once, until its terminus where it meets Highway 28 again, across from the old Ponderosa Ranch.

◖ Flume Trail

Proceeding directly from the mild to the wild, on the opposite end of the biking spectrum is the Flume Trail. Probably the most famous single mountain-biking trail in the West, the Flume Trail can be ridden in different ways. The most common route is to start at Spooner Lake State Park, off Highway 28 just north of its junction with U.S. 50. Follow the trail east from the parking area to just before Spooner Lake's dam, then turn left and follow the wide dirt road toward Marlette Lake. The road travels north alongside North Canyon Creek through increasingly dense aspen groves (gorgeous fall colors can be seen here in late Sept.–early Oct.). The grade gets progressively steeper during the first 4 miles, then in the last mile you drop steeply to the shore of Marlette Lake. Plenty of beginning and intermediate riders just turn around here for a 10-mile round-trip with about 1,100 feet of elevation gain. Those heading for the Flume Trail go left at a signed fork at the lakeshore, follow a dirt road along the water's edge for another mile,

PONDEROSA RANCH

For decades, one of the most popular tourist attractions at Lake Tahoe was the Ponderosa Ranch, a theme park based on the television show *Bonanza*, which depicted the life of the Cartwright family (Pa, Adam, Hoss, and Little Joe) and their fictional struggles on their magnificent Nevada ranch. The popular show, which aired 1959-1973, was partly filmed on a strip of land near Incline Village, including its famous opening scene.

In the 1960s, Bill Anderson, one of the contractors who worked with the film crews building fake outbuildings and roads on location at Tahoe, got the idea to use the sets from the show to create a theme park. He even built an exact replica of the Cartwright house, which never existed at Lake Tahoe but rather was filmed on a Hollywood soundstage, at the Incline Village shooting location. The theme park operated 1968-2003 and featured hayrides, pony rides, staged gunfights, a petting zoo, vintage cars and wagon exhibits, souvenir shops, and an entire false-front Western town, including the Silver Dollar Saloon and the re-created Cartwright ranch house.

When the owners of the 570-acre park put it up for sale at a price tag of $50 million, a consortium of government agencies struggled to come up with the money to buy the land and preserve it from commercial development. Their efforts failed, and in 2004 Incline Village resident David Duffield, founder of the technology company People-Soft, became the new owner of the Ponderosa Ranch. What will happen to the property is anybody's guess, but for now, Duffield says he doesn't plan to reopen the theme park or develop the land.

Regardless, Incline Village still takes pride in its connection to the Ponderosa Ranch. When the TV show *Bonanza* reached its 50th anniversary in 2009, the Incline Village library and historical society hosted lectures and events to commemorate the show and its beloved cast.

Lovers of the *Bonanza* TV show, or those who have fond memories of visiting the Ponderosa Ranch in its heyday, should check out the website www.ponderosascenery.homestead.com for more fascinating trivia about the amusement park and the show.

then are deposited on the Flume Trail's famous single-track. The trail is built on the grade of an old square-box logging flume, which carried water and timber from Lake Tahoe to the silver mines of Virginia City in the late 1800s. The flume's route was carved into the side of the precipitous slope above Lake Tahoe's East Shore. Good bike-handling skills are important here, as the east side of the trail is lined with car-size boulders, and the west side has near vertical drop-offs of up to 1,600 feet. Because the trail follows the route of the old flume, it is almost level—it drops only 40 feet per mile—so your cardiovascular system won't be working hard, just your nervous system. If the trail gets too hairy for you, there is no crime in stopping for a minute, or getting off your bike and walking. Plenty of riders do so,

especially since the lake views are so breathtaking that you don't want to spin by too fast.

After almost 5 miles of this adrenaline-pumping riding, the trail forks again, and most riders bear left on Tunnel Creek Road and descend via the sandy, dusty fire road to Incline Village, dropping 1,600 feet in only 2.5 miles. Some riders who have made it through the entire Flume Trail without a mishap manage to lose control on this final descent, so use caution. If you haven't arranged shuttle transportation, it's a 10-mile ride back to Spooner Lake on a narrow stretch of Highway 28. If a shuttle is waiting for you, your one-way ride will be about 13 miles, with 1,100 feet of elevation gain and 2,000 feet of loss. Most people take about 3–4 hours to complete the one-way Flume trip from Spooner Lake to Incline Village.

© ANN MARIE BROWN

It's tough to beat the lake views from the Flume Trail ride.

For those who don't have patient friends who are willing to pick them up at the end of the ride, the **Spooner Lake Outdoor Company** (775/749-5349, www.theflumetrail.com or www.spoonerlake.com), located at the Spooner Lake parking lot, runs a mountain-bike shuttle service seven days a week. The fee is $15 for a one-way shuttle, or $10 if you rent one of their bikes. Bike rentals are $45–75 per day. Or if you would prefer to tackle the Flume Trail with a knowledgeable guide, the Spooner Lake Outdoor Company will be happy to accommodate you.

There are two options for extending the Flume Trail ride into a longer loop, but both are intended for very strong and experienced riders only. For the first loop option, instead of descending via Tunnel Creek Road, stay right at the junction and keep riding along the ridge for 1.3 miles to another segment of the Flume Trail, called Red House Flume. A right turn on Red House Flume will connect you to a series of fire roads that will bring you back above Marlette Lake. All junctions along the route are well signed, and free maps are available at the Spooner Lake Trailhead. From Marlette Lake, just retrace your tire treads back to Spooner Lake. The total loop ride is about 24 miles and very challenging, with a total 2,600-foot elevation gain. The second option is to loop back via the Tahoe Rim Trail. Go right on Tunnel Creek Road and follow it uphill for only 0.5 mile to the Twin Lakes junction, then follow the Rim Trail south for 5 miles to Hobart/Marlette Road, above Marlette Lake. A right turn here will bring you back to Marlette Lake and Spooner Lake. The total loop ride is 22 miles with 2,000 feet of elevation gain.

South Camp Peak

Another popular mountain-biking destination on the East Shore is the 8,818-foot summit of South Camp Peak, accessible from the Tahoe Rim Trail Trailhead just east of Spooner

Summit on U.S. 50. Although the view of the Lake Tahoe basin at the summit is grand, getting there is half the fun, as you pedal past wildflower-covered slopes and through groves of quaking aspen. The trail is smooth, mostly hard-packed sand all the way, and the grade is fairly moderate for the first 3.8 miles until you near the top, where it steepens considerably. The last 1.5 miles are a serious challenge, with an 800-foot elevation gain. Total mileage out and back to South Camp Peak is 10.6 miles.

BOATING AND WATER SPORTS
Kayaking
The East Shore of Lake Tahoe is one of the loveliest areas for kayaking, with miles of pristine, development-free shoreline. Many kayakers put in at **Sand Harbor** (Lake Tahoe Nevada State Park, 2005 Hwy. 28, 775/831-0494, www.parks.nv.gov, $15 launch fee), then paddle south along a string of secluded coves and

white-sand and boulder-strewn beaches. There are abundant spots where you can pull up on shore for rest stops, swimming, and picnicking, but look carefully before you land; occasional East Shore beachgoers prefer to sunbathe au naturel. You may get an impromptu anatomy lesson. Morning is usually the best time to paddle along the East Shore, before the west winds start blowing across the lake in the afternoon. Another popular put-in spot is at **Cave Rock,** farther south at Lake Tahoe Nevada State Park ($12 launch fee).

Kayak rentals at Sand Harbor are available by advance reservation through **Tahoe Adventure Company** (530/913-9212, www.tahoeadventurecompany.com, $60 all-day rental for single kayaks, $80 all day for double kayaks). **Tahoe City Kayak** (530/581-4336, www.tahoecitykayak.com) offers four-hour kayak tours starting at Sand Harbor ($65–95 per person, including lunch, reserve in advance). **Tahoe**

EAST SHORE

© ANN MARIE BROWN

Kayakers pull up on the boulders that surround Sand Harbor.

Paddle & Oar in Kings Beach (530/581-3029, www.tahoepaddle.com, tours $90–100 per person, rentals $20–30 per hour or $80–120 per day) also rents kayaks and offers tours along the boulder-lined shores of Sand Harbor.

Kayakers with bigger ambitions should check out the **Lake Tahoe Water Trail** map (800/849-6589, www.adventuremaps.net), which shows available boat launches, campsites, lodging, dining, and more for all 72 miles of lake shoreline. And visit the website of the Lake Tahoe Water Trail Committee (www.laketahoewatertrail.org) for information on trip planning, Tahoe paddling events, and the local kayaking community.

Water Sports Outfitters and Marinas

All types of powerboats and personal watercraft can be rented at **Action Watersports** (on the beach behind the Hyatt's Lone Eagle Grille, 967 Lakeshore Blvd., Incline Village, 775/831-4386, www.awsincline.com). They also offer daily two-hour sailing cruises aboard the 55-foot catamaran *Sierra Cloud* ($60 adults, $30 children).

If you brought your own boat or personal watercraft to Lake Tahoe and just need a boat ramp where you can put it in the water, you can do so on the East Shore at Cave Rock (775/831-0494) or Sand Harbor (775/831-0494).

SWIMMING

The Nevada side of the lake is a favorite for swimmers and sunbathers, due to its abundance of undeveloped shoreline and shallow, relatively warm water. On the warmest days of July and August, Tahoe's water temperature within a few feet of the East Shore can be as high as the 70s—as much as 20 degrees warmer than at many other points in the lake. Beachgoers can choose between drive-in, fee-required beaches with picnic tables, restrooms, and other facilities, and secluded hike-in beaches, including

some that are clothing-optional. Residents and visitors staying at the condominium resorts in Incline Village have guest access to two developed beaches, **Burnt Cedar** and **Incline Beach,** that are managed by the Incline Village General Improvement District (775/832-1310).

◖ Sand Harbor

Those who are staying elsewhere on the East Shore can head for the developed beach at Sand Harbor, three miles south of Incline Village (Lake Tahoe Nevada State Park, 2005 Hwy. 28, 775/831-0494, www.parks.nv.gov). This is one of Lake Tahoe's most scenic beaches, a white crescent of sand framed by giant rounded boulders. The beach has a concession stand, a nature trail, and a separate cove for snorkeling and scuba diving. Beach patrol lifeguards are on duty Memorial Day–Labor Day. Parking is $12 per car.

Free, Hike-In Beaches

A vast majority of beachgoers prefer the no-fee option of finding their own beach paradise in the stretch of shoreline immediately south of Incline Village, known as **Hidden Beach.** This land is part of Lake Tahoe Nevada State Park, but there is no official parking area. Beachgoers must park in narrow pullouts alongside Highway 28 and then walk a short distance to the lake. Be sure to obey all No Parking signs and carry out any trash with you. Because these beaches are state owned, dogs are not permitted.

South of Sand Harbor and north of Spooner Summit are more no-fee, hike-in beaches. The best parking and access is at the Forest Service–run Chimney Beach parking lot, 2.9 miles south of Sand Harbor on Highway 28 (although many people also park in pullouts alongside the highway). From the large parking lot, a downhill walk of 0.6 mile is required to reach the lakeshore. From there you can follow trails to the north or south to find your special

© ANN MARIE BROWN

One of Tahoe's best stretches of sand can be found at Sand Harbor.

spot. Walking north about a quarter mile will bring you to the namesake stone chimney at **Chimney Beach.** Walking south leads you to **Secret Cove** and **Secret Harbor.** At either beach, don't be surprised if you run into sunbathers wearing nothing but their birthday suits. Leashed dogs are permitted on these Forest Service beaches.

Farthest to the south is **Skunk Harbor** beach, which requires the longest hike to reach (1.2 miles one-way). The trailhead is located 2.4 miles north of Spooner Summit on Highway 28. The shoreline here is comprised of coarse gravel, compared to the sandier beaches to the north. Dogs are permitted on this beach, and visitors can take a look at the exterior of the **Newhall House,** a stone cottage perched on the shoreline that was built in 1923.

FISHING

The steep shoreline and rocky shoals at **Cave Rock** ($10 day-use fee per vehicle) create one of the few places in Lake Tahoe where shore anglers have half a chance of catching fish, especially rainbow trout and occasionally brown trout. Most shore anglers try their luck with worms, spinners, marshmallows, or salmon eggs. Two launch ramps at the site lead to deep water close to shore. Another spot on the East Shore that is popular with shoreline anglers is the rocky shoreline at **Sand Harbor** ($12 day-use fee per vehicle). If you need to purchase a fishing license or buy tackle or equipment, try Ace Hardware (910 Tahoe Blvd./Hwy. 28, Incline Village, 775/831-2020). Both Sand Harbor and Cave Rock are under the jurisdiction of Lake Tahoe Nevada State Park (2005 Hwy. 28, 775/831-0494, www.parks.nv.gov).

On the other end of the fishing spectrum, fly fishers enjoy catch-and-release fishing at **Spooner Lake** for rainbow, brown, and brook trout. Only artificial lures and single barbless hooks are permitted.

ROCK CLIMBING

Rock climbers were sorely disappointed when craggy, volcanic Cave Rock was closed to climbing in 2003 due to its importance as a Native American cultural site. To climbers, Cave Rock was revered as Tahoe's premier sport climbing crag, with a multitude of difficult routes and fantastic lake views. For now, Cave Rock is closed to climbing, and it looks like it will remain that way permanently. Still, several other rocks on the East Shore are suitable for intermediate climbers, including **Shakespeare Rock** and **Trippy Rock.** Shakespeare Rock towers 400 feet above U.S. 50, a quarter mile north of the Glenbrook turnoff (on the east side of the highway). Trippy Rock is located five miles north of Incline Village on Highway 431. For more information on these sites, contact the Carson Ranger District of Humboldt-Toiyabe National Forest (775/882-2766).

GOLF

Incline Village has not one but two excellent golf courses—the **Championship Course** (955 Fairway Blvd., Incline Village, 775/832-1146 or 866/925-4653, www.golfincline.com) and the **Mountain Course** (690 Wilson Way, Incline Village, 775/832-1150 or 866/925-4653, www.golfincline.com). Designed by Robert Trent Jones Jr. and consistently ranked as one of the top 10 public courses in the country, the Mountain Course is an 18-hole, par 58 maze of boulders, pines, and meandering streams that demands accurate hitting. The midlength course (3,500 yards) is completely natural with no artificial landscaping and has been designated a certified Audubon Cooperative Sanctuary. The course usually plays quickly, but the lake views may slow you down. Rates are a reasonable $75 (twilight rates are $45).

The Championship Course is an 18-hole, par 72, lake-view beauty that was designed by the senior Robert Trent Jones. The course recently underwent a two-year,

multimillion-dollar renovation orchestrated by architect Kyle Phillips. After being closed for two years, it reopened in 2005. Accuracy and distance are required for successful play, with fairways surrounded by ponderosa pines, strategically placed bunkers, meandering streams, and small greens. Course length is 7,100 yards from the back tees. Green fees are $179 (twilight rates are $95). The course clubhouse, The Chateau, was completely redesigned as well and now features The Grille, a lunch spot for hungry golfers.

Farther from the lake, three more courses are found between Incline Village and Reno: **Lake Ridge Golf Course** (775/825-2200, www.lakeridgegolf.com), **Northgate Golf Club** (775/747-7577), and **Wolf Run Golf Club** (775/851-3301, www.wolfrungolfclub.com).

In the Carson Valley area of Nevada, about one hour from the lakeshore, are a consortium of courses known as the **Divine Nine** (www.divine9.com): The Golf Club at Genoa Lakes, Genoa Lakes Golf Resort, Silver Oak Golf Club, Sunridge Golf Club, Eagle Valley East, Eagle Valley West, Dayton Valley Golf Club, Carson Valley Golf Course, and Empire Ranch Golf Course. The Nine's total 171 holes of golf encompass 70,000 yards of terrain—enough to keep any golfer busy for more than a week. Golf packages and special discounts are available for golfers who want to play a majority of the courses.

WINTER SPORTS
Downhill Skiing and Snowboarding

The East Shore of the lake sports two major ski resorts: Mount Rose and Diamond Peak, both just a few miles from Incline Village. Although lift tickets are surprisingly reasonable at both resorts (in fact, midweek deals at Mount Rose are a steal), bargain hunters should be sure to check the website **Snowbomb** (www.snowbomb.com), which frequently offers vouchers for discounted tickets for these two resorts, plus discounts at local lodgings, ski shops, and restaurants. If you have a Costco store near your hometown, you can sometimes buy discounted lift tickets there, or visit www.costco.com.

To save time and money by renting equipment before you arrive at the slopes, head to Village Ski Loft in Incline Village (800 Tahoe Blvd./Hwy. 28, 775/831-3537).

Mount Rose Ski Area (22222 Hwy. 431/ Mount Rose Hwy., 11 miles northeast of Incline Village, 775/849-0704 or 800/754-7673, www.skirose.com, 9 A.M.–4 P.M. daily, Zephyr Chair opens at 8:30 A.M.) has the highest base elevation of any resort at Lake Tahoe (7,900 feet), making its slopes the last place where the snow turns to slush on warm spring days. It's also known for having few, if any, lift lines. Total skiable acreage at the resort is 1,200-plus acres; the longest vertical drop is 1,800 feet. Getting to the summit (9,700 feet) takes only 3.5 minutes, thanks to a super-speedy lift system—an important feature since access to all intermediate and advanced runs is from the top. A total of 60-plus trails, the longest measuring in at 2.5 miles, are serviced by seven lifts. The awesome views from the mountain's slopes take in not just Lake Tahoe to the south but also the Washoe Valley, the Virginia Hills, Reno, and the Nevada desert to the east. Riders and tricksters can jib all day at five terrain parks and two half-pipes.

In 2004, Mount Rose added a large section to its skiable terrain, an area of steep, ungroomed powder called The Chutes, which for many years was out-of-bounds, powder-stash territory, and illegal to enter. The Chutes now has its own chairlift, the Blazing Zephyr, and 16 official double-black-diamond runs. Another 200 acres on the back side of Mount Rose have also been made legal.

Despite the newfound popularity of the

© ANN MARIE BROWN

a stormy day on the slopes of Mount Rose

steep and deep Chutes, this resort is not just for envelope pushers. Plenty of kids learn to ski or ride at **Rosebuds Ski and Snowboard Camp.** And adult beginners can choose from first-timer instruction, rookie classes, and intermediate lessons. With rental equipment and lift tickets, lesson packages cost only $59–89 for adults.

Weekend lift ticket prices at Mount Rose are usually lower than at comparable Tahoe resorts, and deep discounts happen almost every weekday. Full-day tickets are $69 adults, $49 teens 13–17, $42 seniors 65-plus, $19 children 6–12, and $5 for children 5 and under), but many skiers take advantage of Mount Rose's regular weekly bargains, like "Two for Tuesday," when you can buy two adult tickets for the price of one, and "Ladies Day Thursdays," when women receive a full-day ticket for less than half price, plus free lesson clinics. Always buy your tickets on the Web in advance of your trip to save a few bucks. If you are staying in Reno, you can take the **ski shuttle** to Mount Rose, a drive of about 30 minutes. The shuttle runs from major Reno hotels (Nugget, Grand Sierra, Sands, Silver Legacy, Peppermill, Atlantis) twice each morning to Mount Rose Ski Area (a 25-minute drive). Reservations are recommended (775/325-8813, www.tahoeskishuttle.com). The fare is $15 round-trip, but combined lift ticket and shuttle packages are available for $74.

Nearby, the intimate and family-oriented **Diamond Peak Ski Resort** (1219 Ski Way, Incline Village, 775/832-1177, www.diamondpeak.com, 9 a.m.–4 p.m. daily) is located just 1.5 miles from downtown Incline Village. Its 30 runs access 655 skiable acres. The longest run is 2.5 miles, with a vertical drop of 1,840 feet. The resort's summit elevation (8,540 feet) is a little higher than the base elevation at Mount Rose. With average snowfall of only about 350 inches, they often have to make snow, but they are equipped for it. Like at Mount Rose, the vistas from the chairlifts and the slopes take in Lake Tahoe and a wide expanse of Nevada desert. Diamond Peak may not have the most varied and challenging slopes around, but they are among the most scenic; be sure to check out the view from Crystal Ridge. What the resort doesn't have in acreage, it overcompensates for with its breathtaking vistas.

Beginners will be happy here, as the resort has plenty of affordable lessons options. Kids as young as three can attend ski school, and kids as young as four can take snowboarding lessons. A total of six chairlifts service the resort, and three operate with a "Launch Pad" conveyor belt system to make loading and unloading easier. Boarders can bust air at Diamond Peak's freestyle terrain park and superpipe, or if they want to improve their skills, sign up for two- or four-hour freestyle snowboarding clinics. Those seeking more advanced terrain should head to Solitude Canyon.

Lift tickets here are one of the best bargains at Tahoe: All-day tickets for adults are $54, teens 15–17 and seniors 65–69 are $43, youth 7–14 and seniors 70–79 are $20, and seniors 80-plus and kids 6 and under are free. Discounted family packages for one or two adults and one or more children are also available. Free shuttle service to the slopes is available from points in Kings Beach, Crystal Bay, and Incline Village; see www.diamondpeak.com for details.

On most Saturday nights in February and March, Diamond Peak hosts "Last Tracks" starting at 4 p.m. With advance reservations and a separate entry fee (currently $29), skiers and riders get to taste fine wines and nosh on appetizers at the mid-mountain Snowflake Lodge, a spot that is well loved for its horizon-stretching views of Lake Tahoe. Afterwards, as the sun sinks behind the west shore, guests cruise down a freshly groomed intermediate run to the bottom.

Cross-Country Skiing

Cross-country skiers looking for a no-cost place

© ANN MARIE BROWN

Kids make the most of the white stuff at the roadside Spooner Summit Snow Play Area.

to kick and glide can head to **Tahoe Meadows,** on the southeast side of Highway 431/Mount Rose Highway, just below Mount Rose Summit (7.5 miles from Incline Village). This is a great place for moonlight skiing.

Sledding and Tubing

On the East Shore, there are three places where you can bring your own sleds, tubes, saucers, or garbage-can lids and slide down snow-covered slopes. **Tahoe Meadows** (7.5 miles north of Incline Village on Hwy. 431/

Mount Rose Hwy.) has a few mellow hills for young sledders and abundant spots to build snowmen or make snow angels. **Incline Village Snow Play Area** (on Fairway Blvd. next to the Chateau Clubhouse, at the Championship Course driving range) has a gentle hill for sledding. The **Spooner Summit Snow Play Area** (junction of Hwy. 28 and U.S. 50), 12 miles north of Stateline and 12 miles south of Incline Village, has a variety of hills ranging from mild to very steep. There is no fee for the use of any of these areas.

Entertainment and Shopping

NIGHTLIFE

Unless your idea of nightlife is cross-country skiing under a full moon, the only place to find any late-evening action on the East Shore is at the Crystal Bay and Incline Village casinos. The king of them all is the **Cal-Neva Resort** (2 Tahoe Blvd./Hwy. 28, Crystal Bay, 775/832-4000 or 800/225-6382, www.calnevaresort.com), which straddles the California/Nevada state line. Once owned by singer Frank Sinatra, the Cal-Neva has a large indoor showroom for live entertainment, a wedding chapel, and a European-style health spa, as well as all the usual casino and sports-book offerings. Right next door is the **Crystal Bay Casino** (14 Tahoe Blvd./Hwy. 28, Crystal Bay, 775/833-6333, www.crystalbaycasino.com), remodeled in 2004, which offers live music, dancing, live entertainment at the Stage Lounge and the Crown Room, the Crystal Bay Steak and Lobster House, a full-service sports book, and 30 plasma TVs. In the summer months, Crystal Bay Club also showcases performers at its 1,900-seat rooftop stage.

Across the street, the **Tahoe Biltmore Casino** (5 Tahoe Blvd./Hwy. 28, Crystal Bay, 775/831-0660 or 800/245-8667, www.tahoebiltmore.com) has a sports book, dancing, and live entertainment in an old-fashioned nightclub atmosphere at the Breeze Nightclub. At **Jim Kelly's Nugget** (20 Tahoe Blvd./Hwy. 28, Crystal Bay, 775/831-0455), the beer bar is where the action is in summer. If you are diligent, you can taste all 101 beers on the menu and be inducted into the Nugget Beer Drinkers Hall of Fame. Whoopee, you get a T-shirt and a plaque.

Down the road in Incline Village, the Fantasy Forest casino and sports book at the four-diamond **Hyatt Regency Lake Tahoe** (Country Club Dr. at Lakeshore Dr., Incline Village, 775/832-1234 or 800/327-3910, www.hyatt.com) is somewhat more refined. If you get tired of playing keno or betting on football, you can get a massage at the resort's 20,000-square-foot Stillwater Spa, which was added in 2005.

If you are looking for more passive entertainment, check out the evening's offerings at **Incline Village Cinema** (901 Tahoe Blvd./Hwy. 28, Incline Village, 775/546-5951).

SHOPPING

Because of the general lack of commercial enterprises on the East Shore, except for the Incline Village area, shoppers won't have much browsing to do unless they head to Truckee, Tahoe City, Stateline, or South Lake Tahoe. However, Incline Village does have a small shopping center at **Christmas Tree Village** (on Hwy. 28 just west of Village Blvd.), which has a handful of interesting specialty shops: home design, jewelry, and art. A block away is the **Raley's Shopping Center** (on Hwy. 28 just east of Village Blvd.), where you can shop for practical items at a Radio Shack, Ace Hardware, Raley's Supermarket, and the like. **The Village Center** (Mays Blvd. at Southwood) has a half dozen shops of an equally pedestrian nature, including a post office.

FESTIVALS AND EVENTS

The East Shore's, and possibly the entire Tahoe basin's, biggest and most famous annual event is the **◖ Lake Tahoe Shakespeare Festival** (800/747-4697, www.laketahoeshakespeare.com, $15–80), which features two or more of Shakespeare's plays performed at Sand Harbor's natural outdoor amphitheater, which overlooks the lake. Over the course of the month-long festival, about 30,000 ticket holders bring their own picnic dinner (or buy one from one of several food vendors) and wiggle their toes in the sand while watching professional actors

The Lake Tahoe Shakespeare Festival takes place outdoors at Sand Harbor.

perform one of the Bard's comedies or tragedies. The festival, which has been taking place at Lake Tahoe every mid-July–mid-August for some 40 years, is a hit with people of all ages. Purchase tickets in advance, especially if you want to see the show on popular full moon nights, when it's hard to take your eyes off the moonlight reflecting on the lake's surface in order to watch the play.

FAMILY FUN

Kids and adults alike will enjoy a trip to **Virginia City,** site of the 1860s Comstock gold- and silver-mining boom. The under-12 set will certainly want to take a ride on the Virginia and Truckee Railroad and tour the underground mine in the Ponderosa Saloon. Along the way, consider a stop at the **Children's Museum of Northern Nevada** in Carson City (813 N. Carson St., 775/884-2226, www.cmnn.org, 10 A.M.–4:30 P.M. daily, children 2–13 $3, adults $5), where kids are not just allowed to touch the exhibits, they are encouraged to do so. There's a walk-in kaleidoscope, a giant keyboard, and other fun stuff for ages 3–12.

Also in Carson City is the **Nevada State Railroad Museum** (2180 S. Carson St., 775/687-6953, www.nsrm-friends.org, 8:30 A.M.–4:30 P.M. Fri.–Mon. $6 adults, children 17 and under free), which houses a collection of restored historic Virginia and Truckee Railroad cars and locomotives. Steam-train rides are offered in summer.

If your kids are of the video age, they will probably prefer to spend a few hours at one of the East Shore's arcades. Not surprisingly, you'll find them at four Crystal Bay and Incline Village casinos—Cal-Neva, Crystal Bay, Hyatt Regency, and Tahoe Biltmore—giving the kids something to do while Mom and Dad gamble away their college funds.

For a more old-fashioned indoor game, consider knocking over a few pins at **Bowl Incline** (920 Southwood Blvd., Incline Village,

775/831-1900, 11 A.M.–midnight daily). In addition to the bowling lanes, there is a video arcade, billiards, video poker, darts, and the like. If you are concerned about the health of your kids' lungs in cigarette-happy Nevada, the bowling alley is smoke-free on Sunday. And if it's winter and you or your kids are longing for a round of golf, try out Bowl Incline's full-swing golf simulator, which uses real balls and clubs.

Accommodations

INCLINE VILLAGE AND CRYSTAL BAY
Casinos and Hotels

Straddling the California/Nevada border on the North Shore at Crystal Bay, ☾ **Cal-Neva Resort, Spa, and Casino** (2 Tahoe Blvd./Hwy. 28, Crystal Bay, 775/832-4000 or 800/225-6382, www.calnevaresort.com, $49–239) enjoys a spectacular lakeside setting at Crystal Point and houses the oldest operating casino in the United States. The hotel was built in 1937 and was owned by Frank Sinatra in the 1960s. Old Blue Eyes and his cronies Sammy

Davis Jr., Dean Martin, and Marilyn Monroe would pal around here when they wanted to flee the hectic L.A. celebrity lifestyle. Because of its state-line location, the Cal-Neva enjoys an odd twist of geography. Guests can swim from California to Nevada, and back again, in its outdoor pool. All of its 220 guest rooms have lake views, but the best vistas are seen from the pricier rooms on the 7th, 8th, and 9th floors. A few of the "celebrity cabins" have nice views, too. Try to get Marilyn Monroe's cabin if it's available; the lake view is awesome. If you've won a small fortune at the casino, reserve a stay

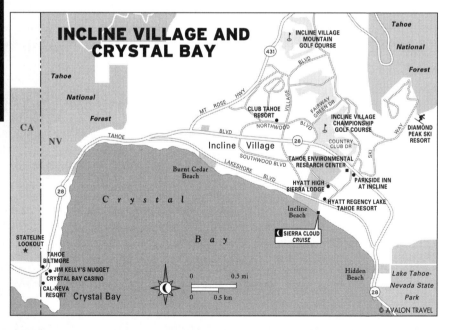

in one of the suites with living rooms and balconies, or the chalets with fireplaces ($229–329). This is definitely a place where you should pay extra money for the better rooms. Stay-and-ski packages are super affordable, especially midweek—as low as $119 for two adult ski tickets at Diamond Peak and a lakeview room. Like most Tahoe casinos, this one has a restaurant, bar, and spa, so you can get all your entertainment in one building. *Condé Nast Traveler* called the Cal-Neva "Nevada's Best Getaway." If you enjoy ghost stories, be sure to take the "tunnel tour," which is usually offered on Friday and Saturday nights.

Located within a few miles of the Mount Rose and Diamond Peak ski areas, and with a secure ski storage area and ski rental shop on the premises, the four-diamond ◖ **Hyatt Regency Lake Tahoe Resort** (111 Country Club Dr., Incline Village, 775/832-1234, www.laketahoehyatt.com, $210–500) caters to the snow bunny crowd. The motto at this megaresort should be "but wait, there's more." The 1920s-era hotel features the Grand Lodge Casino, a heated pool that has both an indoor and an outdoor section (they call it a "year-round swimming oasis"), a fitness club, and the 20,000-square-foot Stillwater Spa—Tahoe's largest day spa, offering all the latest feel-good treatments. If you are celebrating something special with your sweetie, reserve an hour's worth of pampering in the "couples' massage suite," which has its own fireplace. Six restaurants feed the hungry, including the Lone Eagle Grille (775/886-6899 or 775/832-1234, www.loneeaglegrille.com, lunch 11:30 A.M.–3 P.M. Mon.–Sat., Sunday brunch 10 A.M.–3 P.M., dinner 5:30–9 P.M. Sun.–Thurs., 5:30–9:30 P.M. Fri.–Sat., $32–47) with its massive rock fireplaces, open-beamed ceiling, and enviable lake view. Forget skiing; you may never want to leave this place. The Hyatt's 449 rooms come with all the usual four-star hotel amenities, but the six suites on the upper floors of the 12-story

tower are far superior, as you might expect. For the most privacy, book one of the 24 one- and two-bedroom lakefront cottages with fireplaces and private decks ($400 and up), which were remodeled in 2007 and now have designer carpets, 42-inch flat-screen televisions, chenille sofas, and Italian leather chairs. Don't miss the wonderful breakfast buffet at the resort's Sierra Café. If you really want to stay here but don't think you can afford it, check out their midweek specials in winter. A typical deal is two lift tickets at Diamond Peak and a room for two for only $300.

For bargain lodging near Incline Village and Crystal Bay, look no further than the 113 rooms at the **Tahoe Biltmore** (5 Tahoe Blvd./Hwy. 28, Crystal Bay, 775/831-0660 or 800/245-8667, www.tahoebiltmore.com, $39–179). The resort is showing its age, but it's clean and serviceable. Two accommodations are offered: rooms in the main hotel and "cottage" rooms. The cottage rooms are slightly lower priced and are grouped together with about six units per building. They are much larger than many of the hotel rooms, but unfortunately, they aren't soundproof. Light sleepers may hear people coming and going from the casino all night. Dogs are permitted in the cottages for an extra $20 per night. If you are planning a summer stay, be forewarned that the Biltmore has no air-conditioning, and the rooms can be stuffy. Rates include a huge, cholesterol-raising breakfast at the Biltmore Café. In the winter months, check for stay-and-ski package deals, or Sunday–Wednesday deals dropping as low as $45 for two nights. The Biltmore is far and away the best deal in town, but remember, you get what you pay for.

Condominium-Style Resorts

Located near the Hyatt Regency Lake Tahoe Resort, the ◖ **Hyatt High Sierra Lodge** (989 Incline Way, Incline Village, 775/832-0220, www.hyatt.com, $275–700) is an upscale

© ANN MARIE BROWN

It's a bit like Waikiki at the Hyatt's beach on summer weekends.

time-share resort with 60 two-bedroom condominiums for rent. Like at the neighboring Hyatt, the lake views are incredible. The condos can sleep 4–6 people and have private balconies, gas fireplaces, fully equipped kitchens, and master bedroom suites with king beds. Guests can take advantage of concierge service, babysitting referrals, and other typical resort perks, including use of a 500-foot private beach. If you don't want to cook, you can walk to the neighboring Hyatt's three restaurants.

One mile outside downtown Incline Village, the unpretentious **Club Tahoe Resort** (914 Northwoods Blvd., Incline Village, 775/831-5750 or 800/527-5154, www.clubtahoe.com, $145–250) rents two-bedroom condos for a real bargain compared to other places in the area. Affordable stay-and-ski packages are available, too. The units are more than 1,000 square feet in size and can easily sleep six people in a master bedroom, smaller second bedroom, and upstairs loft area. Rental units have a full kitchen,

two bathrooms, fireplace, washer/dryer, two televisions, and everything else you'd expect. There's nothing terribly fancy about the place, but for an affordable family or small-group vacation, it works just fine.

Vacation Rentals

Lodging options in the Incline Village area are fairly limited, so vacation home rentals take up the lodging slack. Whether you want a condo, a cabin, or a luxury home to rent, one of these three companies can find it for you from the hundreds of vacation properties available in the area: Incline Vacation Rentals (901 Tahoe Blvd./Hwy. 28, Incline Village, 800/831-3304, www.inclinevacations.com), Vacation Station (930 Tahoe Blvd./Hwy. 28, Incline Village, 800/841-7443, www.vacationstation.com), and Incline at Tahoe Realty (811 Tahoe Blvd./Hwy. 28, Incline Village, 888/686-5253, www.inclineattahoe.com).

Motels and Lodges

The no-frills **Parkside Inn at Incline** (1003 Tahoe Blvd./Hwy. 28, Incline Village, 775/831-1052 or 800/824-6391, www.innatincline.com, $59–189) is just the ticket for skiers who don't have stacks of extra cash under their mattresses. The 38 rooms are set in a two-story motel-style building. The rooms are large, basic, and clean, and you can't ask for more than that at this price. Guests have access to an indoor pool, sauna, and hot tub. A continental breakfast is served on weekends only (daily during peak tourist season) in the common room. Even though this is Nevada, the Inn at Incline is a completely nonsmoking property. Stay-and-ski packages are quite affordable. Diamond Peak Ski Resort is only a mile away.

Campgrounds and RV Parks

Located 7.5 miles north of Incline Village on Highway 431, at 9,300 feet in elevation, the small, 24-site **Mount Rose Campground** (775/882-2766, $17, reserve at 877/444-6777 or www.recreation.gov) is run by the Forest Service and has restrooms, water, and a dump station. It can accommodate small trailers and RVs up to 16 feet long. If you are planning to climb to the summit of 10,778-foot Mount Rose, this is a great place to camp. The trailhead is right across the highway. A major trailhead for the Tahoe Rim Trail is nearby at Tahoe Meadows.

For those who don't mind hiking or biking for a few miles to reach their campsite, **Lake Tahoe Nevada State Park** (775/831-0494, www.parks.nv.gov) allows camping at no charge in three developed campgrounds— Marlette Peak, Hobart, and North Canyon. Each campground has a toilet and four or five campsites with picnic tables, fire rings, and bear-resistant food and trash storage boxes.

SPOONER LAKE

Many visitors complain that it's hard to find lodgings with real "nature appeal" around Lake Tahoe, since so much of the shoreline has motels, hotels, and other businesses packed in right next to each other. That's what makes the **◖Spooner Lake Wilderness Cabins** (near Spooner Summit, 775/749-5349, www.spoonerlake.com, $95–188 for two people in spring, summer, and fall; $160–319 for two people in winter) so special. Set inside the boundary of Lake Tahoe Nevada State Park, the two Scandinavian-style cabins were constructed in 2002 with beautiful hand-hewn logs, and they are surrounded by nothing but forested parkland. It takes a little effort to get to the cabins. Spooner Lake Cabin is set on a knoll near Spooner Lake, a 0.75-mile walk (or bike ride, snowshoe, or cross-country ski) from the parking lot. It sleeps 4–6 people. The more intimate Wildcat Cabin is a 2-mile walk (or bike ride, snowshoe, or cross-country ski) and has a great long-distance view of Lake Tahoe and Emerald Bay. Two people fit nicely in Wildcat; four would be a stretch.

The cabins can be accessed year-round, and they are equipped with a propane cooking stove and some kitchen supplies, a wood-burning stove for heat, propane lights, a queen-size bed, and a full-size futon. In place of a bathroom, guests use a composting toilet. (There's no shower or tub at either cabin.) Each cabin is provided with two gallons of water per day, so you don't have to haul that in, but you do need to bring your own food or plan to hike/bike/ski/snowshoe out for meals. This is an ideal getaway for summer visitors who want to bike the famous Flume Trail (the trailhead is right here) or just sit on their own private deck and read a book in the warm Tahoe sun.

EAST SHORE

© ANN MARIE BROWN

Mountain bikers can spend the night at the Wildcat Cabin at Spooner Lake.

Food

INCLINE VILLAGE AND CRYSTAL BAY
Breakfast

The locals love **The Wildflower Café** (869 Tahoe Blvd./Hwy. 28, Incline Village, 775/831-8072, 7 A.M.–2:30 P.M. Mon.–Sat., 8 A.M.–2 P.M. Sun.), a 1950s-throwback breakfast joint that knows how to do justice to pigs in a blanket (two pancakes wrapped around link sausages), biscuits and gravy, and home fries. They do lunch, too—a variety of burgers and sandwiches including all the classics, like tuna melts and Reubens. Everything is under $12.

American

Always dazzling diners with its drop-dead-gorgeous lake view, the **⬤ Lone Eagle Grille** at the Hyatt Regency Lake Tahoe Resort (111 Country Club Dr., Incline Village, 775/886-6899 or 775/832-1234, www.lonee-aglegrille.com, lunch 11:30 A.M.–3 P.M. Mon.–Sat., Sunday brunch 10 A.M.–3 P.M., dinner 5:30–9 P.M. Sun.–Thurs., 5:30–9:30 P.M. Fri.–Sat., $32–47) features a high, open-timbered ceiling, two massive rock fireplaces, and hearty American food (spit-roasted duck, rack of lamb, grilled king salmon, elk chops, and beef tenderloin). This is not a restaurant for penny-pinchers; two people probably won't leave without dropping at least $150 on dinner. This is why you might want to come here for lunch instead, when entrées are priced around 20 bucks and you can enjoy the fabulous lake view in daylight. Or come at any time, sit in the massive bar/lounge, and order from the less-expensive bar menu. In summer, you can nab an outside table, and even in winter you can bundle up and sit outside at the large gas fire pit. There may be no better spot for an après-ski drink.

The Hyatt has two other restaurants, both less expensive, more casual, and sadly lacking the Lone Eagle Grille's lovely lake view: Ciao Mein and Sierra Café. The latter is known for its extensive breakfast buffet, which includes lots of homemade muffins and pastries.

The hippest place in Incline for new American food is **Bite** (907 Tahoe Blvd./Hwy. 28, Incline Village, 775/831-1000, www.bite-tahoe.com, 5–10 P.M. Thurs.–Tues., $8–18). A huge variety of tapas-style small plates are available here, from outrageously good sliders (Tuscan grilled cheese, BLTs, ahi, and plain old cheeseburgers) to crab cakes, hanger steak, gnocchi, and macaroni and cheese. Even wine is available in small-sized portions, so you can taste several different vintages.

Now here's a distinction: The **Big Water Grille** (341 Ski Way, Incline Village, 775/833-0606, www.bigwatergrille.com, 4:30–9:30 P.M. Wed.–Mon., $28–42) is the highest dining room on the North Shore at an elevation of 6,700 feet, located right below the entrance to Diamond Peak Ski Resort. That great height means that a few choice tables have great lake views (albeit from a distance), which are coupled with an outstanding and creative menu that changes often. Current favorites include the lobster trio (lobster thermidor, lobster soufflé, and a lobster gazpacho) and heirloom tomato soup. The wine list features more than 200 choices, and the bar is often bustling with Tahoe locals, especially during happy hour when appetizers are only $6.

Located across from the monolithic Hyatt, **Austin's** (120 Country Club Dr., Incline Village, 775/832-7778, www.austinstahoe.com, 11 A.M.–9 P.M. Mon.–Fri., 5–9 P.M. Sat.–Sun., $8–20) is a cozy, home-style restaurant that is famous for its comfort food. If you are craving chicken-fried steak (or chicken-fried

chicken, for that matter), you'll find it here, served with a side of mashed potatoes and gravy. But this is not just a meat-and-potatoes place; salad lovers will appreciate the variety and size of the salads. A side of corn bread comes with almost everything. Austin's buttermilk french fries with jalapeño dipping sauce are an Incline Village institution.

Sit back in one of the velvet-covered, high-back booths and enjoy the old-school ambience at **Crystal Bay Steak and Lobster House** at Crystal Bay Casino (14 Tahoe Blvd./Hwy. 28, Crystal Bay, 775/833-6333, www.crystalbaycasino.com, 5:30–9 P.M. Tues.–Sun., $25–45). The menu runs the gamut of quintessential protein-rich American entrées—prawns, salmon, scallops, ribs, rack of lamb, steaks, and prime rib. The namesake steak-and-lobster entrée costs $68, but it's enough food for a family of four. Tableside preparation is their signature. Top off your meal with a port or cognac from the extensive wine list.

California Cuisine

One of the most romantic dining experiences possible at Lake Tahoe can be had at **The Soule Domain** (9983 Cove St., Brockway, 530/546-7529, www.souledomain.com, 6 P.M.–close daily, $19–34). Dinner is the only meal served in this petite, 1930s-era log cabin located next door to the Tahoe Biltmore, and that's because it takes all day to prepare menu items as complex as fresh vegetables baked in pastry shells, grilled lamb chops with basil cashew pesto, and filet mignon pan roasted with shiitake mushrooms, gorgonzola, and brandy. The meaning of the restaurant's name? This place is the "domain" of chef and owner Charles Edward Soule IV. He and his brother Steve have been successfully running The Soule Domain since 1985.

No discussion of continental cuisine in Incline Village would be complete without mentioning **Le Bistro** (120 Country Club

Dr., Incline Village, 775/831-0800, www.leb-istrorestaurant.net, 6–9:30 P.M. Tues.–Sat., $26–30). Located behind the Country Club Mall, Le Bistro's intimate provincial-style dining room is the perfect setting for entrées like quenelle of squab and beef tournedos. Can't decide what to order? Go for the five-course prix fixe menu ($50). Every item, from the baked escargot and romaine salad to the crème brûlée, is *très français*. Chef Jean-Pierre Doignon is a legend in the Lake Tahoe dining scene.

It's hard to classify **Frederick's Fusion Bistro**'s (907 Tahoe Blvd./Hwy. 28, Incline Village, 775/832-3007, http://fredricksbistro.com) eclectic cuisine, which is part Californian and European and part Asian sushi bar. No matter, you'll love your meal here, and the intimate bistro atmosphere of the dining room. That's if you can get past this restaurant's weird location next to the 7-Eleven in Incline Village. A few winners are the braised lamb shank, lobster corn dogs, and pork loin with gorgonzola and candied walnut filling. For dessert, you just have to try the fried Snickers bar.

Most of us sold our fondue pots at garage sales sometime after the 1970s. But **La Fondue** (120 Country Club Dr., Incline Village, 866/739-4893, www.lafonduetahoe.com, 5:30–9 P.M. daily in summer, Wed.–Mon. only in winter, $16–28) delivers a much finer version of the sticky, melted stuff than we ever dreamed of in our avocado-green 1970s kitchens. About a dozen different fondue dishes grace the menu, including the house specialty, a cheese fondue made of swiss gruyère and emmentaler. Dip in some grapes, apple pieces, or French bread, and you're in fondue heaven. Meat eaters will prefer to try the filet mignon, lamb, meatball, or jumbo prawn fondue, or order one of the schnitzels. Dessert is, of course, a sinful chocolate fondue. In the summer, you can dine outdoors.

Italian

For more than 20 years, **Azzara's** (930 Tahoe Blvd./Hwy. 28, Incline Village, 775/831-0346, www.azzaras.com, opens at 5 P.M. for dinner, closed Mon., $17–28) has been dishing out northern Italian meals to hungry Incline Village diners. It's hard to decide between the multiple pasta dishes and house specialties like *frutti de mare* and *melanzane,* but no matter what you order, save room for the unforgettable tiramisu. This is classic Italian food prepared just right. Even the kids will enjoy the meals here. If you're having trouble finding it, Azzara's is in the Raley's shopping center.

Sometimes after a day of skiing, ordering a pizza to go or eat in sounds a lot more appealing than showering and dressing up for dinner. That's where **Mofo's Pizza** (in Christmas Tree Village, 868 Tahoe Blvd./Hwy. 28, Incline Village, 775/831-4999, www.mofospizzaand-pasta.com, 11:30 A.M.–2 P.M. and 5–8:30 P.M. daily, $12–22) comes in. They've been making pizzas for Incline Village residents and visitors since 1986. Their calzones and homemade ravioli are rich and filling, and the 20-item salad bar gives you something to graze on while you wait for dinner.

If your pizza sensibilities are a little more gourmet, try the exotic toppings and whole-wheat pizza crust at **Tomaato's** (120 Country Club Dr., Incline Village, 775/833-2200, www.tomaatos.com, 5–9 P.M. Thurs.–Tues., $10–20), located across the street from the Hyatt. Their calzones are as good as their pizzas, which manage to walk that fine line between thin crust and thick crust. Start your meal with a baked brie salad.

Mexican

At lunchtime, don't get in the way of the door at **T's Mesquite Rotisserie** (901 Tahoe Blvd./Hwy. 28, Incline Village, 775/831-2832, 11 A.M.–8 P.M. daily, $6–20), or you are likely to get run over by a horde of hungry people. T's makes fast food the right way, with a large rotisserie oven that cooks whole chickens to perfection all day long. While you wait to order, the aroma can drive you crazy. Plenty of people order takeout; others find a spot in the crowded dining area or outside on a few picnic tables. In addition to the hormone-free chicken, there's corn-fed beef tri-tip, sandwiches, steak and chicken burritos, and tacos. If you order right, you can feed a small family for about 25 bucks. *Sunset* magazine rated T's tacos as "best in the West."

The colorful **Hacienda de La Sierra** (931 Tahoe Blvd./Hwy. 28, Incline Village, 775/831-8300, www.haciendatahoe.com, 4–10 P.M. daily, $9–18) has everything you want in a Mexican cantina: great margaritas; large portions of fajitas, burritos, and all the classic Mexican dishes; plus unlimited bowls of chips and salsa. Adding to the festive atmosphere, Hacienda de La Sierra's dining area is spacious and brightly hued (tropical artwork and a parrot theme define the decor). In summer, diners can eat outside on the back patio.

Asian

For most visitors, it's a pleasant surprise to find out how good the sushi can be at Lake Tahoe, a couple hundred miles from the ocean. But the Tahoe basin has more than its share of excellent sushi restaurants, and Incline Village's version is **Yoshimi** (882 Tahoe Blvd./Hwy. 28, Incline Village, 775/831-2777, 11:30 A.M.–2 P.M. and 5–9 P.M. Tues.–Sat., $16 lunch, $26 dinner), located in the Christmas Tree Village shopping center. Lunch and dinner are all you can eat here, so bring your appetite for their huge menu of sushi rolls, as well as their beer and sake selection.

The soothing, purple-hued dining room at **Thai Recipe** (901 Tahoe Blvd./Hwy. 28, Incline Village, 775/831-4777, 11 A.M.–9 P.M. daily, $9–17) is the perfect setting for a meal of Thai egg rolls, lemongrass salad, and spinach curry, or any of your other Thai favorites. The restaurant's owner, a retired university professor from Bangkok, makes sure that everything is beautifully prepared and served with warm Thai hospitality.

Practicalities

INFORMATION

Visit the **Incline Village/Crystal Bay Visitors Bureau and Chamber of Commerce** (969 Tahoe Blvd./Hwy. 28 in Incline Village, 775/832-1606 or 800/468-2463, www.gotahoenorth.com, 10 A.M.–4 P.M. weekends and holidays, 8 A.M.–5 P.M. weekdays). If you are traveling to or from Nevada to Lake Tahoe, you might also want to visit the **Carson Valley Visitors Center** (1477 Hwy. 395, Gardnerville, 775/782-8144 or 800/727-7677, www.visitcarsonvalley.org) or **Carson City Convention and Visitors Bureau** (1900 S. Carson St., Carson City, 775/687-7410 or 800/638-2321, www.visitcarsoncity.com).

SERVICES
Medical Care

Both of the following locations offer 24-hour emergency care: **Incline Village Community Hospital** (in the Raley's Shopping Center, 930 Tahoe Blvd./Hwy. 28, Incline Village, 775/833-4100, www.tfhd.com) and **Incline Village Urgent Care** (995 Tahoe Blvd./Hwy. 28, Incline Village, 775/833-2929).

Post Offices

The largest post office on the East Shore is at The Village Center in **Incline Village** (770 Mays Blvd. at Southwood Blvd., 775/831-8994). **Crystal Bay** also has a post office (26 Hwy. 28/Tahoe Blvd. at Crystal Bay Dr.,

EAST SHORE

RENO HIGHLIGHTS

This casino town is called the "Biggest Little City in the World," for reasons that are not entirely clear. It has always been the poor cousin to that other Nevada casino town—glamorous, infamous Las Vegas. Still, the northern Nevada city of Reno has its share of charms, and as a tourist destination it gets better every year. For an interesting day trip, take a 25-mile drive from Incline Village to Reno. Here are some of the highlights you will find:

Nevada Museum of Art (160 W. Liberty St., 775/329-3333, www.nevadaart.org, 10 A.M.–5 P.M. Wed.–Sun., until 8 P.M. on Thurs., $10 adults, $8 students and seniors, $1 children 6-12). The permanent collection in this 55,000-square-foot architectural gem consists of nearly 2,000 works of art organized around the themes of land and environment. Don't miss the rooftop sculpture garden. After a look at the exhibits, take a walk past the lively restaurants, galleries, and shops on California Street.

Truckee Riverwalk (775/825-9255, www.renoriver.org). This picturesque public plaza on the Truckee River in downtown Reno features wildlife art and unique fountains. A collection of trails, benches, parks, cafés, galleries, and boutique shops, Riverwalk mixes the best of Reno's urban and natural environments. Events are held throughout the year.

Fleischmann Planetarium and Science Center (1650 N. Virginia St., University of Nevada at Reno, 775/784-4811, http://planetarium.unr.nevada.edu, noon–5 P.M. Mon.–Thurs., noon–9 P.M. Fri., 10 A.M.–9 P.M. Sat., 10 A.M.–5 P.M. Sun., gallery exhibits are free, planetarium shows are $6 adults, $4 seniors over 55 and children 12 and under). Check out a collection of meteorites, including four that were recovered in the state of Nevada, and enjoy a large-format feature film or a planetarium star show at the SkyDome. Kids will want to step on the scale and find out how much they weigh on the moon or Jupiter.

National Automobile Museum (10 S. Lake St., 775/333-9300, www.automuseum.

org, 9:30 A.M.–5:30 P.M. Mon.–Sat., 10 A.M.–4 P.M. Sun., $10 adults, $8 seniors 62 and over, $4 children 6-18, free for children 5 and under). More than 200 fancy cars are housed here, including cars that have appeared in Hollywood films, cars that belonged to celebrities, and one-of-a-kind models that are like nothing you have ever seen on the road.

Nevada Historical Society Museum (1650 N. Virginia St., 775/688-1190, 11 A.M.–5 P.M. Mon.–Sat., $2 adults, free for children under 18). The state's oldest museum, founded in 1904, holds a wealth of exhibits, photographs, and research materials for history buffs, spanning the ages from prehistoric times to the Nevada mining boom of the 19th century. Take a look at early gambling devices, slot machines, cards, and casino chips, and learn how silver played an important part in Nevada's bid for statehood.

Sierra Safari Zoo (10200 N. Virginia St., 775/677-1104, www.sierrasafarizoo.org, 10 A.M.–5 P.M. daily Apr.–Oct., $7 adults, $6 seniors 55-plus and children 3-12). Get up close and personal with over 200 animals of 40 different species at this open-air zoo.

Festivals and events: Reno loves to party, and the town can think of plenty of excuses for a celebration. Every June, the **Wildest, Richest Rodeo in the West** (775/329-3877 or 800/225-2277, www.renorodeo.com) features the world's best rodeo athletes competing in the fine arts of steer wrestling, bronc riding, bull riding, and more. Later in the summer, **Hot August Nights** (www.hotaugustnights.net) is a week-long celebration of 1950s music and cars. The country's top competitive aviation event takes place at the **Reno National Championship Air Races** (775/972-6663, www.airrace.org) in September, although a tragic crash at the 2011 races have put the future of this event in question. Also in September is Reno's most colorful event: the **Great Reno Balloon Race** (775/826-1181, www.renoballoon.com).

775/831-8994). Both are open 8:30 A.M.–5 P.M. Monday–Friday.

Internet Access
To check your email or surf the Web, go to the **Incline Village Public Library** (one block off Hwy. 28 at 845 Alder Ave., 775/832-4130). Or go to one of several coffee shops in Incline Village, including the Starbucks Coffee at 899 Tahoe Boulevard (775/831-6615).

GETTING THERE
By Air
Visitors can fly into the **Reno-Tahoe International Airport** (2001 E. Plumb La., 775/328-6400, www.renoairport.com) and then rent a car or take bus, shuttle, or limousine service. Several companies offer shuttle or limo service between the Reno-Tahoe International Airport and the Incline Village area: Airport Mini-Bus/Bell Limousine (800/235-5466), Executive Limousine (775/333-3300), Aladdin Limousine (800/546-6009), Sierra West Limousine (877/347-4789), and North Tahoe Limousine (800/832-8213). North Tahoe Checker Cab (866/420-8294) also travels between the airport and Incline Village.

Visitors could also fly into the Sacramento, Oakland, San Francisco, or San Jose airports, then rent a car to drive to Lake Tahoe. Sacramento Airport is about 3 hours from Incline Village; the three other airports are about 4.5 hours away.

By Car
From the San Francisco Bay Area or Sacramento, the primary driving route to Incline Village and the East Shore is to take I-80 east to Truckee and then Highway 267 south to Kings Beach. Incline Village is about 5 miles east of Kings Beach on Highway 28.

Total driving distance is about 130 miles from Sacramento or 220 miles from San Francisco.

From Reno-Tahoe International Airport, take U.S. 395 south for 7 miles to Highway 431 west. Drive southwest on Highway 431 for 20 miles to Incline Village.

By Bus
Visitors can access Truckee or Reno by two major bus lines: **Greyhound Bus Lines** (800/231-2222, www.greyhound.com) or **Amtrak Bus** (800/872-7245, www.amtrak.com). Tahoe Area Regional Transit (TART) (530/550-1212 or 800/736-6365, www.laketahoetransit.com) system buses connect with these bus lines at the Truckee Depot to take passengers to Incline Village.

By Train
The nearest Amtrak train depots are in Truckee or Reno. For schedules and information, contact **Amtrak** (800/872-7245, www.amtrak.com). Tahoe Area Regional Transit (TART) (530/550-1212 or 800/736-6365, www.laketahoetransit.com) system buses connect with Amtrak at the Truckee Depot to take passengers to Incline Village.

GETTING AROUND
Tahoe Area Regional Transit (TART) (530/550-1212 or 800/736-6365, www.laketahoetransit.com) runs between Incline Village and Tahoma year-round, traveling along the North and West Shores and up to Alpine Meadows, Squaw Valley, and Truckee. TART also connects with the South Shore bus line at Meeks Bay in summer. There is currently no public transportation that runs south from Incline Village along the East Shore.

During the ski season, the major ski areas (Northstar, Squaw Valley, Alpine Meadows, Mount Rose, Diamond Peak) have shuttle

EAST SHORE

service to and from designated stops along Highway 28. Contact the individual resorts for details.

In winter, the **Reno Ski Shuttle** (775/325-8813, www.tahoeskishuttle.com) runs from major Reno hotels (Nugget, Hilton, Sands, Silver Legacy, Peppermill, Atlantis) twice each morning to Mount Rose Ski Area (a 25-minute drive). Reservations are recommended. The fare is $15 round-trip, but combined lift ticket and shuttle packages are available.

By Car

All the major **car-rental** agencies are available at Reno-Tahoe International Airport (775/328-6400, www.renoairport.com). To get current updates on road conditions in California, phone 800/427-7623 or visit www.dot.ca.gov. To get current updates on Nevada road conditions, phone 877/687-6237 or visit www.safetravelusa.com.

By Taxi

Several private cab services can get you where you want to go on the East Shore, or pick you up or drop you off at the Reno-Tahoe airport. Contact any of the following services: Truckee Tahoe Transportation (530/582-5828, www.truckeetahoetransportation.com), All-Star Taxi (530/448-2552, www.taxitahoe.com), Anytime Taxi (877/808-8294 or 530/414-4187, www.anytimetaxi.net), North Tahoe Checker Cab (866/420-8294 or 530/587-0666), or Lake Tahoe Taxi (530/577-7000).

CARSON PASS

Carson Pass may be less than an hour from bustling South Lake Tahoe, but psychologically, it's a world away. Named for the famous scout and explorer, Kit Carson, Carson Pass is as noncommercialized as the South Shore is commercialized. There isn't much in the way of visitor services except for a few scattered cabin resorts, a handful of restaurants, and one major ski area. The largest town, and county seat, Markleeville, has a population of only a few hundred people. In fact, all of Alpine County has only two residents per square mile. Private property is the exception rather than the rule; a remarkable 93 percent of the county's acreage is public land.

But this doesn't mean that Carson Pass is undiscovered. The region's population is boosted exponentially each year by the thousands of visitors who flock here in summer for hiking, mountain biking, and some of the best fishing anywhere in the Sierra, and in winter for an array of winter sports. Those who choose to visit come for the area's natural wonders. High volcanic peaks, alpine lakes, aspen groves, wildflower fields, and dramatic Sierra scenery wait to be explored. The home of Kirkwood Ski Resort, this area is well known for consistently receiving more snowfall than anywhere else in the Sierra—often as much as 700 inches per year. The remarkable volcanic landscape lends itself well to alpine and cross-country skiing, snowboarding, and snowshoeing. For the

HIGHLIGHTS

LOOK FOR **(** TO FIND RECOMMENDED SIGHTS, ACTIVITIES, DINING, AND LODGING.

(Markleeville: Turn back time with a walk along the streets of Markleeville, which are lined with 19th-century buildings, including the quaint Old Webster School at the Alpine County Museum (page 246).

(Autumn Colors: Timing is everything if you want to witness one of California's best shows of fall colors along the roads of Hope Valley and Carson Pass. The prolific groves of quaking aspens generally attain their peak shades of gold, amber, and red somewhere between mid-September and mid-October (page 247).

(Carson Pass Summit: Stop in at the visitors center located at Carson Pass Summit to learn about the journeys of the great scout Kit Carson and the thousands of emigrants who passed through this area (page 247).

(Zip Tahoe: Let gravity be your adrenaline on Kirkwood's year-round zipline course. You'll "fly" through the tree canopy, 80 feet above the ground (page 248).

(Frog Lake: For a short, easy introduction to the scenic wonders of Carson Pass, take this 1.8-mile round-trip hike from Carson Pass Summit to Frog Lake. Most of the summer you'll be able to admire myriad wildflowers along the way (page 252).

(Lake Margaret: This longer hike in the Carson Pass area is a great way to spend a half day. A nearly five-mile round-trip hike with relatively short uphill stretches brings you to the shores of lovely Lake Margaret, where swimming, fishing, and sunbathing are favored activities (page 255).

(Dogsledding: Dash through the snow in an open sleigh drawn by eager, panting husky dogs and veteran dog musher Dotty Dennis (page 263).

intrepid skier who prefers trackless snow, miles of backcountry terrain wait to be explored.

Anglers, too, consider Carson Pass to be a gold mine, with hungry trout lurking in more than 60 lakes, multiple streams, and the world-famous Carson River. Hikers swarm to the area

in July to see one of California's best wildflower shows, and then return in late September for an incredible fall foliage display. Campers and hot-springs aficionados flock to Grover Hot Springs State Park, which in addition to its natural hot springs, has lovely meadows and pine-dotted

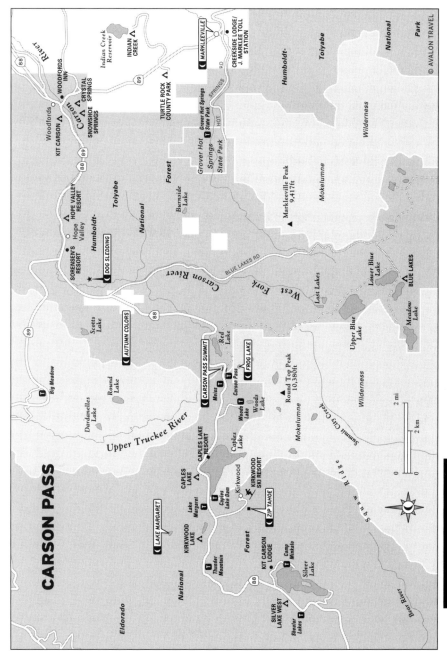

CARSON PASS

CARSON PASS

woods. But the busiest weekend of the year occurs each July, when the annual Markleeville Death Ride takes place. One of California's premier cycling events, the Death Ride consists of a daunting 129-mile route with a total 15,000 feet of elevation change. Even if you'd never think of riding in a bike tour of this magnitude, it's worth showing up just to watch the spectacle.

PLANNING YOUR TIME

If you are a hiker, biker, angler, nature photographer, snowboarder, or skier, you'll easily find enough activities to keep you busy in the Carson Pass area for a week, a month, or more. Casual sightseers and those who prefer the city amenities of South Lake Tahoe will probably be content with a half-day drive through this area. Be sure to visit the quaint hamlet of **Markleeville,** where the main street is a throwback to the 19th century. And take the scenic drive up and over 8,573-foot **Carson Pass** itself, where you can stop in at the log-cabin visitors center and learn about the thousands of emigrants who passed this way before you, or take the short, flower-filled hike to **Frog Lake.**

Sights and Entertainment

◖ MARKLEEVILLE

The quaint town of Markleeville, with its 100-yard-long main street, is well worth a stop. Founded in 1861 during the Nevada silver rush, the town once boasted a population of nearly 3,000 people, but today it has only 1,000, and that includes the outlying areas. Most of the town's original 19th-century buildings still stand. Locals and visitors hang out on the front porch of the **Markleeville General Store** (14799 Hwy. 89, 530/694-2448, 10 a.m.–6 p.m. daily). Don't be surprised if you find a dog sleeping on the two-lane highway that runs through town. In summer and early fall, pay a visit to the **Alpine County Museum** (1 School St., Markleeville, 530/694-2317, 11 a.m.–4 p.m. Thurs.–Mon., Memorial Day–Oct., free). The museum consists of the Old Webster School, a one-room schoolhouse built in 1882, and an old log jail from the mid-1800s, constructed with seemingly impenetrable iron doors, two hand-riveted iron cells, vertical log walls, and a log foundation. Farming, mining, and lumbering tools are on display, as well as some Washoe Indian baskets and artifacts. Donations are accepted.

GROVER HOT SPRINGS STATE PARK

Located three miles from Markleeville, Grover Hot Springs State Park's (530/694-2248, www.parks.ca.gov) main attraction is its natural mineral springs, which were discovered by John C. Fremont, the explorer credited with the first sighting of Lake Tahoe. Unlike most hot springs, Grover's water contains little sulfur, so it doesn't have a strong "rotten-egg" smell. The warmer of the park's two concrete pools is regulated between 102 and 104°F, although where the water springs from the ground it is a scalding 148°F. A cool-temperature pool is a more popular option in the summer months. The park also has a year-round campground and hiking and mountain-biking trails. The pools are open year-round except for Christmas, New Year's, and Thanksgiving, and a brief period in September for maintenance, but hours vary widely, so call ahead. Weekends and holidays can be very busy; the wait time to enter the pools during peak periods can be as long as two hours. An $8 fee per vehicle is charged to enter the park; pool fees are $7 adults, $5 children 16 and under.

SHOWSHOE THOMPSON

Sacramento farmer John A. Thompson, better known as Snowshoe Thompson, was Tahoe's first skier and the man who carried the mail across the Sierra in the winter months. A resident of Diamond Valley in Alpine County, he skied through the heart of winter in the mountains hundreds of times, beginning in 1856 and continuing for two decades. Had it not been for his weekly mail runs, there would have been no communication between the eastern and western slopes of the Sierra for a six-month period each year.

Thompson did not use any single route, but varied his path according to the weather and snow conditions. Most commonly, he traveled from Hangtown (Placerville) to Woodfords (near Markleeville), then followed the route of the Mormon Emigrant Trail (today the route of Highway 88) to Genoa, Nevada, then known as Mormon Station. He routinely passed through Kirkwood and the Carson Pass area on this three-day journey eastward. The return trip usually took only two days.

A Norwegian immigrant, Thompson was born Jon Torstein-Rue in 1827. He learned to ski in the Telemark region of Norway, then left his native country at the age of 10. His handmade, 10-foot-long skis were fashioned from green oak and lashed to his boots with leather straps. At the time, these heavy, unwieldy contraptions were known as "snowshoes." Thompson's were said to weigh 25 pounds. In addition to the burden of the skis, Thompson carried as much as 60-100 pounds of mail on his back. The mail sack contained not just letters but also medicine, emergency supplies, clothing, books, and whatever else the people of Genoa needed.

Using one long pole for balance and support, Thompson skied 25-40 miles per day to keep his delivery on schedule. He wore a Mackinaw jacket and a wide-brimmed hat, and covered his face with charcoal to prevent snow blindness. The isolated residents of Genoa were so thrilled at his arrival they would drop whatever they were doing to watch the tall blonde Norwegian ski down from Genoa Peak. He regularly boasted that he never got lost and never got scared. When a storm became an "inconvenience," he would find a big boulder, clear its surface of snow, and dance Norwegian folk dances until the skies cleared.

In 1866, Thompson married an Englishwoman named Agnes Singleton. They farmsteaded in Diamond Valley in the warm months, and Agnes gave birth to a child in 1867. Thompson taught his only son and many other children to ski, and showed his neighbors how to make their own "snowshoes." He was famous for showing off his racing and jumping skills. In 1872, he was clocked skiing at 55 miles per hour, and successfully ski-jumped 180 feet.

Snowshoe Thompson died of appendicitis in 1876, and his grave can be seen in the town cemetery in Genoa, Nevada. Despite his great service to the people of Nevada, he was never paid a single cent for delivering the U.S. mail.

◖ AUTUMN COLORS

The Carson Pass area is well known for its spectacular show of fall colors put on by the dense groves of quaking aspens that line both sides of the pass. Optimal viewing typically occurs mid-September–mid-October, but it's always wise to phone one of the area's resorts to get an update on current conditions. Some of the most popular spots for photographers and leaf lovers are right along the road by Sorensen's Resort, on the north side of Highway 88 in the pastures of Hope Valley, near Red Lake, on the north side of Caples Lake, and on the road to Woods Lake Campground.

◖ CARSON PASS SUMMIT

At the top of Carson Pass, elevation 8,673 feet, is a log-cabin visitors center run by the U.S. Forest Service, a trailhead that leads into the Mokelumne Wilderness, and a monument to the great explorer and scout Kit Carson. The Carson Pass Information Station (209/258-8606, summer and fall only) sells maps and guidebooks and provides free information to visitors. It's located at Carson Pass Summit on Highway 88 ($5 parking fee), nine miles west of the junction of Highways 88 and 89 and five miles east of Caples Lake. Just east of Carson Pass, you can take a short walk to see large boulders painted with the names of gold-seeking pioneers who followed the route of the historic Emigrant Trail. If you have the time, be sure to take the short, one-mile walk to Frog Lake or the longer hike to Winnemucca Lake.

◖ ZIP TAHOE

Just ask Einstein: Gravity is its own thrill ride. Kirkwood Mountain Resort's zipline course, Zip Tahoe (209/258-7330, www.zip-tahoe.com, $125 per person), which consists of nine segments with platform decks in between, can reach speeds of 35 miles per hour. Situated about 80 feet above the ground, the zipline bobs and weaves through the tree canopy, poking out from the trees just often enough to provide lovely Sierra views. The entire zipline tour lasts about three hours and includes an all-terrain vehicle and chairlift ride to the course. Ever since Heavenly closed its zipline in 2010, this is the only zip course in the Tahoe region, and it's open year-round. In the winter, you zip right above the snowboarders and skiers.

FESTIVALS AND EVENTS

The biggest event in the Carson Pass region is the **Markleeville Death Ride** (www.deathride.com), held each year in July. This is one of California's premier cycling events, which brings even expert riders to their knees with its staggering 15,000 feet of elevation change and 129-mile distance. Even if you'd never consider riding in a bike tour of this magnitude, it's worth showing up in July just to watch the spectacle. The second most popular event is the **Kirkwood Wildflower Festival** (www.kirkwood.com), usually held in late July. The festival consists of guided flower hikes in the morning, and live music, arts and crafts, and food and wine in the afternoon.

dogsled tour at Kirkwood in Carson Pass

© ANN MARIE BROWN

CARSON PASS

FAMILY FUN

Ranger programs are available for children 7–12 at the campground at **Grover Hot Springs State Park** (530/694-2248 or 530/694-2249, www.parks.ca.gov). Nighttime campfire programs, usually held on Saturday nights, cover topics such as bears, mountain lions, the forest ecosystem, and the history of Alpine County. Most programs are about one hour long.

Kirkwood Ski Resort (209/258-6000 or 877/547-5966, www.kirkwood.com) has a multitude of activities that are suitable for kids, from scaling the Adventure Center's climbing wall and zooming down the zipline in summer to tubing and dogsledding in winter.

Recreation

HIKING

The following hikes are listed from north to south along Highway 89 and from east to west along Highway 88. For more information on these trails, contact the Eldorado National Forest, Amador Ranger District (26820 Silver Dr., Pioneer, 209/295-4251, www.fs.fed.us/r5/eldorado).

Dardanelles and Round Lakes

- Distance: 7.6 miles round-trip
- Duration: 4 hours
- Effort: Moderate
- Elevation change: 1,500 feet
- Trailhead: Big Meadow
- Directions: From the T-junction of U.S. 50 and Hwy. 89 in Meyers, drive 5.3 miles south on Hwy. 89 to the Big Meadows parking area on the left (west) side of the highway. Park near the restrooms.

Nowhere is it more clear that the land around Lake Tahoe was shaped by diametrically opposed forces—fire (volcanic action) and ice (glaciers)—than on this pleasant day hike to Dardanelles and Round Lakes. The trip begins at the large Tahoe Rim Trail parking lot at Big Meadow. Pick up the trail from the south side of the parking-lot loop and follow it to a crossing of Highway 89 in about 200 yards. On the far side of the highway, the trail ascends through red-fir and lodgepole-pine forest to expansive Big Meadow, a lovely place to visit at wildflower time, when it is covered with buttercups. After a too-brief level stroll through the meadow grasses, you head back into the trees for another mile of climbing. After a short, steep descent from a saddle, you'll reach a junction at two miles out and turn sharply right on the Meiss Meadow Trail toward Christmas Valley, leaving the Tahoe Rim Trail behind (you'll return to this junction to continue to Round Lake later). In about 200 yards, turn left at the next junction, cross a creek, and walk the final 1.2 miles to Dardanelles Lake. This last level stretch is pure pleasure—it is lined with aspen and alder trees, which put on a colorful display in autumn, and odd-shaped volcanic outcrops. A highlight is a massive western juniper tree that appears to be the granddaddy of them all.

At 7,740 feet in elevation, Dardanelles Lake is a stunner, with a striking granite backdrop and plenty of spots for picnicking, swimming, or camping. This is a deservedly popular spot. Spend as long as you wish here, then backtrack to the Tahoe Rim Trail junction, turn right for Round Lake, and follow the trail 0.75 mile to its shores. Round Lake provides a stark contrast to Dardanelles Lake. It is about twice as large, brownish green in color, and surrounded by dark volcanic rock, not granite. Although not as scenic as Dardanelles Lake, it, too, provides excellent swimming, plus good fishing for cutthroat trout.

Hot Springs Creek Waterfalls

- Distance: 3 miles round-trip
- Duration: 1.5 hours
- Effort: Easy
- Elevation change: 200 feet
- Trailhead: Grover Hot Springs State Park
- Directions: From the junction of Hwy. 89 and Hwy. 88 in Hope Valley, drive east on Hwy. 88/89 for 7 miles to Woodfords, then turn south on Hwy. 89 and drive 6 miles to Markleeville. Turn right (west) on Hot Springs Rd. and drive 3.5 miles to the Grover Hot Springs State Park entrance ($8 per vehicle fee). Continue past the entrance kiosk, then take the left fork past the campground to the signed trailhead, a gated dirt road.

A short and easy walk from the campground and hot-springs pool at Grover Hot Springs State Park leads to an early-summer waterfall along Hot Springs Creek. The route begins as a dirt road, but in 0.6 mile it veers off to the left onto a narrower trail. You'll hike through an open forest of Jeffrey and sugar pines with an understory of aromatic sagebrush. Odd-shaped volcanic formations can be seen beyond the trees. Soon the trail moves closer to Hot Springs Creek, and with the stream on your left, the canyon begins to narrow, and the terrain gets increasingly rocky. When the waterfalls are running strong with spring runoff, you will hear them before you see them. The largest of three falls drops about 30 feet over a tower of volcanic rock. The pools below the big fall are filled with trout and make great swimming holes later in summer when the creek flow slows and the water warms up.

Red Lake Peak

- Distance: 4.8 miles round-trip
- Duration: 2.5 hours
- Effort: Moderate

A hiker and her dog walk across the ice at Round Lake.

- Elevation change: 1,500 feet
- Trailhead: Meiss
- Directions: From the junction of Hwy. 89 and Hwy. 88 in Hope Valley, drive west on Hwy. 88 for 9 miles to Carson Pass Summit. The Meiss Trailhead is on the right (north) side of the highway, across from and slightly west of the Carson Pass Information Station. A $5 parking fee is charged.

The hike to Red Lake Peak is a trek for history lovers. When you stand on the 10,063-foot summit, you can imagine what it felt like when explorer John C. Fremont climbed this peak on February 14, 1844, after nearly perishing from weeks of struggling through the snow-covered Sierra, and became the first white man to lay eyes on Lake Tahoe. At the time, what was even better for Fremont and the men of his expedition was that from this high point, they could see the pass that would lead them out of the mountains and down to the Sacramento Valley.

There is no official trail to Red Lake Peak, but so many hikers have made the trip that there is a clearly beaten path to the summit, which is also a popular backcountry skiing and snowboarding destination in winter. From the Meiss Trailhead parking lot, follow the Pacific Crest Trail west and then north, switchbacking gently uphill through acres of mule's ears and sagebrush. At a saddle above Meiss Meadow, 1.3 miles from the start, you'll see a cattle pond and just beyond an unmarked spur trail on the right that heads up the southwest slope of Red Lake Peak (although you can't see the summit from here). The spur trail leads very steeply up to a notch, from which you can see both Lake Tahoe and Red Lake Peak's volcanic summit block. The last stretch to the top has the worst gradient yet; the final few yards will require some hands-and-feet scrambling, but it's manageable for most. In addition to the view of Lake Tahoe, about 20 miles away, the summit also offers views of Hope Valley, Round Top

Peak, Elephants Back, and the Mokelumne and Desolation Wildernesses.

Showers and Meiss Lakes

- Distance: 10.2–11.4 miles round-trip
- Duration: 5–6 hours
- Effort: Moderate
- Elevation change: 1,500 feet
- Trailhead: Meiss
- Directions: From the junction of Hwy. 89 and Hwy. 88 in Hope Valley, drive west on Hwy. 88 for 9 miles to Carson Pass Summit. The Meiss Trailhead is on the right (north) side of the highway, across from and slightly west of the Carson Pass Information Station. A $5 parking fee is charged.

Because it is located near an equestrian campground, Showers Lake is quite popular with the horsey set, but it's worth a look for two-legged visitors as well. Although the lake is pleasant enough for a quick swim, the hike to reach it is more of a highlight than the destination itself. That's because the trail departs the Meiss Trailhead at Carson Pass and wanders through some remarkable Sierra scenery, providing a brilliant wildflower display in midsummer and splendid ridgetop views year-round. The trail follows the same route as the path to Red Lake Peak to the saddle above Meiss Meadow, 1.3 miles from the trailhead, where the views spread wide. For many, this spot is a satisfying destination by itself. Where the Red Lake Peak spur takes off to the right, you continue straight, heading steeply downhill into boggy but beautiful Meiss Meadow, the headwaters for the Upper Truckee River, and then bear left for Showers Lake. The trail meanders up open flower-covered slopes and into occasional groves of lodgepole pines, and crosses the Upper Truckee twice. After a moderate climb, the last 0.5 mile is a 350-foot descent to Showers Lake at 8,790 feet, the highest lake in the Upper Truckee River basin. If you still have energy on the way back, you might want to take the fork on the south side of Meiss Meadow that leads 0.6 mile gently downhill to Meiss Lake, a shallow and warm body of water. Fishing is not permitted in this lake, but swimming (or wading, for very tall people) is recommended. If you visit both lakes, your distance for the day will be 11.4 miles.

◖ Frog Lake

- Distance: 1.8 miles round-trip
- Duration: 1 hour
- Effort: Easy
- Elevation change: 200 feet
- Trailhead: Carson Pass
- Directions: From the junction of Hwy. 89 and Hwy. 88 in Hope Valley, drive west on Hwy. 88 for 9 miles to Carson Pass Summit. Park in the lot on the left (south) side of the highway, next to the Carson Pass Information Station. A $5 parking fee is charged.

Hikers seeking a brief introduction to the Carson Pass area will enjoy this easy, short stroll to Frog Lake. The trail starts alongside the Carson Pass Information Station and meanders just under a mile to the lakeshore. After an initial climb of about 0.5 mile, the grade levels out. Note the contorted shapes of the lodgepole pines that grow along this path, a result of the heavy snow load they face each winter. During the peak of the July flower season, the lupine bloom and the seemingly endless acres of mule's ears are spectacular. Turquoise-colored Frog Lake is just off the trail on the left; the distinct shape of Elephants Back, an old lava dome, rises behind it, and many choose to make the easy climb to its summit. Many hikers get inspired by the scenery here and continue another 1.4 miles to Winnemucca Lake, with a total elevation gain of only 500 feet from Carson Pass. You can also reach that lake by starting at Woods Lake Campground.

Round Top Peak and Winnemucca Lake Loop

- Distance: 6.8 miles round-trip
- Duration: 4 hours
- Effort: Strenuous
- Elevation change: 2,200 feet
- Trailhead: Woods Lake
- Directions: From the junction of Hwy. 89 and Hwy. 88 in Hope Valley, drive west on Hwy. 88 for 10.5 miles to the Woods Lake Campground turnoff on the left (south) side of the highway, 1.5 miles west of Carson Pass. Turn left and drive 1 mile to the trailhead parking area, which is 0.5 mile before the campground. A $5 parking fee is charged.

As with most hikes in the Carson Pass area, this trail is incredibly popular all summer long, but especially during the peak of the wildflower bloom in July. As many as 300 people per day will hike to Winnemucca Lake on summer weekends. Although many people just walk out and back to the lake starting from either the Carson Pass or Woods Lake Trailheads, you might as well pack the most you can into this trip by hiking the full loop to Winnemucca and Round Top Lakes, and taking the spur trail to the summit of 10,381-foot Round Top Peak, an ancient volcanic vent that is the highest peak in the Carson Pass area. The trip begins at the Woods Lake Trailhead; campers can start right from their tents, while everyone else has to start at the trailhead parking lot 0.5 mile before the camp. The path wanders through the forest for a while, then breaks out onto open slopes with a straight-on view of Round Top Peak. The outlet creek from Winnemucca Lake flows merrily on your right; the hillsides to your left are completely covered with flowers during the height of the season. In a mere 1.9 miles, you reach the shore of Winnemucca Lake, a gorgeous blue-green gem that is set directly below Round Top Peak and surrounded by mule's ears,

© ANN MARIE BROWN

Dogs and their people enjoy hiking the Winnemucca Lake Loop.

scarlet gilia, Indian paintbrush, and a host of other colorful flowers. At the lake, you'll see plenty of other hikers who have arrived on the other trail from Carson Pass to the northeast, but your loop continues to the west for another mile of ascent to Round Top Lake. Heading there, you'll leave most of the crowds behind. Beautiful Round Top Lake is considerably smaller than Winnemucca, but its deeply carved glacial cirque is quite dramatic, and a few stands of whitebark pines provide shade for picnickers.

At Round Top Lake, you've gained almost 1,200 feet from your start at Woods Lake, but Round Top Peak still towers imposingly 1,000 feet above you. Experienced, sure-footed hikers shouldn't miss the chance to climb it by following the obvious use trail from the lake's east end. The path struggles up, up, and up over the peak's volcanic slopes. You will need to use your hands as well as your feet as you near the top; most hikers are satisfied with attaining a false summit a few yards below the actual summit, as the going gets quite hairy in the last stretch. Truthfully, it doesn't matter how high you go; the views are dazzling from just about everywhere along Round Top's knife-thin ridge.

Rest on a high point—and your laurels—and take in the marvelous vista of the Dardanelles, Lake Tahoe, Caples Lake, Woods Lake, Round Top Lake, Winnemucca Lake, and Frog Lake, all to the north. Although this view is certainly captivating, perhaps more dramatic is the southward vista of deep and immense Summit City Canyon, which drops 3,000 feet below Round Top. On the clearest days, Mount Diablo in the east San Francisco Bay Area can be seen, 100 miles to the west.

After backtracking to the base of the peak, finish out your loop with a descent on the Lost Cabin Mine Trail alongside Round Top Lake's outlet creek, through more wildflower gardens, and past the structures of an old mine

CARSON PASS

backpackers heading back to Woods Lake at Carson Pass

site, back to the campground at Winnemucca Lake. Walk through the camp and down the access road back to your car.

Fourth of July Lake

- Distance: 9.4 miles round-trip
- Duration: 5 hours
- Effort: Strenuous
- Elevation change: 2,200 feet
- Trailhead: Woods Lake
- Directions: From the junction of Hwy. 89 and Hwy. 88 in Hope Valley, drive west on Hwy. 88 for 10.5 miles to the Woods Lake Campground turnoff on the left (south) side of the highway, 1.5 miles west of Carson Pass. Turn left and drive 1 mile to the trailhead parking area, which is 0.5 mile before the campground. A $5 parking fee is charged.

One way to escape the crowds of wildflower aficionados and scenery lovers at Winnemucca

and Round Top Lakes is to take this hike to Fourth of July Lake, which leaves the most heavily visited areas of Carson Pass behind and descends 1,000 feet on a merciless grade to the lake. Several routes will get you there, but the most scenic is to follow the 2.8-mile path from Woods Lake Campground to Winnemucca and Round Top Lakes, then depart the loop trail and take the left fork near Round Top Lake that leads west and then south to Fourth of July Lake. The trail reaches a rocky divide in 0.6 mile, and from there you can look almost straight down 1,000 feet to the lake. With only 1.3 miles of trail remaining, the grade is brutally steep. This steep and rocky descent—and ensuing ascent—is what stops the crowds from flocking here, although the wildflowers along this stretch are often some of the best in Carson Pass. (When the flowers aren't blooming, you might want to skip Fourth of July Lake altogether and head for other destinations.) After stumbling through the precipitous descent to the lake, you'll reach its shoreline and find good fishing for brook and cutthroat trout. Late in summer, as the lake level drops, a sandy beach becomes exposed—a perfect spot for a well-earned swim.

Emigrant Lake

- Distance: 8.6 miles round-trip
- Duration: 4 hours
- Effort: Moderate
- Elevation change: 900 feet
- Trailhead: Caples Lake dam
- Directions: From the junction of Hwy. 89 and Hwy. 88 in Hope Valley, drive west on Hwy. 88 for 13.5 miles to the west side of Caples Lake and the trailhead parking area by the dam (4.5 miles west of Carson Pass).

Although the mileage is substantial along the trail to Emigrant Lake, the grade is so gentle you may wonder if you are still in the Sierra.

In fact, the trail is basically flat for the first 2.5 miles, as it parallels the southwest shore of Caples Lake, traveling under the shady canopy of big conifers. You'll pass traces of the old emigrant trail along this route, but there is little evidence left of the multitudes who once traveled this way. But just when you get into cruising mode, you do have to do some work. Almost all the elevation gain takes place in the last 1.8 miles, beginning soon after the trail reaches the end of Caples Lake. You'll ascend alongside Emigrant Creek, crossing it once, then march up a final few switchbacks to the lake at 8,600 feet. There's only one trail junction to worry about, 3.4 miles out, where you bear left. Emigrant Lake is a spectacular sight, set in a glacial cirque with steep granite walls rising up to Covered Wagon Peak and Thimble Peak. Swimming, sunbathing, and scenery-admiring are the preferred activities here.

© ANN MARIE BROWN

Lake Margaret

◖ Lake Margaret

- Distance: 4.8 miles round-trip
- Duration: 2.5 hours
- Effort: Easy/moderate
- Elevation change: 450 feet
- Trailhead: Lake Margaret
- Directions: From the junction of Hwy. 89 and Hwy. 88 in Hope Valley, drive west on Hwy. 88 for 13.7 miles to the Lake Margaret Trailhead on the north side of the road (0.2 mile west of Caples Lake dam and 0.1 mile east of the Kirkwood Inn).

For an easy hike in the Carson Pass area, you just can't do better than this trail to Lake Margaret, which requires only gentle climbing and descending, and reaches the lake in a mere 2.4 miles. Most children five and up will be very comfortable on this trail and will certainly enjoy a swim in Lake Margaret. The path begins with a descent from the parking lot through a forest of red firs and lodgepole pines. It then meanders through an eclectic mix of terrain: across granite slabs, alongside meadows, across Caples Creek (a favorite area of fly fishers), past a couple of small ponds, and through more dense forest. At two miles, after a second creek crossing, you'll find yourself in a lovely grove of aspens and, in season, knee-high wildflowers. The final stretch to the lake is the most strenuous ascent of the day, but still nothing to complain about. When you reach the top, you get your first look at lovely Lake Margaret, elevation 7,500 feet. Surrounded by granite slabs, the intimate-size lake provides just enough room for all comers to find their own spots for picnicking, fishing, or swimming. A few tiny islands and multiple shoreline boulders make for fine sunbathing. Although this trail is a great walk anytime it is snow-free, plan your trip for the July wildflower bloom, and you will be astonished at the beauty here.

CARSON PASS

Thunder Mountain

- Distance: 7.2 miles round-trip
- Duration: 4 hours
- Effort: Moderate
- Elevation change: 1,450 feet
- Trailhead: Thunder Mountain
- Directions: From the junction of Hwy. 89 and Hwy. 88 in Hope Valley, drive west on Hwy. 88 for 16 miles to the Thunder Mountain Trailhead on the south side of the road, 1.8 miles west of the Kirkwood Ski Resort access road and 4 miles east of Silver Lake.

Although the Thunder Mountain Trail can be hiked as a 10-mile loop, the first leg offers such fine views and excellent scenery that the vast majority of hikers walk it out and back for a 7.2-mile round-trip. The trail begins with a moderate ascent through a lovely lodgepole-pine and red-fir forest, then emerges from the trees on a sagebrush- and mule's ear–covered ridge, just below the snow deflectors above the highway at Carson Spur. From here on, you enjoy expansive views as you wander across an exposed landscape marked by strange volcanic mudflow formations, each one more odd looking than the next. Lichens on their nubby surfaces give them an orange and greenish cast. The trail passes to the west of the Two Sentinels, elevation 8,780 feet, and follows the line of the ridge above Kirkwood Ski Resort. The only thing that mars the otherwise compelling scenery is the sight of the condominiums and development in Kirkwood Valley. Continuing along the ridgeline, the trail passes Martin Point and warning signs for out-of-bounds skiing at Kirkwood. A few switchbacks lead to a small saddle below a massive volcanic crag on the left and the high point of Amador County (9,410 feet) on the right, which is actually two feet higher than Thunder Mountain. Shortly beyond the saddle, a use trail leads northwest a few hundred feet to the top. The main trail continues around the back of this high ridge to a three-way junction, where you head right for Thunder's 9,408-foot summit. The peak is marked by a metal pole and superb views of the Desolation Wilderness to the north, Round Top Peak to the east, Silver and Caples Lakes, below, and the Mokelumne and Emigrant Wildernesses to the south. If you search around, you should be able to locate a summit register. Read the pithy remarks of others, and then add a few of your own.

Minkalo Trail to Granite Lake

- Distance: 2 miles round-trip
- Duration: 1 hour
- Effort: Easy
- Elevation change: 300 feet
- Trailhead: Camp Minkalo at Silver Lake
- Directions: From the junction of Hwy. 89 and Hwy. 88 in Hope Valley, drive west on Hwy. 88 for 20 miles to the Kit Carson Lodge turnoff on the north side of the road, at Silver Lake. Turn north and drive past Kit Carson Lodge. Go left at the first fork and right at the second fork to reach the parking area for Minkalo Trail, 1.5 miles from Hwy. 88. Walk back on the road for about 150 feet to pick up the trail.

Silver Lake is owned and managed by the Eldorado Irrigation District, providing much-needed water for the folks "down the hill" in the Sierra foothills. The lake has numerous private homes and a few resorts and camps on its edges, making it seem somewhat less wild than nearby Caples Lake. Still, the big blue lake and its large, solitary Treasure Island is quite scenic, and this trail from its eastern shoreline leads to Granite Lake in only one mile—a walk of less than a half hour with a climb of only 300 feet. The path crosses Squaw Creek and meanders uphill through a granite landscape of big boulders and slabs (watch for trail cairns to keep you on the path). The trail leads right to Granite Lake's shoreline, which makes a fine destination for

© ANN MARIE BROWN

Granite Lake is an easy walk from the trailhead off Highway 88.

casual hikers and families. True to its name, the lake is lined with granite. A swim and a picnic here could get your kids hooked on the Sierra for life. Those who want more exercise can continue for another two miles to Hidden Lake, which is unfortunately not as scenic as Granite Lake, and loop back to the Minkalo Trailhead by descending to Plasse's Resort, then following the trail along the east side of Silver Lake back to Minkalo Camp.

Shealor Lakes

- Distance: 3 miles round-trip
- Duration: 2 hours
- Effort: Moderate
- Elevation change: 800 feet
- Trailhead: Shealor Lakes
- Directions: From the junction of Hwy. 89 and Hwy. 88 in Hope Valley, drive west on Hwy. 88 for 21 miles to the Shealor Lakes Trailhead on the north side of the road, 1.2

miles west of Silver Lake's dam and 0.5 mile east of the Plasse's Resort turnoff.

The best swimming in the Carson Pass region may well be at the granite-lined Shealor Lakes, and the lakes certainly win top honors in the scenery department as well. But aside from the tempting waters, the brief, rewarding trip to Shealor Lakes is all about polished granite. Even for the geologically challenged, it's not hard to picture the glaciers moving through here. The trail starts out in a red-fir and lodgepole-pine forest and climbs for 0.5 mile up a granite-studded slope to a ridgetop. At the top, you are rewarded with an amazing view looking north toward the Desolation Wilderness; pointy Pyramid Peak is an obvious landmark. Once you've reached this high ridge, the next mile to the lakes is all downhill, traveling over exposed granite slopes into the basin that cradles the Shealor Lakes. Trail cairns mark the way, but as long as you are descending, you'll be heading for the lakes, which are in plain sight. This means that most of the work will be on your return, when you have to climb back up out of the lakes' basin, but no matter; the scenery is so gorgeous that it's worth every step. There are two Shealor lakes, but most people go no farther than the first, largest one. Surrounded by polished granite slabs, with a stand of trees on the south side that allows for a few camping spots, the lake is the perfect place to bring a book and spend a day.

BIKING

No discussion of biking in the Carson Pass area would be complete without singing the praises of the annual **Markleeville Death Ride** (www.deathride.com), which takes place in July. The Death Ride brings even expert riders to their knees with its staggering 129-mile length and 15,000 feet of elevation change. The route begins and ends in Markleeville and goes out and back across three Sierra passes—Carson, Ebbetts, and Monitor. Each year, hundreds of cyclists sign up for the chance to pedal all or part of the epic ride.

To prepare for the Death Ride, a challenging training ride is the out-and-back from **Woodfords to Lake Alpine** (80 miles). From Woodfords, take Highway 89 south past Markleeville to Highway 4, then turn west and crank up a strenuous seven-mile ascent over Ebbetts Pass. Beyond the summit, you'll descend to Hermit Valley, then climb up again through some nasty switchbacks to Mosquito Lake. From there, you have a big sigh of relief as you coast to Lake Alpine, where you can get some much-needed snacks at the store and café. Don't get too relaxed, however, as you have to turn around and retrace your tire marks for the ride back to Woodfords.

For those with more sensible biking aspirations, the Carson Pass area offers a multitude of trails. Mountain bikers looking for an easy cruise will enjoy the dirt road that leads to **Burnside Lake** from the junction of Highways 88 and 89 in Hope Valley (13 miles round-trip with 1,100 feet of elevation gain). The lake makes a fine swimming destination. More-experienced mountain bikers looking for some technical challenges will enjoy the 8.4-mile single-track ride on the Tahoe Rim Trail to **Round and Dardanelles Lakes.** The trail begins at the Big Meadow Trailhead on Highway 89 (5.3 miles south of Meyers and 5.7 miles north of Hope Valley) and follows the Tahoe Rim Trail south through Big Meadow and on to the lakes.

A variation on this route is to follow the Tahoe Rim Trail to a fork 0.5 mile before Round Lake, then turn right (north) on the trail to **Christmas Valley.** This very technical downhill stretch will make you glad you have a full-suspension bike (or wish you had one if you don't). When the trail reaches pavement, turn right and follow the old road back to the trailhead. This makes a loop of about seven miles.

From the same Big Meadow Trailhead, super-advanced mountain bikers take off on **Mr. Toad's Wild Ride,** otherwise known as the Saxon Creek Trail. This treacherous point-to-point ride travels from the Big Meadow Trailhead to Oneidas Street in South Lake Tahoe. Some claim that the route is so boulder strewn and technical that it is simply not rideable. But that doesn't stop people from trying. For details, see *Biking* in the *South Shore* chapter.

On summer weekends at **Kirkwood Ski Resort,** you can ride up Chairs 1 and 2 with your bike, then pedal around a network of 13.5 miles of dirt roads and trails across the ski area, and 25-plus miles of trails just outside the ski area. The most popular ride is to Caples Crest for a spectacular view of Caples Lake and the Mokelumne Wilderness. Lift access is available only on summer weekends 10 A.M.–4 P.M. , early July–early Sept.; tickets are $32 adults, $17–22 children.

Bike rentals and route advice are available at Hope Valley Outdoors at Hope Valley Resort (14655 Hwy. 88, Hope Valley, 530/694-2266, www.hopevalleyoutdoors.com), and at Kirkwood Adventure Center (1501 Kirkwood Meadows Dr., Kirkwood, 209/258-7294 or 877/547-5966, www.kirkwood.com). Rentals are $55 per day, $40 per half day.

BOATING AND WATER SPORTS

Boat rentals are available at Caples Lake Resort and Silver Lake Resort. At **Caples Lake** (1111 Hwy. 88, one mile east of Kirkwood, 209/258-8888, www.capleslakeresort.com), the marina is open 7 or 8 A.M.–6 or 7 P.M. in summer and fall. Twelve- and 14-foot aluminum boats with 7.5 horsepower motors are available for fishing or just cruising the lake. Rates are $30–40 for two hours, $50–65 for four hours, or $80–100 for eight hours. If you'd rather travel under your own power, kayak and canoe rentals are $20–25 for two hours, $30–35 for four hours, or $50 for eight hours. If you have your own boat, the launch ramp is open 7 or 8 A.M.–8 P.M. Launch fees are $10–15.

Rafting and White-Water Kayaking

In the early-summer months (May–July), the **East Fork of the Carson River** provides exciting white-water action in its rugged, rock-walled canyon. Guided day trips are available from Tahoe Whitewater Tours (530/581-2441 or 800/442-7238, www.gowhitewater.com).

For calm-water kayaking on one of Carson Pass's many lakes, kayak rentals are available at Kirkwood Adventure Center (1501 Kirkwood Meadows Dr., Kirkwood, 209/258-7294 or 877/547-5966, www.kirkwood.com) located in the Red Cliffs Day Lodge at Kirkwood Mountain Resort, at Hope Valley Outdoors in Hope Valley Resort (14655 Hwy. 88, Hope Valley, 530/694-2266, www.hopevalleyoutdoors.com) or at Caples or Silver Lake.

SWIMMING

The best place for swimming, aside from the multiple mountain lakes you can hike to, is at **Grover Hot Springs State Park** (530/694-2248, www.parks.ca.gov), where hot springs bubble up from the ground and the water is channeled into two concrete pools of varying temperature. The pools are open year-round except for Christmas, New Year's, and Thanksgiving, and a brief period in September for maintenance. An $8 fee per vehicle is charged to enter the park; pool fees are $7 adults and $5 children 16 and under.

FISHING

The Hope Valley and Carson Pass area is known as one of the greatest fishing regions in the Sierra Nevada. From April to October, the **West Fork Carson River,** which runs through Hope, Faith, and Charity Valleys, offers excellent trout fishing. It flows alongside Highway 88 and Blue Lakes Road, providing easy access, and is regularly stocked with rainbow and cutthroat trout. A fishing access area is located on the northwest side of the T-junction of Highways 88 and 89 in Hope Valley. You're more likely to find solitude if you access the river along Blue Lakes Road.

Fishing is also good in the Upper and Lower **Blue Lakes** themselves, 12 miles up Blue Lakes Road from Highway 88. The primary catch is rainbow trout, with occasional brook trout and cutthroat trout. Fish here early in summer before Pacific Gas and Electric Company drops the lake level.

The **East Fork Carson River** is a fly fisher's dream. From Hangman's Bridge (south of Markleeville) downstream to the Nevada state line, you must use artificial lures with single barbless hooks. The river has rainbows, Lahontan cutthroat, brown trout, and mountain whitefish. If you're not familiar with fly-fishing, or want to sharpen your skills, sign up for lessons with **Horse Feathers Fly Fishing School** (530/694-2399), which operates out of Sorensen's Resort.

Caples Lake and **Silver Lake** both have excellent fishing for rainbow, brown, and

CARSON PASS

mackinaw trout. You can rent boats at either lake and try your luck at trolling, or fish from shore. For the intrepid angler who can't wait for the snow to melt, ice fishing is possible in both Caples and Silver Lakes.

Fishing licenses, flies, bait, and tackle are available at Woodfords Station, the Markleeville General Store, Carson River Resort, Hope Valley Outdoor Center, Kirkwood General Store, and Silver and Caples Lakes.

HORSEBACK RIDING

The handsome steeds at the **Kirkwood Corral** (1501 Kirkwood Meadows Dr. at Hwy. 88, Kirkwood, 775/790-5929, www.kirkwood. com) have been a picturesque fixture in Kirkwood's meadow for more than 100 years. Although the horses were removed for a few summers during 2005–2007 due to environmental concerns, they are back again and ready

© ANN MARIE BROWN

CARSON PASS

Horses graze the meadow at Kirkwood.

to ride. One- and two-hour rides are available daily in summer.

WINTER SPORTS
Downhill Skiing and Snowboarding

At **Kirkwood Ski Resort** (1501 Kirkwood Meadows Dr. at Hwy. 88, Kirkwood, 209/258-6000 or 877/547-5966, www.kirkwood.com, 9 A.M.–4 P.M. daily), the operative word is *snow,* and it's Tahoe's deepest and driest. For most of the last decade, the resort has had the deepest snowpack of any ski area—not just at Lake Tahoe, but anywhere in North America. Average annual snowfall is more than 500 inches—some years more than 700 inches—and this is quality stuff, typically the driest snow in the entire Sierra. Powder hounds, rejoice.

Kirkwood skiers and riders received big news in February 2012, when the resort announced that it had been purchased by Vail Resorts, Inc.—the same company that owns Heavenly and Northstar in Tahoe as well as several resorts in Colorado. Kirkwood season pass holders can now use their passes at Northstar and Heavenly, and vice versa. In addition to the ski resort, Vail Resorts bought the land at the mountain's base, with commercial development in mind. This means that sleepy little Kirkwood will soon have a multi-million-dollar "mountain village" with shops, restaurants, condos, and the like. Expect to see big changes in the next few years, starting with the addition of a handful of new high-speed quad chairlifts. Today, Kirkwood has ski-in, ski-out lodging, plus activities for nonskiers like evening snowcat tours, grooming cat rides, tubing, and snowshoeing at the Kirkwood Cross-Country Center, but expect much more in the near future.

The alpine slopes at Kirkwood feature steep chutes, plenty of tree skiing, big cliffs, and powder-filled open bowls. Fourteen lifts serve almost 70 runs, which are carved over 2,300

© ANN MARIE BROWN

Kirkwood has terrain for all levels, including beginners.

in California to offer such a program. A special area called Beacon Basin is reserved as an avalanche transceiver training area.

Snowboarders have plenty to cheer about at Kirkwood, too. It has three terrain parks, including a 350-foot-long superpipe with 18-foot walls. Beginning riders and skiers don't get left behind. The gentle terrain at Kirkwood's Timber Creek has been rated as one of the top learning areas in the country. This is long, gentle, beginner terrain in a separate area of the mountain with its own lodge and three lifts. The Mighty Mountain Children's School teaches kids ages 4–12 how to ski and ages 5–12 how to snowboard. All-day packages for kids including lessons, rentals, and lunch are $115. Every Sunday, a child 12 and under can ski free with a parent paying for an adult lift ticket (only one child per adult). Learning programs for adults include three-day programs in which students are guaranteed to learn to ski or ride on the first day ($199–209), and one-day packages for as low as $69 on weekdays that include rentals, lessons, and a limited lift ticket.

A day spent skiing or riding at Kirkwood will cost less than at most of the Tahoe resorts. All-day lift tickets for adults are $72–82, teens 13–18 and seniors 65–69 are $61–65, children 6–12 and seniors 70 and up are $20–22, and children 5 and under are $9. To save a few bucks on Kirkwood lift tickets, buy them in advance at Kirkwood's website. Or if you plan to ski two days in a row on nonholidays, you can buy a discounted two-day ticket.

If you are staying on Tahoe's South Shore and you don't want to drive through snowy Carson Pass to get to Kirkwood, catch a ride on the Powder Express shuttle (888/353-6173, www.kirkwood.com), which leaves from numerous points between Stateline and the South Lake Tahoe Y every morning. The shuttle fee is $15 round-trip (the return bus leaves Kirkwood at 4:30 P.M.).

acres of skiable terrain. The longest vertical drop is a respectable 2,000 feet; the longest run is 2.5 miles. Kirkwood's base elevation is 7,800 feet, which is higher than all other Tahoe-area resorts except Mount Rose, and snow depths even at the bottom of the mountain are generally more than 20 feet. Its top elevation is 9,800 feet.

For those who prefer fresh tracks, Kirkwood also features some of the best backcountry skiing anywhere in the Tahoe basin, with great terrain, extreme "steeps," and easy access. When the access gates to the backcountry are open, skiers and riders can find great lines heading out of Kirkwood in all directions, and the mountain vistas are sublime. The resort capitalizes on this with Expedition Kirkwood, a school that teaches backcountry skills, including avalanche awareness and survival techniques. Kirkwood is the only resort

Cross-Country Skiing and Snowshoeing

More than 80 kilometers of groomed cross-country ski and snowshoe trails are available at **Kirkwood Cross-Country and Snowshoe Center** (1501 Kirkwood Meadows Dr. at Hwy. 88, Kirkwood, 209/258-7248 or 877/547-5966, www.kirkwood.com), located across the highway from the downhill ski resort, next to the Kirkwood Inn. With a base elevation of 7,800 feet, there is usually dependable snow here at Kirkwood when it's getting thin, icy, and pathetic at other cross-country resorts. All trails are machine groomed each morning and have skating, gliding, and snowshoe lanes. The trail system is divided into three interconnected sections, which cover more than 4,000 acres. Trailside warming huts and a day lodge are available for drinks, snacks, and a place to get warm by a blazing fire. Snowshoers are allowed to go everywhere skiers can go, and dogs are allowed on two short but fun trails, including one that circles Kirkwood Meadow. A special one-kilometer loop trail is set aside for young children. It circles around a meadow by the day lodge and has life-size outlines of forest animals and other fun interpretive signs.

All-day trail passes are $22 for adults 19–64, $17 for teens 13–18 and seniors 65–69, $12 for seniors 70 and up, and $8 for children 11–12. Children 10 and under ski free. Trail passes for dogs are $4. All skiing and snowshoeing equipment rentals are available; cost is about $22 per day for either sport. Adult beginner packages, which include cross-country skiing lessons, trail passes, and rentals, are $48. Guided snowshoe hikes are often available, including a special full-moon snowshoe one night each month in winter ($30).

At the **Hope Valley Outdoors** (Hwy. 89/88 junction, Hope Valley, 530/721-2015, www.hopevalleyoutdoors.com), located in a yurt in the meadow at Pickett's Junction (one mile west of Sorenson's Resort, just south of the junction

of Hwy. 89 and Hwy. 88), you can rent cross-country and telemark skis ($15–20) and snowshoes ($14–16). Cross-country ski lessons and guided tours are offered by advance reservation. Sixty miles of trails, some of which are groomed, are available nearby in the national forest. There is no fee for using the trails, but donations are accepted. Dogs are welcome on the trails.

For do-it-yourselfers, two Sno-Parks are found about 500 feet apart on Highway 88 at Carson Pass and Meiss Meadow. Both have parking for about 40 cars. As at all California Sno-Parks, you must purchase a Sno-Park permit ($5 per day or $25 per year; contact the Eldorado National Forest at 530/644-6048 for a list of places that sell them) in order to park your car and access the trails. From the **Carson Pass Sno-Park,** you can ski or snowshoe the intermediate Wilderness Boundary Trail, which connects with Woods Lake Road and the trail from Meiss Sno-Park. From **Meiss Sno-Park,** you can ski or snowshoe the easy route to Woods Lake (you have to cross the highway to access the trail) or head north to Meiss Meadow on an unmarked route that roughly follows the Pacific Crest Trail.

A third Sno-Park is located at Blue Lakes Road and Highway 88, three miles west of the T-junction of Highway 88 and 89, but because snowmobiles are allowed, this Sno-Park is not as popular for cross-country skiing and snowshoeing. For an easy cross-country glide, many skiers park along the road near the junction of Highways 88 and 89 in **Hope Valley,** then ski around the meadows near the junction or along the Burnside Lake Road to **Burnside Lake** (13 miles round-trip). Two miles north of this junction on Highway 89 is the meadow at **Grass Lake,** another good place for easy skiing. A three-mile trail leads to Hope Valley. Both of these areas are great for moonlight skiing.

Sledding and Tubing

Kirkwood gets in on the tubing action with its

© ANN MARIE BROWN

Carson Summit offers many access points for skiers heading into the backcountry.

Slide Mountain Tubing Hill (1501 Kirkwood Meadows Dr. at Hwy. 88, Kirkwood, 209/258-7210 or 877/547-5966, www.kirkwood.com, noon–4 P.M. weekends and holidays only), located near Red Cliffs Day Lodge. Tubing rates are $14 per person for a half day or $20 all day, and that includes the tube and a handle tow that carries you back up the slope. Kids must be at least four years old or three feet tall to go tubing, but if yours are too little, take them to the Village Snow Play Area instead, where they can build forts, snow castles, snowmen, or whatever else they can think of, and no fees are charged.

Snowmobiling

Lake Tahoe Adventures (3071 Hwy. 50, South Lake Tahoe, 530/577-2940 or 800/865-4679, www.laketahoeadventures.com) specializes in introducing beginners to snowmobiling with a two-hour tour around Hope Valley and Charity Valley. Helmets, gloves, and boots are included in the price; tours cost $115 for single riders and $155 for two riders on one machine (holiday rates are slightly higher).

Dogsledding

In Hope Valley, 30-year veteran sled-dog musher Dotty Dennis and her pack of frisky pups at **Husky Express** (775/782-3047, www.highsierra.com/sst/) will take you on a five-mile, hour-long ride. Dotty and her dogs operate out of the Highway 88 meadow by the Scott Lake turnoff, 1.5 miles west of the Highway 88/89 junction. The dogsleds have a load limit of 375 pounds each, with room for two adults and one or two small children. Rates are $250 per sled; reservations are required. If you get hooked on dog mushing, Dotty offers a comprehensive hands-on mushers course and a skijoring clinic.

KIT CARSON & HIGHWAY 88

For many Western history fans, the name Kit Carson is synonymous with the definition of a true "mountain man." An icon of the American West, Christopher "Kit" Carson lived from 1809 to 1868 and made his living as an explorer, guide, fur trapper, soldier, and Indian agent. Carson Pass, Carson City, Carson Valley, and the Carson River are all named for him, and his adventurous life was the subject of more than two dozen novels between 1849 and 1923. Despite the fact that Carson was both applauded and vilified for his dealings with Native Americans, he was depicted as a hero in more than a half-dozen silent and talking movies of the early 20th century.

Carson fought in the Mexican-American War and the Civil War, and played a major role in battles against the Blackfeet and Navajo. But he is best known for being the right-hand man of explorer John C. Fremont. Fremont hired him as a guide on an 1840s expedition to map trails through the Rocky Mountains, the Great Basin, and the Sierra Nevada. Among his many accomplishments on these trips with Fremont, Carson discovered the scenic trans-Sierra route that is now known as Highway 88.

At the summit of Carson Pass (8,673 feet in elevation) stands a historical marker denoting the site of the Kit Carson Tree, on which Carson inscribed his name in 1844 while guiding Fremont's expedition across the Sierra Nevada in the middle of winter. Drawing on his experience as a fur trapper, Carson taught the expedition party how to camp, stay warm, and survive in the rough winter weather. Despite the warnings of local Native Americans, who cautioned the party against traveling through the snow-covered mountains, the men made the trip from Nevada's Carson Valley to California's Sacramento Valley in about five weeks. Five years later, a party of Mormons built an official trail across Carson Pass. During the California gold rush, this became the most-traveled route across the Sierra and a critical corridor in the push for westward expansion.

Accommodations and Food

MARKLEEVILLE AND HOPE VALLEY
Motels and Lodges

The intimate, 11-room **Creekside Lodge** (14820 Hwy. 89, Markleeville, 530/694-2511 or 866/802-7335, www.markleevilleusa.com, $80–180) is located in downtown Markleeville right next to the historic Wolf Creek Restaurant and Cutthroat Bar. The recently renovated rooms are decorated in mountain-lodge style, with colorful quilts, historic photographs and prints, and wrought-iron lamps and headboards. Eight rooms have king beds, two have queen beds, and one suite is set up for families with a king bed, two twin beds, and a kitchenette. All rooms have telephones and satellite television.

For budget lodging in the Carson Pass area, you won't find a better deal than the 20-room **Woodfords Inn** (20960 Hwy. 89, Woodfords, 530/694-2410, $79–99). Rooms have one queen bed or two doubles. Rates are low partly because it's a half-hour drive to Kirkwood and six miles to Markleeville. All rooms have cable television and VCRs, and there is a hot tub on the premises.

One more option in downtown Markleeville is the **J. Marklee Toll Station** (14856 Hwy. 89, Markleeville, 530/694-2507, www.tollstation.com, $85–125), which has five ultrabasic rooms and one cabin.

Cabins

Located in a dense grove of quaking aspens in Hope Valley, **❰ Sorensen's Resort**

(14255 Hwy. 88, Hope Valley, 530/694-2203 or 800/423-9949, www.sorensensresort.com, $115–295 for two) is a deservedly popular spot. Set on nearly 170 acres, the cabin resort was first developed in the 1920s by Danish sheepherders. Much of the architecture is Norwegian in style, and each of the 30 cabins is unique. Some have gas fireplaces or woodstoves, and a few cabins are pet friendly (rates vary based on cabin size; the largest units sleep six and cost about $450 per night). The resort is well suited to both serious outdoor recreationists and romantics looking for a weekend getaway. The resort's café serves three meals a day, and cross-country skiing is popular in winter. A wide variety of excursions and organized activities are available year-round, from history hikes to watercolor painting classes to bird-watching to astronomy lessons.

If you want to fish the world-class trout waters of the East Fork Carson River, book a stay at the cabins at the **Carson River Resort** (12399 Hwy. 89, Markleeville, 877/694-2229, www.carsonriverresort.com, $90–170), just 2.5 miles south of Markleeville. This no-frills resort is a perfect base for fly fishers, with a general store that can supply the wet or dry flies you forgot and the few groceries you'll need for basic sustenance. Many of the cabins are cute little log structures, which were sold as building kits by Sears and Roebuck in the 1940s. The River Cabin is the most coveted since it sits a stone's throw from the East Fork Carson. Pets are allowed in most cabins for a small extra fee. The resort also has RV spaces, a campground, and gas and propane for sale.

Campgrounds and RV Parks

The campground at **Grover Hot Springs State Park** (530/694-2248, www.parks.ca.gov., $35) is a favorite of bathers and others who believe in, or at least enjoy, the healing power of mineral waters. Located three miles outside downtown Markleeville, the park has two pools—one hot and one cool—plus a 76-site campground for tents or RVs up to 24 feet long, which has showers, water, flush toilets, picnic tables, and fire pits. Reserve at 800/444-7275 or www.reserveamerica.com.

The Carson River Ranger District of Toiyabe National Forest runs five campgrounds (775/882-2766, $16) in the lands around Markleeville and Woodfords: **Crystal Springs, Snowshoe Springs, Kit Carson, Hope Valley,** and **Markleeville Creek.** Each have only 10–20 sites. All campgrounds are first come, first served except Hope Valley, which can be reserved in advance at 877/444-6777 or www.recreation.gov.

Just outside Markleeville, **Turtle Rock County Park** (17300 Hwy. 89, 530/694-2140, $10–15) has 26 sites for tents or RVs up to 35 feet long set in an open pine forest. And a few miles off Highway 89 near Indian Creek Reservoir, the Bureau of Land Management runs the 29-site **Indian Creek Campground** (775/885-6000, $14–32), which can accommodate RVs up to 30 feet long and has a few luxuries, including hot showers, flush toilets, and an RV dump station. Boating, fishing, and swimming are popular here. No reservations are available for the camp's individual sites; it's first come, first served, unless you want the group campsite that holds 40 people. To reserve the group site, call the BLM Carson City District Office (775/885-6000).

The private **Hope Valley Resort** (800/423-9949, sites $20–45, trailer $85–95), run by the folks at Sorensen's, has 25 sites alongside the West Fork Carson River for tents or RVs up to 36 feet long, with full hookups, flush toilets, and showers. If you are a tent camper, you'll love the three walk-in sites. If you don't care to rough it, rent their 1947 housekeeping trailer with a front deck that overlooks the river.

Additionally, the Pacific Gas and Electric utility company manages a series of campgrounds at **Blue Lakes** ($23), a popular fishing and boating spot on Blue Lakes Road near Hope Valley. The camps are situated between 12 and 14 miles from Hwy. 88, so it's a long drive to get here (and get back out for groceries). Elevation is 8,200 feet. No reservations. For more information, contact the Amador Ranger District of Eldorado National Forest (209/295-4251).

Lastly, the **Carson River Resort** also has campsites and RV spaces for rent (12399 Hwy. 89, Markleeville, 530/694-2229, www.carsonriver resort.com, $20–35), as does **Sorensen's Resort** (14255 Hwy. 88, Hope Valley, 530/694-2203 or 800/423-9949, www.sorensensresort.com).

Food

The center of all activity in Markleeville, **Wolf Creek Restaurant and Cutthroat Saloon** (14830 Hwy. 89, Markleeville, 530/694-2150, www.markleevilleusa.com, 8 A.M.–9 P.M. daily in summer, winter hours vary, $8–30) serves three meals a day on the weekends and two during the week in its historic three-story building. The structure was moved to Markleeville in 1885 from its original site in Silver Mountain City, which was once the Alpine County seat (now it's a ghost town). The menu runs the gamut from simple hamburgers and hearty salads to baby back ribs, pan-seared salmon, and calamari piccata. It's all delicious mountain fare, served up with a big dose of Markleeville atmosphere. Cozy up next to the pot-bellied stove with a glass of zinfandel and thank your lucky stars that towns like this still exist.

If it's Friday or Saturday night, head to **Stonefly** (4821 Hwy. 89, Markleeville, 530/694-9999, www.stoneflyrestaurant.com, 5–9 P.M. Fri.–Sat., $20), an Italian café that is so hip and cool that it only needs to be open two nights a week. Wood-fired pizzas are a big attraction, covered with trendy toppings like baby kale, pine nuts, and beets. Other offerings are equally gourmet: wood-fired Dungeness crab, polenta with mushrooms,

and a house-made ricotta. The menu is short and sweet and changes with the season, so go with an open mind. Everything is prepared in the open kitchen and served in the colorful, cozy dining room, or outside on the patio in the summer months.

Another dependable bet for three meals a day year-round is the café at **Sorensen's Resort** (14255 Hwy. 88, Hope Valley, 530/694-2203 or 800/423-9949, www.sorensensresort.com, café hours 7:30 A.M.–4 P.M. and 5–8:30 P.M. daily, breakfast and lunch $7–15, dinner $17–30). You can pop in for breakfast or lunch any time, but dinner is by reservation only, and most spots in the small dining room are taken by the resort's guests, so be sure to call early in the day. Homemade soups, beef burgundy stew, grilled salmon, barbecued chicken, seafood pasta, and New York steak round out the classically American menu. Don't miss the homemade berry cobbler.

For a quick stop for breakfast or lunch, or for the latest fishing advice or local gossip, stop in at the historic **Woodfords Station** (290 Hwy. 88 at Markleeville turnoff, Woodfords, 866/694-2930, www.woodfordsstation. com, 7 A.M.–6 P.M. daily, $4–8). Have a seat in the old Pony Express stop and try the McWoodford's egg, ham, and cheese sandwich for breakfast or a slice of Lynda's quiche. A variety of hot and cold sandwiches are served, plus chili or the soup of the day and a passel of pies and milk shakes. All that, and you can buy a fishing license, too.

An equally casual menu is offered at **Hope Valley Café** (14655 Hwy. 88, Markleeville, 530/694-2323, 8 A.M.–5 P.M. daily, $8–12). Hamburgers, veggie burgers, and salmon burgers are served up with microbrews and imported beers on tap. Have a meal and rent a kayak, fishing pole, or mountain bike at the same time. And lovers of quality baked goods, you'll be in your element. Pies and cookies are their specialty, but everything sweet is freshly made and delicious. Everybody who stops here leaves happy.

Groceries and supplies are available at the **Markleeville General Store** in downtown Markleeville (14799 Hwy. 89, 530/694-2448, 10 A.M.–6 P.M. daily) and at the store at **Carson River Resort** (877/694-2229). If you need to do some serious stocking up, your best bet is to head to South Lake Tahoe, a 40-minute drive.

SILVER LAKE, CAPLES LAKE, AND KIRKWOOD
Cabins

The Highway 88 corridor has a handful of cabin resorts located right on the shores of Caples and Silver Lakes. Try **Caples Lake Resort** (1111 Hwy. 88, Kirkwood, 209/258-8888, www.capleslakeresort.com) for a convenient fishing or skiing getaway. Located just one mile from Kirkwood Ski Resort, the resort has nine cabins and six lodge rooms that are just a stone's throw from Caples Lake. The rustic cabins have kitchens, bathrooms, and gas fireplaces, and can accommodate 2–6 people ($130–375 in summer, $150–300 in winter). The lake-view lodge rooms ($100–150 in summer, $100–180 in winter) have private bathrooms, but they are across the hall, so bring your bathrobe. A continental breakfast is included with the lodge rooms, but not the cabins. A sauna, small store, and boat rentals are available.

A more luxurious option on Silver Lake is the ◖ **Kit Carson Lodge** (Hwy. 88, Silver Lake, 209/258-8500, www.kitcarsonlodge.com), situated on 12 acres on the eastern end of Silver Lake, just out of sight of Highway 88. The resort is deservedly popular, with naturally landscaped grounds surrounding wood-and-stone cabins that have decks, fireplaces, kitchens, and private baths located right on the shore of Silver Lake. The resort owners have done justice to the concept of "rustic elegance" and the prices reflect that. In addition to 19 cabins ($1,875–2,435 per week mid-June–end of Aug.,

$240–365 per night with a two-night minimum end of Aug.–mid-Oct.), eight bed-and-breakfast rooms are available in two fourplex units ($130–172 per night all season). Although the bed-and-breakfast rooms aren't quite as intimate and spacious as the stand-alone cabins, each has a private deck that looks out onto the lake. Breakfast and dinner are available in the resort's restaurant, which is adjacent to a small art gallery featuring paintings and sculptures of the Sierra. A swimming beach, boat rentals, and nearby hiking trails keep guests busy with a choice of activities. In winter, the resort keeps only one or two cabins open for cross-country skiers and snowshoers ($250–345 per night).

Condominium-Style Resorts

For skiers and riders, lodging is available right at Kirkwood Ski Resort. **Kirkwood Accommodations** (800/967-7500, www.kirkwood.com) rents privately owned ski-in/ski-out vacation homes, condos, and town houses at Kirkwood Towers, The Lodge at Kirkwood, Meadowstone Lodge, the Mountain Club, Snowcrest Lodge, and other Kirkwood properties. Typical lodging rates during ski season weekends and holidays are $220–400 per night for two people in a studio unit or hotel-style room, but can drop as low as $139 midweek during nonholiday periods. Two-bedroom units that can sleep six people go for $299–599 per night. "Stay and ski free" packages are the best deals, but these are only available during nonholiday periods.

Campgrounds and RV Parks

The U.S. Forest Service runs four campgrounds near Silver and Caples Lakes: Woods Lake, Silver Lake East, Caples Lake, and Kirkwood Lake (530/644-6048, www.fs.fed.us/r5/eldorado, $20–44). Silver Lake East is the largest camp, with 62 sites that can be reserved in advance at 877/444-6777 or www.reserveusa.com. The other three campgrounds are

Spacious tent sites are nestled among the lodgepole pines and firs at Woods Lake Campground.

first come, first served, and each has 12–34 sites. A major trailhead into the Mokelumne Wilderness is located at scenic ◖ **Woods Lake Campground,** which has a compelling view of Round Top Peak from many of its sites. Woods Lake camp is suitable for tents only, as is Kirkwood Lake. The other two camps can accommodate RVs up to 40 feet long. Caples Lake Campground is right across the highway from Caples Lake.

The 42 sites at **Silver Lake West Campground** (530/295-6810, www.eid.org, $25) are owned by the Eldorado Irrigation District and managed by a concessionaire. Reservations are not taken. Restrooms and water are available. The maximum length for a trailer or motor home is 24 feet.

The private **Plasse's Resort** (209/258-8814, www.plassesresort.com, $28–35 tents, $33–47 RVs) at Silver Lake has a 60-site campground for tents or RVs up to 32 feet long, plus flush

toilets, showers, laundry, a dump station, and a small store and restaurant. Canoe and kayak rentals are available.

Food

First opened in 1864 by Zachary Kirkwood and in operation ever since, the ◖ **Kirkwood Inn and Saloon** (Hwy. 88 across from Kirkwood, 209/258-7304, 8 A.M.–9 P.M. daily in summer, 3–9 P.M. daily in winter, $9–26) is a throwback to early times in the Carson Pass area. Housed in the original log cabin, the inn is a great place for a hearty meal after a day tearing up Kirkwood's "steeps" or a long hike to an alpine lake. Even if you are just driving through Carson Pass, be sure to stop and have at least one meal here. Have a seat by the roaring fire or straddle a bar stool at the rustic bar, and you'll swear you've been transported to the 19th century. Look for the bullet holes left in the walls from Prohibition days. The dinner menu consists of hearty salads, burgers, and hot sandwiches, or more substantial fare like New York strip steak, campfire chicken, pork tenderloin, and a variety of pastas. Barbecue ribs are a specialty. The inn is open for three meals a day most of the year. A breakfast here is the perfect way to fuel up for a day exploring Carson Pass.

The dining room at **C Kit Carson Lodge** (Hwy. 88, Silver Lake, 209/258-8500, www. kitcarsonlodge.com, lunch 11 A.M.–3 P.M. , dinner 6–9 P.M. Tues.–Sat., early June–late Oct., lunch $5–10, dinner $16–36) is probably best known for its Sunday brunch, although its nightly dinners are exemplary as well. Entrees are on the expensive side, but the classic American cuisine (duck, salmon, filet mignon) is well prepared and graciously served, and the airy and bright dining room is a perfect setting for any meal.

If you are staying and playing at Kirkwood Ski Resort, you'll find several choices for casual meals: Timber Creek Bar and Grill, Red Cliffs Cafeteria, Monte Wolfe's, and Bub's Sports Bar and Grill. An honorable mention goes to **Bub's Sports Bar and Grill** (209/258-7225, 3–8 P.M. Mon.–Fri., 11 A.M.–9 P.M. Sat.–Sun.,

$9–15) for its location right across the street from the Cornice Express lift and its tasty hamburgers and brick-oven pizzas; this is a great spot to take the kids or hang out with your buds. But the best of the resort's dining options is the **Off the Wall Bar and Grill** (inside The Lodge at Kirkwood, 209/258-7365, 11 A.M.–4 P.M. weekdays, 11 A.M.–9 P.M. Sat.–Sun., $10–35). In winter, you can warm up by the fire while you chew on a prime rib sandwich or some blue-cheese-smothered potato skins, or dine on something more refined like a mixed green salad with prosciutto and figs. On weekend evenings, enjoy an elegant dinner of Southwest and Pacific Rim cuisine featuring entrees like fresh lobster ravioli with goat cheese and curry, scallops Rockefeller on a bed of wilted spinach, or filet mignon with wild mushroom bordelaise. Diners enjoy the big view of the slopes and Kirkwood's ridgeline from Thimble Peak to Martin Point.

Groceries and supplies are available at the **Kirkwood General Store** (1501 Kirkwood Meadows Dr., 209/258-7294), but for serious stocking up, the 40-minute drive to South Lake Tahoe is your best bet.

Practicalities

INFORMATION

The **Alpine County Chamber of Commerce and Visitors Center** (530/694-2475, www. alpinecounty.com) is located at 3 Webster Street in Markleeville. The best source of information on outdoor activities is the **Amador Ranger District** of Eldorado National Forest (26820 Silver Dr., Pioneer, 209/295-4251, www.fs.fed.us/r5/eldorado), which operates a visitors center just off Highway 88 in Pioneer. In summer and fall, the volunteers at the Carson Pass Information Station at Carson Pass Summit on Highway 88 (209/258-8606) are a great source for information. Or contact

the **Pacific Ranger District** in Pollock Pines (530/644-2349, www.fs.fed.us/r5/eldorado).

SERVICES
Medical Care
The nearest hospital is located in South Lake Tahoe, about a 40-minute drive from Carson Pass: **Barton Memorial Hospital** (2170 South Ave., South Lake Tahoe, 530/541-3420, www. bartonhealth.org). South Lake Tahoe also has two 24-hour emergency-care centers: **Tahoe Urgent Care** (2130 Hwy. 50, South Lake Tahoe, 530/541-3277) and **Stateline**

Stop in at the Alpine County Visitors Center in Markleeville.

© ANN MARIE BROWN

Medical Center (150 Hwy. 50, Stateline, 775/589-8900).

Post Offices

A post office is located in downtown Markleeville (14845 Hwy. 88, 530/694-2125). Kirkwood has its own post office located in the Kirkwood General Store (1501 Kirkwood Meadows Dr., 209/258-7294).

GETTING THERE
By Air

Visitors can fly into the **Reno-Tahoe International Airport** (2001 E. Plumb La., 775/328-6400, www.renoairport.com) and rent a car to drive to Carson Pass, about a 90-minute drive. Visitors could also fly into the Sacramento, Oakland, San Francisco, or San Jose airports. Sacramento Airport is about two hours from Carson Pass; the other airports are about four hours away.

By Car

From South Lake Tahoe, take Highway 89 south to Meyers, then turn south (left) to stay on Highway 89. Drive 11 miles to Hope Valley, then turn east or west on Highway 88. East leads to Markleeville in 13 miles; west leads to Carson Pass in 9 miles, and Caples and Silver Lake beyond. It takes about 40 minutes to drive from South Lake Tahoe to Carson Pass.

From Sacramento, Stockton, or the San Francisco Bay Area, the primary driving route to Carson Pass is to follow Highway 88 east through Jackson. From Sacramento, take Highway 16 east and then Highway 49 south to Jackson, then take Highway 88 east to Carson Pass. From the San Francisco Bay Area, take I-580 east to Tracy, then take I-205 east to I-5 north. In Stockton, take Highway 4 east to Highway 99 north to Highway 88 east.

From Reno, take U.S. 395 south to Gardnerville, Nevada, then take Highway 88 west to Carson Pass.

By Bus

The nearest bus terminal is in South Lake Tahoe at the South Y Transit Center on U.S. 50. From there, you would have to rent a car to access Carson Pass.

GETTING AROUND

Carson Pass is accessed from South Lake Tahoe and Meyers by traveling south through 7,735-foot Luther Pass on Highway 89, then connecting to Highway 88 at Pickett's Junction in Hope Valley. A left turn on Highway 88 will take you east to Markleeville; a right turn will take you up and over Carson Pass and to Kirkwood Ski Resort. Highway 88, which crosses 8,573-foot Carson Pass, roughly follows the route blazed by pioneers Kit Carson and John Fremont when they discovered Lake Tahoe in 1846. The region can also be accessed from the east (U.S. 395 and Nevada) by traveling over 8,314-foot Monitor Pass on Highway 89, but this pass is usually closed in the winter months. Or it can be accessed year-round from the west on Highway 88 through the small towns of Jackson and Pioneer.

The Carson Pass area is much more remote than any of the other regions covered in this book. In and around Carson Pass and Hope Valley, you can drive for miles without seeing any businesses or services, although year-round there are enough visitors to this area that you can usually flag down a passing car. It is best to be sure that your vehicle is in good working condition before traveling around Carson Pass, as the nearest garage of any size is in South Lake Tahoe, and even getting tow truck service will probably take considerable time. (The tiny town of Markleeville has a small garage, but with very limited services. The best you can hope for is that they might be able to fix a flat tire.) Cell phone service is fair to good, so you usually won't have to travel too far without being able to pick up a signal.

In winter, you should carry chains for driving around the Carson Pass area. The pass itself is perched at 8,573 feet, so it is much higher, and subject to worse weather, than Echo Pass on U.S. 50, the next pass to the north. Chains are sometimes required for crossing Carson Pass even if you have a four-wheel-drive vehicle. To get current updates on road conditions in California, phone 800/427-7623 or visit www.dot.ca.gov. To get current updates on Nevada road conditions, phone 877/687-6237 or visit www.safetravelusa.com. If you are traveling to Carson Pass from South Lake Tahoe in the winter months to ski at Kirkwood, consider leaving your car in South Lake and riding the bus instead (current cost is only $15 round-trip). phone 800/427-7623.

BACKGROUND

The Land

GEOLOGY

The tale of Lake Tahoe began about 400 million years ago when the land that is now the Sierra Nevada lay quietly beneath an ancient sea. This landmass was made up of thick layers of sediment that were piled thousands of feet deep. As the number of layers continued to build, pressure caused the bottom layers to be folded, twisted, and compressed into rock forms. Eventually these massive rocks were thrust upward above the sea's surface by movements of the Pacific and North American continental plates. In the process, a mountain range was formed—what would eventually become the **Sierra Nevada,** the longest and highest single mountain range in the contiguous United States.

As the mountains rose, molten rock welled up from deep within the earth and cooled slowly beneath the layers of rock and sediment, forming the substance we know as **granite.** Over eons of time, erosion gradually wore away almost all the overlying sediment and exposed the granite underneath. Today, much of the rock seen around Lake Tahoe is granite. With its salt-and-pepper appearance, created

© ANN MARIE BROWN

© ANN MARIE BROWN

It will take more than two men to move this glacial boulder.

by a random distribution of light- and dark-colored minerals, it is easy to distinguish from other types of rock.

Next, around 10 million years ago, the entire block of the mountain range was uplifted and tilted to the west. A few million years later, two parallel **faults**—or fractures in the earth's crust—evolved in the block, and the landmasses on both sides of the faults continued to rise. On the west side, the Sierra Nevada was created, with upthrown fault blocks forming the South and West Shores' highest peaks, including Freel Peak, Monument Peak, Pyramid Peak, and Mount Tallac. On the east side, the equally dramatic Carson Range came into being. In between, the land between the two parallel faults sank and created the valley that would later hold the Lake Tahoe basin.

The major structure of the Tahoe Sierra was now formed and only required a few finishing touches. About two million years ago, **lava** began to flow from Mount Pluto and other volcanoes on the north and east side of the basin. The lava formed a plug across the huge basin's northeastern outlet. Rivers, streams, and snowmelt that flowed into the dammed basin filled it with water to a depth several hundred feet higher than Lake Tahoe's current level. Eventually a new outlet was eroded through the lava dam, creating the present course of the Lower Truckee River and stabilizing the lake level at its current depth. Today, the Lower Truckee River by Tahoe City remains Lake Tahoe's only outlet, although 63 separate tributaries and two hot springs pour into the lake.

Another series of geologic events put the final touches on the Lake Tahoe area. Several times during the past million years the planet cooled, one of a series of **ice ages** descended, and the entire Sierra Nevada mountain range was engulfed in snow and ice. **Glaciers,** or rivers of ice, went to work on the exposed granite, moving slowly down established river valleys on the western side of the lake and carving the broad

U shapes of Emerald Bay, Fallen Leaf Lake, and Cascade Lake. It is uncertain how many times glacial ice moved through the Tahoe area, advancing and then retreating, although there is evidence that at least three major glaciations occurred. Only the sturdiest chunks of granite withstood the glaciers' onslaught. Softer, weaker rock was chiseled away and ground into rubble by the fierce power of the glaciers' grinding ice and rock. The gravel left behind by the melting glaciers formed hills that are known as lateral and terminal **moraines.** One such wall of rubble forms the basis for Highway 89 just south of Emerald Bay, where the road follows the line of a narrow moraine between Cascade Lake and Lake Tahoe. Emerald Bay is encircled by an incomplete moraine. Had the moraine been completed, Emerald Bay would be a separate lake, like nearby Cascade Lake, not a part of Lake Tahoe.

The sum total of these varied geologic events formed the Lake Tahoe we know today. The lake's statistics are laced with superlatives. With a deepest point of 1,645 feet near Crystal Bay, Tahoe is the 3rd-deepest lake in North America (after Great Slave Lake in Canada and Crater Lake in Oregon) and the 10th deepest in the world. Its average depth is 989 feet, and with 193 square miles of surface area, the lake holds almost 39 trillion gallons of water. Lake Tahoe is 22 miles long and 12 miles wide, with approximately 72 miles of shoreline. It is the largest alpine (high-elevation) lake in North America. Several million tons of water evaporate from its surface every day, yet this decreases the lake level by only one-tenth of an inch. Still, it is estimated that because the lake's surface is so vast, if the water that evaporates every 24 hours could be recovered, it would supply the daily requirements of a city the size of Los Angeles.

CLIMATE

Elevations in the Tahoe basin range from the lake's elevation of 6,223 feet to 10,881 feet at Freel Peak's summit on the South Shore. Given that range, the climate change can be dramatic. Summertime temperatures can reach 90°F at the lakeshore, but it can snow any month of the year on the highest peaks.

Generally, the climate at Tahoe is quite mild year-round, with daytime temperatures in the high 70s or low 80s (Fahrenheit) in summer and nighttime temperatures in the 40s or low 50s. Typical rainfall in the months of July, August, and September is less than 0.5 inch, ensuring plentiful days of summer sunshine at the lake. June–August is usually ideal for outdoor recreation and lazing around the lake.

Winter days average 36°F, and nights will often drop below 20°F. Lake Tahoe typically sees about 275 days of sunshine per year. Precipitation is common in winter, with the average annual snowfall at lake level averaging 10–12 feet. At the higher elevations of Tahoe's ski areas, the annual snowfall averages 25–40 feet. Starting as early as mid-November and often lasting into April, the season of snow beckons skiers, snowboarders, and winter sports aficionados from all over the globe. Because the timing of snowfall and snowmelt vary greatly from year to year, always phone ahead for condition updates before planning your trip.

Spring and fall are usually cooler and wetter than summer, but often still quite pleasant. Rain occurs occasionally in the spring and fall months, with average annual rainfall totaling just over eight inches. April and May are often called the "mud months" because of the wealth of wet soil and rushing streams from snowmelt.

Because of the immense size of Lake Tahoe, its huge volume of water is in constant motion, with the cold water on the surface sinking while warmer water rises from the deep. Although Emerald Bay has frozen over a few times in recorded history, the main body of the lake never has. The water is notoriously cold, though. Even in the summer heat of August, when the air temperature might reach the high

© ANN MARIE BROWN

Unlike Lake Tahoe, small Grass Lake sometimes freezes over.

80s, the lake's surface temperature to a depth of about 10 feet tops out at 68°F. In February or March, the surface temperature is 40–50°F. Below a depth of about 600 feet, the water is a constant chilly 39°F year-round.

ENVIRONMENTAL ISSUES

Despite the impressive statistics of the massive lake, it is not the size or depth of Lake Tahoe that is its most prized feature, but rather the **clarity** of its water, which is considered to be 99.8 percent pure, about the same as distilled water. This is partly due to the fact that 40 percent of the precipitation that falls in the Lake Tahoe basin lands directly on the lake, so it has no opportunity to be contaminated. The remaining percentage drains through coarse granitic soil, which serves as an excellent filter.

John LeConte, the third president of the University of California at Berkeley, completed the first study of Tahoe's water quality in 1884. Using a technique developed by Pietro Secchi,

LeConte attached a rope to a white disk, similar to a 10-inch-wide dinner plate, and lowered it into the water. The **Secchi disk** disappeared from view 103 feet below the lake's surface. Continuous monitoring of the lake using a Secchi disk began in 1968 under the direction of renowned scientist Dr. Charles Goldman of the U.C. Davis Tahoe Research Group. This led to the alarming discovery of a decrease in the lake's clarity. The Secchi disk could be seen clearly at 102 feet deep in 1968. By 1996, it could only be seen 77 feet deep. In 2005, it was visible only 73.6 feet below the lake's surface.

The problem with maintaining Tahoe's clarity lies in the fact that there is little intake or outflow of fresh water, so pollution and sediment that enter the lake stay there for a very long time. Logging activities that occurred around the lakeshore 150 years ago still affect the water clarity today. Of the 63 tributaries that feed into the lake, only one watershed is large enough to be considered a river—the

Upper Truckee River, which enters the lake in the city of South Lake Tahoe. The lake's only outflow is the Lower Truckee River in Tahoe City, by Fanny Bridge. (The river flows northwest to Truckee and then turns east and travels through downtown Reno and into Pyramid Lake.) It is estimated that about 25 percent of the lake's water comes from the Upper Truckee. Unfortunately, so does a lion's share of sediment. The Upper Truckee River was channeled and restricted to create room for the South Lake Tahoe airport, golf courses, and subdivisions. Where the river meets the lake, wetlands and marshes were permanently altered in order to construct the Tahoe Keys marina and town houses. Moving and straightening a river leads to erosion of its banks, which leads to sedimentation. Removing a river's natural wetlands means there is no longer any filtering system in place before the water reaches a lake. The resulting sedimentation leads to the ideal conditions for algae to flourish, and that leads to a lake that is no longer blue but greenish in color, and no longer clear but obfuscated. Compounding the damage, we've added fertilizers and other pollutants to the lake, and auto emissions from car traffic on the lake's highways.

Out-of-state visitors to California notice an abundance of cars on highways and roads bearing a familiar blue slogan: Keep Tahoe Blue. Created by the **League to Save Lake Tahoe,** the car tags were an ingenious marketing effort designed to raise money for and create awareness of the need to preserve Tahoe's famous water clarity. The nonprofit league was formed in 1957. Its numerous successes have included stopping plans to build a bridge over Emerald Bay and high-speed freeways around the lake, and a ban on carbureted two-stroke watercraft engines, such as those found on older personal watercraft and outboard motors. The league also hosted the 1997 Presidential Forum at Lake Tahoe, when President Bill Clinton and Vice President Al Gore took a tour aboard the U.C. Davis lake-monitoring vessel with members of the Tahoe Research Group. The league manages an office and Environmental Education Center (2608 Hwy. 50, 530/541-5388, www.keeptahoeblue.org) in South Lake Tahoe, where visitors can learn about ongoing efforts to preserve Tahoe's water clarity.

Several state-run agencies also work to protect Lake Tahoe. The **California Tahoe Conservancy** acquires sensitive lands around the lake and preserves them from development. The conservancy's major focus is on saving wetlands, meadows, and marshes, which are important filters for sediment and pollutants. Only an estimated 30 percent of the lake's wetlands and meadows still exist today. Where wetlands have already been altered by development, the conservancy attempts to return them to their natural state. The **Lahontan Water Quality Control Board** is responsible for water quality on the California side of the lake. The **Tahoe Regional Planning Agency** (www.trpa.org) regulates all types of development around the lake, from big issues such as public transportation, logging, and erosion control to smaller matters like the size of private driveways and business signage. Its multiple projects fall under the umbrella of an Environmental Improvement Program (EIP), which is funded by the federal government and the California and Nevada state governments. This gives Washington a say in the health of Lake Tahoe as well. Adding to the federal stake at the lake, the U.S. Forest Service owns nearly 80 percent of the land around Lake Tahoe.

All in all, the management of Lake Tahoe is a political pea soup, with several regulatory agencies performing frequently overlapping functions. But that's not surprising, considering the fact that the lake is a national treasure, and its shoreline lies in five separate counties, two states, one incorporated city (South Lake Tahoe), and several unincorporated towns. The good news is that everyone seems to agree that

LEAVE NO TRACE

When hiking in Tahoe, follow the Leave No Trace Principles of outdoor ethics:

Plan Ahead and Prepare

- Prepare for extreme weather, hazards, and emergencies.
- Schedule your trip to avoid times of high use.
- Visit in small groups. Split larger parties into groups of 4-6.

Travel and Camp on Durable Surfaces

- Durable surfaces include established trails and campsites, rock, gravel, dry grasses, or snow.
- Protect riparian areas by camping at least 200 feet from lakes and streams.
- Good campsites are found, not made. Altering a site is not necessary.
- Concentrate use on existing trails and campsites.
- Walk single file in the middle of the trail, even when wet or muddy.
- Keep campsites small. Focus activity in areas where vegetation is absent.

Dispose of Waste Properly

- Pack it in, pack it out. Inspect your campsite and rest areas for trash or spilled foods. Pack out all trash, leftover food, and litter.
- Deposit solid human waste in catholes dug 6-8 inches deep at least 200 feet from water, camp, and trails. Cover and disguise the cathole when finished.
- Pack out toilet paper and hygiene products.
- To wash yourself or your dishes, carry water 200 feet away from streams or lakes and use small amounts of biodegradable soap. Scatter strained dishwater.

Leave What You Find

- Preserve the past. Examine, but do not touch, cultural or historic structures and artifacts.
- Leave rocks, plants, and other natural objects as you find them.

- Avoid introducing or transporting nonnative species.
- Do not build structures, furniture, or dig trenches.

Minimize Campfire Impacts

- Campfires can cause lasting impacts to the backcountry. Use a lightweight stove for cooking and enjoy a candle lantern for light.
- Where fires are permitted, use established fire rings, fire pans, or mound fires.
- Keep fires small. Only use sticks from the ground that can be broken by hand.
- Burn all wood and coals to ash, put out campfires completely, then scatter cool ashes.

Respect Wildlife

- Observe wildlife from a distance. Do not follow or approach them.
- Never feed animals. Feeding wildlife damages their health, alters natural behaviors, and exposes them to predators and other dangers.
- Protect wildlife and your food by storing rations and trash securely.

Be Considerate of Other Visitors

- Respect other visitors and protect the quality of their experience.
- Be courteous. Yield to other users on the trail.
- Step to the downhill side of the trail when encountering pack stock.
- Take breaks and camp away from trails and other visitors.
- Let nature's sounds prevail. Avoid loud voices and noises.

preserving Tahoe's water quality is of utmost importance not just for the health of the lake but also for the economic prosperity of the region. How that preservation takes place will be a subject of much controversy and debate as long as people choose to live in the Tahoe basin.

Flora

With elevations ranging from 6,200 feet at Tahoe's lake level to well over 10,000 feet on the basin's highest peaks, plus a combination of granitic and volcanic soils, the Tahoe region provides a wide mix of environments for a variety of flora, from giant conifers to the tiniest of alpine wildflowers. Tahoe supports four separate life zones for plants. The Yellow Pine Zone covers the lowest elevations, up to about 6,500 feet. The Red Fir Zone includes elevations from 6,500 feet to 9,000 feet. The Subalpine Zone covers elevations from 9,000 to 10,500 feet, and the Alpine Zone covers the few areas that are above 10,500 feet.

YELLOW PINE ZONE

The conifers of the Yellow Pine Zone, the region nearest Tahoe's shoreline, can be identified by a few easy-to-remember characteristics. The three-needled **Jeffrey pine** is the most common tree in the Tahoe basin, growing at elevations from 6,000 feet to 10,000 feet. It is a favorite of many Sierra tree lovers because of the unique scent of its bark, which smells sweet, like vanilla or butterscotch. Sometimes the odor is so strong that it wafts over you from several feet away; other times you must put your nose right up to the tree's bark crevices to smell it. The Jeffrey pine has distinct, jigsaw-puzzle bark (it's especially pronounced on older, wider trees), and its cones have spines that point downward, not outward, so they are easy to pick up and handle. This rugged tree is often seen growing on granite slabs seemingly without the aid of soil.

Similar to the Jeffrey pine is the **ponderosa pine,** a species that is also known by its clearly delineated, jigsaw-puzzle-style bark and needles bundled in groups of three. The ponderosa's needles grow up to 10 inches long, and its cones are prickly to the touch. Generations of schoolchildren have been taught the mnemonic "prickly ponderosa and gentle Jeffrey" to remember how to distinguish the two pines' cones.

The **sugar pine** is the tallest and largest of more than 100 species of pine trees in the world. Old trees frequently reach 7 feet in diameter and 200 feet tall. This venerable pine has unmistakable cones, befitting a tree of its size: up to 20 inches in length, the longest of any conifer. The cones hang down like Christmas ornaments off the tips of the sugar pine's long branches. While they are still green, they weigh up to five pounds. Unlike the ponderosa and Jeffrey pine, the sugar pine's needles are bundled in groups of five.

Often seen in the company of Jeffrey, ponderosa, and sugar pines is the **incense-cedar,** which can be identified by its lacy foliage and thick, shaggy bark that is similar to that of a coastal redwood tree. The incense-cedar has unusual needles that are completely flat at the ends, as if they have been ironed. The tree emits a slight spicy odor that some say is reminiscent of the scent of pencils. The incense-cedar's name is hyphenated because it is not a true cedar.

The second most common tree at Lake Tahoe is the **white fir.** Its sturdy, white-gray trunk commonly reaches a width of five feet. The white fir's needles grow in flat sprays that are distinctly two-dimensional. Most people recognize white firs because the young ones look like little Christmas trees; indeed, this is a commonly marketed Christmas tree in California. Older trees easily attain heights of 150 feet.

A few deciduous trees also make an appearance around Tahoe's lakeshore, the most noticeable being the **quaking aspen.** This broad-leaved tree gets its name from its round leaves on flat leaf stems that flutter in the slightest breeze. Quaking aspens grow near streams and meadows or on moist slopes from 6,000 to 10,000 feet in elevation. In autumn, the aspen sports a spectacular coat of golden yellow. Especially noteworthy groves of quaking aspens can be seen along the shores of Fallen Leaf Lake on the South Shore and near Marlette Lake on the East Shore.

Other colorful deciduous trees that flourish near water are **willows** and **mountain alders.** Five separate species of willows grow alongside Tahoe's streams, most in the shape of small trees or large shrubs. The willow's leaves are long and narrow and turn bright red in autumn. Mountain alders, which often grow alongside willows, have rounder leaves with jagged edges and a dense network of veins. Alders form dense thickets that are almost impenetrable to humans. They have very small cones that look like tiny pinecones.

At areas around Lake Tahoe where the forests open up, wet mountain meadows are common, and within them bloom a variety of wildflowers in early summer: pink shooting stars, red and yellow western columbine, bright yellow coneflowers, red or orange paintbrush, and false hellebore (corn lilies), among many others.

RED FIR ZONE

As you hike uphill from the lake, you quickly leave the sugar and ponderosa pines behind and enter the Red Fir Zone, also called the Upper Montane Zone. Jeffrey pines from the Yellow Pine Zone grow well in these higher elevations,

© ANN MARIE BROWN

Tahoe's aspens turn golden in autumn.

too, but the namesake red fir and lodgepole pine predominate. The deeply shaded forests in this zone also contain western white pines and western juniper. **Red firs** are easy to identify because of their reddish-brown, deeply furrowed bark. They can grow up to six feet in diameter and are often seen in pure groves made up of only their own kind. Depressions at the bases of the biggest trees are sometimes used by bears as winter dens (the same is also true for white firs). **Lodgepole pines** are the only two-needled pines in the Sierra. They earned their name because Native Americans used their dependably straight and slender trunks as poles for their tepees and lodges. Ironically, their Latin name is *pinus contorta* (contorted pine). Adding to the confusion, throughout history the tree has been mistakenly called a tamarack, which is actually a deciduous conifer that does not grow anywhere in the Sierra. (You'll find a Tamarack Lake in the Desolation Wilderness, bordered by lodepole pines, just off the Pacific Crest Trail a few miles from Echo Lakes.) The lodgepole's bark is thin and scaly, and its needles are in bundles of two.

Finally, the **piñon pine** is a tree that grows only on the dry slopes of the Nevada side of the lake, often in fields or sagebrush and in the occasional company of western junipers. This hardy tree bears large meaty nuts that were a staple of the Washoe Indians' diet, as well as a favorite food of many birds and animals.

Aside from the big conifers, one small plant common in the Red Fir life zone is worth a special mention. It is the **snow plant,** a red, thick, asparagus-like plant that has no green leaves. It is one of the first flora to make an appearance as the snow melts; early-season hikers will often see it protruding from the forest floor amid piles of melting snow. A member of the heath family, snow plant is so tough and determined to sprout that it can sometimes push up through asphalt.

SUBALPINE ZONE

Still higher, near timberline at 9,000–10,500 feet, only a few hardy trees survive: western white pines, western junipers, whitebark pines, and mountain hemlocks. The **western white pine** is a gray-barked pine with blue-green needles in bundles of five. The tree has eight-inch-long cones that are often slightly curved. Western white pines rarely exceed 100 feet tall, but their long limbs curve gracefully upward. **Western juniper** (also called Sierra juniper) is another distinctive tree of the Subalpine Zone, and it is easy to identify because of its bluish-green, scalelike needles and spiraling trunk, which makes it appear as if the tree twisted in circles as it grew. The roots of this hearty tree will tunnel through crevices in granite, so it often looks as if the western juniper is growing right out of rock. Western junipers in the Sierra can live as long as 2,000 years. As the juniper ages, its trunk becomes stripped of bark and bleached to a light blond. The juniper produces an abundance of blue-purple "berries" in the summer months, which are well loved by birds and were once used by humans for making gin. These are actually not berries at all but the juniper's cones. The western juniper is especially common around Carson Pass and Meiss Country. One huge specimen with a seven-foot-wide diameter can be seen on the trail to Dardanelles Lake.

The wind-battered and low-growing **whitebark pine** often looks more like a shrub with multiple small trunks than a single tree; at its tallest it grows to about 35 feet. Its cones are purple, egg shaped, and two inches long, with seeds that are highly coveted by Clark's nutcrackers, chickarees, and chipmunks. These trees, too, are common around Carson Pass.

The **mountain hemlock** is easily spotted by its uppermost branches, which droop downward or sideways, as if they are taking a bow. Naturalist John Muir was a great fan of the mountain hemlock and wrote a lengthy ode to them in his first book, *The Mountains of California*. The hemlock has greenish-blue foliage that is distinct when viewed close up; its needles are dense and completely cover the stems they grow on, like a soft coat of fur.

The dominant plants that grow in the high meadows of the Subalpine life zone are **sedges,** not the grasses found in lower-elevation meadows. Wildflowers at these elevations include many of the same species of the Red Fir life zone, although the higher the elevation, the more likely the plants will be of a smaller, more compact variety.

ALPINE ZONE
Finally, at 10,500 feet and above lies the region that only hardy Tahoe hikers will see: the Alpine life zone above the timberline, where trees are rare to nonexistent. Plants that grow here are typically very small, mainly because of harsh winds. The growing season is very short, making these alpine environments extremely fragile and easily disturbed by human presence. Cushions or mats of colorful flowers like penstemon and phlox brighten the generally stark landscape of gray, rocky slopes. Some of the loveliest of these matlike plants are the mountain heaths or heathers, including John Muir's beloved cassiope, which can be seen along the shores of the lakes in the Desolation Wilderness's Crystal Basin.

Fauna

Many visitors to Lake Tahoe hope to catch a glimpse of some interesting wildlife. In this regard, Tahoe often delivers. The following is a brief guide to some of Tahoe's most commonly seen, or most notable, animal denizens.

LARGE MAMMALS
Black Bear
The only kind of bear that lives near Lake Tahoe, or anywhere in California, is the black bear. Although the fearsome grizzly once roamed here and is immortalized on the California flag, grizzlies have been extinct in the Golden State since 1924. Black bears have a somewhat misleading name—they are more commonly brown, blond, or cinnamon colored, only rarely pure black. Often they have a white patch on their chests. The smallest of all North American bears, they weigh as much as 450 pounds, can run up to 30 miles per hour, and are powerful swimmers and climbers. Despite the adult bear's enormous size, bear cubs weigh only a half pound at birth.

Black bears will eat just about anything, but their staple foods are berries, fruits, plants, insects, honeycomb, the inner layer of tree bark, and fish and small mammals. Contrary to popular belief, black bears do not hibernate. A pregnant female will "den up" in winter and usually give birth while she is sleeping, but this is not true hibernation. Male black bears are often seen roaming for food in winter.

Mule Deer
Occasionally seen in the forests around Lake Tahoe, most commonly on the East Shore or near Carson Pass, the mule deer is one of our largest American deer and can weigh up to 200 pounds. The deer gets its name from its ears, which are large and rounded. Mule deer in the Sierra have a white patch on their rumps and a black-tipped tail. The antlers on the bucks, which develop in summer, are usually an elegant, matched set of four points on each side. Tahoe's mule deer migrate downslope to the Carson Valley in winter, so visitors are more likely to see them in the Tahoe basin in

© ANN MARIE BROWN

The smallest of all North American bears, black bears weigh as much as 450 pounds, can run up to 30 miles per hour, and are good tree-climbers.

the summer months, when food is plentiful. Still, mule deer are nowhere near as common in the Tahoe basin as they are at similar elevations elsewhere in the Sierra. The tall mountains surrounding the basin, combined with Tahoe's severe winter weather, serve as a discouraging barrier.

Mountain Lion

The most reclusive of all of Tahoe's creatures, the mountain lion is the largest cat in North America and is best distinguished from afar by its two- to three-foot-long tail. The adult cat's body minus its tail is often six feet long; a male cat typically weighs 250 pounds. The mountain lion is tawny except for its underside, which is white. It usually lives where deer, its main food source, are plentiful. Because mountain lions have large territories, probably only two or three live in the entire Tahoe basin. There have been no mountain lion attacks on visitors

to Lake Tahoe, although a few attacks have occurred elsewhere in California. Although you probably won't see a lion, you might be lucky enough to find its tracks. The large, catlike footprints are easy to distinguish; they are four-toed prints that do not show claws.

Coyote

Many Tahoe visitors report seeing a wolf or a fox near the highway, but what they usually have seen is a coyote. (Wolves do not live in the Sierra; foxes are quite small and rarely seen during the day.) The coyote is a doglike animal with a grayish-brown coat; its back slopes downward toward its tail. An average-size coyote weighs about 30 pounds and stands about two feet tall. Coyotes can run as fast as 40 miles per hour and make a series of "yip" cries, often followed by a howl. Across California, the coyote has acclimated well to the presence of humans and is generally unafraid of them.

WINTER WILDLIFE

When the coldest days of winter arrive, how do Tahoe's animal residents survive? Humans turn on the furnace and bundle up in boots and warm coats, but how do mammals and birds stay warm and safe? Here's a short list of some of Tahoe's more common creatures and their winter survival techniques:

Pine marten: In winter, these small members of the weasel family grow long hairs between the toe pads on their feet. This keeps their feet warm and enables them to travel on snow.

Short-tailed and long-tailed weasel: The coats of these two weasel species turn white in the winter, except for the tip of their tail, which stays black. The weasels white coats have more space between each hair, which gets filled by air and acts as insulation.

Coyote: You're more likely to see Tahoe's coyotes in winter than in summer, although they are commonly spotted year-round. In winter, the coyote grows a thicker, blondish-brown fur coat that is easily spotted against white snow. Coyotes can often be seen hunting for mice or squirrels in the snow-covered meadows.

Chickaree, or Douglas squirrel: This small gray squirrel is one of the noisier squirrels, possessing a large selection of chattering calls and trills. In the autumn, chickarees stockpile conifer cones at the base of trees for the upcoming winter. They need easy access to their storehouses because they do not hibernate during the winter months but are active year-round. In the winter, they use holes in trees as nests and often visit backyard bird feeders.

Yellow-bellied marmot: Commonly seen in the Desolation Wilderness during the summer, marmots hibernate in rock caves during the winter. They must gain enough weight during the short summer season or they may die of starvation while hibernating.

Bear: These large, furry mammals eat all spring, summer, and fall to get ready for winter. Although many species of bears hibernate, Tahoe's bears sleep hard in winter but don't actually hibernate. They usually "hunker down" in a tree hollow or some type of cave, but on warm, sunny winter days, they will occasionally come out of their dens to look for food. While the female bear sleeps, she gives birth to her young. The babies (typically two) burrow into their mother's fur and snuggle with her until spring.

Bald eagle: Lake Tahoe does not freeze over in the winter, so bald eagles can catch fish in the lake year-round. A greater number of bald eagles are spotted in the winter months at Tahoe than in the summer. Approximately 10 to 15 individual eagles overwinter in Tahoe.

Mountain chickadee: These little birds are frequent visitors to backyard bird feeders year-round, and depend largely on humans for a wintertime food source.

SMALL MAMMALS
Bobcat

A stocky feline about twice the size of a house cat, the bobcat is easily recognized by its short, "bobbed" tail, only four inches long. Bobcats are mostly nocturnal but are sometimes seen hunting during the day. Their coats are gray-brown in winter and reddish-brown in summer, and marked with black spots and bars. The bobcat's ears have short tufts above them.

Raccoon

This black-masked invader is sometimes seen scavenging around campgrounds, particularly in the evenings, or drinking and feeding at rivers or lakes. The raccoon has distinctive rings around its tail and a large, gray-brown body that can weigh as much as 40 pounds. Despite its girth, the raccoon is a good swimmer and climber and can run as fast as 15 miles per hour. Its fingerlike toes are useful for washing its food.

Porcupine

Only the rare Tahoe visitor gets to see the elusive yellow-haired porcupine, a mostly nocturnal mammal that is characterized by its body covering of thousands of quills, or sharp, hollow spines. (Dogs, however, seem to have a knack for finding them—usually with very unhappy results for the dog.) The porcupine's quills lie flat when the animal is relaxed but stand straight up when it is threatened. Porcupines spend most of their time high in trees, where they eat twigs and bark, but will waddle across meadows or forests in search of a new feeding tree. Porcupine tracks face forward and inward; the animal walks pigeon-toed. The most common sightings of porcupines at Lake Tahoe are on the South Shore near Fallen Leaf Lake and Camp Richardson.

Snowshoe Hare

Brown in summer and white in winter, this large member of the rabbit family is a master of disguise. The snowshoe hare derives its name from its huge hind feet, which act like snowshoes and allow the animal to "float" across the snow, without sinking in. The hare has distinctive, three-inch-long ears that stand upright and are marked by black tips.

Yellow-Bellied Marmot

The largest and most curious member of the squirrel family, the yellow-bellied marmot is frequently seen in Tahoe's high country. About seven inches tall and as long as two feet, the bold marmot has no enemies and is frequently seen sunning itself on high boulders. The marmot's coat is buff to brown, and its belly is yellow. The animal is most often seen on talus-lined slopes or near rock piles at high elevations. If you see two or more marmots together, they are often wrestling or chasing each other. You may hear them make a high-pitched whistling sound. Some people refer to marmots as woodchucks or groundhogs.

Pine Marten

This large, slender member of the weasel family has a brown back, light head and underbelly, pointed nose, long bushy tail, and distinctive orange patch at its throat. Two to three feet long and with a sleek, acrobatic physique, the solitary pine marten is rarely seen by visitors, as it spends most of its time high in trees, hunting for squirrels and birds.

Beaver

First introduced to the Sierra by fur trappers, then later by the California Fish and Game Department, the nonnative beaver has prospered around Lake Tahoe because of the region's many waterways lined with aspen and willow groves. The trees' inner bark is the beaver's favorite food. The beaver has a flattened tail that makes a distinctive slapping sound on the water. Its webbed hind feet make it an agile swimmer. Adults are typically three feet long (including the tail) and weigh 50–60 pounds. Beavers mate for life, and if their mate dies, they never mate again.

Pika

A resident in alpine environments higher than 9,500 feet, the pika is a small relative of the rabbit that busily collects green grasses, then stacks them in the sun and dries them for winter food and insulation. The creature does not hibernate, so it needs to keep a full larder of dried grasses for its winter nourishment. The diminutive pika is most often seen on talus-lined slopes or rocky hillsides and is easily recognized because of its small, rounded ears and absence of a tail.

Squirrels

The number and variety of squirrels and their close relations around Lake Tahoe can be quite daunting to the amateur naturalist trying to identify them. One of the easiest-to-spot species is the **golden-mantled ground squirrel,** a common sight at elevations above 6,000 feet. Frequently mistaken for large chipmunks, these cute squirrels can be correctly identified by their lack of the chipmunk's facial stripe. Otherwise, they look much the same, with one white stripe on each side of their brown bodies, bordered by a heavy black stripe. The golden-mantled ground squirrel must fatten itself up all summer to prepare for winter hibernation.

The **western gray squirrel** is the common gray-coated squirrel seen throughout California, with a long bushy tail and white belly. Western gray squirrels are great tree climbers and are mostly seen below 6,500 feet. The gray squirrel population around Lake Tahoe took a hit in the 1950s, when local residents set out poisons to stop the animals from damaging their houses. Their numbers are now back to normal.

The hyperactive **Douglas squirrel,** or **chickaree,** is much smaller than the western gray squirrel, and it's colored a mix of brown and gray. This perky, constantly chattering squirrel remains active throughout the year and is frequently seen both on the ground and in trees, where it cuts thousands of pinecones for its winter stash. The Douglas squirrel is easily excited and makes a high-pitched trilling sound that can be mistaken for the cry of a bird.

The **California ground squirrel** is best identified by a silver, V-shaped pattern on the shoulders of its grayish-brown coat. Its body is similar to that of the western gray squirrel, but it does not have a bushy tail. Although it can climb trees, the California ground squirrel is most often seen on the ground. The animals hibernate in winter, so you'll only spot them during the summer months.

Chipmunks

Not one but several kinds of chipmunks are found at Lake Tahoe. All are colored in various shades of golden brown and have a distinctive white stripe on both their body and face. Generally, chipmunks at higher elevations hibernate and those at lower elevations do not. Like their cousins the squirrels, chipmunks eat nuts, seeds, and fungi, which they carry around in their fur-lined cheek pouches. Chipmunks hibernate in winter.

BIRDS
Steller's Jay

Nobody visits Lake Tahoe without seeing the Steller's jay, a bold and raucous bird who makes his presence known. The western cousin of the East Coast's blue jay, the Steller's jay has a distinctive black topknot of feathers that point backward, affording him a regal look. The jay's body is about 10 inches in length and a deep, pure blue. When on the ground, the Steller's jay hops; it does not walk. If you are eating a sandwich when one is near, keep a vigilant guard; the jay has no qualms about stealing food.

Clark's Nutcracker

Similar in size and behavior to the Steller's jay (noisy and cantankerous, and often seen scouting at campgrounds and picnic areas for food), the Clark's nutcracker is light gray with white and black patches on its tail and wings. The birds are often spotted among the upper branches of whitebark pine trees, where they quarrel with each other as they collect pine nuts. The Clark's nutcracker stores nuts and seeds for winter in a massive granary, usually located on a south-facing slope. One pair can cache as many as 30,000 nuts and seeds in autumn. In spring, the birds can recall the placement of every single nut and will retrieve them to feed their young.

Raven

Frequently mistaken for the smaller crow, the common raven is a remarkably intelligent bird that is often seen scrounging for leftovers near campgrounds and picnic areas. Ravens are about two feet long, with glossy black feathers and a curved beak, and a strange call that sounds something like a croaking noise. While flying, they will also sometimes make a series of clicking sounds. In spring, the male raven performs a spectacular aerial dance for its mate—swooping, diving, and barrel rolling—while making loud cries.

Woodpeckers

Plentiful around Lake Tahoe, a variety of woodpeckers are frequently seen and heard amid the conifer forest. With some variation, they are all black and white with a dash of flaming red on their heads or necks (although in some species only the males bear the red patch). Most common is the **hairy woodpecker,** which is often mistakenly identified as a downy woodpecker. The hairy is much larger than the downy—about the size of a robin—and has a much longer bill. The male has a bright red neck patch. Both woodpeckers have a vertical white stripe on their black backs, and both drill into dead trees to find insects.

The **white-headed woodpecker** is seen mostly in pine forests, where it eats pine nuts and insects. White-headed woodpeckers do not drill like most woodpeckers; instead they look for food by pulling bark off trees with their beaks. The white-headed woodpecker is all black except for its white head and wing patch. The male has a small red patch on the back of its neck.

Also a member of the woodpecker family, the **red-breasted sapsucker** has a bright red "hood" that extends down below its throat. The rest of its body is speckled black and white, but it flashes a white rump and shoulder patches when it flies. Unlike many woodpeckers, the sapsucker feeds by drilling holes in live trees, then waits for the holes to fill with sap, which attracts insects—hence the name "sapsucker." Both the male and female of the species look alike.

The **northern flicker** is another common woodpecker seen around Lake Tahoe. This foot-long bird is mostly brown and gray with some red under its wings, but it is most easily spotted by its bright white rump, which is obvious in flight. The male has a dash of red on its cheeks. Flickers will drill into trees for insects or feed on the ground, poking in the earth for ants. They have tongues as long as three inches that are particularly well adapted for sucking up ants.

Nuthatches

Three types of nuthatches commonly make an appearance in Tahoe's forests: the **red-breasted,** the **white-breasted,** and the **pygmy.** These compact birds have short necks and tails, and they travel down tree trunks headfirst looking for insects. Their upside-down stance makes them unmistakable. All three species are gray and white and 4–6 inches long.

Mountain Chickadee

The most common bird in the Lake Tahoe basin, the small, gray mountain chickadee has a black cap, a black stripe under its chin, and a white stripe above its eyes. It is often seen hanging upside down on branches, searching for insects and seeds. You'll know the call of a chickadee by its three-note whistle, which travels down the musical scale with each note.

Western Tanager

One of the most colorful birds of the forest, the male western tanager is a favorite of many bird-watchers. His orange-red head, bright yellow body, and black wings and tail make him as bright hued as a pet-shop bird, and an unforgettable sight. The female's markings are much more subdued but still a colorful gold and olive. The orange on the male's head disappears in autumn when it is time to migrate.

American Dipper

One of naturalist John Muir's favorite birds, the dipper (also called the water ouzel) is an unusual songbird that is often seen amid the spray of waterfalls. Although it is colored a nondescript gray, the dipper lives an extraordinary life, diving underwater to feed on insects and larvae. The bird has a third eyelid that closes over its eyes to protect it from spray, a flap of skin that closes over its nostrils to keep out water, and an extra-large oil gland that waterproofs its plumage. It often builds its nest behind a waterfall, then flies back and forth through the torrent to feed its young. When searching for food in a stream, it can walk underwater.

California Gull

Many a first-time Tahoe visitor has been surprised to see gulls—a species associated with the seashore—hanging out on Tahoe's beaches. The California gull is well adapted to almost any environment where it can scavenge for garbage, insects, and fish. The **ring-billed gull,** which has a black stripe around its bill, also makes an appearance on Tahoe's shoreline.

Great Horned Owl

The only living creature that will prey on a skunk, the magnificent great horned owl can stand up to two feet high and calls out a haunting "hoo, hoo, hoo" at night. This owl is a terrific nocturnal hunter that can take down animals as large as the snowshoe hare. The bird's distinct ear tufts, or "horns," are its namesake feature. When a great horned owl perches and flies, it appears to have no neck.

American Bald Eagle

Even if you've never seen one before, you'll have no trouble identifying the national bird. The bald eagle's white "bald" head and white tail on its otherwise dark brown body are dead giveaways, even from a distance. While soaring, the eagle's wings can expand to more than seven feet. Bald eagles are commonly seen around Emerald Bay, where a pair or two often nests near aptly named Eagle Point, and at Kiva Point, near the Forest Service's Taylor Creek Visitor Center. Seen from up close, the eagle

has a huge, yellow, hooked bill, which it uses for tearing up fish. Typically about a dozen bald eagles make their home at Lake Tahoe, and they are more often seen in the winter months.

Osprey

This large raptor is a specialist in high-flying fishing. Dark brown (almost black) and white, the bird will hover above a lake, then plunge feetfirst to capture fish. It is well known for its keen eyesight, which is more than 10 times that of a human. Occasionally the osprey is mistaken for a bald eagle, because it, too, has a white head, but the osprey is a much smaller bird, with a wingspan of only five feet. Also, ospreys display more white on the underside of their wings when they fly.

Canada Goose

The largest bird that most visitors will see at Lake Tahoe, the Canada goose feels comfortably at home on the lake's shoreline, as it does in many places in North America. The goose can be as much as four feet in length and will stand three feet high with its long neck extended. Their bodies are brown and white, but their necks are glossy black with a wide stripe of white beneath their chins. Elevated platforms installed by the Forest Service at the marsh at Pope Beach have provided the birds with a safe place to nest.

FISH
Rainbow Trout

A favorite of anglers throughout the Sierra, the rainbow trout is a colorful fish with a pink-to-red band along the centerline of its body, with darker green above and a lighter green below. The fish also has black spots on its back and fins. To a greater extent than any other trout species, rainbows have vast variation in their coloration, particularly from one body of water to another. Rainbow trout will grow up to 24 inches in large lakes, but only half that size in streams.

© ANN MARIE BROWN

Canada geese on the shoreline

Brown Trout

Brown trout are not as dark colored as you might surmise from their name; they vary from golden to olive to cinnamon colored, with light tan bellies. The fish is easily recognized by the large dark spots on its head and back, and red spots on its lower sides. It is the only trout in California that has both black and red spots, although it is not a California native. Brown trout in the Sierra originally came from a strain of fish in Germany or Scotland. The brown trout is generally very wary and more difficult to catch than the rainbow trout. Many fish will grow to old ages and trophy sizes, longer than two feet.

Mackinaw Trout

This monster of the deep is the coveted prize of many sport fishers. The fish has a gray, spotted body that varies from pale gray to almost black. The average size of a mackinaw in Lake Tahoe is 3–5 pounds, but fish as large as 10 pounds are fairly common. Occasionally a 20- to 30-pounder will be caught; the lake record

is more than 37 pounds. Mackinaw are also found in Fallen Leaf Lake and Donner Lake; they prefer deep, cold water most of the year. The trout is not native to the Tahoe area and was first introduced for sportfishing in 1894. In other areas of the country, mackinaw are simply known as lake trout.

Kokanee Salmon

A distant cousin of the sockeye salmon, the foot-long kokanee is a landlocked salmon that is blue-green above and silvery white below, with a smattering of black spots. Most people know the kokanee in its spawning colors, when its body turns bright red and the male develops a protruding, hooked jaw. During the autumn spawn, they are easily seen in Taylor Creek near the Forest Service visitor center on the South Shore. Kokanee salmon are not native to Lake Tahoe; they were planted in the 1940s to serve as a sport fish and have thrived well. Despite their small size, they are strong fighters and provide exciting fishing.

History

TAHOE'S FIRST VISITORS

Three separate tribes of the Washoe Indians spent summers at the shores of Lake Tahoe for thousands of years. Every year, as the days lengthened and warmed, the Washoes would travel from their winter homes in the Carson Valley to the shores of the lake, where they would harvest piñon nuts, fish in the lake's bountiful waters, and hunt the abundant game. The women of the tribes made woven baskets of exceptional artistry from the lakeshore's willows and grasses.

The huge lake did not appear on the radar of European Americans until 1844, when explorer John C. Fremont first sighted it during a February snowstorm. Fremont had been traveling for several months with the legendary scout Kit Carson and an expedition of 34 men, attempting to locate and map a waterway described by earlier geographers as the Buenaventura River, which supposedly flowed through the Sierra Nevada and into the Gulf of Mexico or San Francisco Bay. They had also heard tales of a big lake located somewhere high in the Sierra. Although Fremont's Washoe Indian guides warned him against traveling through the mountains in winter, the explorer pushed on, facing fierce weather, extreme deprivation, and arduous treks through deep snow. Fremont's famous diary entry from the night before his sighting of Lake Tahoe read: "We had tonight an extraordinary meal—pea soup, mule, and dog."

In the morning, when the skies had partially cleared, Fremont and mapmaker Charles Preuss climbed to the 10,651-foot summit of Red Lake Peak, 20 miles southwest of Lake Tahoe near what is now Carson Pass. Hoping to locate a suitable route through the mountains and down to the Sacramento Valley, they spied not only the pass but a section of the legendary lake

as well. Overjoyed at finding a way out of the snowy Sierra, the group set off immediately to the west and traveled down the South Fork of the American River to Sutter's Fort, a 16-day trek. Although Fremont did not lose a single man during the entire expedition, two of his party went mad from starvation and exhaustion. Only half of the party's 67 pack animals made it through the arduous trip; the rest had frozen or were eaten.

NAMING THE LAKE

After recovering from the journey, Fremont named the mystery lake "Bonpland" after a French botanist and explorer who had traveled with him on previous expeditions. The name never came into common usage, nor did Fremont's mapmaker's chosen name, the plain "Mountain Lake." By 1853, the official cartographers for the State of California had renamed Tahoe "Lake Bigler" in honor of the third governor of California, John Bigler. Bigler, to his credit, had led a rescue effort to the snowbound Donner party on the north shore of the lake in 1852. The lake's name stuck loosely for about a decade until 1862, when a federal cartographer for the Department of the Interior, William Henry Knight, began a crusade for the name Tahoe, which was believed to be the Indian name for the lake, translating to "big water" or "high water." (Today we know that the Washoe Indians called the area "Da'ow-a-ga" for "edge of the lake," but early explorers heard the unfamiliar sounds as "Tahoe.") Knight argued that Governor Bigler had not distinguished himself enough for history to name such a remarkable lake after him. In fact, after the Civil War broke out, Bigler was accused of being a Southern sympathizer and fell into public disfavor. Knight's arguments were convincing, and "Tahoe" became the moniker

TAHOE'S PLACE NAMES

Al Tahoe: This street and neighborhood in South Lake Tahoe was named for a hotel that once stood in the area, built in 1907 by Almerin (Al) Sprague. He named it after himself: the Al Tahoe Hotel.

Carson Pass: The pass and the river were named for Christopher (Kit) Carson (1809–1868), the scout and guide who aided John C. Fremont in his early explorations of the Sierra Nevada. Although the famous mountain man was illiterate, he dictated his autobiography, which became a best seller.

Dicks Peak and Dicks Lake: This peak and lake in the Desolation Wilderness was named after Captain Richard "Dick" Barter, who was known as the Hermit of Emerald Bay. He lived alone on Fannette Island for many years and spent his days drifting around the lake in a small rowboat.

Donner Lake, Pass, and Peak: All were named for brothers George and Jacob Donner, who with James F. Reed led the Donner Party of emigrants across the Sierra Nevada. Caught by an early snowstorm in October 1846, the party was marooned for the winter near what is now Donner Pass. More than three dozen members lost their lives to starvation and exposure. The Donner Party is remembered most for the fact that some of its survivors resorted to eating the bodies of their dead companions.

Jobs Peak and Jobs Sister: These two peaks south of Heavenly Ski Resort were named for Moses Job, a storekeeper who lived in Carson Valley, Nevada, in the 1850s. Jobs Sister is the second-highest mountain in Tahoe at 10,873 feet, topped only by nearby Freel Peak at 10,881 feet.

Lola Montez Lake and Mount Lola: The lake and peak near Donner Summit were named for a mid-1800s European dancer and showgirl who eventually settled in Grass Valley, where she ran a saloon and kept a pet bear. Throughout Lola's extravagant life she made colorful news for a variety of reasons, but she was perhaps most famous for her affairs with powerful men, including King Ludwig I of Bavaria, who made her a countess.

Markleeville: This small town in Carson Pass was named for settler Jacob Marklee in 1864, who lived at the site of what is now the Alpine County Courthouse. Marklee was killed in a gunfight a few years later.

Mount Pluto: The centerpiece of Northstar-at-Tahoe Ski Resort, Mount Pluto was one of the last volcanoes in Tahoe to erupt. Pluto is the name of the Roman god of the underworld and is named for plutonic rock, evidence of volcanic activity.

Mount Tallac: One of only two place names in the Tahoe basin that are derived from Native American names, Tallac is from the Washoe Indian word *dala'ak* (big mountain or great mountain). The only other Tahoe place name derived from the Washoe language is *tahoe* itself, which comes from *Da'ow* (big water or lake).

Ophir Creek: This stream near Mount Rose bears a biblical name referring to a "land of gold." A handful of towns throughout the Gold Country have also borne the name Ophir, but most of them no longer exist.

Truckee: The town and the river were named for a northern Paiute Indian chief who guided a party of emigrants across the Sierra in 1844. His name meant "all right" in the Paiute language.

---

with staying power. It did not become official, however, until 1945, when the California legislature put its seal on the name.

THE COMSTOCK LODE AND THE 1859 GOLD RUSH

Despite all the wrangling over what to call it, Tahoe remained little more than the peaceful gathering place of the Washoe Indians for

another 15 years after Fremont's sighting, although hundreds of emigrants traveling from the eastern United States to the goldfields and farmlands of California passed near its shores. None stayed long; they were bound by the hope of a prosperous future and single-mindedly sought their destination.

The quiet was shattered in 1859 with the discovery of the massive Comstock Lode of silver ore in Virginia City, Nevada, just east of Lake Tahoe. The timing of the strike was fortuitous, as the Union needed funds to finance the Civil War, and silver provided it. Miners and prospectors rushed in to Nevada from points west, where the California gold rush was already winding down. Whether they arrived from the north, at Donner Pass, or the south, at Carson Pass, they had to circle around Lake Tahoe to get to Virginia City. In a few short years, the Bonanza Road on the South Shore (now the route of Highway 50 and Pioneer Trail) was carved through the mountains, and it became the primary route to Nevada from San Francisco and Sacramento. Dozens of way stations, tollhouses, inns, stores, and livery stables sprung up along its path. Virginia City soon grew to be the second-largest city in the West, after San Francisco, and the road around Lake Tahoe was so busy that wagon drivers sometimes had to wait for hours before they could break into the nonstop stream of traffic. In 1860, one observer counted 350 wagons passing by in a single day.

The Comstock Lode provided silver ore, but the mines required massive quantities of lumber to shore up their tunnels, and the new boomtowns of Nevada required fuel for their boilers. With the densely wooded slopes of Lake Tahoe only 30 miles from the Comstock mines, the commerce of logging became as lucrative as mining. A timber empire was created, with an elaborate system of flumes, steamboats, barges, and incline railways utilized to transport lumber to Virginia City. The town of Glenbrook had four lumber mills by 1875, including the largest one run by lumber baron D. L. Bliss. Beginning on the east side of the lake and then spreading to most of its shoreline, thousands of pine trees that were hundreds of years old were felled to fuel the mines. The easy availability of these timber-rich forests led to their annihilation. Trees were felled, then transported by oxen or narrow-gauge railway

to the lake, where they were floated in large rafts to the lumber mills. After a while, this system was deemed too inefficient, so lengthy wooden flumes were built along the East Shore hills, then filled with water in which the timber was floated to the Glenbrook mills. To transport the milled lumber, a rail system was constructed from Glenbrook over Spooner Summit to Carson City. Another railway, known as the Great Incline, was built at the Hobart mills on the North Shore. In Carson City, the Virginia and Truckee Railroad served as the connecting link to the mines.

The appetite of the Comstock Lode was insatiable. Between 1860 and 1885, the entire East Shore was denuded. If the Comstock ore hadn't eventually played out, not a single tree would have been left standing anywhere around the lake.

Sadly, the environmental damage from this massive logging effort still affects the lake today. Vast amounts of sediment, which negatively impact Tahoe's water quality, entered the lake from the indiscriminate logging. The second- and third-growth trees that have grown up in place of the original logged forests are mostly moisture-loving red and white firs, which are not as well adapted to the Tahoe environment as the original pines were. A drought that began in the late 1980s weakened many of these firs; since then many have been killed by disease and an infestation of bark beetles. Although to the casual observer Tahoe's tree-lined shores may look rich and healthy, the forests still suffer the aftereffects of greed from more than a century ago.

THE RESORT ERA

By the close of the 19th century, wealthy families throughout California and Nevada had gotten word of the wonders of Lake Tahoe. Despite the rape of its landscape by lumber barons and mining engineers, the lake's virtues had been extolled by popular writers of the day, such as J. Ross Browne of *Harper's Weekly,* Horace Greeley of the *New York Times,* and humorist Mark Twain. The elite from San Francisco, Sacramento, and Nevada City flocked to the lakeshore, and luxurious hotels and resorts were constructed to accommodate them in fine style. Many marveled at the industrial wonders of the Glenbrook mills as much as the scenic beauty of the lake itself.

With the completion of the Central Pacific Railroad through Truckee in 1869, a critical link was made in the transcontinental rail line. Travel to the Tahoe area had become immensely easier than it was for the struggling emigrants who passed through here only two decades earlier. A passenger could board a train in San Francisco and be at the lakeshore in only nine hours. Tahoe-bound travelers disembarked at the Truckee depot, then took a 14-mile stagecoach ride to Tahoe City. Later, the stage was replaced by a narrow-gauge train, which traveled along the scenic Truckee River to the city (today the same route is a paved bike path). At Tahoe City, tourists could stay and play in the town's Grand Central Hotel, or board a steamship to cruise to Campbell's Hot Springs Resort on the North Shore, Tallac House on the South Shore, Glen Brook House on the East Shore, or a number of other lakeside resorts ranging from the rustic to the pretentious.

Until the 1920s, automobile use was not widespread and good roads had not yet been built, so steamships were the preferred mode of passenger travel at the lake. The steamers carried not just people but also mail, cargo, farm animals, groceries, and everything else that was needed by those who settled or vacationed at the lake. Vessels as large and grand as the 200-passenger SS *Tahoe* plied the waters, providing essential and nonessential services. The hour when the "mail boat" arrived was one of the high points of the day, when visitors would converge on the pier to see the "Graceful Lady" dock. When this ship and others like it outlived their usefulness, they were scuttled into the lake's depths.

The State of Nevada legalized gambling in 1931, and the resort era led to the onset of the casino era when Harvey's Gambling Wheel Saloon and Gambling Hall opened its doors. Gambling at Lake Tahoe proved to be so popular that by the 1940s, winter roads were regularly plowed to provide year-round access. By the 1950s, Tahoe had become both a summer and winter resort, and its fate as a major snowsports destination was sealed by the success of the 1960 Winter Olympics, held at Squaw Valley USA.

ESSENTIALS

Getting There and Around

BY AIR

The closest major airport to Lake Tahoe is **Reno-Tahoe International Airport** (2001 E. Plumb La., 775/328-6400, www.renoairport.com) in Nevada, a 30-minute drive from Incline Village on the northeast shore of the lake or a one-hour drive from South Lake Tahoe and Stateline on the south shore. The medium-size airport has two main terminals that serve Alaska, Allegiant, American, Delta, Horizon Air, Southwest, Ted, United, and US Airways airlines. Scattered among the gates are the usual cabal of airport shops: a Peets Coffee,

Pizza Hut, Taco Bell, Burger King, golf shop, and several gift shops and newsstands. Also, since Reno is in the gambling-friendly state of Nevada, travelers will find an abundance of slot machines throughout the airport. While waiting for your plane, you will be continually annoyed by these machines spouting the cry, "Wheel of Fortune!"

Tahoe-bound travelers can also fly into **Sacramento International Airport** (www.sacairports.org), which is a 2.5-hour drive from Lake Tahoe. Relatively small and pleasantly uncongested, Sacramento Airport is served by

© ANN MARIE BROWN

these airlines: Alaska, American, Continental, Delta, Frontier, Hawaiian, Horizon, Jet Blue, Mexicana, Northwest, Southwest, United, United Express, and US Airways. A typical array of airport restaurants and boutiques can be found here: Starbucks, Cinnabon, Burger King, Baja Fresh, several bookstores and souvenir shops, and the like.

Visitors might also want to look into flights at **San Francisco International Airport (SFO)** (www.flysfo.com) or the San Francisco Bay Area's two other major airports, in Oakland (www.oaklandairport.com) and San Jose (www.sjc.org). It is a four-hour drive from San Francisco or San Jose to Lake Tahoe; Oakland is about a half hour closer. Flights into Oakland or San Jose are often less expensive than flights into SFO.

Smaller airports are located at South Lake Tahoe and Truckee, but neither one has commercial service.

Airport Shuttles and Limousines

Shuttle services run between the Reno-Tahoe International Airport and both the South and North Shores. To get to the South Shore, contact South Tahoe Express (866/898-2463, www.southtahoeexpress.com, $27.50 per adult one-way or $49 round-trip), which offers several scheduled runs daily. To get from Reno Airport to the North Shore, contact North Lake Tahoe Express, which offers scheduled service 3:30 A.M.–midnight daily (866/216-5222, www.northlaketahoeexpress.com, $40 per person one-way, $75 round-trip, discounts for multiple people in your party).

For a more private and also pricier ride, on-demand limousine service is offered by Bell Limousine (775/786-3700 or 800/235-5466, www.bell-limo.com), Executive Limousine (775/333-3300, www.exlimo.com), or No Stress Express (775/885-9832, www.nostressexpress.com).

BY RENTAL CAR

Several major car-rental companies are located at Reno-Tahoe International Airport:
Advantage (800/777-5500, www.advantage.com), Alamo (877/222-9075, www.alamo.com), Avis (800/331-1212, www.avis.com), Budget (800/527-0700, www.budget.com), Dollar (800/800-3665, www.dollar.com), Enterprise (800/261-7331, www.enterprise.com), Hertz (800/654-3131, www.hertz.com), National (800/227-9058, www.nationalcar.com), and Thrifty (800/847-4389, www.thrifty.com).

Travelers flying into Sacramento or the San Francisco Bay Area airports also have their pick of all the major car-rental companies. Once you have arrived in Tahoe, you can also rent cars from Enterprise Rental Car in South Lake Tahoe (530/544-8844) and Truckee (530/550-1550).

Suggested Driving Routes

Visitors to Lake Tahoe coming from the west (**Sacramento** or the **San Francisco Bay Area**) should use **U.S. 50** to access the South Shore and **I-80** to access the North Shore. U.S. 50 splits off I-80 in downtown Sacramento and travels east through Placerville and over Echo Summit to South Lake Tahoe (about 2 hours or 100 miles from Sacramento and 3.5 hours or 200 miles from San Francisco). For visitors heading to the North Shore, I-80 continues east from Sacramento for another 90 miles to Truckee. At Truckee, take Highway 89 south for 15 miles to Tahoe City.

Visitors traveling to Lake Tahoe from the east (**Reno**) can take **U.S. 395** south for seven miles to Highway 431 west. Drive southwest on Highway 431 for 20 miles to Incline Village on the northeast shore of the lake. Or, to reach the South Shore directly, take U.S. 395 south from Reno through Carson City, then take **U.S. 50** west to South Lake Tahoe (about one hour or 60 miles). Or, to reach points near Tahoe City or the West Shore, take I-80 west from Reno for 32 miles to **Truckee**. In Truckee, connect to Highway 267 and travel south to the lakeshore at Tahoe Vista or Kings Beach (12 miles), or connect to Highway 89 and travel south to Tahoe City (15 miles).

To get current updates on road conditions on the California side of Lake Tahoe, phone 800/427-7623 or visit www.dot.ca.gov. To get current updates on Nevada road conditions, phone 877/687-6237 or visit www.safetravelusa.com.

One note: When crossing into California by automobile, all visitors are subject to agricultural inspections. These inspections are run by the California Department of Food and Agriculture (CDFA). The inspection may be as simple as an officer stopping your car momentarily to ask you where you have been traveling and if you are carrying any fruits, vegetables, or plants from other states. Be sure to declare anything you are carrying. In very rare cases, vehicles are searched. As a general rule, most out-of-state produce and plants should be kept out of California, unless they have been properly inspected by the CDFA. For more information on current regulations, phone the CDFA at 916/654-0462 or 800/675-2427.

BY RENTAL RV

RV rentals in Reno cost about the same as elsewhere in California and Nevada, which is basically the same nightly price as a stay in a good hotel. And like at hotels, your price will vary widely whether you are traveling during the high season (summer) or low season (Oct.–Apr.). For an RV that can sleep up to five people (about 32 feet long), expect to pay about $150–250 per night in the low season and as much as $250–450 per night in the high season (May–Sept.). On a night-by-night basis, you can save a little money by renting an RV for a week. Seven nights' rental will run about $1,400 during the low season, $2,000–2,500 during the high season. But don't forget to tack on the mileage fee. Most companies allow 100 free miles per day, and then charge a flat rate for extra mileage (typically about $0.30 per mile).

Also, plan to spend a small fortune on gasoline—most RVs get 6–10 miles to the gallon. The smallest rigs may get a whopping 14 miles per gallon.

The biggest and oldest RV rental company in Reno is Sierra RV (9125 S. Virginia St., Reno, 775/324-0522 or 800/972-8760, www.sierrarv.com). It rents RVs of all shapes and sizes, from 20-foot Class B motor homes that sleep only two to 35-foot motor homes that sleep eight. All are fully contained models with kitchen, bath, color TV, CD player, generator, and microwave. Pets and smoking are not permitted. The daily rate for 3–6 days is $100–300 (depending on the size of the rig and your travel dates); the weekly rate is $800–2,000. As with most RV rental companies, you get only 100 free miles per day. You'll pay $0.29 per mile for the first 2,000 extra miles.

If you'd rather go with a national chain, try **Cruise America** (Reno KOA at Boomtown Casino, 2100 Garson Rd., Verdi, 775/824-0576 or 800/671-8042, www.cruiseamerica.com), just off I-80.

In Sacramento, RV rentals are available at two Cruise America locations (800/671-8042, www.cruiseamerica.com). Expect to pay about $500 for three nights in the low season (Oct.–May) or $650 in the high season (June–Sept.) for an RV that can sleep six people. You can save a little money by renting an RV for a week. Seven nights' rental will run about $1,000 during the low season, $1,500 during the high season. But don't forget to tack on the mileage fee of $0.29 per mile.

GETTING AROUND
By Car

Except on the most crowded summer and winter holidays, driving a car around Lake Tahoe is quite easy. Parking, on the other hand, is another matter, especially at some of the top sightseeing destinations. If you are visiting the South Shore in summer, consider leaving your car at

Be sure to watch for wildlife crossing the road.

your lodging and taking the **Nifty Fifty Trolley** (530/541-7149, www.bluego.org). On the North Shore, public transportation is readily available through Tahoe Area Regional Transit and the **Tahoe Trolley** (TART, 530/550-1212 or 800/736-6365, www.laketahoetransit.com). In the winter months, almost all the ski resorts around the Tahoe basin are accessible by free public transportation. Check the website of the resort you are planning to visit for details.

When visiting Tahoe from November to April, know that chains may be required on any road at any time. Always carry chains in your car and know how to put them on your drive wheels. To get current updates on road conditions on the California side of Lake Tahoe, phone 800/427-7623 or visit www.dot.ca.gov. To get current updates on Nevada road conditions, phone 877/687-6237 or visit www.safetravelusa.com.

Maps

For visitors to the South Shore, a street map of South Lake Tahoe, Stateline, and its environs is available for a small fee from South Shore visitors centers. Hikers, mountain bikers, and others who want to explore beyond the highways will want a detailed trail map, such as the Lake Tahoe Recreation Map or Desolation Wilderness Trail Map published by **Tom Harrison Maps** (415/456-7940, www.tomharrisonmaps.com). These are available for a fee at most Tahoe outdoor stores and visitors centers or by ordering direct. Another good map for outdoor recreationists is the Lake Tahoe Trail Map by **Adventure Maps** (800/849-6589, www.adventuremaps.net), also available for a fee from Tahoe outdoor stores and visitors centers or by ordering direct.

Tours and Shuttle Buses

Discover Lake Tahoe Tours (530/542-1080, www.demotours.com, $50 adults, $35 children) offers narrated shuttle bus tours around the lake and to Virginia City most of the year. They also offer tours from the South Shore to Yosemite National Park and San Francisco.

In the summer months, the **Nifty Fifty Trolley** (530/541-7149, www.bluego.org) provides narrated tours combined with shuttle service along the length of the South Shore. The trolleys are open-sided buses—replicas of 19th-century streetcars with polished oak seats and brass poles—that allow riders to enjoy the fresh mountain air while they travel. Riders can get on and off as often as they like with a $5 all-day pass. Also in summer months, the **Tahoe Trolley** (800/736-6365, www.laketahoetransit.com) travels along much of the North and West Shores.

The South Shore casinos offer their own free shuttles to and from most lodgings along the U.S. 50 corridor. Most major ski resorts on both the North and South Shores also offer free winter ski shuttles from various locations to the slopes. Contact the individual resorts, or see the specific chapters in this book, for more information.

Tips for Travelers

BEFORE YOU GO

If you're visiting Lake Tahoe for the first time, you may be surprised to find that this mountainous region is by no means remote or cut off from the trappings and comforts of civilization. In fact, Tahoe has all the amenities of most small cities. Within a few miles of any spot around the lake's perimeter, you'll find major chain grocery stores, restaurants of both the upscale and hole-in-the-wall variety (and everything in between), lodgings of all types, gas stations, post offices, and even coffeehouses and day spas. This greatly relieves the pressure of packing for your trip to Tahoe. If you choose to, you can leave almost everything at home except for the clothes on your back. Anything you need, you can buy, particularly in the big towns of Tahoe City, Incline Village, South Lake Tahoe, and Stateline.

In the summer months, a few personal items you might want to pack are **hiking boots** or sturdy shoes for walking, and a small **day pack** or fanny pack. Even nonhikers are often inspired to take a walk on one of Lake Tahoe's myriad trails. Sturdy shoes or hiking boots are far more comfortable, and a lot safer, than the casual sightseeing shoes you might wear around town. A small day pack or fanny pack is useful for holding a bottle of water, a snack, and your camera.

It's also wise to bring a variety of **clothing for layering.** Weather changes constantly in the Sierra Nevada; it's smart to pack rain gear, jackets, and clothes for both warm and cool weather—even though you may spend your entire vacation in nothing but shorts and a T-shirt.

Numerous boat tours and cruises on the lake are available from both the North and South Shores; see the specific chapters for each region for more information.

The general rule of thumb for summer trips to Lake Tahoe: Bring warm clothes for evenings (especially if you're camping) and layers for daytime. Always carry lightweight rain gear with you, as summer afternoon thunderstorms are common. Spring and fall are cooler, so pack warmer layers.

For winter trips to the lake, always carry **snow chains** for your car tires, even if you have a four-wheel-drive vehicle. Although most of Tahoe's roads and highways are kept plowed in winter, chains are often required. It is far less expensive to buy chains for your car at a big-box store in a large city (Wal-Mart–type stores carry chains, as well as auto supply stores) than it is to buy or rent them at Lake Tahoe.

FOREIGN TRAVELERS
Entering the United States and California

Generally, citizens of foreign countries who wish to visit the United States must first obtain a visa. To apply for a visa, applicants must prove that the purpose of their trip to the United States is for business, pleasure, or medical treatment; that they plan to remain for a limited period of time; and that they have a residence outside the United States as well as other binding ties that will guarantee their return abroad.

However, under the Visa Waiver Program, citizens of 36 foreign countries do not need a visa for travel to the United States, provided they are staying no more than 90 days. The countries are: Andorra, Australia, Austria, Belgium, Brunei, Czech Republic, Denmark, Estonia, Finland, France, Germany, Greece,

Hungary, Iceland, Ireland, Italy, Japan, Latvia, Liechtenstein, Lithuania, Luxembourg, Malta, Monaco, the Netherlands, New Zealand, Norway, Portugal, San Marino, Singapore, Slovakia, Slovenia, South Korea, Spain, Sweden, Switzerland, and the United Kingdom.

As part of the customs process, the U.S. Department of Agriculture screens all foreign visitors at their first point of arrival in the United States (usually, at the airport). Foreigners must declare, in writing, all fruits, vegetables, fruit and vegetable products, meat, meat products, and dairy products that they have brought from another country. Failure to declare an apple or orange, or a leftover sandwich containing meat, can lead to a major delay in getting through customs.

Once a foreign visitor is inside the United States, he or she may travel freely from state to state. However, all visitors (foreign or not) are subject to additional agricultural inspections when entering California by automobile from bordering states. A California Department of Food and Agriculture (CDFA) officer may stop your car momentarily to ask you where you've been traveling and if you are carrying any fruits, vegetables, or plants from other states. In rare cases, vehicles are searched. Most out-of-state produce and plants should be kept out of California. For more information on current regulations, phone the CDFA consumer help line at 800/675-2427 or 916/654-0462.

Finally, there is no compulsory or government insurance plan in the United States. Foreign travelers are advised to purchase travel and health insurance in case of an emergency.

Money and Currency Exchange

Most large banks in the United States exchange major foreign currencies. Several major American banks (Wells Fargo, Bank of America, Bank of the West, and others) are found in the cities of South Lake Tahoe, Incline Village, and Tahoe City. Large international airports such as Reno-Tahoe also have currency exchange offices in their terminals.

While traveling in California, your best bet is to use traveler's checks and credit cards for purchases (both are accepted widely), and use an ATM (automated teller machine) to get cash. ATMs are found at various locations around the lake.

Electricity

Electrical current in the United States is 110 volts. A hair dryer or electric shaver from England or Germany won't work here without an adapter, which is available at most travel stores.

Foreign-Language Assistance

Within the United States, you may phone 888/US1-INFO (888/871-4636) for free access to emergency services and travel assistance in more than 140 languages.

California and Nevada Laws

You must be 21 years of age to purchase and/or drink alcohol in California or Nevada. Drinking and driving is a serious crime in both states; the simple act of having an open container of alcohol in your car, even if it is empty, is punishable by law. If you are arrested for driving under the influence of alcohol, you must submit to a chemical test to determine blood alcohol content.

Sending text messages or talking on a handheld cell phone is illegal while driving in California or Nevada. It is legal to talk on your phone if you are using a hands-free device (earpiece). Also, you must wear a seat belt while driving or riding in a car in California or Nevada.

Smoking is prohibited on public transportation and in all public buildings in California. Restaurants and bars also prohibit smoking. For the most part, you aren't allowed to light up unless you are in a private space or outside in an open area. If someone asks you to put out your cigarette, it's best to do so, because chances are good that they have the law on their side. In Nevada, the opposite is true—smoking is allowed almost everywhere, unless a business has its own individual policy about smoking. You must be 18 years of age to purchase tobacco products in California or Nevada.

Gambling is legal in the state of Nevada for persons over the age of 21.

Taxes and Tipping

The Nevada state sales tax is 6.85 percent, but local taxes as high as 1.0 percent are usually added on top of that. The California state sales tax is 8.25 percent, but local taxes as high as 1.25 percent may be tacked on, adding a total 9.5 percent to almost everything you buy.

At sit-down restaurants in either state, it is customary to tip 15 percent on top of the bill. The tip is your payment to your food server for good service. Most servers count on your tip as part of their day's pay.

TRAVELING BY RV

Recreational vehicles (RVs) are welcome at Lake Tahoe, although some drivers may find it difficult to negotiate them on mountain roads and through the lakeshore traffic. If you are planning to camp in your RV, check the *Accommodations* sections of this book to see which campgrounds have sites specifically for RVs, including hookups and dump stations.

TRAVELING WITH CHILDREN

Families and Lake Tahoe are a perfect match. Tahoe is an ideal place to teach kids about nature and the environment. Kids invariably have fun in the outdoors, and with all the kid-friendly activities around the lake, parents are never left wondering what to do with their charges. At Tahoe, kids can go for hikes, climb on rocks, learn about the local flora and fauna, ride bikes, toast marshmallows, go rafting, ride horses, go skiing or sledding or snowboarding, go boating, or just hang out in a meadow and

be kids. The list of possible activities for kids at Lake Tahoe is endless—just as it is for adults. And if your kid is more inclined toward "man-made" activities, Tahoe also has a good supply of gaming arcades, bowling alleys, miniature golf courses, climbing walls, ziplines, and the like.

TRAVELING WITH PETS

Traveling with your pet to Lake Tahoe is a reasonable proposition, given the number of area hiking trails and other outdoor activities where pets are permitted. Some (but not many) lodgings allow pets, and most campgrounds do as well. Always contact lodgings in advance to make sure they permit pets, and to let them know that you plan to bring yours. Where pets are allowed, there is often an additional fee or deposit charged. Remember that if you choose to camp with your pet, he or she should be in your tent, RV, or car at night, or you risk having your pet tangle with a bear or other wild animal. Pets should never be left unattended at any time, and you should always clean up after your pet.

HEALTH AND SAFETY

If you should happen to have a medical problem while you are visiting Lake Tahoe, you'll be in good hands. Several hospitals and 24-hour emergency medical centers are located around the lake. On the South Shore, there is **Barton Memorial Hospital** (2170 South Ave., South Lake Tahoe, 530/541-3420, www.bartonhealth.org) as well as two 24-hour emergency-care centers: **Tahoe Urgent Care** (2130 Hwy. 50, South Lake Tahoe, 530/541-3277) and **Stateline Medical Center** (150 Hwy. 50, Stateline, 775/589-8900).

On the North and East Shores, there is **Tahoe Forest Hospital** (10121 Pine Ave. at Donner Pass Rd., Truckee, 530/587-6011 or 800/733-9953, www.tfhd.com), **Incline Village Community Hospital** (880 Alder Ave., Incline Village, 775/833-4100, www.tfhd.com), or

FUN WITH FIDO

There's only one place your dog wants to be, and that's with you. And since Tahoe offers a lot for a doggie to do, why leave him or her at home when you go on vacation?

Reserve a **pet-friendly lodging** in advance. Always state clearly that you want to bring your dog and inquire about the current rules and fees for pets. Usually you will be asked about the size and breed of your dog; some lodgings only allow small dogs or "friendly" breeds. Most lodgings charge a per-night fee for your dog; many require a deposit. Pet policies change from time to time, so make sure you know what you're signing up for before forking over your credit card.

Some excellent dog-friendly accommodations on the South Shore are the Fireside Lodge, Motel 6, Best Western Timber Cove Lodge, Super 8 Motel, 3 Peaks Resort and Beach Club, Park Tahoe Inn, and Avalon Lodge. Favorite doggie lodgings on the North and West Shores are the cabins at Tahoma Meadows Bed and Breakfast near Homewood or those at Rustic Cottages in Kings Beach. Sporty dogs choose the Cedar House Sport Hotel in Truckee, while rafting dogs prefer the River Ranch Lodge near Alpine Meadows, and snowshoeing and hiking dogs hoof it to the Lost Trail Lodge.

Budget-minded dogs will prefer to **camp** rather than paying for a roof over their heads and HBO each night. Most campgrounds allow leashed dogs, except for a few private ones, like Camp Richardson. Advance reservations are a necessity in the summer months.

With your sleeping arrangements secured, you're ready to have fun. Swimming dogs will enjoy a **dog paddle** in some of the lake's calmer waters. The best beaches that permit dogs are at Fallen Leaf Lake on the South Shore; Kiva Beach on the southwest shore; Chimney, Hidden, and Secret Beaches on the East Shore; and Lake Forest Beach and Coon Street Beach on the North Shore. If your dog is a retriever, don't forget the tennis balls.

Seafaring dogs have options, too. If your dog has good balance and won't tip the boat over, you can go **kayaking.** Kayak Tahoe leads guided tours along the East Shore and Emerald Bay, and good dogs are permitted. Or rent a kayak and paddle on your own (if you have a big dog, rent a double kayak). Dogs are also permitted on the inflatable **rafts** that float the Truckee River from Tahoe City to River Ranch. Dogs can ride as passengers on the **boat taxi** at Echo Lake ($5 for dogs, more for humans). Take the boat to the far side of the upper lake, then hike back along the shoreline; or ride the boat both ways.

Incline Village Urgent Care (995 Tahoe Blvd./ Hwy. 28, Incline Village, 775/833-2929).

Winter is often the most accident-prone time at Lake Tahoe, and this is mostly because of the hazards created by winter driving. The most important rule for driving in snow or ice is to *slow down.* From November to March, always carry chains in the trunk or your car or truck, even if your vehicle has four-wheel drive. You may be required by law to use them, or you may simply need them if you get stuck in an icy or snow-packed parking lot.

Winter can also bring hazards for ill-prepared skiers and snowshoers. Always check the weather report before setting out for outdoor adventures in winter, and always dress in multiple layers, including an outer layer that will keep you dry. It's a good idea to carry an extra set of clothes, and especially shoes and socks, in your car. Don't forget to wear sunscreen in the winter months; the sun may be lower in the sky, but its reflection off the snow combined with Tahoe's high elevation can be a recipe for skin damage.

In the summer months, by far the biggest dangers to be faced at Lake Tahoe are those created by visitors who don't follow posted rules and regulations. Food storage rules top that list. If you are picnicking or camping, always store your food away when you aren't eating so

If your dog is a landlubber, romp in the woods instead. Dogs are allowed on all **hiking trails** in Tahoe National Forest and the Desolation Wilderness, but not in state parks like D. L. Bliss and Emerald Bay. For an experience your dog can brag about back home, in summer go for a ride on the **cable car** at Squaw Valley USA (there is no charge for leashed, well-behaved dogs), then hike back downhill through beautiful Shirley Canyon.

In the winter months, your dog can go **skiing.** No, dogs can't ride on the chairlift, but two cross-country ski resorts allow dogs on some of their trails: Kirkwood Cross-Country in Carson Pass and Tahoe Cross-Country on the North Shore. All of Tahoe's Sno-Park trails are also open to dogs.

At a few outdoor **restaurants,** your dog can join you (but always check with management beforehand). Two popular dog-friendly spots are the picnic tables outside of Sprouts Café and the Burger Lounge in South Lake Tahoe. Dogs always enjoy a good picnic, so pack a basket of doggie treats and human food and head out to Kiva Beach (South Shore) or Lake Forest Beach (North Shore) for supper and sunset on the sand.

Before traveling with your dog, pack a few essentials: a six-foot leash, a collar with easily readable identification tags, and pick-up bags, so you can help to keep Lake Tahoe beautiful and clean.

© ANN MARIE BROWN

Take Fido along with you on the Winnemucca Lake Loop Trail.

that you don't attract bears and smaller critters like squirrels and chipmunks. Although Tahoe's bears are black bears, not grizzlies, and not threatening to humans, they will do just about anything to get human food. Don't tempt them.

Pay special attention to signs posted at trailheads and campgrounds. If a sign says Stay Back from the Edge, obey it. Be wary of waterfalls, slick hiking trails, and cliffs and ledges with steep drop-offs. Remain on the trails to avoid getting lost or getting yourself into a hazardous situation. Always carry a good trail map. If you are heading out for a hike, tell someone where you are going and when you will be back.

Carry a pack filled with the essentials for a day out, and a few emergency items.

A few more rules to live by: Don't drink water from streams and lakes without purifying it; carry and use a filter for purifying water from natural sources, or pack along bottled water. While you're at it, take along extra water and food; if you don't need it, you can give it to someone who does. Many visitors come to Tahoe from lower elevations and are surprised at how thirsty they feel even before they start to exercise. Tahoe's dry air and high elevation can easily create conditions for dehydration; drink more water, and carry more water with you than you think you will need.

While hiking, be aware of your surroundings: Pay attention to the direction you've traveled and landmarks you've passed. Keep an eye out for approaching storms, and stay off exposed ridges and peaks if a thunderstorm is threatening. Watch yourself and your companions for symptoms of altitude sickness and problems encountered from high elevation.

ACCESSIBILITY

Many of Lake Tahoe's best attractions and sites are accessible to visitors in wheelchairs. On the South Shore, these include the Taylor Creek Visitor Center and the Stream Profile Chamber, the Tallac Historic Site, Inspiration Point at Emerald Bay, the Heavenly Gondola, Kahle Park, and Vikingsholm. Some of the South Shore's best beaches are also wheelchair accessible, including Zephyr Cove and Nevada Beach. The popular boat cruises on the paddle wheelers MS *Dixie* and *Tahoe Queen* are also accessible.

On the North and West Shores, accessible sights and beaches include the Gatekeeper's Cabin Museum, William Kent Beach, and Donner Memorial State Park. On the East Shore, the Tahoe Meadows area near Incline Village and Mount Rose has a beautiful 1.3-mile wheelchair-accessible trail, and Spooner Lake State Park has several wheelchair-accessible areas.

Public transportation around Lake Tahoe, through Blue Go on the South Shore and Tahoe Area Regional Transit on the North Shore, is also accessible. Also, there are numerous paved biked paths around Lake Tahoe, which are well suited for wheelchair travel.

For more information on accessibility at Lake Tahoe, contact the **Tahoe Area Coordinating Council for the Disabled** (530/544-1127, www. tahoeareacoordinatingcouncilforthedisabled. com). Their website contains an excellent list of lodgings, campgrounds, attractions, restaurants, and transportation services that are accessible. All of Lake Tahoe's visitors centers also have information on accessible sights, attractions, lodgings, and restaurants.

INFORMATION AND SERVICES

If you've just arrived in town, the best sources for all-around information, maps, and brochures are the area visitors centers. On the South Shore, head to the **Lake Tahoe Visitors Authority**'s Nevada office (169 Hwy. 50, 3rd Fl., Stateline, 775/588-5900, www.tahoesouth. com), located across from Lakeside Inn and Casino, or its California office (3066 Hwy. 50, South Lake Tahoe, 530/544-5050, www. tahoesouth.com), located next door to the Lake Tahoe Historical Society Museum near El Dorado Beach. For recreation information, go to **Explore Tahoe: An Urban Trailhead** (4114 Hwy. 50, South Lake Tahoe, 530/542-2908, www.cityofslt.us) or the **U.S. Forest Service office** (35 College Dr., South Lake Tahoe, 530/543-2600, www.fs.fed.us/r5/ltbmu).

On the North Shore, head to the **Tahoe City Visitors Information Center** (380 N. Lake Blvd., Tahoe City, 530/581-6900 or 888/434-1262, www.gotahoenorth.com). For information about Truckee and nearby areas, try the **Truckee Donner Visitors Center** (10065 Donner Pass Rd., Truckee, 530/587-8808, www.truckee.com). And in Incline Village, go to the **Incline Village/Crystal Bay Visitors Bureau and Chamber of Commerce** (969 Tahoe Blvd./Hwy. 28 in Incline Village, 775/832-1606 or 800/468-2463, www.gotahoenorth.com).

RESOURCES

Suggested Reading

GEOLOGY

Hill, Mary. *Geology of the Sierra Nevada.* Berkeley, CA: University of California Press, 1975. Even though it is more than 30 years old, this useful book is still of great interest to Tahoe hikers and travelers with inquiring minds who marvel at glacially sculpted wonders such as Emerald Bay, and the granitic and volcanic peaks surrounding Lake Tahoe. Multiple illustrations and photos help to explain the results of the forces of geology in action.

Konigsmark, Ted. *Geologic Trips: Sierra Nevada.* Mendocino, CA: Bored Feet Press, 2003. Written for the layman, this book interprets more than 100 of the most famous geologic landmarks in the Sierra Nevada, from Half Dome in Yosemite to Emerald Bay and Cave Rock at Lake Tahoe. It's a fun read even for those who are geologically challenged.

HUMAN HISTORY

Calabro, Marian. *The Perilous Journey of the Donner Party.* New York, NY: Clarion Books/Houghton Mifflin, 1999. For children who want to learn more about the tragedy of the Donner Party, this book tells the tale from the perspective of 13-year-old Donner Party survivor Virginia Reed. The author includes an epilogue on many of the party's survivors and reprints in its entirety a letter written by Virginia after she was rescued. The book won a California Library Association Beatty Award for a young-adult book that promotes awareness of California history.

Dixon, Kelly J. *Boomtown Saloons: Archaeology and History in Virginia City.* Reno, NV: University of Nevada Press, 2005. This scholarly but approachable account of the excavation of four historic saloon sites in Virginia City presents scientific evidence of what life was truly like in the great silver-mining era. Using historical photographs and maps and modern-day technology such as DNA analysis, the author's research supports the theory that Western saloons were not as wild as legend leaves us to believe, but rather that they served an important and complex social role in their communities.

Donner Houghton, Eliza P. *The Expedition of the Donner Party and Its Tragic Fate.* Lincoln, NE: University of Nebraska Press, 1997. Originally published in 1911, this book was written by George Donner's youngest daughter, Eliza, who was only four years old at the time of the Donner Party's ill-fated journey. Her recollections were later substantiated by her older siblings and other survivors. She also recounts parts of her life story after the party's rescue, detailing the difficulties of being known as a member of the infamous Donner family.

Frohlich, Robert. *Mountain Dreamers: Visionaries of Sierra Nevada Skiing.* Arnold, CA: Coldstream Press, 1997. Ski aficionados will enjoy this account of the development and promotion of ski resorts at Lake Tahoe, Yosemite, and elsewhere around the Sierra. The story begins with the original 12-foot-long wooden skis, the first rope tows, and the introduction of the American public to skiing, and leads up to today's high-tech equipment and megaresorts.

Frohlich, Robert, and S. E. Humphries. *Skiing with Style: Sugar Bowl 60 Years.* Arnold, CA: Coldstream Press, 1999. The story of one of the oldest and grandest ski resorts in the West is told in detail, complete with more than 100 black-and-white photographs and quotes from Sugar Bowl's first investors, ski instructors, and managers. The focus of the book is on Hannes Schroll, the man who in the 1930s envisioned and created a European-style resort similar to those from his native Austria, but many other characters who played a part in Sugar Bowl's history also are featured.

Landauer, Lyndall Baker. *The Mountain Sea: A History of Lake Tahoe.* Honolulu, HI: Flying Cloud Press, 1996. Written by a respected historian and past editor of the Lake Tahoe Historical Society's newsletter, this is the most complete version of Lake Tahoe's history in print. For readers who wish to learn more about Tahoe's resort era, the Comstock boom and subsequent development of roads around the lake, the grand steamships of the late 19th century, or the beginning of the gambling era, this hard-to-find book is the ultimate reference.

Lavender, David. *Snowbound: The Tragic Story of the Donner Party.* New York, NY: Holiday House, 1996. A kid-friendly book covering the chronicles of the ill-fated Donner Party, it also features dozens of black-and-white photographs and illustrations. Unlike many Donner Party books, this one focuses more on the overall dangers and hardships of emigrant travel than on the infamous Donner cannibalism, providing a more general description of the suffering endured by the pioneer wagon trains that crossed the Sierra Nevada in the mid-19th century.

Lekisch, Barbara. *Embracing Scenes About Lakes Tahoe and Donner: Painters, Illustrators, and Sketch Artists, 1855–1915.* Lafayette, CA: Great West Books, 2003. Providing an unusual take on Tahoe history, this book contains brief biographies, diary entries, and letters of more than 150 artists who drew their inspiration from the Tahoe region, including reproductions of their paintings, illustrations, and sketches.

Lekisch, Barbara. *Tahoe Place Names: The Origin and History of Names in the Lake Tahoe Basin.* Lafayette, CA: Great West Books, 1988. This is the book you need if you find yourself wondering what "Tallac" means (it is "Great Mountain," and it's the only mountain at Lake Tahoe that has a Washoe name) or pondering the origin of the moniker "Heavenly Valley" (it was a purely commercial invention, thought up by the ski resort's marketing team). The book also serves as a great introduction to Tahoe's long and varied history; for example, descriptions of Snowshoe Thompson's remarkable feats are listed under the Thompson Peak entry. The January–February 1844 diary of Charles Preuss, who with explorer John Fremont was one of the first white men to see Lake Tahoe, is reprinted as an appendix.

McLaughlin, Mark. *Sierra Stories: True Tales of Tahoe* and *Sierra Stories: True Tales of Tahoe Volume Two.* Carnelian Bay, CA: Mic Mac

Publishing, 1997 and 1998. Both books contain a series of short and fascinating biographies of some of Tahoe's most interesting characters, including "Lucky" Baldwin, Nelly Bly, Mark Twain, D. L. Bliss, a ragtag assortment of miners, and the bold pioneer women of the West.

Mullen, Frank Jr. *The Donner Party Chronicles: A Day-to-Day Account of a Doomed Wagon Train, 1846–1847.* Reno, NV: Nevada Humanities Committee, 1997. Of the dozens of books available on the Donner Party tragedy, this one also serves as a guide to present-day evidence of the Emigrant Trail, including color photographs of still-existing wagon ruts and landmarks. The author provides a day-by-day chronicle of the Donner Party's travels from the Midwest to California, following the misleading route advice of an enterprising land speculator.

Oberding, Janice. *Legends and Ghosts of the Lake Tahoe Area.* Reno, NV: Thunder Mountain Productions Press, 2004. Written by an expert on ghosts and paranormal activity, this volume tells the ghostly stories of Tahoe travelers and visitors, from the Donner Party to Marilyn Monroe. If you ever suspected that the Cal-Neva Resort or the Thunderbird Lodge might be haunted, this book is for you.

Scott, Edward B. *The Saga of Lake Tahoe: A Complete Documentation of Lake Tahoe's Development Over the Last 100 Years.* Antioch, CA: Sierra-Tahoe Publishing Company, 1957. Part history book and part photo collection, this volume documents Lake Tahoe's history from 1857 to 1957, with nearly 300 photographs and a large foldout map of the lake. It includes authentic images of the Bonanza Trail, the Tahoe lumber industry, and the steamships and wooden vessels that once sailed Tahoe's waters.

Stewart, George R. *Ordeal by Hunger: The Story of the Donner Party.* New York, NY: Mariner Books, 1992. Written by a noted historian who taught for more than 50 years at the University of California, Berkeley, this book is considered to be the definitive history of the Donner Party's trials. Stewart incorporates the survivors' diaries and other historical documents in his account.

Strong, Douglas Hillman. *Tahoe: An Environmental History.* Lincoln, NE: University of Nebraska Press, 1984. The only book available that details Tahoe's complex environmental problems and their historical origins, this book is a fascinating account of the damage done by 19th-century logging and farming and 20th-century urbanization, and the difficult political and scientific processes required to preserve the lake today.

Strong, Douglas Hillman. *Tahoe: From Timber Barons to Ecologists.* Lincoln, NE: University of Nebraska Press, 1999. An environmental history of the Lake Tahoe area, this book tells the history of the Tahoe area from its use by the indigenous Washoe people to the present. To whom does Tahoe belong, and how should the area be used? This book examines the struggle among contending forces with widely different answers to this question, and includes original photographs by local photographer Jim Hildinger.

Wheeler, Sessions, and William W. Bliss. *Tahoe Heritage: The Bliss Family of Glenbrook, Nevada.* Reno, NV: University of Nevada Press, 1997. More than a century ago, Duane L. Bliss, the namesake of the West Shore's D. L. Bliss State Park, built a lumber empire on the shores of Lake Tahoe. This story tells Bliss's enterprising saga, including his transition from lumber baron to railway builder to owner of the renowned Glenbrook Inn.

NATURAL HISTORY

Arno, Stephen F. *Discovering Sierra Trees.* Yosemite National Park: Yosemite Association and Sequoia Natural History Association, 1973. Beautifully illustrated, this brief, 89-page tree guide gives thorough and easily digestible descriptions of 19 conifers and 17 broad-leaved trees of the Sierra. The author's lyrical writing is a pleasure, even if you are far from the nearest Jeffrey pine or mountain hemlock.

Blackwell, Laird R. *Wildflowers of the Tahoe Sierra: From Forest Deep to Mountain Peak.* Redmond, WA: Lone Pine Publishing, 1997. This compact and indispensable wildflower guide, written by a Sierra Nevada college professor, details the common colorful blooms of the Tahoe basin. High-quality color photographs and descriptive text make it easy to identify more than 100 flowers, and the spiral-bound book is small enough to fit in a pocket or backpack.

Carville, Julie Stauffer. *Hiking Tahoe's Wildflower Trails.* Redmond, WA: Lone Pine Publishing, 1989. A longtime resident of Tahoe, author Julie Carville shares her local knowledge about where to see the best wildflower displays. A combination hiking-trail book and wildflower field guide, this book describes in detail a variety of hikes for all ability levels and nearly 300 wildflowers that you may see along the trails. Featuring more than 100 illustrations and some color photos, this book was previously published by Mountain Gypsy Press and titled *Lingering in Tahoe's Wild Gardens: A Guide to Hundreds of the Most Beautiful Wildflower Gardens of the Tahoe Region.*

Graf, Michael. *Plants of the Tahoe Basin: Flowering Plants, Trees, and Ferns.* Berkeley, CA: University of California Press, 1999. Filled with hundreds of beautiful full-color photographs, this comprehensive guide covers more than 600 species of flowering plants, the majority being wildflowers. The book is organized taxonomically (alphabetized by scientific classification) rather than by flower color, which may prove challenging to beginners, yet is a great way to learn about plant families, genera, and species. For each flower, identification clues are provided, as well as notes on where in the Tahoe basin to find it.

Haulenbeek, Rod. *Tree Adventures at Tahoe.* Carnelian Bay, CA: Wide Eyed Publications, 1995. In this small self-published volume, the author takes readers on an intimate tour of Tahoe's most interesting trees. The book serves as a personal travel companion, pointing out not just interesting facts about the trees but also the highways, towns, geology, and wildlife around them.

Horn, Elizabeth L. *Sierra Nevada Wildflowers.* Missoula, MT: Mountain Press Publishing Company, 1998. Good photographs accompany descriptions of more than 300 species of flowering plants and shrubs. Unlike most flower identification guides, this one is organized alphabetically by scientific classification (not by color of flower), which could prove problematic for novices. Still, the photographs and descriptions are useful, and the information is solid.

Laws, John Muir. *Sierra Birds: A Hiker's Guide.* Berkeley, CA: Heydey Books, 2004. Perfectly sized to fit in a hiker's back pocket, this beautifully illustrated, thoroughly annotated, and uniquely arranged guide is one that anyone can use to identify birds in the Sierra Nevada. Includes over 200 species of birds, arranged by color and size.

Paruk, Jim. *Sierra Nevada Tree Identifier.* Yosemite National Park: Yosemite Association,

1997. This practical guide to the Sierra's 20 conifers and 24 broad-leaved trees provides useful tips on tree identification as well as an interesting natural history of each species.

Stokes, Donald, and Lillian Stokes. *Field Guide to Birds: Western Region.* New York, NY: Little, Brown, and Company, 1996. Utilizing more than 900 full-color photographs, the authors have created an unintimidating bird guidebook that is respected by novice and expert birders alike. General identification information is provided for each species, as well as feeding, nesting, and other characteristic behaviors.

Tekiela, Stan. *Birds of California Field Guide.* Cambridge, MN: Adventure Publications, 2003. This pocket-size guide is easy to carry along the trail and includes gorgeous close-up photos of each bird. Although it is not as comprehensive as the Stokes guide, it's a better choice for hikers and backpackers.

Wiese, Karen. *Sierra Nevada Wildflowers.* Helena, MT: Falcon Publishing, 2000. This wildflower guide is loaded with clear, easy-to-see photographs of more than 230 wildflowers specific to the Sierra Nevada. In addition to the expected descriptive information, each listing includes an explanation of the flower's genus or species name and other interesting facts.

OUTDOOR RECREATION

Bonser, Carol, and R. W. Miskimins. *Mountain Biking South Lake Tahoe's Best Trails* and *Mountain Biking North Lake Tahoe's Best Trails.* Bishop, CA: Mountain Biking Press/ Fine Edge Productions, 1997 and 1998. These two slim volumes feature about 40 rides apiece in the South and North Shore areas. Although some of the information is outdated, the books serve as a good general guide to trail rides around the lake, and both include useful appendices on mountain-biking skills, bike maintenance, and roadside repairs.

Carville, Mike. *Rock Climbing Lake Tahoe.* Helena, MT: Falcon Publishing, 1999. More than 1,000 routes at a dozen major climbing areas around Lake Tahoe are described, including Donner Pass, the Truckee River Canyon, Christmas Valley, Echo Pass, Lover's Leap, Phantom Spires, Eagle Creek Canyon, East Shore Crags, Sugarloaf, Pie Shop, and Indian Springs. Due to the 1999 publication date, some of the information is outdated (access roads have closed; regulations have changed), but the maps and cliff drawings are excellent. Bouldering, toproping, and ice climbing are also briefly covered.

Haggard, Stephen Rider. *Fly Fishing the Tahoe Region.* Truckee, CA: Aquabonita Books, 2002. Everything a fly-fishing angler needs to know to fish 77 streams and 97 lakes in the Desolation Wilderness, Truckee and Carson River drainages, and other Tahoe regions is in this book, including information on hatches, directions and access, nearby lodging and services, and angling regulations.

Hauserman, Tim. *The Tahoe Rim Trail: A Complete Guide for Hikers, Mountain Bikers, and Equestrians.* Berkeley, CA: Wilderness Press, 2008. This second edition of the Tahoe Rim Trail guide was written with an enjoyable dose of humor. The book divides the 165-mile Rim Trail into eight segments, each described in detail, with attention paid to the needs of the trail's three user groups: hikers, bikers, and horseback riders. Worthwhile side trips off the trail are also described. The author is a member of the Tahoe Rim Trail Board of Directors and has walked every inch of the trail.

Jackson, Lorene. *Mountain Biking Lake Tahoe: A Guide to Lake Tahoe and Truckee's Greatest Off-Road Bicycle Rides.* Helena, MT: Falcon Publishing, 2006. Expert mountain biker Lorene Jackson describes her favorite routes, from easy cruising along the Emigrant Trail to hard-core technical rides on segments of the Tahoe Rim Trail. The ride descriptions include GPS-compatible trail maps and route profiles, mile-by-mile directional cues, difficulty ratings, average riding times, and best seasons to ride.

Jeneid, Michael. *Adventure Kayaking from the Russian River to Monterey, Including Lake Tahoe, Mono Lake, and Pyramid Lake.* Berkeley, CA: Wilderness Press, 1998. Although this book includes only two kayak tours in the Lake Tahoe area, it features accurate instructions on put-in sites, suggested paddle routes and campsites, notes on the presence of powerboats or picnickers, information on local birds and wildlife, and a detailed map for each route. Armchair readers will enjoy the author's first-person kayaking anecdotes.

Jeheid, Michael. *Cross-Country Skiing California.* Berkeley, CA: Wilderness Press, 2000. Covering 22 cross-country ski resorts, including a half dozen near Lake Tahoe, this book has driving directions, a description of each resort's offerings, information on trail passes and rental fees, and suggestions on accommodations. A general introduction to cross-country skiing and a wealth of how-to advice is included. The author is a certified cross-country ski instructor.

Libkind, Marcus. *Ski Tours in the Sierra Nevada: Lake Tahoe* and *Ski Tours in the Sierra Nevada: Carson Pass, Bear Valley, and Pinecrest.* Glendale, CA: Bittersweet Publishing Company, 1995. With tours for every level of cross-country skier, from beginner to expert, these two books provide useful information for those who wish to kick and glide across dozens of routes around Lake Tahoe and Carson Pass. Each ski trail description includes clear directions to the starting and ending points, a topographic map, and ratings for overall difficulty, trail length, and elevation change.

McNamara, Chris. *South Lake Tahoe Climbing.* South Lake Tahoe: Supertopo, 2004. This comprehensive rock-climbing guide to various sites near the South Shore (Christmas Valley, Echo Pass, Lover's Leap, Phantom Spires, Wrights Lake) includes lots of interesting climbing history, as well as practical where-to and how-to information and gorgeous climbing photos.

Pike, Charlie. *Paddling Northern California.* Helena, MT: Falcon Publishing, 2001. This kayaking guide contains only a smattering of Lake Tahoe tours, but it offers detailed maps with put-in information and trip landmarks, a useful introduction on how to prepare for a kayaking trip, and appendices of local paddling organizations and information resources.

Soares, Mark. *Snowshoe Routes: Northern California.* Seattle, WA: The Mountaineers, 2002. Descriptions of 66 different snowshoe trails in Northern California, including Lake Tahoe, Mount Shasta, Lassen Peak, Yosemite, and the Eastern Sierra. For each route, the book shows total distance and time of hike, elevation, and difficulty levels from easy to strenuous. Clear maps are provided, with easy directions to trailheads and driving directions from major Northern California cities.

White, Michael. *Snowshoe Trails of Tahoe.* Berkeley, CA: Wilderness Press, 2005. Now in its second edition, this book details 65 snowshoe trips in the Lake Tahoe area, complete with topographic maps of the routes. Each trip includes a difficulty rating, directions to the trailhead, and a detailed description of the route. The book begins with important tips on preparing for your snowshoe adventure, such as weather-watching, safety procedures, and equipment checklists.

Yesavage, Jerome. *Desolation Wilderness: Fishing Guide*. Portland, OR: Frank Amato Publications, 1994. Hikers and backpackers who want to catch golden, rainbow, brook, and brown trout in the Desolation Wilderness will be pleased with this diminutive 64-page guide, which details more than 60 lakes. The book includes tips on what types of trout are found where and how to fish for them, plus where to find backpacking campsites (take the camping information with a grain of salt, however; the book is quite old, and many regulations have changed). The author is active in CalTrout (a nonprofit organization dedicated to preserving trout habitat) and an avid fly fisher.

PHOTO COLLECTIONS

Bachand, Thomas. *Lake Tahoe: A Fragile Beauty*. San Francisco, CA: Chronicle Books, 2008. With an introduction by Dr. Charles R. Goldman, founder and director of the Tahoe Research Group at U.C. Davis, this landscape-format book of 80 stunning color plates captures the sublime beauty of the lake while also illustrating its fragility, as a result of development and global warming. The book also includes some of Carlton Watkins's early photographs of the lake.

Bell, Jim. *Tahoe's Gilded Age: A Photographic Portfolio from 1881–1919* and *Memories of Tahoe: A Photographic Portfolio from 1920–1959*. Carnelian Bay, CA: Publishers Press, 2005. These two books of historical photographs were compiled by local Tahoe City photographer Jim Bell. The history of development and life at Lake Tahoe from the 1880s to the late 1950s is chronicled in these pages. Each book begins with a spirited narrative of the times, written by Chaco Mohler of Tahoe City.

Cameron, Robert, and Warren Lerude. *Above Tahoe and Reno: A New Collection of Historical and Original Aerial Photographs*. San Francisco, CA: Cameron and Company, 1995. One in a series of aerial photography books by Robert Cameron, this coffee-table book focuses not just on the natural beauty of Lake Tahoe and its environs but also the manufactured marvels of bustling Reno, Nevada.

Goin, Peter. *Lake Tahoe: Images of America*. San Francisco, CA: Arcadia Publishing, 2005. This black-and-white photo collection is filled with historical images from Lake Tahoe's past, with accompanying commentary on each image.

Goin, Peter, and C. Elizabeth Raymond. *Stopping Time: A Rephotographic Survey of Lake Tahoe*. Albuquerque, NM: University of New Mexico Press, 1992. This book puts Tahoe history in perspective. Photographer Peter Goin juxtaposes more than 100 of his modern-day photographs of the lake and its surrounding landscape with 19th-century archived photographs, creating a visual record of Tahoe's evolution. Writer Elizabeth Raymond supplies the historical text and photo captions.

Paul, Jon. *Visions of Lake Tahoe*. South Lake Tahoe: Jon Paul Gallery, 2005. Visit this photographer's gallery in South Lake Tahoe, and you will surely want to take home this book of breathtaking images of the lake basin. There's almost no text in this book at all; the beautiful pictures speak for themselves.

Pesetski, Larry. *A Journey to Lake Tahoe and Beyond*. Sierra Vista Publications, 2005. This coffee-table book of stunning color images shows Tahoe in all four seasons and at all hours of the day. Many close-ups of plants and animals are also included.

Scott, E. B. *The Saga of Lake Tahoe, Volumes I and II*. Antioch, CA: Sierra Tahoe Publishing, 1957 and 1973. These two volumes combine to create a detailed pictorial history of Lake Tahoe, featuring hundreds of Scott's black-and-white photographs.

Index

List of Maps

www.moon.com

DESTINATIONS | ACTIVITIES | BLOGS | MAPS | BOOKS

MOON.COM is ready to help plan your next trip! Filled with fresh trip ideas and strategies, author interviews, informative travel blogs, a detailed map library, and descriptions of all the Moon guidebooks, Moon.com is all you need to get out and explore the world—or even places in your own backyard. While at Moon.com, sign up for our monthly e-newsletter for updates on new releases, travel tips, and expert advice from our on-the-go Moon authors. As always, when you travel with Moon, expect an experience that is uncommon and truly unique.

KEEP UP WITH MOON ON FACEBOOK AND TWITTER
JOIN THE MOON PHOTO GROUP ON FLICKR